LANDSCAPE IT YOURSELF

A HANDBOOK FOR HOME GARDENERS

PLANT FINDER STRIP ▶

To find the names of the plants that would be most suitable for your garden and your needs, place the edge of the PLANT FINDER STRIP along the bottom of each Plant Chart, adjusting as necessary. Using a pencil, or a pen, mark your basic requirements for height, foliage, flowers, fruit, plant hardiness zone, landscape use, autumn color, drought resistance, or any other factor that is on the chart and is appropriate. Then, moving from the top of the chart down, or from the bottom up, note which plants fulfill all the requirements for your own garden. After you have selected a small group of plants that are suitable for your landscape, turn to the alphabetical descriptions for each plant that appears on the Plant Chart and read the descriptions. Without having to leave your home you can learn exactly which plant will thrive on your property. Happy planting and good growth!

cut line

cut line

cut line

cut line

PLANT FINDER STRIP

YOU CAN ✸✸✸✸✸✸✸✸✸✸✸

LANDSCAPE IT YOURSELF

A HANDBOOK FOR HOME GARDENERS

by HAROLD GIVENS ✸✸✸✸✸✸✸✸✸

HARCOURT BRACE JOVANOVICH ✸ NEW YORK AND LONDON

Library of Congress Cataloging in Publication Data
Givens, Harold D.
    Landscape it yourself.
    Bibliography: p.
    Includes index.
    1. Landscape gardening.   I. Title.
SB469.3.G57   712'.6   76–14436
ISBN 0–15–147679–9

First edition
B C D E

Acknowledgments

For practical garden pointers,
the author wishes to thank the Garden Club of Berkeley, California,
and the Garden Club of Santa Cruz, California.

To Beth, Howard and Jimmy

Contents

Preface

You don't have to be a skilled landscape designer to create a charming and lush garden. With your own ideas and some guidance you can have a personalized garden to suit your life style and to provide privacy and recreation, or for any other use. Doing your own landscaping adds new dimensions to the enjoyment of gardening.

Landscaping is the creation of a living composition; a beautiful landscape is the product of a logical approach and careful planning. This book is a clear and practical beginner's guide. It will show you how you can have a garden that will live and grow with you.

LANDSCAPE IT YOURSELF emphasizes serviceable design in planting, cultivation, and care of new properties, as well as relandscaping established gardens. The methods suggested in this book can be used in landscaping urban, suburban, and country dwellings—large and small homes, mobile-home parks, retirement clusters, and apartment complexes. It is also of use for civic and organization buildings. Every mode of living invites gardens that are compatible with the surrounding architecture and the climate and that are also functionally beautiful.

The approaches discussed have been developed during nineteen years of teaching landscape gardening and have been tested by thousands of students. Freedom of expression within the natural terrain is stressed. This means using natural forms and composition to achieve your own definition of beauty and function.

There have been great changes in garden design in recent years. Established rules are now broken as often as they are followed. However, the knowledge of classical rules of design is a valuable tool for implementing your own ideas. "Central axis lines," "equivalent balance," and other technical terms are used only when they are appropriate.

Dozens of plot plans are included to illustrate how design principles can be used and how they can be adapted or ignored—with success! Plot plans in this book are merely procedural guides. Use these rules of design and the plot plans in both preliminary planning and in actual field layout for your own land. You will enjoy adapting them to your own needs and bending and blending them to create a truly personalized garden.

Once you have used this book to guide your planning, the next problem is the selection and purchase of appropriate plants. "What should I plant here?" is always the big question. This book offers a unique easy-to-use system of plant selection charts. You can use them to choose—almost without effort—the exact plants for your garden. These charts are not just lists of plants, but operative plant selection devices that include all the plant categories you need:

Trees
Conifers
Shrubs
Vines
Groundcovers
Perennials
Annuals
Bulbs

Plant names—Latin and common—sizes, temperature, and growth zones are listed. Flowering plants, evergreens, and deciduous plants are identified and their landscaping uses are indicated. Each plant is also numerically keyed to its complete description. The descriptions include the height, shape, and usual use of the plants, flowers —when they can be expected and what color they will be—shape and abundance of foliage, pruning, propogation, cultivation, and specific ideas for plant use.

The unique feature of this book is the clear Plant Selection Charts for every part of the United States: north, south, east, and west. An easy-to-read hardiness zone map is included so that you know which plans will survive in your garden. First, find your own region and your own zone, mark its number on the Plant Selection Charts, and then proceed. It is easy! You can have beautiful color—any color—flowers and foliage, vines and groundcovers, leafy and needled trees, hedges, woodplants, shrubs, annuals and perennials, vegetables and herbs—any type of garden you want—with low maintenance and high returns in beauty and comfort.

Although LANDSCAPE IT YOURSELF is directed to the home owner with a small or medium size garden, it can also be used to landscape plots or areas larger than one acre. This book is based upon a lifetime of professional experience and I sincerely hope it will help you to design and develop a truly fine garden.

Harold Givens

HOW TO LANDSCAPE
YOUR GARDEN

1

Making Plans

A lovely garden satisfies many senses. Fragrant plants placed in strategic locations carry scented breezes on a hot day; soft-textured shrubs beside a patio or path delight the touch; a pine tree rustling in the wind fires the imagination, and the vibrancy of floral blooms is a visual delight.

To create a personalized landscape requires the selection of specific elements from a myriad of possibilities. Your garden plan is a working guide to the artistic and useful arrangement of all elements into one harmonious unit. Manmade structures, such as patios, paths, and fences, and natural elements, such as hills, slopes, and ponds as well as the shape, color, and texture of foliage and flowers should all be considered. Careful planning produces gracious, beautifully accented vistas; utilitarian buildings are hidden from sight, and a feeling of unity with nature is created.

Planning is also important because gardens can be expansive. The wrong tree or shrub—one that is not suited to the climate—will not prosper, nor will you be happy if you locate plants, trees, or shrubs without considering their mature height and shape, and their growth patterns. Thinking ahead must be part of your plan.

Is your family growing—in number as well as age? Do they have changing interests and hobbies? What about changes in your financial resources? Is your neighborhood changing? Should you consider the eventual replacement of a tricycle path with a volley-ball court as your children grow? Might you someday need a screen or fence to shut out traffic noise? These are the types of questions that good planning will take into consideration.

A garden plan is the guide that directs the development of your property for the utmost enjoyment of outdoor living—by all members of your family.

WHAT KIND OF GARDEN DO YOU WANT?

The first step in making a garden plan is to list the major factors that you must take into account (your house, for instance) and the selected features (flower bed, arbor, etc.) you wish to include in your garden. Here is a sample list:

House
Garage
Driveway
Barn (or other structure)
Patio
Children's play area
Rose garden
Flower bed
Vegetable garden
Tool shed
Arbor
Utility-storage facilities
Clothes reel
Water sources
Walks and paths

In making your own list, be careful to include all structures and natural elements that will affect your garden planning. Also, choose all features with care. Add any features that you think would be nice in your garden. Think about how each will be used and how often it will be used. Decide what is best for your family based on your own life style.

Sketch 1.1   **SOME USUAL GARDEN COMPONENTS**

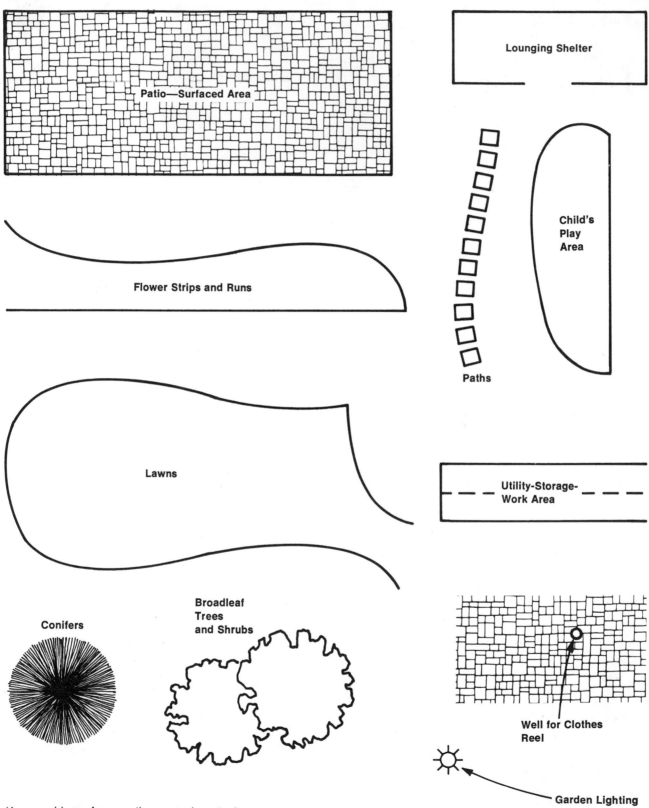

Your problem: Arrange the several parts into a functionally related and harmoniously coordinated composition that is adaptable to the area and your family needs.

Sample Plans

Sketch 1.1 illustrates some typical garden components. Which of these features would you want in your garden? Figure 1.1 is a sample plan for combining these components into a harmonious whole. Here are some of the features that make this plan attractive:

The surfaced patio for day and evening social events can also support a clothes reel and provide a surface for small children's games.

The partially shaded lounging area is perfect for late afternoon snacks.

The fragrant flower bed is adjacent to the patio.

The large lawn provides a cool expanse but also unites the patio and shrubs in the back of the property.

The play area is pleasingly curved, is in full view of the house and every other part of the garden, and can be expanded onto the lawn.

The utility-storage-work area is screened from sight, and it protects equipment from rain and snow.

The stepping-stone path allows for circulation of traffic.

Trees offer balance and protection from the wind.

Shrubs provide color and texture and unite natural and manmade elements.

Studying Sketch 1.1 and Figure 1.1 will show you how plans are created. A plan is the organization on paper of your own landscaping ideas.

Figure 1.2 is simpler. It is an open informal design, but it is still carefully organized and very serviceable. Notice how the trees in the background provide balance and shade. If you have a comparable area, you might use this or a similar plan. Sample plans can and should be modified for your needs and your property. Your own taste and style is what your garden is all about.

Putting It on Paper

Now that you have studied two sample plans, you can start work on your own land and your own plans. Begin by preparing a large work surface, such as a dining-room or kitchen table. You'll need three or four sheets of good quality paper. The sheets should be large enough to accommodate a sketch, in scale, of your property. Use a scale of ⅛ inch to 1 foot. Here are some dimensions:

> 1 inch = 8 feet
> 5 inches = 40 feet
> 6 inches = 48 feet
> 10 inches = 80 feet

A rectangular plot 100 feet by 80 feet would require sheets of paper at least 18″ x 18″. A good margin makes working easier and neater.

If you don't have large drafting paper, wrapping paper or shelving paper might be used instead. You will also need a compass, a medium-size french curve, two ordinary wooden rulers—one of these should be at least 18 inches long—some sharp pencils, and a good eraser. If you don't have a french curve, you can use a rounded template cut from cardboard, or some other pleasingly curved edge. These basic tools are shown in Sketch 1.2.

WHERE DO YOU BEGIN?

Walk out of your house and stand in the middle of your yard. As you look around, contours, conditions, and problems become apparent. A landscape picture should take shape in your mind. Now, back to your house and some paperwork. Resist the urge to complete your design in one or two sittings. Relax, think through every step as you work. Make several trial plans if you wish. The idea of a plan is to make most of your mistakes on paper.

Figure 1.1 **A SERVICEABLE DESIGN FOR A SMALL TO MEDIUM GARDEN**

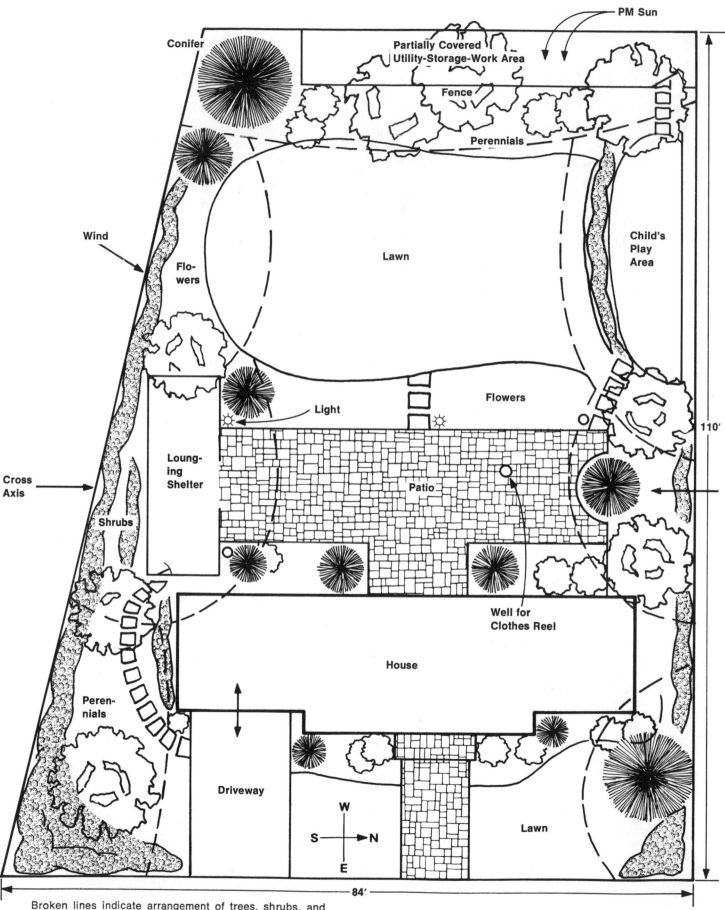

Broken lines indicate arrangement of trees, shrubs, and
structures in units or groupings, and the units are tied
together—united by means of blenders.

Figure 1.2   A SERVICEABLE DESIGN FOR A SMALL TO MEDIUM PROPERTY

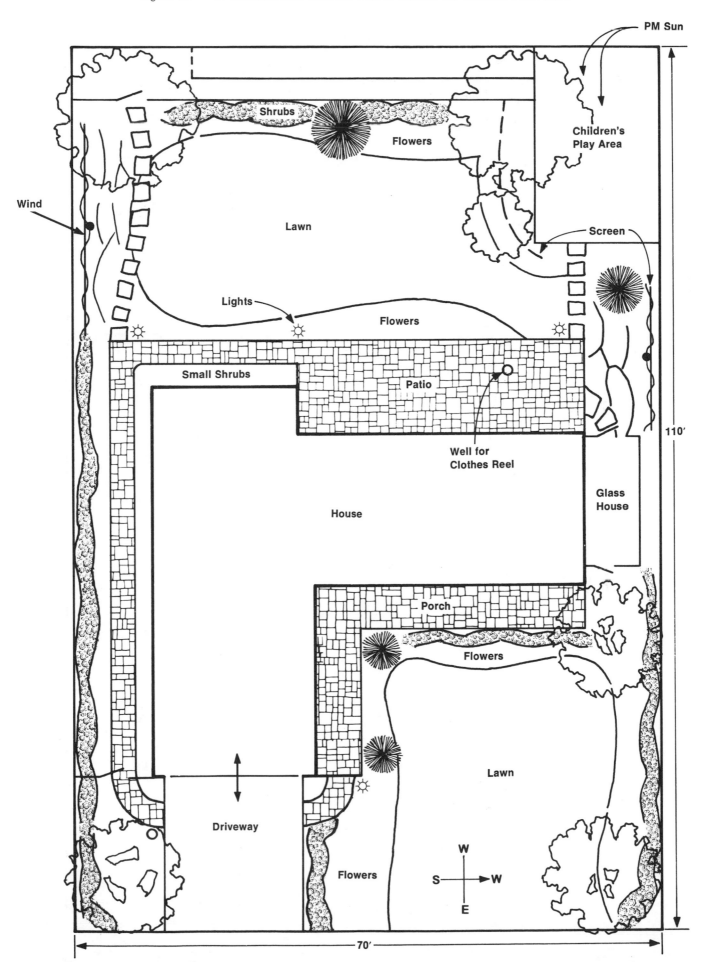

Sketch 1.2   **DRAWING TOOLS**

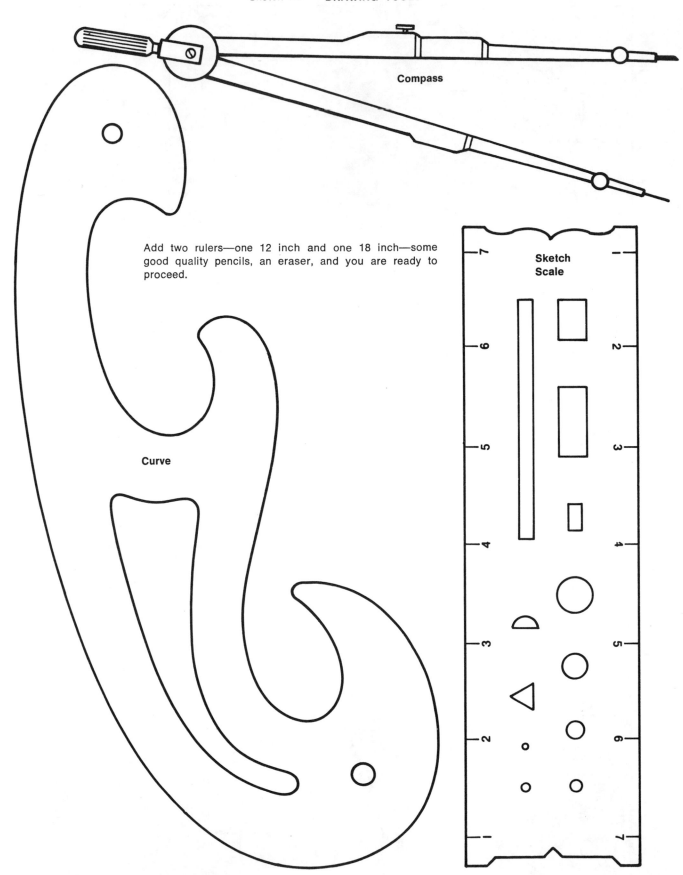

Compass

Add two rulers—one 12 inch and one 18 inch—some good quality pencils, an eraser, and you are ready to proceed.

Curve

Sketch Scale

Start your plans by answering these seven basic questions about your property:

1. What sort of house do you have?
2. How is the house situated on your property?
3. How large is the plot or acreage? What is the shape of the plot?
4. Is it usually windy or mild and calm?
5. What is the prevailing climate?
6. What is your plant hardiness zone?
7. How close is your nearest neighbor? Do you want more privacy? Or do you want to share an open garden without formal boundary between your land and the adjacent property?

Let's consider some detailed sample answers to these questions. Note how the situations described in the sample answers differ from yours, and how they are similar. Answer each question in your mind, as it is discussed in the sample.

Type of Architecture

The relationship of house and garden styles is obvious. Your house is the most dominant feature in your landscape, and you should make sure that the style of your garden is compatible with the architecture of the house. Your garden should blend house and land into a single picture.

Each group of settlers who came to North America brought the building styles and techniques of their homeland. But because the building materials of the homeland were not always available here, the settlers adapted the traditional styles. In Louisiana and the St. Lawrence valley, the French replaced stone with stucco; small masonry and adobe suited the hot, dry areas under Spanish influence; in the Northeast, Dutch-style roofs were often used. Traditional English styles appeared in most regions. The English houses were of two basic types: large mansions in the South, and small many-gabled, half-timbered houses in the North. The New England climate forced a lowering of the roof line and simplification of room plans and exterior trim.

In modern times, especially since World War II, mass housing and community planning have greatly influenced home design. New building materials and techniques of pre-fabrication have brought about many modern styles.

What is the style of your house? Of what material is it constructed? How does it relate to the surrounding landscape? Do you like natural, informal effects, or stylized patterns? Would a formal or informal garden be best with your own home and life style?

→ Draw the outline of your own property on the paper you have prepared for your plot plan.
→ Draw the outline of your own house situated on your property.

How the House Is Situated

The position of your house in relation to the garden—in front, alongside, or in the back of the house—will affect your choice of plants and other garden features. If a garden faces east, such features as a patio, children's play area, or lounging area will not be a problem. However, if the garden receives strong afternoon sun, that sun might evaporate moisture from the soil and cause problems with certain plants. People with nearly identical houses, on similar lots, in the same community, are not always able to have the same sort of garden.

If a garden area is very large, manmade fences or shade trees can be used to protect shrubs and flowers from drying sun or strong winds. Vine-covered structures are also sometimes used for shade fences.

→ Draw a directional sign or symbol showing North, South, East, and West in relation to your own property.

Size and Shape of Your Property

Is your property long and narrow, or wide and short? Is it quadrangular, triangular, or irregular? Is it circular or angular, amorphous or geometric in shape? The shape of your house and property will greatly influence which features can be used in your garden and where they can be located.

A long narrow garden presents many restrictions, but it also offers an opportunity for elegant long-distance vistas and effects. An angular property of even moderate size has more potential for creative design than a geometrically regular garden; an angular garden will accommodate more and larger garden features.

Level properties are easier to landscape than sloping or undulating lots, but the latter offer additional opportunity for unique designs and unusual effects. A sloping garden may include interesting stone walls, impressive broad steps, or terraces, with sectional features and almost vertical plant arrangements. A steep slope at the rear of the lot would allow you to use partially imbedded rock to support an exquisite evergreen planting to visually extend your garden.

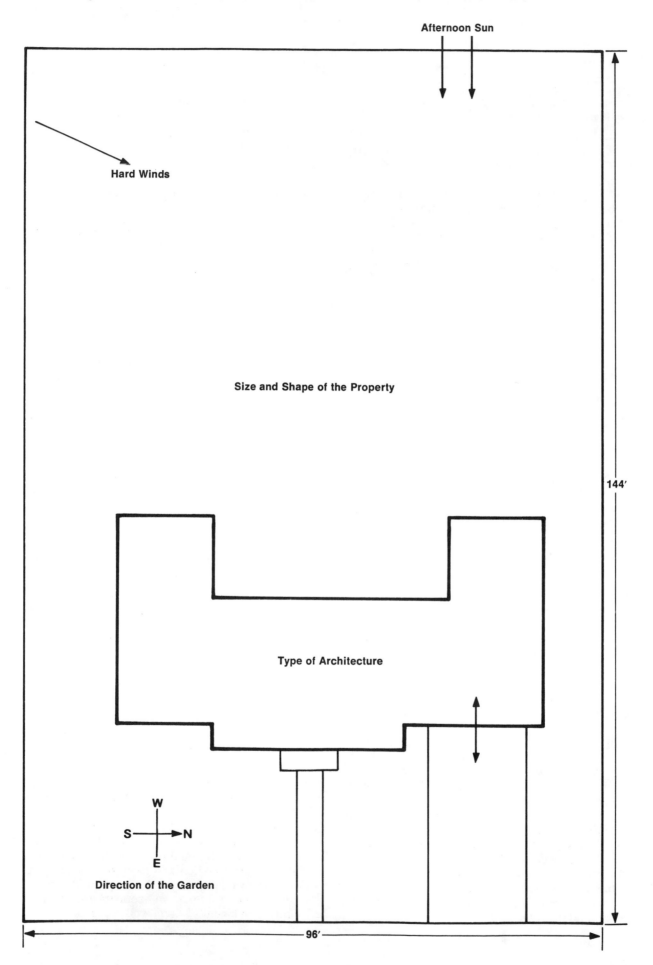

Figure 1.3   DIRECTION OF THE GARDEN, AFTERNOON SUN, AND HARD WINDS

If your lot is small to average in size, you must carefully plan which features to include in your garden. Swimming pools, game courts, and vegetables take large areas; rock gardens, flower beds, small putting greens, or old-fashioned croquet runs require less. A barbecue or cooking area will usually require more room than you might think because you must plan for tables, chairs, and nearby service pieces.

The size of your garden will determine many of its plantings, but the amount of time you can spend in gardening and maintenance and the size of your budget are equally important factors. It could cost $10 a square foot for a small but exquisite rose garden, or less than one-tenth of that amount if you work with nature and create a more rustic garden or a sand garden.

Direction and Velocity of Winds

We touched briefly on this when discussing garden direction. Almost every locality occasionally experiences winds of high velocity. Such winds can be devastating to an unprotected garden. Your plan should show from which direction these winds might be expected. Look at Figure 1.3. You do not want strong winds to sweep across a lounging area, pool, or children's play area. Nor do you want them to affect flowers or ornamental plantings. Azaleas, camellias, and rhododendrons have little chance of success unless they have good moisture, morning sun, and protection from both strong afternoon sun and cold northern winds. Careful planning will permit you to shift features of your landscape to provide necessary protection for flowering plants.

By indicating the direction of afternoon sun and cold winds you can provide protection where it is needed. One way is to place vulnerable plants near the house or another building; another is to protect and shield them with trees. See Figure 1.4. Planning ahead will prevent later disappointment. When the effects of such exposure are inevitable, you can at least select species and varieties of plants that are relatively wind-resistant. Furthermore, you can use certain hardy plants, such as those suggested in Sketch 1.3, to create a wind screen.

→ Draw a line on your plot plan to show how the prevailing winds cross your property.

Summer and Winter Temperatures

In the margin of your garden design, make two notations:

Average summer daytime temperature: _____
Coldest winter temperature: _____

These notations shall act as a constant reminder and will guide you in selecting plants appropriate to your climate.

Your Plant Hardiness Zone

It is important to find your temperature zone on the Plant Hardiness Zone map, Figure 1.5. This map is a guide in the selection of flowers, shrubs, trees, groundcovers, vines, and bulbs that are adaptable to your climate. If you are located in Zone 4 or 5, for example, it would be foolish to invest in plants requiring the milder temperature of Zones 9 or 10. This appears obvious, but unless you are familiar with the cold-resistant peculiarities of many plants, improper selection can easily occur. Some plants fare well in both warm and cold climates, but need special soil; there are other individual peculiarities, too.

Zoned plant lists are included in the plant selection section starting on page 94.

Privacy, Boundaries, and Lot-line Fences

Is yours a community where boundary-line fences are the custom? You should not build any fence without considering local styles and specifications. A boundary-line fence is perhaps the only element of your own personalized garden that is really part of the community as well as part of your property, and, therefore, it is best to take community sentiment into consideration. This is sometimes difficult; too often local fencing styles are just not suitable for your house, garden, or taste. In this case, you should consider masking the fence with shrubs and vines.

If you have a professional erect your fences, avoid disappointment by telling him exactly what you want. If you build the fence yourself, discuss the project with adjacent neighbors; if the fence will also benefit them, they might help with the construction.

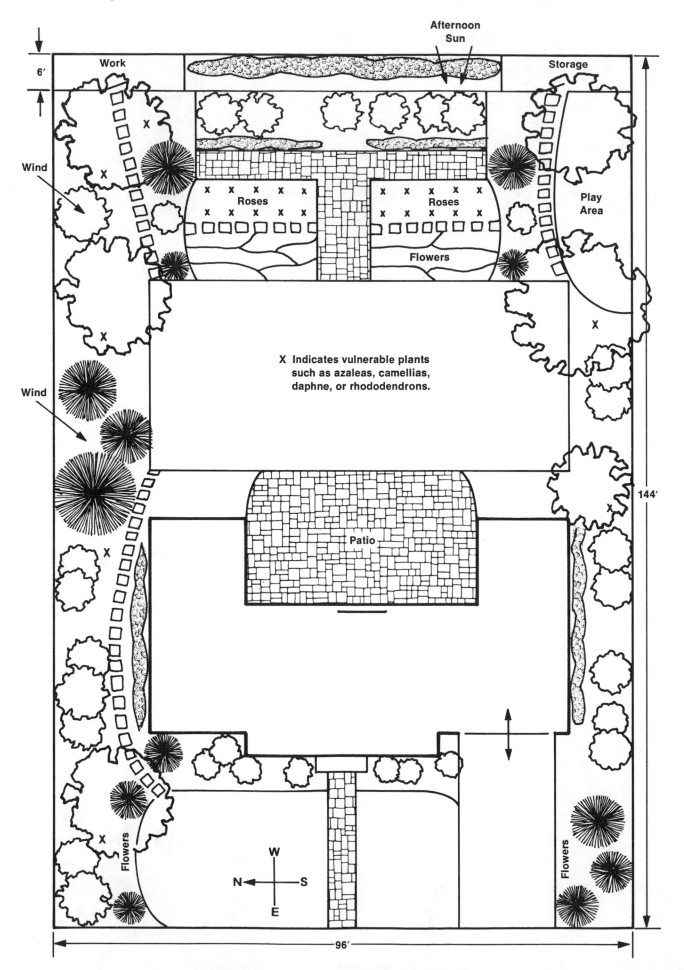

Figure 1.4   **TYPICAL LOCATIONS FOR PLANTS DAMAGED BY AFTERNOON SUN**

Sketch 1.3　**A TYPICAL WIND-RETARDANT, EVERGREEN PLANTING**

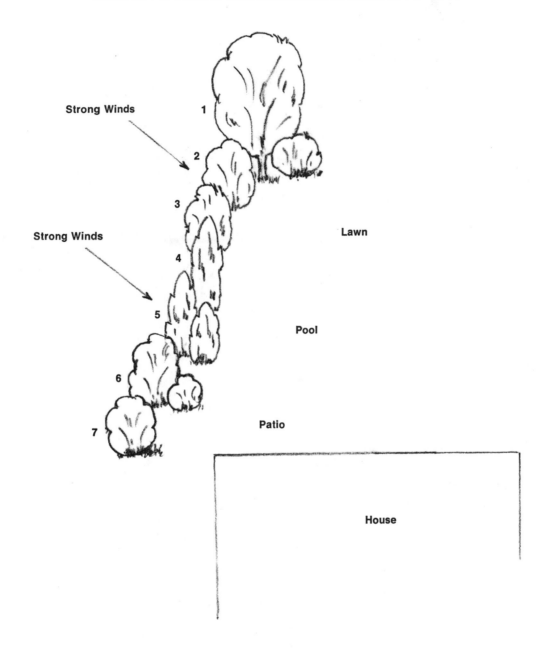

1—*Ulmus parvifolia* (Chinese elm tree)	25–35′
2—Escallonia	8–9′
3—Escallonia	8–9′
4—*Juniperus chinensis columnaris glauca*	12–15′
5—*Juniperus chinensis torulosa*	8–12′
6—*Ligustrum vulgare* (Privet growing naturally)	8–10′
7—*Ilex cornuta* (Chinese holly)	8–10′

The above plants will grow taller if permitted to do so, which will increase the scope of wind protection.

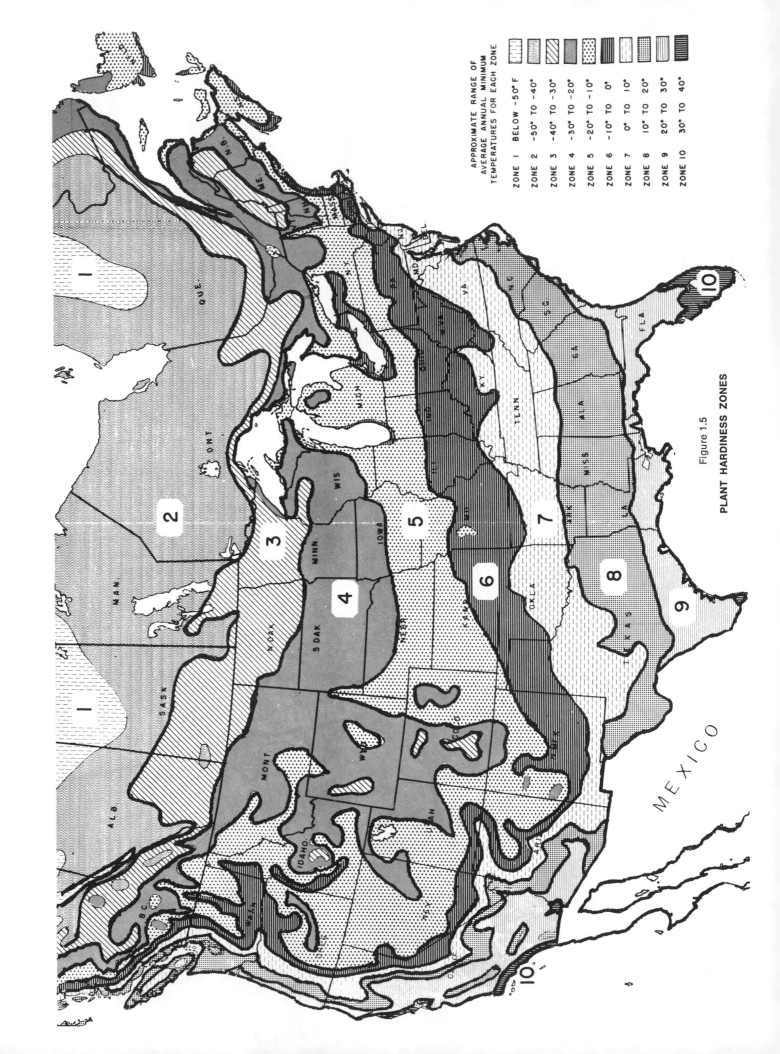

APPROXIMATE RANGE OF
AVERAGE ANNUAL MINIMUM
TEMPERATURES FOR EACH ZONE

ZONE 1   BELOW −50° F
ZONE 2   −50° TO −40°
ZONE 3   −40° TO −30°
ZONE 4   −30° TO −20°
ZONE 5   −20° TO −10°
ZONE 6   −10° TO 0°
ZONE 7   0° TO 10°
ZONE 8   10° TO 20°
ZONE 9   20° TO 30°
ZONE 10 30° TO 40°

Figure 1.5

PLANT HARDINESS ZONES

Photo 1.1

Rhythmic beauty in a fence.
(Garden of Dr. and Mrs. John Bolderick)

Backyard-line fences are usually the maximum legal height and are built for privacy and protection. Frontyard fences are generally more decorative than serviceable and should gracefully define the property. There are many attractive types that are similar to the conventional post-rail or basket-weave fence. The trick is to find a style that harmonizes with everything and everyone.
→ Draw a line on your plot plan to indicate where you might want fences on your property.

GROUND WORK

Until now we have been discussing problems above ground. Now let's look at the ground level —and beneath. There are three basic ground-level factors that determine how the above-ground-level plants will fare. The following must be considered:

1. What sort of soil do you have? Is it clay, sandy, or sandy rocky?
2. What is the general slope of the land in relation to your house? What about other sections of the property?
3. What about drainage? Is it good? Will changes be necessary?

Think back to the garden features that you and your family want. Look back at the list on page 13. As you consider each of the beneath-the-ground factors, remember that they strongly affect what you can have in the above-the-ground landscape.

The Soil

The real fun of landscaping is the selection of plants. However, you can't choose the right plants unless you have some idea of what your soil is like. Although a professional might pick up a handful, sniff it, and be able to identify the content exactly, if you are on your own you will probably need to buy a "soil test kit", available at a local nursery. You might also send soil samples to your Agricultural Extension Service. These state facilities provide reliable information, and they are usually prompt and helpful.

A gardener has very little control over climate, rainfall, wind, and humidity, but he really can control—to some extent—the soil content of his garden.

Soil is the very substance of the earth. Thousands, probably millions, of years ago its formation first began. Soil was once plant life, rocks, minerals, bones, everything! The action of the sun, frost, earth changes, ice ages, and erosion served to break down all these components into small and still smaller particles. Most soils in gardens are composed of minerals from rock particles; decayed organic matter—such as leaves and animal matter—called humus; microscopic living organisms, such as bacteria; water, which holds dissolved minerals and salts; and pockets of air.

There are three general types of soil that most gardeners and landscapers are concerned about: clay-like soil, sandy soil, and loam soil.

Clay soil is one of the most difficult for the landscaper. It can hold water and be very heavy. It is very slow drying, and if left uncultivated after a long rain, it will form a hard crust that makes penetration almost impossible at times, and difficult at best. Usually sand and humus must be added to clay soils and then tilled into the clay. This is tough work, but it must be done.

Sandy soils are not as heavy-textured as clay soils. They warm up quickly in the spring and are easy to work. However, they do not retain the moisture that a clay soil does, and they often require the addition of quantities of organic matter and clay.

Loam is a gardener's delight; it is ideal for most plants. Loam soil is usually porous enough for good drainage, has some air pockets, and contains the minerals necessary for healthy, normal plant growth. It is the right combination of clay, sand, and organic matter or humus.

What kind of soil do you have? What special soil preparation will be necessary? How much will it cost in time and money? These are all questions that must be answered before any garden plan can be completed.

Grading and the Use of Walls

Your property is either completely level or there is some slope in part of your land. If there is a slope, which is probable, then some grading may be required.

The house *must* be on higher ground than the area around it; it must be slightly elevated and at the top of a slope. Naturally, all water must drain away from the house. The front yard of a house is usually designed to slope away from it. Be sure to provide a slope of at least several inches from the level of your house to the level of the edge of your yard.

If there is an area in the center of your property in which water accumulates, filling will be necessary. Intermittent elevations might be leveled, and the finished grade should be sloped either from one side or the other and drain toward the lowest level. Note the grading in Figure 1.6.

Many lots slope considerably over their entire length, and they offer a good opportunity for a garden of exceptional variety and interest. If grading plans are made well in advance, it is even possible to have a graceful wall that acts as a retaining wall (to hold back soil) and that also provides opportunities for landscaping features.

Whether the land is level or sloping, a wall can be a handsome and serviceable addition to any garden. There are three basic kinds of garden walls: free standing walls, retaining walls, and seat walls. Within all three categories, height, size, and style may vary considerably. Walls can be constructed of a variety of materials—adobe, brick, block, concrete, stone, concrete block, wood —the possibilities are almost endless.

Figure 1.6　**THE SLOPING LOT**

A sloping and slightly undulating lot from a 16 foot elevation in the back to street level in front.

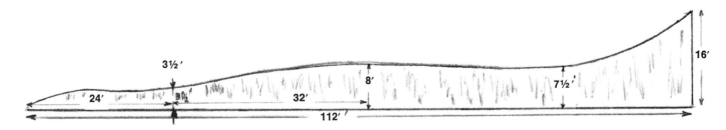

Some leveling for house, front and back yards. A 2-foot wall (rock or reinforced concrete) at base of remaining slope. A cross drain at base of wall at A. Area C is slightly sloped from the house, D is level, and E slopes slightly from the house.

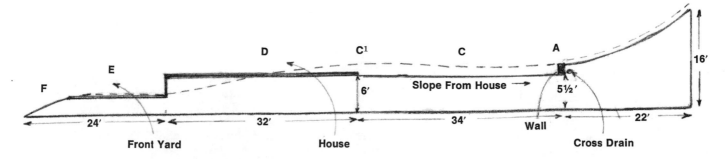

Free Standing Walls

Free standing walls are permanent fences. Since there are usually ordinances that control fences, especially when used on the property line, be sure to check local building codes and secure the required permits.

A free standing wall constructed of brick, particularly used brick, would be a real challenge for the amateur. If you plan to use stone, ashler, or rubble, you might find it helpful to take a few lessons in stone cutting, fitting, and arrangement, the use of mortar, handling a quarryman's cutters and saws, and the craft of layering cut and uncut stones. Sketch 1.4 illustrates some popular stone walls. A stone wall will need a stabilizing foundation to prevent tilt and cracking in the cold, and should extend well below ground level to insure that it is safe and secure.

Sketch 1.4 **TYPES OF STONE FOR WALLS**

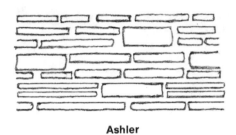

Ashler

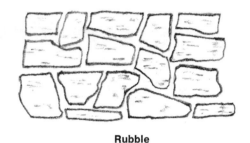

Rubble

Retaining Wall

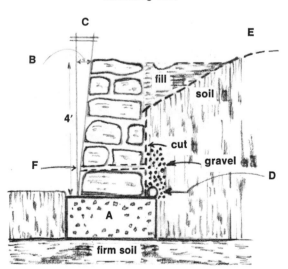

A—Concrete base set on firm soil
B—5″ batter or slope back
C—Batter frame
D—Horizontal drain tile set in gravel
E—Original slope
F—Weep hole to help drain water from behind wall
Mortar: Thoroughly mix 3 parts sand (clean), ½ part fireclay, and 1 part cement.

Photo 1.2

Interesting patterns are formed by a garden wall constructed of used brick.

Photo 1.3

Retaining wall provided with drainage holes. (Home of Melvin and Helen Jory)

Retaining Walls

The principal function of a retaining wall is to hold back the soil behind it. A multi-level garden terraced by curved or straight walls can be very beautiful. Solid walls of over 3 feet, especially retaining walls, are an engineering project, and therefore a word of warning is in order. Building such a wall requires knowledge and skill. Materials used, foundations, resistance to pressure, batter, water, and land movement, drainage, methods of reinforcement, use of mortar, and material preparation must all be calculated. Effects of temperature changes and, of course, the need to arrange the stones, brick, or other materials artistically, add to the problems. If you are not a civil engineer, it is best to get professional advice. It might be better to have a tall retaining wall constructed by a licensed contractor than to attempt it yourself. If you do want to try wall-building, however, be sure to check local building codes and ordinances and to secure the required permits.

Low retaining walls of local stone, carefully fitted together with mortar, are beautiful and relatively easy to construct. Make sure the foundation is below the front line and that the construction is sturdy.

In some retaining walls, soil is used between loose stones instead of mortar. This forms planting pockets which enable the wall to house attractive small plants. The planting can be done as the wall is constructed. Sketch 1.5 offers diagrams of two types of stone retaining walls—one using mortar and the other using soil between the stones.

Sketch 1.5   **RETAINING WALLS**

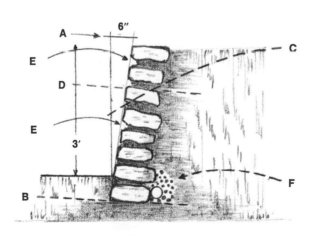

A—Batter frame
   Approximately 2″ batter or slope-back per 1′ of wall
   height
B—Firm base, below level of cut
C—Original slope
D—Slope rock slightly downward from front to back
E, E—Planting pockets
F—Horizontal drain tile laid in gravel

Seat Walls

Seat walls can frame a patio, form a water feature or planting box, separate a driveway from an adjacent garden, or serve any number of utilitarian functions. They can be separate or free standing, or retain a raised flower bed. Seat walls are within the ability of an amateur mason or builder. They are chair height—14 to 16 inches high—and built of brick, stone, wood, or other materials.

Concrete, brick, or stone walls may be capped to form seating. Either the same material or 10-inch wood planks can be used. Sometimes the entire wall is made from wood: 2-inch thick redwood planks are attached to redwood or cedar posts, and bolts or rustproof nails are used to hold the boards together. See Sketch 1.6. All the lumber, except the seating caps, should be treated with preservative and stained with an oil-free stain. The caps sometimes look best when allowed to weather naturally.

→ Draw a line on your plot plan to indicate a wall if you think it will be one of the landscape features you want to include.

Drainage

Many homeowners experience annoying or destructive drainage problems each winter, and the problems often continue into spring, or persist all year. Sometimes the problem is water seeping onto your land from an adjacent garden that is on a slightly higher elevation. This boggy situation can destroy valuable perennials, shrubs, and trees.

Seepage can be avoided by preventive measures. The correct placement of drainage facilities is the logical answer. If your own drainage work doesn't help, consult the proper local city or county government department.

Figure 1.7 shows the placement of a 4-inch diameter subsurface drainpipe, which is detailed in Sketch 1.7. It runs the full length of the property with a slight fall. Seepage from neighboring property and excess rain water during the winter are intercepted and carried away.

If you live where there is excessive rain, establish a drain line along the foundation of your house. Connect it with a main drainage system.

Sketch 1.6 **WOOD RETAINING-SEAT WALL**

A—14" to 18" high (average)
B—Rot-resistant boards nailed or bolted to 4" by 4" redwood or cedar posts
C—Capped to act as a seat

Figure 1.7   SUBSURFACE DRAINPIPES

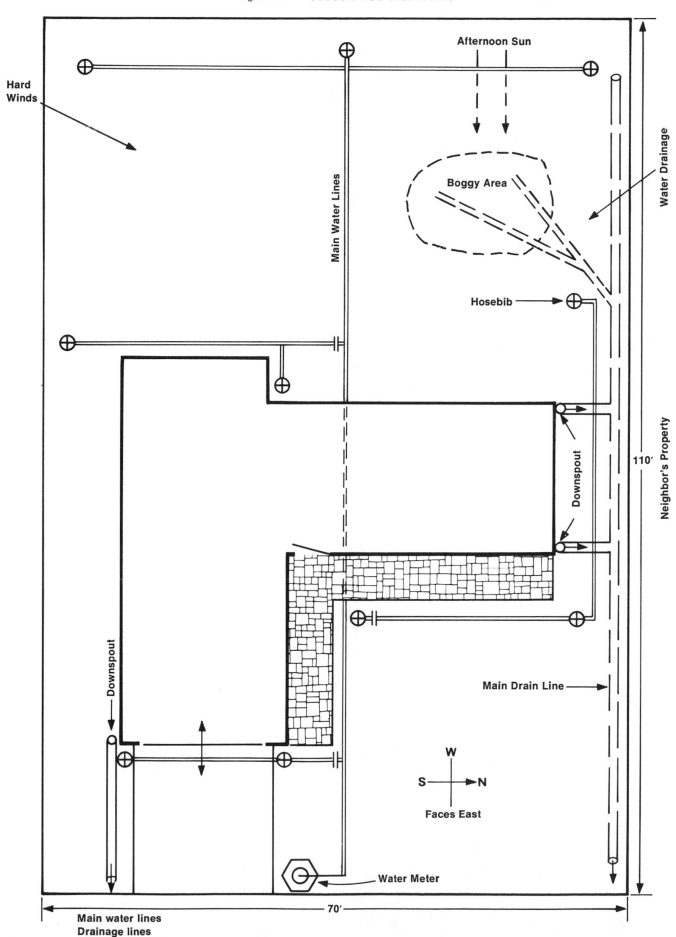

Leaders, gutters, and downspouts will carry away excess water from the roof of your house.

We've discussed the problem of unwanted water. But there are also times when you need water and don't have enough of it. An easy and ample water supply to every part of your property is very important. Main water lines should be legally connected to your municipal or county water supply or to your own pump or source. Check with the proper city or county department about restrictions, requirements, and permits if they are needed. All main-line pipes should be of standard size. As your garden develops, a secondary water system may be needed. It can be connected to the main lines laid earlier.

→ Draw lines on your plot plan to indicate where you think drain routes would best be positioned on your property.

→ Draw the main water lines on your plan using a double line or color line.

Sketch 1.7 **DRAINAGE**

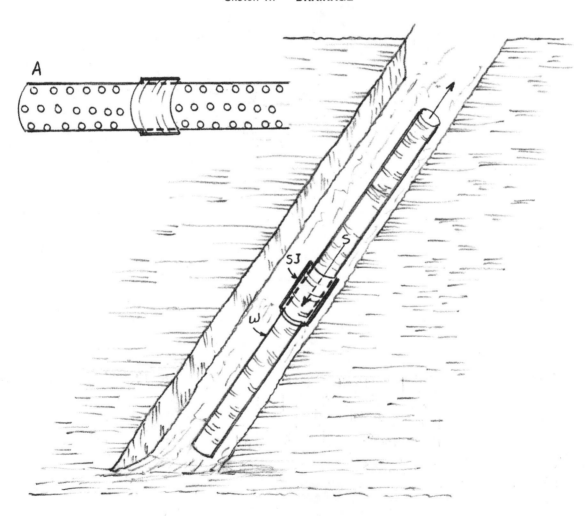

Plastic slip-joint drain pipe:
 A—Holes in underside of pipe to admit water
SJ—Slip joint—S snugly slips into Slip-joint SJ
 W—Water enters the pipe through holes in the underside of the pipe and drains away.
Use perforated pipe for general seepage areas and field drainage and non-perforated type for main drain lines.

An appropriate and well-placed light welcomes your guests at the garden gate.

The strong vertical lines of a tree are balanced by a horizontal line of shrubs and flowers.

A strategic light displays a garden scene and guides the way. ▶

A sloping property is transformed into a quiet and relaxing outdoor living room by the use of a rock wall and skillful implementation of the several principles of design.

Petunias seem to be made for containers of any shape and size. ◣

The tall spikes of these purple blooms are graceful and lovely. ▶
Lupines also can be found in blue, pink and white.
The annual seeds may be planted in open ground.

Harmony and compatible textures can be found even in small mobile home gardens.
Correct landscaping can add stability and permanence to even a transient home.

Long arching branches of weigela in full bloom artfully dominate the garden scene.

An edging of purple alyssum pleasantly defines the garden.

An occasional flowering shrub livens up the entire shrub planting.

A garden in the winter presents possibilities for a new and different kind of beauty.
The configuration of the leafless trees creates a wonderland that can be admired from the snug indoors.

2

Designing Your Garden

PRINCIPLES OF GARDEN DESIGN

Several important *guiding principles* should influence the type, size, and arrangement of your garden's features and plants. These principles are essential to the development of good composition and harmony. They will orient your thinking toward continuity between house and garden. Nine design factors are critical:

Lines	Texture
Balance	Color
Composition	Harmony
Scale	Cheerfulness
Proportion	

Understanding the principles of line, balance, composition, scale, and so on, will give an awareness of the *how, where* and *why* of the integral parts of any garden plan. Equally important, appreciation of these factors will further the *feel* of the art of design, a sensory perception of the things you do. The garden plan in Figure 2.1 illustrates the design principles we will be discussing.

Understanding the principles of design will help you place everything in proper perspective and enable you to relate each part gracefully to all others. This is particularly important if you wish to stray from established trends and develop a unique and personalized garden.

Lines

Let's consider four types of lines—vertical, horizontal, curved, and straight—plus the skyline. Look for these lines in nature whenever you have the opportunity: vertical tree trunks, spreading branches parallel to the ground, the curve of a stream, the sharp angle of a jutting cliff. Study them in well-designed gardens too.

Walk into a garden and observe the lines of the house. Your eyes first pick up the vertical ones because they are strongest—the corners, doors, windows if they are relatively narrow. If you concentrate on these vertical lines for some moments, they become monotonous and eventually irritating. Mentally balance them by means of horizontal lines—the roof line, eaves, line of consecutive windows across the house, foundation planting of shrubs. The effect completely changes. The horizontal lines produce a balancing effect upon the vertical ones, and harmony results.

Now look around the garden itself. Here, too, are lines. Vertical lines of tree trunks and columnar evergreens, also the horizontal or *balancing* lines of tree branches, low shrubs, perhaps a fence along the property line or an attractive wall defining an elevation. Do the lines of paths enhance a gracefully curved lawn? Are there long, colorful runs of perennials? Extend your observation to the undulating skyline defined by the tops of trees and shrubs. It should be smoothly informal and very natural in effect. Lines combine to produce a harmonious relationship and animate the scene.

In good garden design, lines emphasize balance, character, and beauty, and they help tie the various units together and lead your eyes all over the landscape. This is emphasized in Figure 2.1. Practice observing the versatility of lines so you can put them to work in your own garden design.

Figure 2.1   SOME BASIC PRINCIPLES OF GARDEN DESIGN:
LINES, BALANCE, COMPOSITION, SCALE, PROPORTION,
TEXTURE, COLOR, HARMONY, CHEERFULNESS

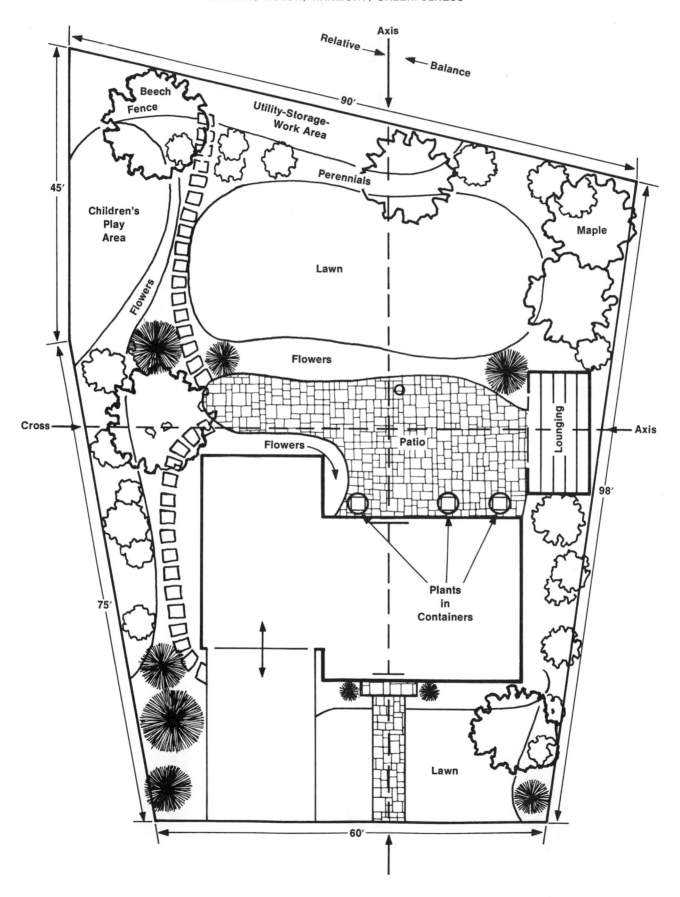

Photo 2.1   (Home of Melvin and Helen Jory)

Crisp clean lines of sheared hedges enhance the balance
and beauty of a front yard.

Balance

Balance has a stabilizing effect. It is important
not only in lines, but everywhere in the landscape.
→ Draw a line on your plot plan through the
center of your property from front to back, as is
done in Figure 2.1. This line is merely a device
for easy organization of elements.

In informal design, the collective interest and
force of composition on the right is reasonably
equivalent to that on the left, but in a very natural
way. A lounging shelter on one side is theoreti-
cally balanced by a tree unit on the other, for
instance, or a beech in the far left corner balances
a maple in the far right. Such balance must not
be obvious however, merely inherent in the overall
scheme. Emphasis is therefore placed upon unit
relationships and a general continuity of interest.
Overall balance is then attained principally by
skillful arrangement of the whole mass of shrubs
and trees, garden features, and structures. Observe the relationships in Sketch 2.1.

Once you are aware of the *aesthetic feel* of
balance, you will be able to manipulate equivalent
landscape masses to obtain the exact effect you
wish as you proceed with the development of your
own garden project.

Composition

To the garden designer, composition means an
orderly and appropriate arrangement of the several elements in his plan. The real challenge is to
organize the various parts into units of related
and harmonious interest and to unify them by
tying them all together with appropriate plants.

You probably selected each piece of furniture
in your living room with very definite service in
mind, but you did not scatter them helter-skelter
over the room. You took great care to assemble
related units, to place the units advantageously
and to tie them together in some overall arrange-

Photo 2.2   (Author's home)

Foundation planting—to bring a long house into pleasing
proportion.

Sketch 2.1   **COMPOSITION**

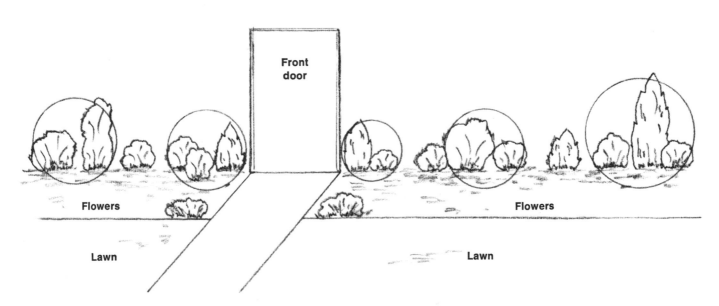

Example: A foundation planting—along the front of your
house. For the non-professional, it is easier to arrange
the richly appropriate, in-scale shrubs in groupings or
units and then tie the units together with *blending* shrubs
to form a cheerful, colorful and *naturally* harmonious
composition.

ment. Your garden is your outdoor living room. There, too, you should strive for a pleasing association of parts, unity of effect, and consistency of style. This holds true even in the most radical departures from design trends.

Scale

Everything in your garden must be in scale with your house and lot. A small house on a small to medium lot requires scaled-down shrubs, trees, and vines; smaller secondary structures, such as a pool or shelter, and a relatively small lawn. Even the garden furniture should be in scale.

Avoid planting trees with an eventual height of 150 feet on a property 50 feet wide and 100 feet long. The trees would grow out of scale and dwarf the house and lot. Trees 35 to 40 feet in height will be in scale, look well, and complement the character of your house and the beauty of your garden composition.

Proportion

Everything in your garden must be in pleasing proportion: the lawn, pool, patio, vertical structures, fence panels, even shrubs, trees, and flower beds must conform to the rules of proportion to look well.

Generally, proportion is the relationship of length to breadth that is pleasing to our eyes. The accepted rule is a ratio of 3 to slightly under 5, or a rectangle somewhat less than twice as broad as it is high, or twice as long as it is wide. However, exactness of dimension is not required. In fact, exactness might become obvious in the composition and, to some degree, spoil it. Just keep the general rule in mind.

Figure 2.2 illustrates proportion in design. The size of the pergola is in good proportion with the rectangular area and its plant elements. The pool relates proportionately to the entire rectangular composition and to the several elements comprising the area—the lounging shelter, paved areas, and the lawn panels. The patio is in pleasing proportion with the house and the pool area. Everything is in good proportion, one feature with the other.

Texture

Texture has several ramifications in an estate or park-size landscape, but in a small to medium-size property, it derives mainly from the limbs, branches, and foliage of plants. The effect may be soft and smooth or rough and sharp. Compare the strong and rugged mien of a gnarled oak with the feathery texture of a smoke tree.

In the realm of foliage, texture generally refers to the size, form, density, and expressive characteristics of leaves. The delicate, lacy texture of gypsophila (baby's breath) produces a feeling of softness. Betula populifolia (birch) has a light and lively texture that imparts a sense of airiness and movement. The lush density of needle-leaf evergreen foliage suggests the smoothness of velvet—soft, expensive, and strong of character. The large, impressive leaves of maple trees present a coarser texture but seem strong and dependable.

Since every plant has a particular texture, in the arrangement of shrubs, trees, and flowers in your garden, you must consider plant association. Delicately textured shrubs beside large, leathery-leaved ones, rather like a garment made of chiffon and burlap, is not pleasing. With few and very special exceptions, plant materials in a particular grouping should be of similar texture. Even the plants used to tie groups together are more effective if they have related textures.

Color

Everything in your garden has color—structures, ground cover, plants, even the soil. The sky adds constantly changing effects. Snow in winter alters the appearance of the landscape, but there still is color.

Many homeowners consider color principally from the standpoint of flower plantings. However, some busy home gardeners consider flowers a maintenance problem and prefer creating an *all-green* garden. This type of composition is feasible, but most often a few flowers are eventually added to brighten the scene.

Figure 2.2. **PROPORTION**

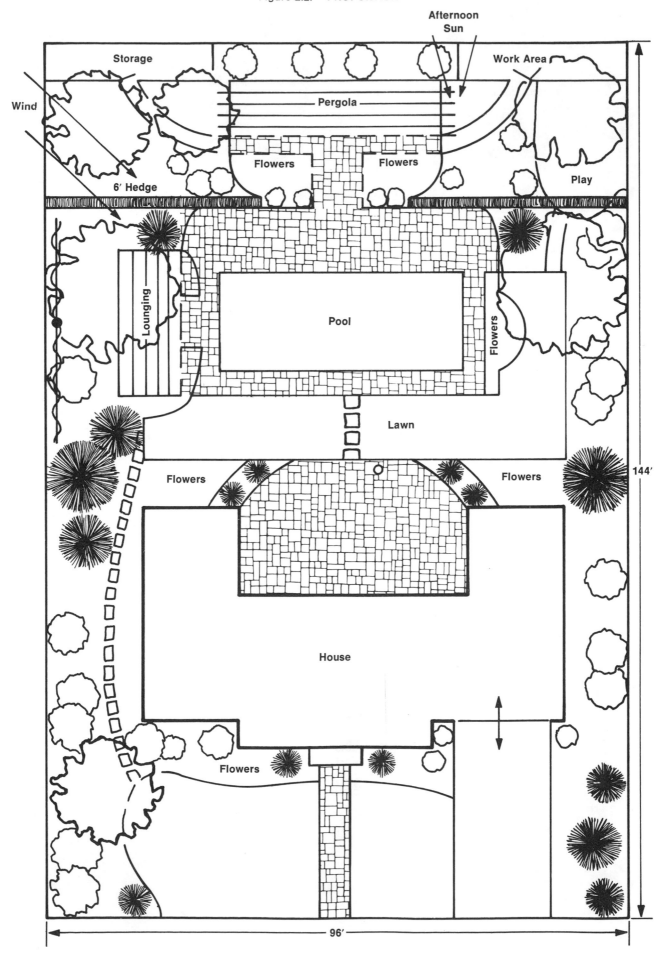

The All-Green Garden

The attractiveness of an all-green garden depends heavily upon attractive association of plant forms, quality of lines, and, particularly, the structural characteristics of smaller trees. Of prime importance are harmonious textural values and a progressive variation of tints and shades of green woven through the composition to add variety and sparkle.

In this type of garden, emphasis is on free-flowing design and skillful association of quality (though not necessarily expensive) plants. Including an occasional contrasting accent tones up the landscape picture. If a light and airy effect is desired, concentrate on open plantings of light-to-medium-textured shrubs and trees. Structures should usually be simple in design and not massive. Equally important is the organization of shades of green and the size and texture of plants, particularly in their groupings, to create pleasing interest in the vertical and horizontal planes, effective transition from one part of the garden to another, and proportional balance and scale throughout. These and other elements of garden design are tools with which to construct an unusually effective all-green garden.

The Garden with Flowers

In conventional garden design, flower color is an orderly part of the whole plan. However, the colors of shrub and tree foliage are also included in the overall concept. Flowers play a major role in creating seasonal interest, and bulbs, annuals, and perennials should be arranged to produce colorful floral pictures in spring, summer, and fall. A few flowering shrubs and trees and some that turn their foliage into beautiful colors in autumn will lengthen your garden's period of seasonal color.

Give considerable thought to selecting pleasing predominant colors for each blooming season and to the related combinations of flowers, shrubs, and trees in your garden. Carefully consider the whole scene and the entire flowering season. Poor combinations can detract from the effectiveness of the most beautiful flowering plants.

Harmony

Harmony in garden design is the compatible arrangement of all landscape elements into an aesthetically pleasing composition that achieves unity of effect. It requires careful manipulation of plants and structures in accordance with other design principles and with your own desires. Whether your preference is a quiet, relaxing garden or a stimulating one, colors and elements must be harmoniously arranged to produce the particular effect you want.

Harmony throughout is the key to a successful garden.

Cheerfulness

Although cheerfulness is not, strictly speaking, a design principle, it is an important factor to keep in mind when planning any garden. The intangible benefits of a garden that reflects good cheer through judicious use of open spaces, colorful flowers, and areas of bright sunlight certainly should not be overlooked.

DEVELOPING YOUR GARDEN DESIGN

Now that you are acquainted with the few guiding principles of design, you can arrange the several essential parts of your garden into a workable plan. They include:

Structures	Special gardens
Surfaced areas	Garden circulation
Children's play unit	Garden lighting
Lawns	

Organization is a vital part of garden design. It is very easy to overlook grading and construct a children's play area on a back slope, for example, and a year later find that winter water drains in the wrong direction and that the play unit is where the patio should be.

To prevent such costly errors you should follow a progressive procedure in your garden development and subsequent garden construction. Although every property differs a little from every other and each homeowner has his own design picture in mind, all must follow a logical course.

Arrangement of Garden Features

The garden plan in Figure 2.3 contains features discussed in Chapter 1: lawns, a sizable patio,

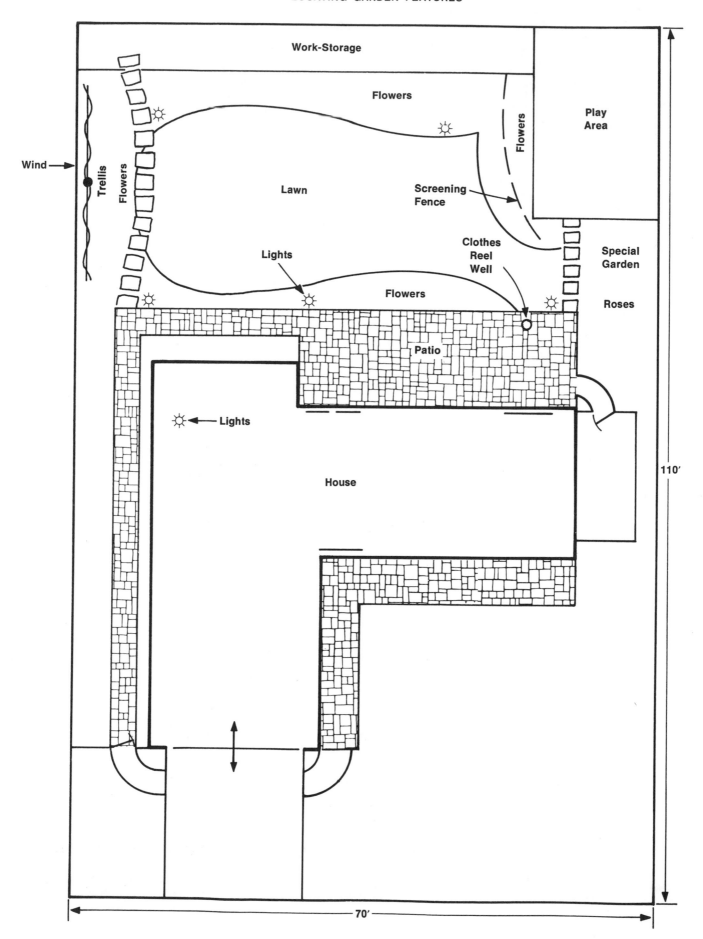

Figure 2.3   **LANDSCAPING THE SMALL PROPERTY:
LOCATING GARDEN FEATURES**

children's play unit, a small rose garden, flower plots and drifts, a trellis, utility-storage facilities, provision for a clothes reel, and some garden lighting. These features require walks and paths, surfaces, water lines, and underground electric lines for garden lights. We will consider all these elements in the following sections.

For homeowners who have larger properties and wish additional features arranged in a more sophisticated design, there is an expanded plan in Chapter 3.

You are already familiar with the influencing factors, house style, shape of lot, and so forth, and the very necessary preparatory ground work discussed in Chapter 1 and have indicated them on your design paper. Now place beside you the list of garden features you yourself have selected, and proceed to design your own personal garden.

PLACING MAJOR UNITS

Structures

Major structures should be placed first in your design. Features such as a pool or lounging shelter are not part of our immediate plan but are included in the next chapter. However, we have included a utility-storage unit, which is of great importance to everyday garden maintenance. In the realm of good garden design, nothing is more difficult to locate inconspicuously than a utility area.

The conventional utility-storage unit requires a storage structure for tools, spray materials, supplies, and power equipment; it is large enough to stack peat moss, leaf mold, bags of fertilizer, pots, flats, and containers. However, there is seldom room for lumber or piles of soil and sand.

Left open to view this miniature warehouse impairs the aesthetic qualities of your garden, so you contrive to screen it by means of artistic fences, structures, or hedge. There is a much better way to handle this problem, one that is feasible in many gardens. A little way in from your rear line fence—6 or 7 feet is sufficient—construct a parallel fence part or all the way across your lot, as indicated in Figure 2.4. Cut in a relatively wide gate. Cover half the area with roof-type sheet plastic, divide it into work sections, and you have a completely isolated utility area of enormous value. See also Sketch 2.2. Sur-

facing is advisable, but alternatively cover the ground with fine gravel.

→ Draw a utility-storage area on your plot plan, if your garden will accommodate one, and set up a special working plan for the entire unit.

Garden Supply

Set aside a section of your utility area for storage of garden supplies. A waterproof locker built against the rear fence is advisable for sprays, tools, and equipment. It will of necessity be rather shallow, but unrestricted length will increase its versatility. Sliding doors are a nice addition but not essential.

Lumber Storage

Every homeowner is aware of the periodic need for lumber somewhere in his garden or home: long 1- by 2-inch strips for repairs, 4- by 4-inch posts, 2- by 12-inch boards to construct a raised flower bed, or logs for the fireplace.

In your utility area, build a level and lengthy lumber rack along the rear fence, elevated a little to prevent contact with the ground. Two or three years supply may easily be stored and covered.

Plant Propagation Facilities

Successful plant propagation requires not only technical skill but proper equipment, soil mixtures, and, equally important, a convenient working unit with mixing table, cutting bench, tool board, pot and flat stand, and a convenient water tap. Sketch 2.3 illustrates a successful arrangement.

The type of utility area we have been discussing provides space for these handy facilities. Locate your work area parallel to the rear fence and under the plastic roofing, being sure to leave a passageway amply wide for a transportation cart or wheelbarrow.

Soil Supply

Construction of five or six relatively small, consecutive bins along the rear fence line is suggested. These will contain soil, sand, leaf mold, peat moss, and prepared soil mixture, all essential gardening requirements. This unit is also covered with sheet-plastic roofing for protection from snow and rain.

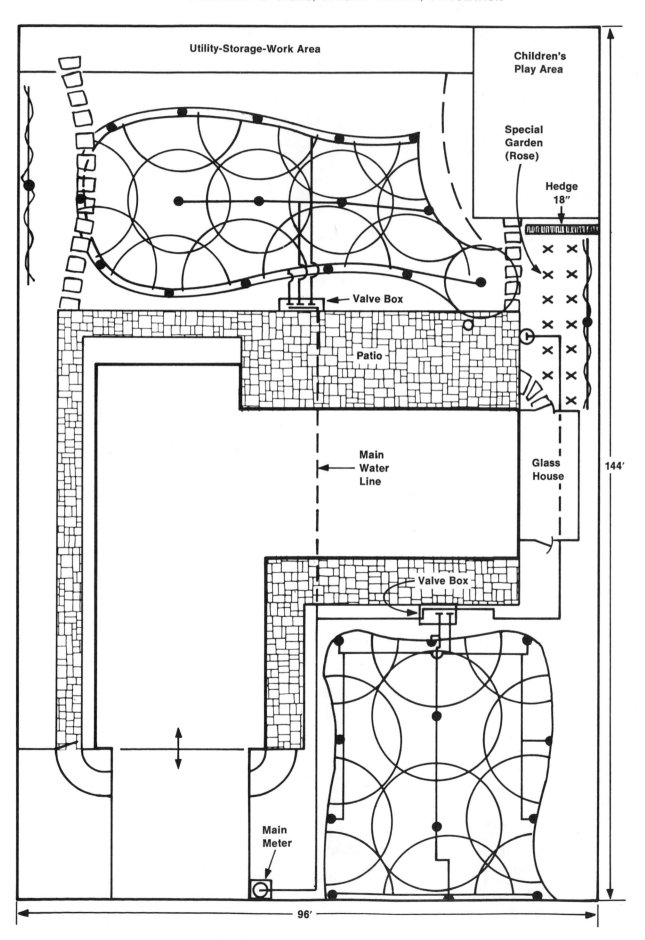

Figure 2.4   **LANDSCAPING THE SMALL GARDEN: UTILITY-STORAGE, SPRINKLING SYSTEMS, SPECIAL GARDEN, CIRCULATION**

Photo 2.3

A handy little garden supply room behind the house.

(Home of Joe and Dolores Bettancourt)

Sketch 2.3   **PLANT PROPAGATION FACILITY**

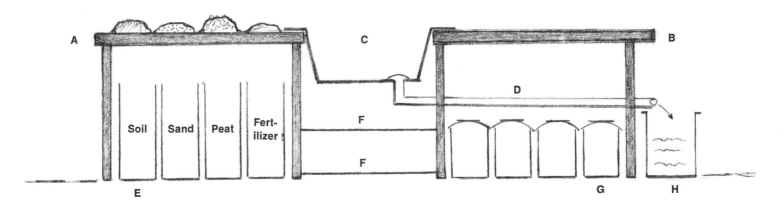

A—Soil, sand, peat, fertilizer mixing table
B—Work table for cuttings, seed-flat preparation, dividing
C—Sink for water requirements
D—Sink drain into drainage facility or receptacle
E—Series of movable bins for soil, sand, peat, fertilizer
F—Pot storage
G—Series of plastic containers for miscellaneous storage
H—Sink drain receptacle (if required)
Attach drop-in-place or hinged doors to the three compartments for neat, cabinet-like appearance and for safety.

Sketch 2.2   **GARDEN EQUIPMENT SUPPLY-STORAGE UNIT**

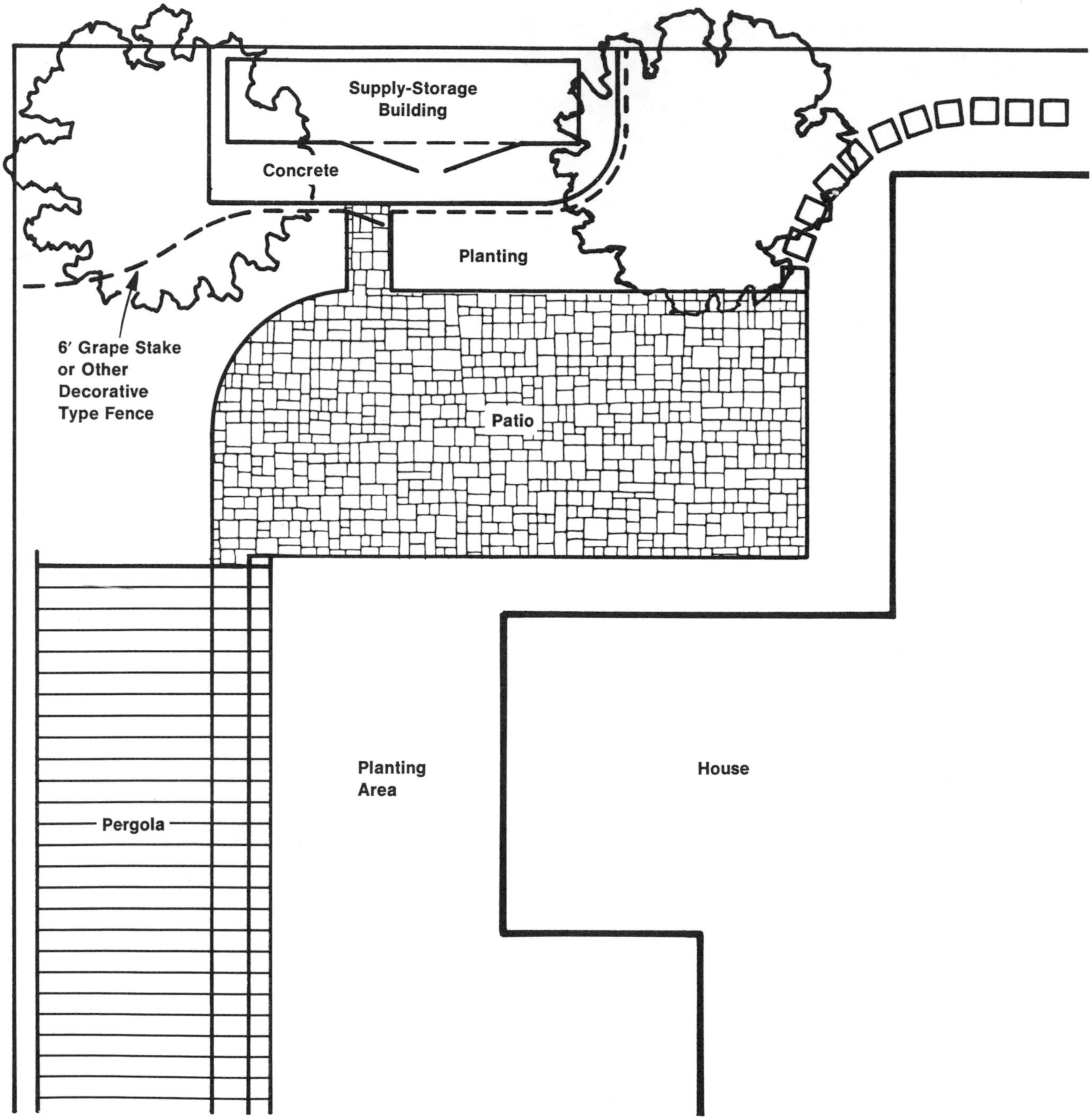

Supply-Storage
Building

Concrete

Planting

6' Grape Stake
or Other
Decorative
Type Fence

Patio

Pergola

Planting
Area

House

Photo 2.4

Use of brick, natural stone, and gray gravel is harmonious and pleasing.

Photo 2.5

Red tile laid to form pleasing patterns around the pool or in the patio.

Water Supply to Utility Areas

A convenient water supply and facility should be provided in the plant propagation unit. Purchase a used kitchen sink and add a sizable wooden drainboard made of 2- by 4-inch redwood and separated a little for free drainage. In addition to a faucet, install a second pipe and attach a hose bibb. Connect the water pipes to your main water line before beginning garden planting.
→ Determine the approximate location of your water facility, and indicate the line on your plot plan.

Other Types of Utility Storage Areas

Many properties will not accommodate the size and type of utility area we have discussed. If not, a small, shelved, and fully equipped lean-to room constructed as a part of your house or garage is excellent for equipment storage. Neat metal structures designed for the purpose are available through garden supply stores and mail order companies. These may be strategically located and blended into the landscape with shrub and small tree plantings.

Surfaced Areas

Your garden should offer a social setting with emphasis on action within an aesthetic environment. Action requires surfaced areas. Therefore many good gardens are designed with spacious surfaces to accommodate garden parties, small business groups, teenage activities, and even dancing in the color and sparkle of a natural setting. Brightly colored garden furniture enlivens the social atmosphere.

Concrete surfacing is acceptable, but the market offers paving materials of such diverse forms and textures that you should consider alternatives. Strive toward a strict consistancy in surface material and patterns. If precast material is used, set it firmly on a poured concrete base for stability and permanency. Neutral to slightly colored surfaces are preferable. Never coat them with paint, for they quickly would become worn and unsightly.

Patio Floors

In the average garden, the patio floor is the first surface to be laid. Because the patio is related to both house and garden, it should be compatible with both and act as a unifying element. In this role, concrete is excellent, but new or used brick is much more interesting. Bricks are easily laid on a freshly poured base with mortar to bind them firmly. Another and quite satisfactory method of laying bricks is to thoroughly compact the soil base, spread a 2-inch layer of fine sand, level and firm it down, and lay the bricks on the sand. Maintain a perfectly level surface as you proceed. Finally, sweep fine sand over the completed patio surface to fill the spaces between the bricks. Bricks are easily laid in patterns to increase interest. But remember, the entire patio surface must have a slightly higher elevation than the lawn to permit drainage.

If precast surfacing material is used for the patio, it should be sufficiently subdued in color and pattern to avoid conflicting with the house and yet lively enough to associate favorably with adjacent floral elements in the garden. Precast surfacing is quite expensive and should be professionally laid.

→ Outline and shade a patio surface on your sketch.

Drying-yard Surfaces

Drying yards are seldom indicated on a design or established as a separate unit in the modern garden. Limited clothes lines, however, are perfectly in order even in urban gardens if strung tautly over a brick or concrete surface in a rather remote part of the garden. If they are kept taut by means of turnbuckles (see Sketch 2.4), they are scarcely noticed.

The patio is an excellent location for a removable clothes reel. At the time of construction, install a small, round well of desired size—say, about 2 inches in diameter—completely through

Sketch 2.4 **CLOTHES LINES**

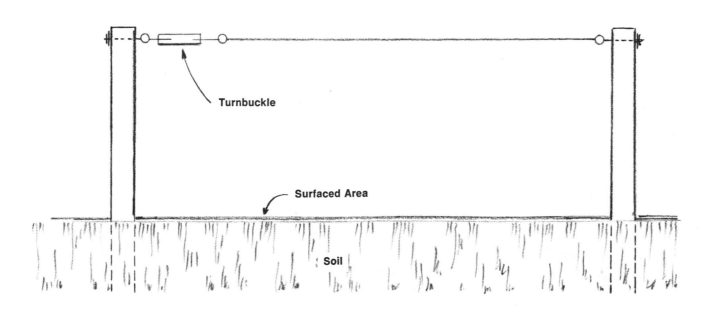

If lines are kept tight by use of turnbuckles, they are barely noticeable.

the surface. Purchase a rubber plug that will tightly close the opening when not in use. Obtain a wooden dowel that will snugly slide down into the well and extend above the surface enough to firmly support the metal reel-holder that slips over it. The clothes reel is then quickly and easily placed in position or removed when not in use. This type of receptacle is indicated in Figure 2.3.
→ Mark the location of a clothes line in your garden or a clothes reel on your patio.

Floor Surfaces in Structures

Floors of garden structures that are used for lounging or serving food should be surfaced. To preserve continuity and unification of elements, within a given feature unit, floors are usually the same kind and color throughout. When, on the other hand, structures are located in different parts of the garden and are not part of a distinct unit, the respective floors may vary.

Flat stone is often used, preferably in natural tones of light browns or tans—warm, lively colors. Slate gives a durable feeling but is neutral or rather dark. Be sure to lay all stone floors on a newly poured concrete base for stability.

Water Lines Under Surfaces

Main water lines to major sections of your garden must be established prior to the construction of surfaces. It is critical that you indicate these water lines on your developing garden design, as was done in Figure 2.4.

Secondary water lines are connected to the nearest main line and laid to such structures as lounging shelters, pergolas, and patios before their floors or other obstacles are constructed.
→ Primary and secondary water lines should be clearly marked on your plot plan.

Children's Play Unit

There are several special requirements in the design and location of a play unit for small children. It must be large enough to accommodate your children plus a few friends and you will probably want it to be in view of the house. On the other hand, the inevitable clutter created by children at play should be at least partially concealed.

With careful planning you can meet all these requirements. For example, it is not necessary for a play area to be rectangular or have the appear-

ance of a box. On most properties it may curve neatly into a planting bay and become part of a natural unit.

To a great extent, your garden design determines the location of a play unit. Since it is only a temporary feature, do not give it a dominant location or allow it to determine permanent garden arrangements. Regardless of temporary importance, a children's play unit is only a part of the whole composition and should be placed logically for later removal or conversion to another use.
→ Draw a play area on your plan if one is required.

Screening the Play Area

In a small backyard, the play unit may be partially screened from the major portion of the garden by a relatively slender and slightly curved fence, as indicated in Figure 2.3. The view from the house remains unobstructed, but a sizable percentage of the garden is shielded. A low to medium shrub planting is often used for partial screening. Be sure to use soft-textured species without thorns.
→If you wish to include a screening element, indicate it on your sketch.

Play Apparatus

Competition among companies that manufacture recreation apparatus is resulting in attractive designs and versatile combinations. Play units designed for one child or a dozen are now available in colors that appeal to children and in forms that do not mar the landscape. Spend some time investigating the choices available, and select with care.

Surface Material

Because small children occasionally fall from play apparatus, it is imperative that you provide some type of shock-absorbing surface material. There are several options. Sand is universally used but presents two problems: it is attractive to pets and is easily carried into the house on clothing. Tanbark has excellent protective qualities; however, when damp it has a tendency to stain clothing. Fine pine or fir shavings are very good. They deteriorate rather rapidly, necessitating renewal each year or two, but the partially decomposed material is an excellent organic additive for the

Photo 2.6

Reduce the number to 2 or 3 and make it all yourself from your own design.

garden soil. Hardwood shavings are slightly abrasive, creating the possibility of skin irritation.

Your city park and recreation department researches play-area surfacing material for your locality. Ask them for assistance in making a selection for your specific situation.

Enclosure

Enclosing the play unit will contain loose surface material and help define the children's play space. Enclosures are usually 12 inches in height and may be constructed of metal, concrete, brick, or wood. Metal is acceptable only if the upper surface is sufficiently capped to prevent cuts. Permanent concrete and brick requires 2- by 8-inch splinter-free lumber caps along the entire top to prevent serious bruises. Experience indicates that 2- by 12-inch surfaced lumber enclosures capped with 2- by 8-inch boards are attractive, serviceable, and economical.

Photo 2.7

A compact unit of play equipment for the small garden. Fruitless mulberry for shade. L to R—Chinese elm, juniperus chinensis pfitzeriana, xylosma, juniperus chinensis pfitzeriana, common privet. Home of H. D. Givens, Jr.

Photo 2.8

Construct one of your own design.

PLANNING LAWN AREAS

Volumes have been written about lawns, but in this work we are interested in *your* lawns. They play an exceptional role in the landscape and must be given explicit consideration at the time of garden planning. Only on your drafting paper are you able to see clearly the extent of your lawn, its shape, its association with other garden elements, and the role it plays in their unification. Like all other landscape features, lawns must take their place gracefully within the overall design composition. Glance at Figure 2.3 and note how the lawn relates to other elements. It is accessible to the play area and the patio and serves to unify the patio and back section of the garden. This lawn is relatively large because in a small backyard there are usually few major features. This limits physical activities primarily to the patio and lawn.

Front lawns are equally important. They are often relatively large to create a feeling of expanse. The proportions must be pleasing, however, and kept within reasonable scale. In a way, your front yard is your name plate. It reflects your thinking, character, and attitude.

→ Draw the front and back lawns on your developing plan.

Photo 2.9

Quiet privacy in a plant protected patio.

(Home of Melvin and Helen Jory)

Lawn Curbing

Permanency, appearance, and ease of maintenance are essentials that must not be neglected in the development of lawns. There are several contributing factors that determine success or failure in these areas, and they begin with a seemingly unimportant item—the lawn curbing.

The guiding rule for lawn curbing is simple: keep it inconspicuous. There are several types of curbing on the market, and you should investigate the feasibility of each in your specific case. Wood lawn curbing is professionally acceptable anywhere and relatively permanent. It reduces damage to mower blades and is very adaptable to the use of power edgers. Furthermore, it is easily repaired or replaced.

Some supply companies offer specially sawed wood lawn curbing that is remarkably flexible for curved installation. If this is available and your choice, copiously apply a nontoxic wood preservative to increase its life by several years. I use 1- by 4-inch redwood boards 12 or more feet long. Those that are to be sharply curved are soaked overnight to increase flexibility.

To install curbing, drive a row of 2- by 4-inch treated stakes deeply into the ground 6 feet apart completely around the outline of the lawn area (more will be needed on curves). Next, nail the curbing temporarily to the stakes from the lawn side at a height commensurate with the final grade of the lawn. Allow water-soaked boards to dry in place. Then apply wood preservative, which is available at paint stores. Nail the curbing permanently after the inevitable changes in final grade.

Preparing the Lawn Area

Grading

Carefully establish the general grade of the lawn area, thoroughly mix the soil with organic material, and leave the lawn curbing temporarily an inch above the anticipated final grade. A second grading with a rake or other hand-held implement will follow the installation of sprinklers.

Sprinklers

A sprinkler system will save you water, time, and energy. Plan toward spray-head control and the use of coarse or fine sprays—that is, simulated rain or mist. Coarse sprays contend better with winds. Adapt conventional systems by increasing

Sketch 2.5

TYPICAL FOUR-LINE LAWN SPRINKLER VALVE-CONTROL ASSEMBLY (VALVE BOX)

Fittings:

1. 1–¾″ Tee

2. 1–¾″ elbow
   1–¾″ x 2″ nipple

3. 1–¾″ Tee
   1–¾″ x 2″ nipple

4. 1–¾″ Tee
   1–¾″ x 2″ nipple

5. 1–¾″ elbow
   1–¾″ x 2″ nipple

A, B, C, D are cut to
desired length.

6. 1–¾″ valve
   1–¾″ x 2″ nipple
   1–¾″ union

7. 1–¾″ valve
   1–¾″ x 2″ nipple
   1–¾″ union

8. 1¾″ valve
   1–¾″ x 2″ nipple
   1–¾″ union

9. 1–¾″ valve
   1–¾″ x 2″ nipple
   1–¾″ union

10. 1–¾″ Tee
    2–¾″ x 2″ nipples
    2–¾″ unions

11. 1–¾″ Tee
    2–¾″ x 2″ nipples
    2–¾″ unions

12. 1–¾″ Tee
    2–¾″ x 2″ nipples
    2–¾″ unions

13. 1–¾″ Tee
    2–¾″ x 2″ nipples
    2–¾″ unions

SL—Sprinkler lines

Check-valve is to
prevent water from
returning from the
sprinkler system to
the main water sup-
ply. Its assembly
may differ according
to type and location
and restrictions.

the volume and pressure at the point of distribution, the sprinkler head. To accomplish this, simply break the overall sprinkler system into shorter valve-controlled lines and place the heads on each line a foot or two closer together. Regardless of water pressure and volume at the meter, you are in complete control. See Sketch 2.5. If the water pressure is high, open two control valves instead of one. When wind is a factor, a partially opened valve permits coarser sprinkling. These adaptations increase the cost of materials and installation very little. Figure 2.4 illustrates the versatility of this type of installation and the control attained. In the back lawn, the ¾-inch pipe along the far edge has one quarter-head sprinkler and five half-head sprinklers approximately 12 feet apart. The line on the patio side has five half-heads and one full head. The middle line has one half-head and three full heads. All are finest quality, pop-up adjustable brass heads. Each line is directly connected to an individual valve in the control box. The valve cluster is connected to the main water line in a manner that permits each valve to operate individually. All heads are attached to ½-inch risers from the ¾-inch line, and the line and risers are purposely set so each head is ½ inch inside the curb to permit a lawn-edger blade to pass freely between curb and head.

It is obvious from the illustration that there is complete and overlapping water coverage. This is most important, for it will prevent dry spots under adverse conditions.

The sprinkling system for the front lawn is laid out in the same manner. Each water line is *underloaded* with quarter, half, and full pop-up adjustable heads connected to a valve control box, assuring ample water coverage under all conditions and complete control at all times.

→ Make a separate, scale drawing of sprinkler systems for your lawns before attempting installation. It is easier to make changes on paper than after the pipe has been cut.

The mechanics of installing a sprinkler system are simple and easy. A few good tools are necessary: two pipe wrenches, a pipe vise, two 6-inch C clamps, a hack saw, a set of pipe dies, a pipe reamer to ream the inside edges of the cut pipe, a coarse file to smooth the outside edge of the cut, two saw horses, a 10-foot plank to hold the pipe vise, pipe and fittings, and a can of cutting oil. The major tools can frequently be rented.

Final Soil Preparation

Proper preparation of the seed bed assures a healthy and vigorous lawn for many years. Quantities of organic material should be added until the soil body is lose to a depth of 8 or 10 inches. There are several reasons for this: to avoid heavy compaction, promote ready acceptance of water and nutrients, increase moisture-retaining qualities, encourage normal bacterial action in the soil, and provide a deep and free root run for lawn plants.

Final Grade

The seed bed must now be raked to distribute the soil evenly and remove all deleterious material. Sketch 2.6 illustrates the process. At the same time, the surface soil is finely pulverized and leveled against the curbing.

The curbing is now raised or lowered to conform to the final compacted grade. Nail the curbing securely to the stakes, and saw the outside of the stakes on a 45-degree slant from the upper surface of the curbing. This makes them almost unnoticeable. Curb assembly is illustrated in Sketch 2.7.

Lawn Selection

The kind of lawn you select is very important. Various species of grass respond differently to temperature, location, usage, sun or shade, wind and weather. Realistically analyze your specific lawn situation with these factors in mind.

Here are a few of the commonly used grasses, with some pertinent information on their characteristics and usage.

COMMON BERMUDA GRASS: This hardy and aggressive grass prefers full sun and good drainage. It will tolerate considerable acidity, poor soil, and heavy usage. Be careful, however: it progresses rather rapidly by runners and is difficult to control. For this reason it is not suggested for the average small to medium garden. It is widely used for large plantings in southern parts of the country.

BLUE GRAMA: This is a very drought-resistant grass and is usable in cool, dry regions that are subject to low rainfall and limited water supply. The Great Plains area is an example. It is a low growing type that will not tolerate heavy use.

CARPET GRASS: This one is relatively coarse but produces a thick turf if grown in moist, sandy loam. It is widely used in temperate to warm areas of the country.

CHEWINGS FESCUE: This is an excellent grass that mixes well with compatible types, such as the bents, ryes, and bluegrasses. It grows well in cool, rather humid regions, adapts to shady sites, and tolerates quite heavy usage.

COLONIAL AND HIGHLAND BENTGRASS: These fine, high quality grasses are widely used in the northeastern, northwestern, and western states, the cooler and rather moist sections of the country. They are fine-blade grasses excellent for formal lawns that are meticulously maintained. Bentgrasses give a finer texture and more refined appearance to a chewings or red fescue lawn, for instance. They are particularly appropriate for front lawns where use is not too extensive. Adequate watering and frequent mowing are mandatory for maximum beauty.

Sketch 2.6   **LAWN PREPARATION: FINAL GRADE**

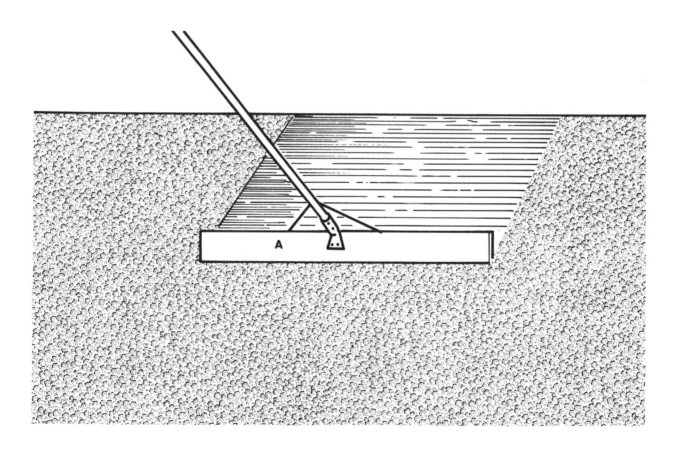

Construct a wood straight-edge for leveling and smoothing lawn seed bed.

A—a 1″ x 4″ x 3′ piece of fir with a strong, well braced handle attached.

Pre-dampen the soil to make it crumbly. Pull the wide straight-edge over and over the soil surface (as you would the back of a garden rake); it will quickly and easily crumble, level, and smooth the soil surface. (The back of the garden rake is too light and narrow to be practical.)

KENTUCKY BLUEGRASS: Here is a grass for many locations and uses. It is hardy, has a delicate blue sheen, and is used singly or in combination with other grasses for backyard lawns, parks, and recreation fields. It is at its best in the cooler and somewhat humid sections of the country and prefers good drainage and nearly neutral soil. A fair amount of moisture and occasional feeding are required to keep it looking well. Merion is a beautiful variety of Kentucky blue but requires a higher level of soil fertility, particularly nitrogen.

PERENNIAL RYE GRASS: This wide-blade grass is generally used in mixed lawns through sections of the western, southern and Atlantic regions. I suggest you inquire about new, fine-leaved varieties.

RED FESCUE: This variety will do well in shaded parts of your garden if the soil is fairly fertile and well drained. Like Kentucky bluegrass, it prefers the cooler and rather humid sections of the country. However, it will prosper elsewhere if the soil is kept rather moist. It is usually mixed with other varieties, especially with Kentucky blue.

ROUGH BLUEGRASS: This is a grass for shady places in cool, moist regions. It is difficult to grow in hot, dry areas.

TALL FESCUE: This grass grows well in the very warm and dry sections of the southern and central regions and is widely used for large plantings —extensive lawns, parks, athletic fields, and playgrounds. If thickly planted, it forms a tough, serviceable turf.

Although some grasses resist drought and neglect fairly well, all respond to frequent feeding, watering, and mowing at regular intervals. For multi-use lawns, compatible mixtures are generally better than a single variety.

Purchase seed from reputable companies that respect the legal regulations set up by state and federal law. Be sure to read the label on the package or, if you buy bulk seed, be certain that it is the correct variety and that it conforms to legal regulations relative to germination, weed and noxious-weed seeds, any other crop seed, and inert matter.

Sketch 2.7 **LAWN CURB ASSEMBLY**

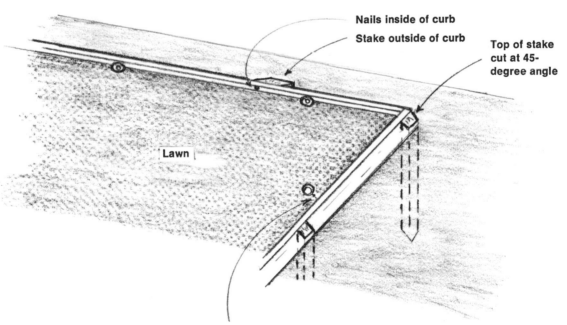

Nails inside of curb
Stake outside of curb
Top of stake cut at 45-degree angle

Lawn

Place pop-up sprinkler heads ½ inch inside of the curb to permit lawn-edger blades to pass freely between curb and head.

ADDING SPECIAL FEATURES AND REFINEMENTS

You have now indicated the principle elements of your garden plan on your design sketch: major water lines, drain lines, fences, surfaces, utility space, children's play area, and lawns. The next step is to add smaller units and refinements.

Special Gardens

Special gardens of unique color and beauty serve as effective points of interest. Note the strategic location of the small rose garden in Figure 2.4. It is at the terminus of the patio and entrance to the lawn, adjacent to the play area, at the entrance of the glass house, and in view of the house. It radiates color to these sections of the garden and helps balance any excess informality with just a touch of the formal.

A good location for a second special display exists on the opposite side of the garden between the trellis and path.

Your developing plan will reveal effective locations for special gardens. Place them carefully to avoid a spotted and dissociated effect.
→ Indicate the placement of special gardens on your plot plan.

Harmony of Outline and Color

The outline or form of a special garden is determined essentially by restrictions of the area and the effect desired. Do you want an element of formality? Or would a bold, informal arrangement in a naturally delineated area be more to your taste? Whatever style you choose, the general outline of a special garden must be simple, related to adjacent elements, and gracefully blended into the local composition.

Give considerable thought to the color arrangement of each special garden. These special groupings do not assume dominant roles in your garden's color scheme but serve rather as highlights in the overall setting. A given unit may be composed of one color, such as a cluster of madonna lilies around a birdbath, a planting of red roses in a shrub bay, or a panel of pink chrysanthemums. The usual planting, however, consists of harmoniously mixed colors that are consistent with seasonal garden-wide flowerings.

Soil and Water

Proper soil preparation is particularly important in special garden areas, for they will probably be planted with choice plants that should not be disturbed for several years. This makes difficult the periodic cultivation necessary for vigorous growth and brilliant displays of color. Thorough initial preparation of the soil with organic material of long-lasting qualities insures maximum results with a minimum of deep cultivation and root disturbance required in the future.

Many times special gardens are in a remote part of the main garden. Handling long lengths of water hose is inconvenient and time consuming. Water pipes should be extended from the nearest main line to each garden unit and fitted with quick-coupling hose bibbs.
→ Indicate these water lines on your plan.

Garden Circulation

Walks and paths have a definite purpose. They provide ease of movement from one part of the garden to another. They should also promote a feeling of continuity throughout the entire composition. Therefore, locate walks and paths judiciously to avoid cutting the overall design into individual strips and peculiarly shaped division, which would diminish garden unification.

Walks

Surfaced walks are needed where foot traffic is relatively heavy: to the front entrance of the house, from the front yard to the back, and to those parts of the garden that are frequented by wheeled implements, such as mowers and carrying carts. Walks should be wide enough to accommodate such traffic easily and should be constructed with both practical and aesthetic factors in mind.

The greater percentage of garden walks are built of concrete. However, untreated concrete surfaces become slippery when wet and may be conducive to slips and falls. This can be prevented by treating the surfaces with a nonskid material at the time of construction. Consult your contractor about the various options available.

The more porous or nonskid type of pre-cast material may be used if perfectly laid over a freshly poured concrete base. There should be a related architectural trend between house and walks, particularly a front walk. Surface materials that reflect a feeling of warmth and friendliness, such as used brick or light brown stone, are especially adaptable.

Photo 2.10

Seasonal beauty along a garden path. Esther Reed daisies, creeping yarrow, *Chamaecyparis pisifera squarrosa minima*, iris.

Paths

Where traffic is light and utility is not the prime consideration, use a path instead of a walk. In the average small to medium garden, a path is more aesthetically effective as it meanders naturally from one element to another, gracefully turning a little here and there to avoid a structure or lead to a point of interest.

Paths vary considerably in construction and appearance. Some gardens gracefully accept well-proportioned gravel paths. In informal design, the gravel should be neutral in color. In many instances, semiformal to formal gardens are noticeably improved by paths of carefully selected colored gravel.

The majority of paths, however, are made of stepping stones which offer an artistic advantage.

Each consecutive stone is an individual source of interest, while collectively they present a linear composition reflective of nature. Natural stone is especially appropriate. Stepping stones of any type should not be painted or their natural appearance otherwise altered.

Paths are meant to be walked upon, so consider carefully the width of the stones and the distance between them. Will your path provide comfortable footing for the elderly, for children? Remember, too, that unevenly laid stones can be dangerous. To prevent tripping, set stones firmly on an even elevation and at regular intervals.

→ Sketch in the walks and paths required in your developing plan.

Garden Lighting

Subtle garden lighting contributes significantly to the charm and elegance of evening garden parties. Fixtures must be in good taste and conform to house and garden styles. In small to medium gardens, ornateness in lights is usually objectionable, but quality is important.

Place lights at strategic vantage points—in the lounging or pool area, beside a striking flower unit, at an intersection of paths, bordering the patio, and in the vicinity of flower border and seats. Study the placement of lights in Figure 2.5 for ideas for your property.

The garden lighting system must be installed prior to laying surfaces so that underground conduits can be conveniently located. A permit is usually required, and the work should be done by a licensed contractor.

Establish indoor controls in handy locations. Switches for backyard lighting located near the back door and switches at the front door for lights in the front yard are most convenient, certainly preferable to having to contend with the inconvenience of a master control somewhere in a remote corner of the garage.

→ Sketch in a system of garden lighting on your plot plan.

Trellises

Trellises are used for two major purposes in the average garden: as plant supports and for screening. In many instances, large and sturdy trellises capable of supporting closely trimmed expanses of pyracantha, evergreen cotoneaster, or hardy vines are valuable screening devices. The two

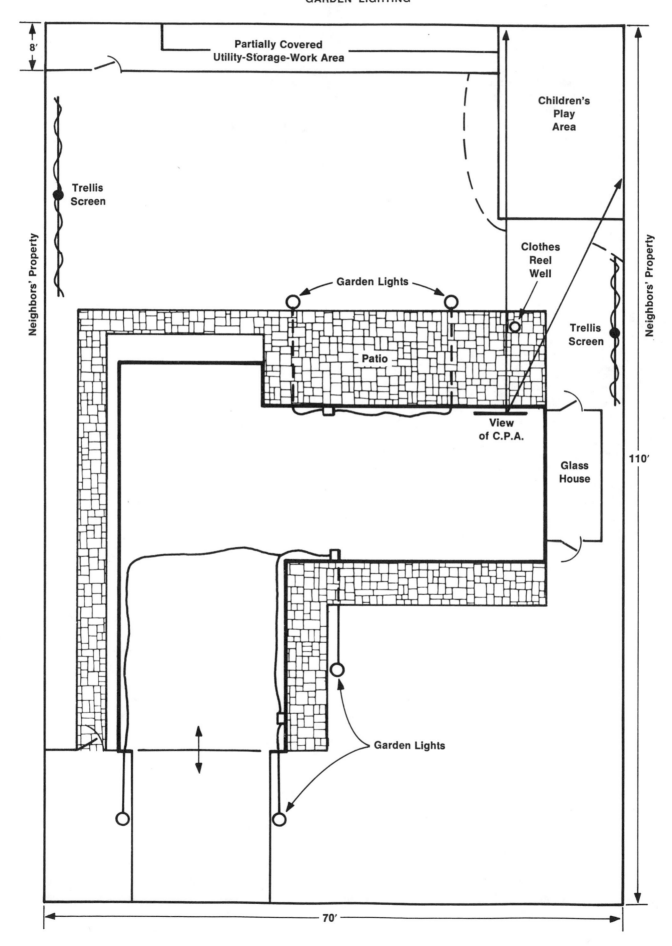

Figure 2.5   LANDSCAPING THE SMALL PROPERTY:
GARDEN LIGHTING

trellises in Figure 2.5, for example, provide privacy from adjacent lots.

Do winds blow directly across your patio or rose garden? Place a wide, sturdy trellis in the path of the wind to break its force. Under these conditions, the sturdiness of the trellis should not be in direct relation to the plant load it is to support but to the force of the wind against it. Invariably, such trellises are located in front of a fence and securely attached to it, but they should also be braced for additional resistance.

The color of a trellis merits consideration. If it is in close proximity to a blue house, for instance, it too might be painted blue. If placed against a natural wood fence, it should probably be of natural wood.

→ Draw one or more trellises on your plot plan, if desired.

We have now placed a selected list of garden features on design paper. However, many homeowners have larger properties and wish to include additional features: a pool, lounging shelter, pergola, larger surfaced areas, and so on. Is your property large? Do you want to include more elements in your garden? If so, Chapter 3 offers numerous suggestions.

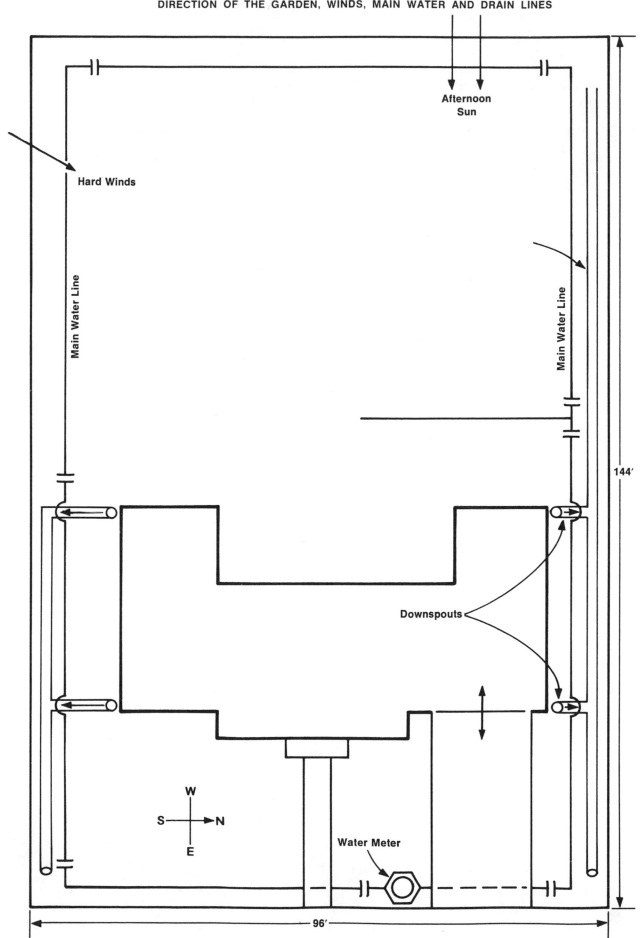

Figure 3.1   **DESIGN FOR LARGER PROPERTIES:**
DIRECTION OF THE GARDEN, WINDS, MAIN WATER AND DRAIN LINES

Applications and Variations of Garden Design

DESIGNING LARGER PROPERTIES

Homeowners with larger properties may include garden features not covered in Chapter 2: for example, greater wind protection, a pool, a lounging shelter, a pergola for special plants, and more extensive surfacing. These can easily be accommodated within a slightly more sophisticated design. The list of features now becomes:

Tall hedge for wind protection	Utility-storage unit
	Children's play area
Pool	Lawns
Lounging shelter	Special gardens
Pergola	Garden circulation
Trellis	Garden lighting
Surfaced areas	

Begin designing the larger property represented by Figure 3.1 in exactly the same manner as the smaller one: plan grading, indicate hard winds and afternoon sun, place drain and water lines, and locate retaining walls (if needed), line fences and the patio. At this point, however, placement of major features—pool, hedge, lounging shelter, pergola, expanded surface area—takes precedence in about that order.

Placing Major Units

Pool

Flanked by its supporting pavement and landscaping, a pool is a desirable and dramatic feature and must be wisely located. It should relate to the whole garden design through association, balance, lines, proportion, scale, and even color. The pool in Figure 3.2 is well positioned in relation to the general garden composition. This is not the only location for a pool, however. Another attractive possible design might place the pool at right angles to the house, in the location of the loung-

ing structure, with balancing composition on the opposite side of the garden.

On the average property, a pool can not always conform to recognized proportion and scale. However, careful composition can help restore balance. If you must use a long, narrow pool, for instance, you might place a vertical structure at one end, a special planting unit at the other, and an expansive surfaced area on one or both sides.

Except on very large properties, pools should not be ornate, but rather constructed along simple lines, usually rectangular or some modification of an oval.

→ Draw a pool, if desired, on your plot plan.

Hedge

Figure 3.2 anticipates hard winds from the back and left of the property. Therefore a 6- or 7-foot hedge is suggested about 25 feet from the back of the lot. If a hedge were not used, the pool, lounging shelter, and pergola might be moved back 8 to 10 feet and an adequate wind deterrent established in the form of trees and tall shrubs. See Figure 3.3.

→ Indicate a hedge, if appropriate, on your design paper.

Lounging Shelter

A lounging shelter must have good proportions and at the same time be in scale with the pool. Its architecture should be relatively simple and conform to that of the house.

→ Draw a lounging shelter on your plan, if one is desired.

Pergola

Many homeowners in warm to hot climates wish to grow specialized plants that will not tolerate excessive heat—azaleas, rhododendrons, for

Figure 3.2   **DESIGN FOR LARGER PROPERTIES:**
GARDEN LIGHTING   **60**

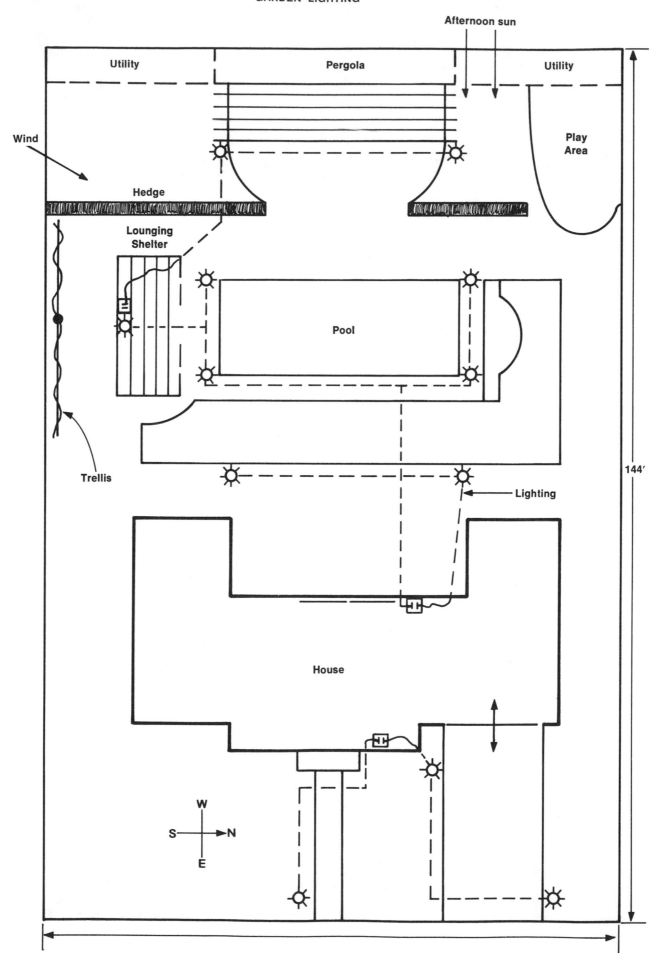

Figure 3.3   FOR LARGER PROPERTIES: TREES AND SHRUBS AS WIND SCREEN   **61**

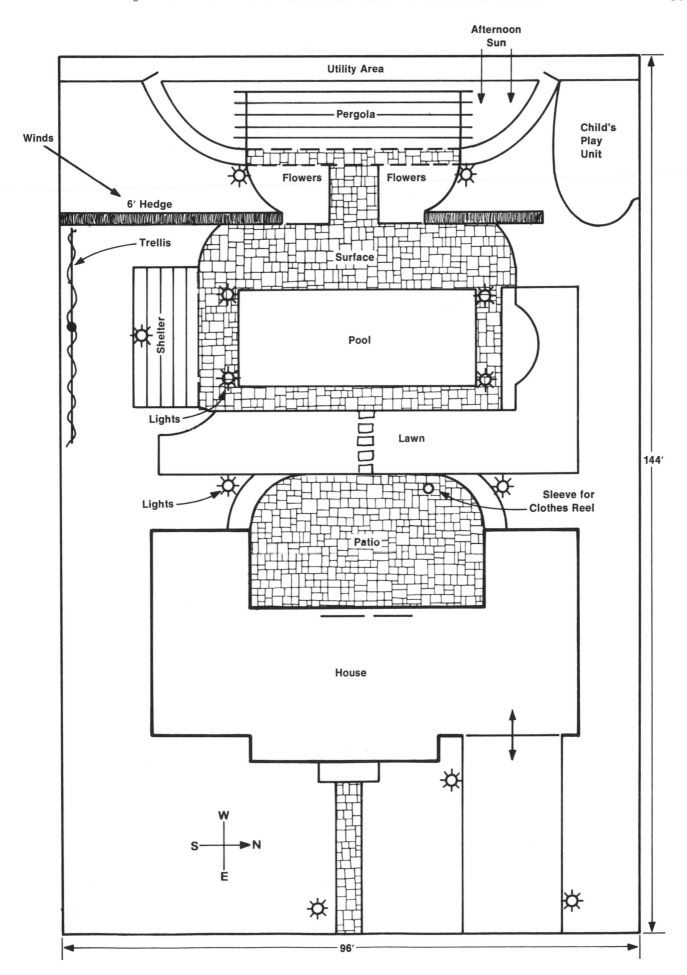

example. A pergola or similar lath structure that filters sunlight provides simple protection for such delicate beauties. Installing an overhead mist-type watering system inside the pergola will further improve the climatic environment. Sunlight filtering is controlled by the distance between the laths that roof the structure. The interspace averages the width of a lath.

Although a pergola should not be ornate, it also should be more than a rectangular box. Like all other garden features, a pergola should be considered part of your overall landscape design. Give it a natural setting. Fit it, for instance, into an arrangement of needle-leaf evergreens that are not tall enough to obstruct sunlight, or place it at the terminus of a cross axis with a rather low shrub planting, as in Figure 3.7. Carefully positioned, a pergola takes its place unobtrusively in the unit composition, protecting and displaying a collection of plants that in turn enhance the color and character of the whole area.

In most gardens, natural wood is the best material for a pergola because it is least conspicuous. Remember that the structure must not compete with the plants it covers.

Completing Your Design

Continue the design of the larger property by locating lawns and planning a sprinkler system, as shown in Figure 3.4. Then place the lesser features, as outlined for the smaller composition in Chapter 2: surfaces, patio, children's play area, utility-storage facility, garden lighting, special garden units, walks and paths. See Figures 3.5 and 3.6. Finally, dress it all with trees, shrubs, vines, and flowers, using the same principles of design explained earlier. Figure 3.7 includes all the features we have been discussing. Figure 3.8 is a similar arrangement without the pergola.

YOUR GARDEN CAN BE FORMALIZED

The garden designs in the preceding Figures are essentially informal. They attempt to imitate nature as closely as possible under restrictive circumstances, and they are balanced in a natural way that is not obvious.

In a formalized garden design, lines are

instantly obvious and garden elements are geometrically located. In Figure 3.9, the main axis begins at the doorway, bisects the patio and rectangular lawn, and is terminated by a specially selected tree in the background.

Two parallel secondary axis lines in the form of identical walkways are established on both sides of the main axis and are equidistant from it. In reality, they are right-angle extensions of the patio, and each is terminated by carefully matched conifers.

The long narrow panels between the walkways on either side have the same dimensions and are planted with similar types of creeping conifers. The two parallel panels on the outside of the walkways differ a little in length and plantings but are the same in width and appearance.

On the patio, and in line with the secondary axis, are two identical tubs and plants. Two identical jars exactly frame the semicircular part of the patio. Two broadleaf trees terminate the ends of the patio and are matched by larger broadleaf trees in the background.

This geometrical arrangement of lines and features might at first appear overly sophisticated for the small to medium property, but fortunately this is not true. You can soften the series of lines by skillful use of plant materials and still retain their formal identity.

The two creeping conifer panels create the illusion of widening the lawn area and softening the walkways. The perennial panel is a richly colored unit of attractive flowers running almost the entire length of the garden and persisting through spring, summer, and fall. Its counterpart on the opposite side of the garden is an attractive rose planting that produces impressive color through spring, summer, and into fall.

The two trees at either end of the patio are flowering plums, whose brilliant flowers in spring and purplish foliage in summer contribute immensely to the garden's color. The axis tree in the background produces autumn foliage.

The side planting on the left is a mellow arrangement of conifers, and the cross axis is terminated on the right by another conifer. The entire planting is minimal but strong, colorful, and beautifully effective.

Although we took a few liberties in our use of flowers, shrubs, and trees to mellow and color this plan to suit a small garden, it still is basically formal. All the principles of design are even more strictly adhered to than with informal planning.

A formalized garden, like any other, is to be lived in. It is an outdoor living room for your entire family and must be practical. Thus, in Figure 3.9, the patio is protected from wind, and

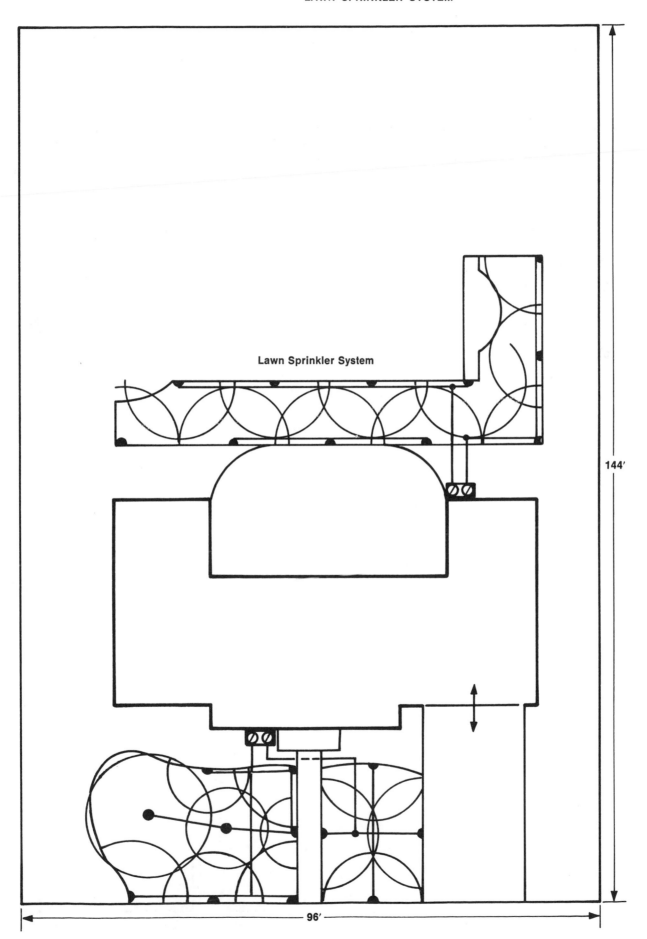

Figure 3.4   **DESIGN FOR LARGER PROPERTIES:**
LAWN SPRINKLER SYSTEM

Lawn Sprinkler System

144′

96′

Figure 3.5 **DESIGN FOR LARGER PROPERTIES: LOCATING GARDEN FEATURES** **64**

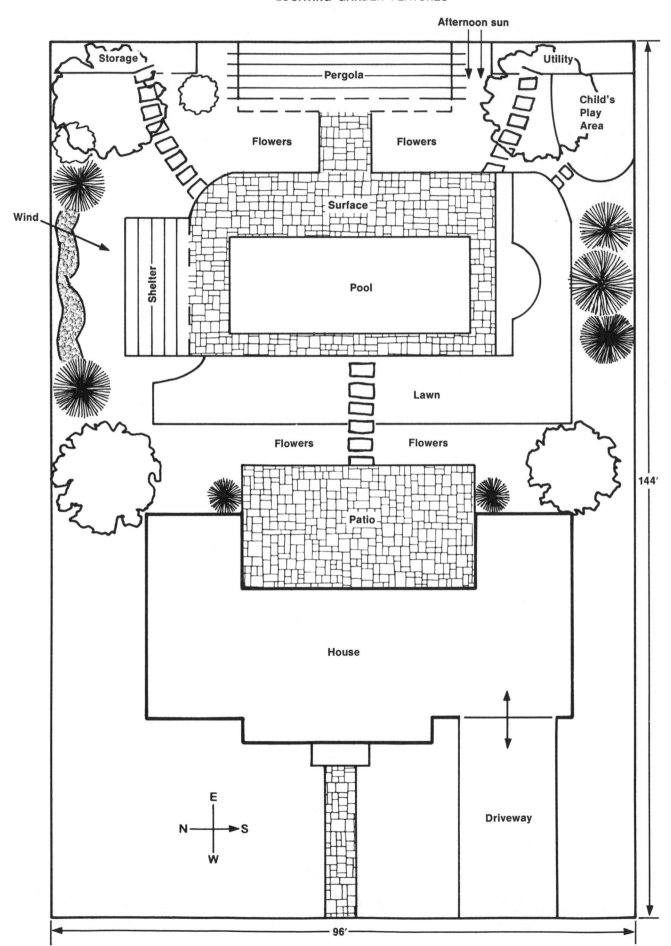

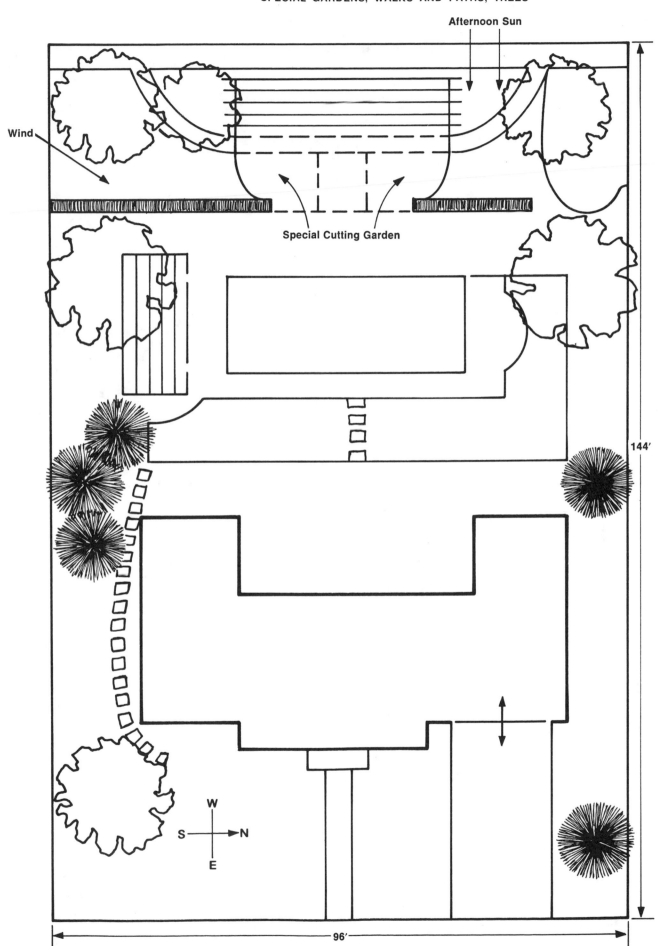

Afternoon Sun

Wind

Special Cutting Garden

144'

W
S — N
E

96'

Figure 3.7   **DESIGN FOR LARGER PROPERTIES: THE COMPLETED PLAN**   **66**

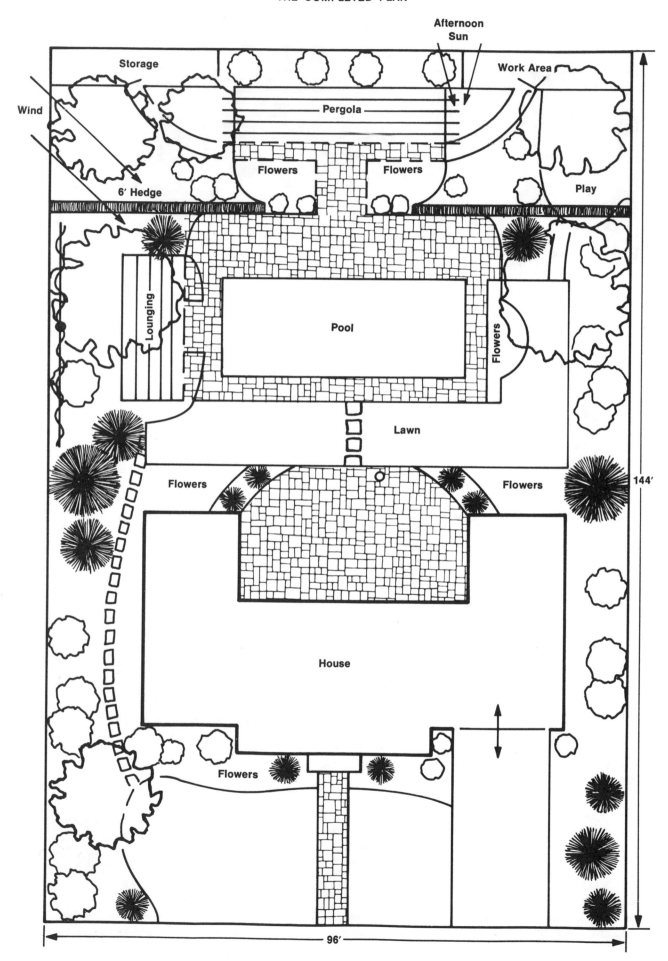

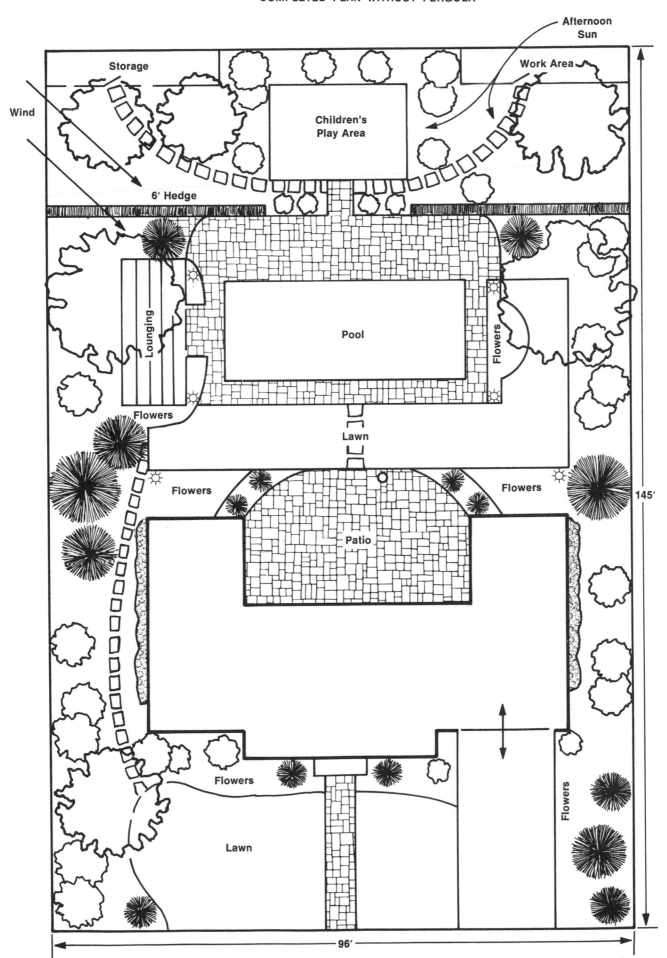

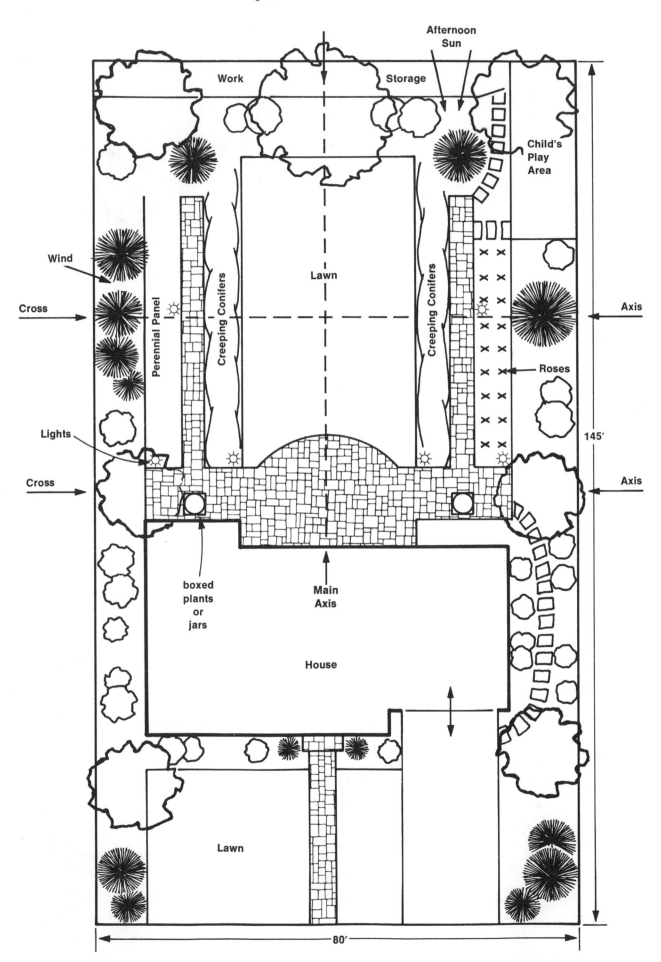

Figure 3.9   **FORMALIZED GARDEN**

there is shade for the children's play area. The plan also provides surfaced distances for children's tricycling, room for garden furniture and for a cookout or other entertaining, roses and other flowers for indoor decorating, a work-storage area, and a sizable lawn.

RELANDSCAPING THE ESTABLISHED GARDEN

So far we have been discussing designs for a new garden, that is, how to landscape more or less bare areas. But what if you purchase a house on a landscaped property and find the garden layout unsatisfactory? Relandscaping is the only solution.

The task will be much less difficult because of your knowledge of planning a *new* property. Every principle we have discussed will be applied in redesigning the established garden, and the procedure is almost the same.

Like planning for a new property, relandscaping is done progressively. Where do you begin? Go into your garden and take inventory. What is already there, and what important elements should be added? For example, main water and drain lines should be installed if none exist or if present lines are inadequate.

→ On a large drawing pad, sketch everything in your garden to scale—lawn, trees, structures, paths, walks. Show the entire garden exactly as it is. Meticulous drawing is important because, for reasons of economy, you are intent upon retaining everything that is adaptable to your new design, including as much of the lawn and as many shrubs and trees as possible. Use Figure 3.10 as an example of an established garden.

Next, decide on the features you want in your new plan. Do you need a play area for small children? a large patio for garden parties? protection from wind? Will you have to add a work-storage area, outdoor lighting, a clothes reel? Make a list of the features you want to include and keep it beside you as you proceed.

Lay a sheet of good quality tracing paper over the original sketch on your drawing pad and securely fasten the two together. Figure 3.11 is an example. You now know what you want in your design and you can see what presently exists.

❊ ❊

Redesigning the Garden

Compare Figures 3.10 and 3.11. In Figure 3.11 we have added a patio and located the work-storage area across the back of the property, permitting removal of the old storage shed. The children's play area, which dominates the entire garden has been relocated. Now is also the time to consider garden lighting and a well for a clothes reel in the patio floor.

→ Draw new structural features in their proper location on the overlay paper.

Next comes the lawn. Do you wish to change its size or shape? Is a sprinkling system needed?

→ Outline the lawn you desire and add a sprinkling system, if required.

The structural part of your plan is now complete. The overlay is marked with your new design, and, by looking through the tracing paper, you can see exactly to what extent your garden must be changed, what can be saved and what must be removed.

The next factor to be considered is the plantings. Keep existing trees wherever possible; shrubs are far easier to remove or add.

Look again at Figures 3.10 and 3.11. Note that we retain the trees across the back of the property. However, we are adding a screen of carefully arranged conifers, two large and several smaller ones, along the left property line. They will shield the patio from wind and form a magnificent backdrop. This change requires removal of the existing broadleaf tree in that area. The right side of the garden is simply and effectively redesigned by adding a broadleaf tree near the corner of the house and one in the background, in place of the old storage shed. A conifer grouping in between is tied to the two tree units by blending shrubs. After additional shrub units are located in the background planting, the composition is complete. See Figure 3.12.

→ Sketch in new trees and shrubs on your overlay paper and draw an X over any existing plantings that must be removed.

You have now redesigned your garden and can see at a glance the extent of required changes and which plants and structural features will be retained. This type of logical procedure guides the nonprofessional garden planner to a very satisfactory conclusion with a minimum of difficulty, and is applicable to property of any size or shape.

Figure 3.10 **RELANDSCAPING THE ESTABLISHED GARDEN: BEFORE RELANDSCAPING**

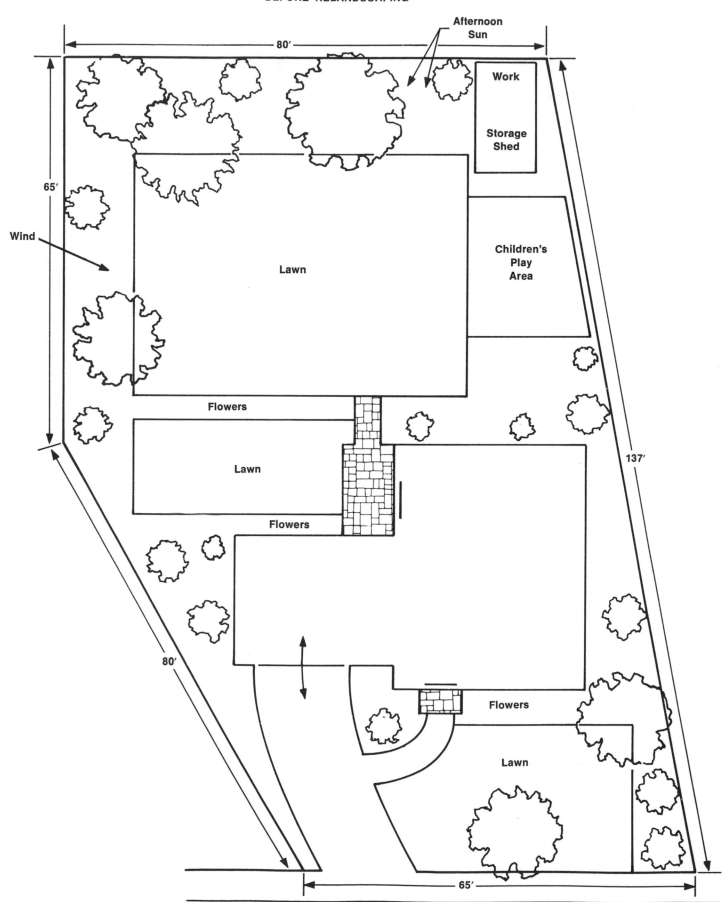

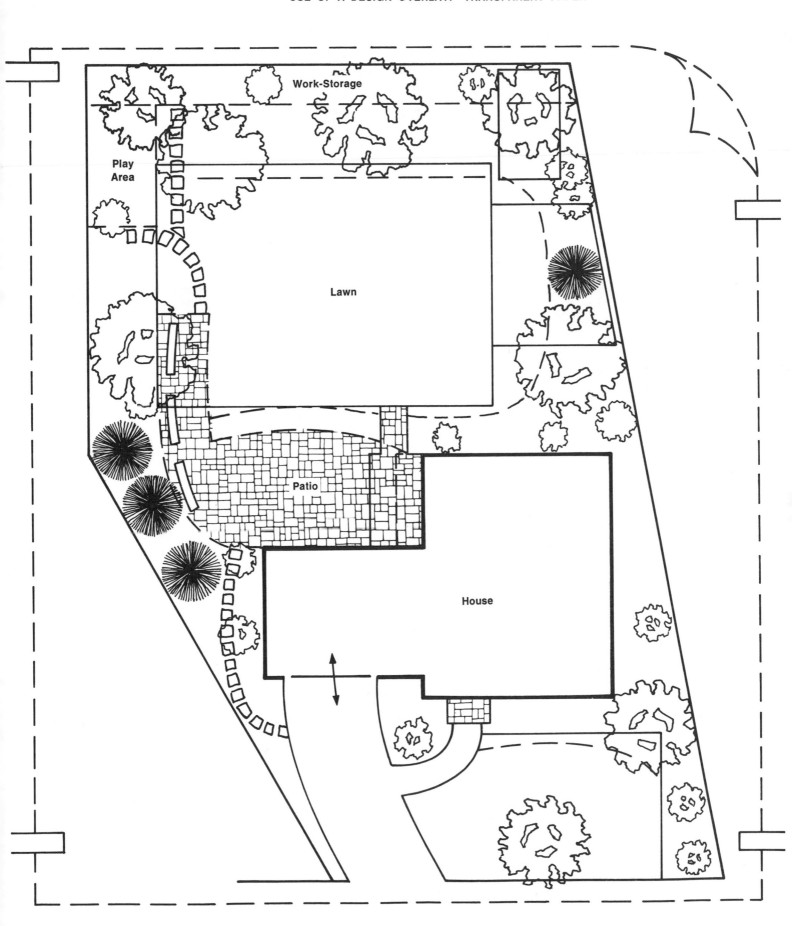

Figure 3.12   **RELANDSCAPING THE ESTABLISHED GARDEN**

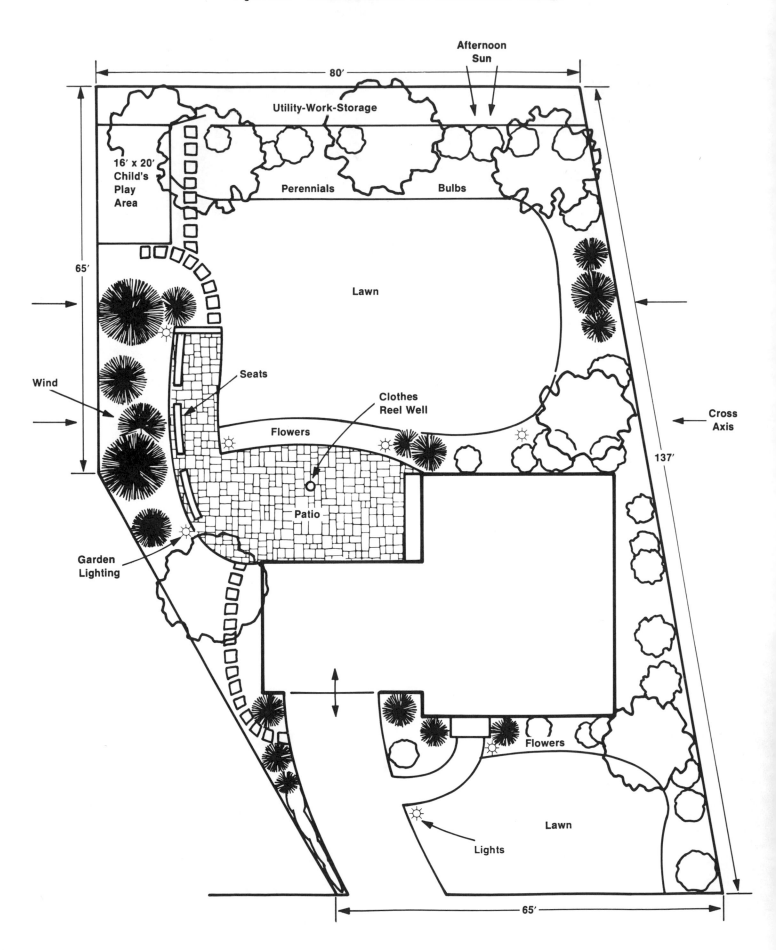

Redesigning the Front Yard

Redesign your front yard using the same step-by-step procedure. Remembering that your front yard represents you to the public, keep in mind the general mood you wish it to express. For instance, a compact series of tall, dark green conifers might appear melancholy, while gracefully curved lawns bordered with flowering trees and shrubs, bulbs, annuals, and perennials will convey cheerfulness.

Study several of the plot plans we have included and note the use of landscape principles in the design of front yards. The component parts must be in good proportion, the lines pleasing. Balance and scale are critical. These factors combined with careful attention to color and texture will produce a vital composition and exemplify unity of house and yard.

Some homeowners wish to avoid lawns in the front yard. One alternative is gravel spread over asphalt paper previously laid on leveled and compacted soil. White and a deep brick-red are the two colors of gravel most frequently used. If you decide to use gravel in place of a front lawn, make sure its color is compatible with your house and flowers, and with local styles. Groundcovers provide a second alternative to lawns. Ajuga, low conifers, and ivy, for example, are quite attractive if meticulously maintained.

Photo 3.1

Instead of the conventional front lawn.
(Design by Itsuo Uenaka)

SPECIAL SITUATIONS

Retirement Gardens

Commendable progress is being made in the development of highly organized retirement communities. The best urban retirement complexes offer specialized central gardens designed for lounging, walking, reading, and friendly conversation. An abundance of flowers and structural amenities generate interest and pleasure for the residents.

The most common type of retirement community is located in a rural environment and consists of individually owned homes clustered around a multi-service community center. Although the homes are small, each has its private garden. These gardens, in a way, unite the owners with the community, and the community seems to set a keynote for the gardens.

It is obvious that such intimate gardens must be well arranged and reflective of each owner's personality and of community styles. Design and color are important in establishing a happy mood and an interesting character. The designer must bear in mind that the garden components are not just plantings, but an arrangement of natural notes, some in waltz-time and some in a modern tempo.

Figure 3.13 shows three examples of interesting retirement gardens. Lines, balance, color, and points of special interest are as carefully used as in larger gardens. Paths and walks are wide and smooth, hose bibbs are handy and fitted with quick couplers, maintenance is minimal and easy. A relatively large surfaced area is desirable to permit outdoor entertainment of friends.

Mobile Home Gardens

Creating a miniature garden around a mobile home is a real challenge. Simplicity and minimal planting are the major guidelines, but we can offer several more specific suggestions to those who live in mobile homes. Many mobile home parks offer, or at least permit, small lawns beside the concrete pads. If your park follows this practice, use the tiny lawn as a nucleus for your design. You might plant pleasing arrangements of low-growing shrubs along the border lines, closely following the principles of design applicable to any home landscaping. Flower areas are necessarily limited to slender borders and perhaps two or three planting bays. Have borders curve

Figure 3.13　**RETIREMENT GARDENS**

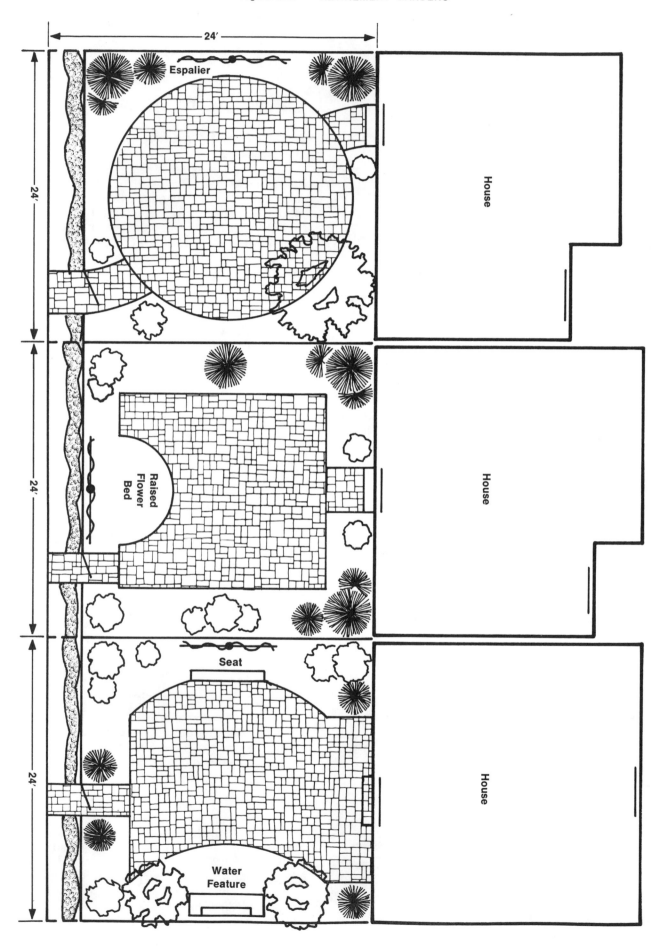

gracefully and make bays as bright and colorful as possible. Hanging baskets in the vicinity of the carport will brighten the whole area and help to enliven the garden. If you have no lawn to work with, plant shrubs along the base of your mobile home and border the shrubs with cheerful flowers.

Whether or not you have a lawn, consider adding two or three small trees to your design. You may want to plant these, and even shrubs, in movable containers. Then you can take them along when you move.

Country Gardens

No other type of landscape offers the designer greater opportunity for both aesthetic and practical planning than the country or farm landscape. Expression of dimensional and seasonal values has almost limitless potential. Vistas may be opened for viewing pastoral scenes. The back garden is easily blended into an orchard to increase enjoyment of spring blossoms and autumn foliage. Distant hills can be framed to form a backdrop of variable interest and ever-changing color.

How can you accomplish this? The orchard, sprawling meadows, and hills are already there. Every natural scene is in place. Your problem lies in developing a design that integrates the distant landscape elements with those in your garden. How? By extending unobstructed visual lines from vantage points in your garden to the distant scenes, and using these lines as planting guides. Although it may be necessary to remove an unimportant obstruction to clear the view, this is a small price to pay for the improvement in your total landscape.

Design your country garden in the regular manner, using the basic rules of area development: grading, establishment of drainage and water lines, soil preparation, and construction of fences, if necessary to protect the garden from farm animals.

→ On a large sheet of paper, carefully draw the area to scale, including all existing elements.

Now look at Figure 3.14. From the main vantage point of the backyard, perhaps where the patio will be, we have drawn a series of broken lines extending beyond the garden limits, toward the distant vistas of orchards, hills, fields. What landscape features would you like to have visible from your patio? Are there meadows, mountains, a lake, a stream? As you design, bear in mind that although fences may delineate the garden, there must be a feeling of expansive relationship to adjacent buildings, connective yards, and roadways.

→ Indicate nearby buildings and the direction of desirable views on your sketch.

The next step is to locate lawns, structural elements, and flower areas on your sketch. If a handball or tennis court is included on your list of garden features, you might place it immediately beyond the garden perimeter and blend it in with appropriate plantings, as in Figure 3.14.

→ Add lawns, structural elements, and flower areas to your sketch.

The major plantings differ somewhat from conventional types. A rural garden, in contrast to one confined to a city lot, imparts a feeling of expanse and openness, of including everything for miles around. Plantings along the theoretical boundary lines of the garden are generally quite low and open: for example, small groupings of flowering shrubs, loosely and very informally blended. Fruit trees are always appropriate. They provide beauty in spring, summer, and autumn, and relate the garden to the surrounding countryside.

Location of the trees is critical to the distant landscape effect. Visualize trees at their mature size and plant them individually and in groups near your vista demarcation lines. Be careful to avoid obstructing distant scenes; attempt to frame fine views attractively. Chestnuts, maples, and oaks naturally tie the garden into the neighboring landscape, creating an exhilarating feeling of beauty, harmony, and expansiveness.

→ Indicate placement of trees and other major plantings on your design paper.

Rock Gardens

Are rock gardens part of your landscape plan? A rock garden may be used in two ways: as a separate area smoothly integrated with adjacent features or as a transitional element leading from one part of the garden to another.

A true rock garden is not a conglomeration of rocks sprinkled with plants, but a unique garden with distinctive characteristics. Large or small, it requires precise planning. It should be treated as a special garden according to the several applicable rules you have learned.

If your lot is relatively level, slightly elevate the rock garden area to assure drainage and increase interest. Is a path through the garden appropriate? Have stepping stones of similar color and kind as the principle rocks meander roughly through the center.

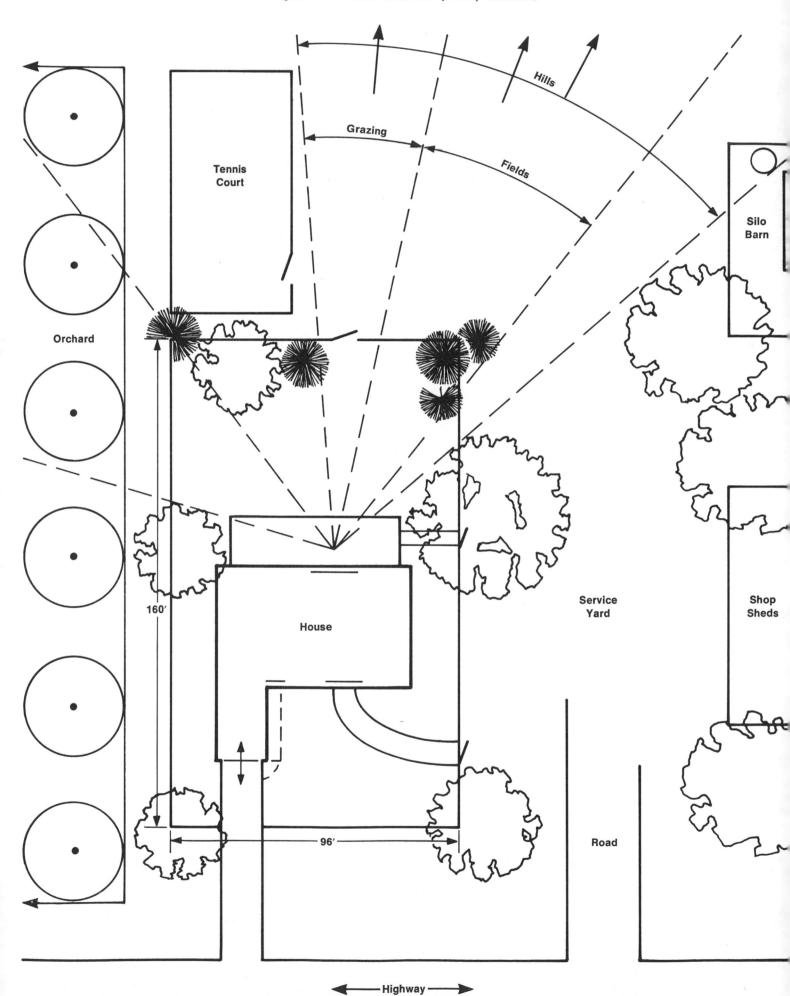

Figure 3.14   THE COUNTRY (FARM) GARDENS

The principle rocks should be natural to your locality and sparsely distributed over the area as though nature had placed them: large single rocks here and there, and a grouping of two, three, or four appearing to have been pushed in the same direction. Altogether, they should form a well-balanced, harmoniously related composition. Don't hesitate to move any of the rocks a little to the right or left as many times as necessary to bring them into pleasing association. Use your own ingenuity, being careful to apply design principles. Sketch 3.1 may be of assistance.

Lines, balance, texture, scale, and color must all be strictly adhered to in planting a rock garden. Low conifers, delicately creeping vines, bulbs, and low-growing perennials are typically rock garden plants. They should be carefully selected and harmonized to produce spring, summer, and fall color and interest.

Sketch 3.1   **ROCK GARDENS**

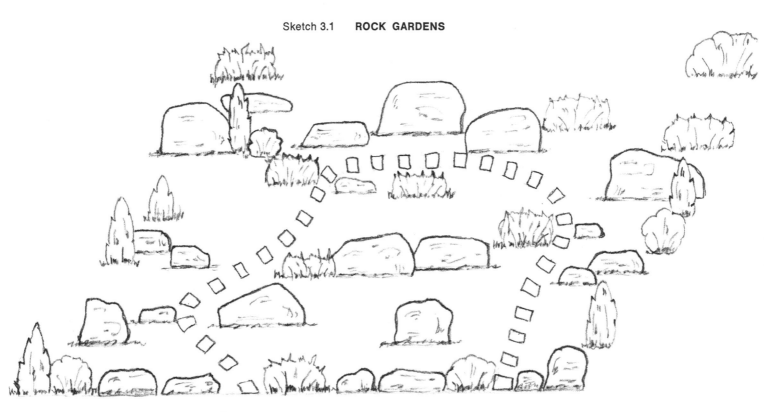

Sketch a pattern for major rock groupings and plants. Then mellow the rock with carefully arranged low-growing broadleaf and conifer shrubs, flowering creepers, and bulbs in season: for spring, perhaps crocus, grape hyacinth, hyacinth, kafir lily, narcissus, Star-of-Bethlehem, tulips; for summer, dwarf agapanthus, sparaxis, sprekelia, tigridia; and for fall, amaryllis, autumn crocus, sternbergia.

When rock gardening on a slope, anchor rocks deeply into the soil for stability.

Hillside Gardens

Many homeowners faced with landscaping a hillside garden feel that their problem is insurmountable. Quite the contrary! Hillsides, either in front or back of the house, offer excellent opportunities for the development of elegant gardens. Large sections of the landscape are seen at once, and the combined effect of the several parts makes a strong and pleasing impression.

A front yard calls for carefully coordinated design. Perhaps a cut in the slope, 3 or 4 feet back from the sidewalk, is called for, and a brick or rock veneered wall legally and solidly constructed. Have wide, meandering steps lead up to the house level by as gentle a slope as possible. Rather steep garden slopes may be tightly groundcovered with ivy. Or consider combinations of large and medium-size rock securely set into the slope in rock-garden fashion. You might then plant the slope with balanced groupings of small conifers, broadleaf shrubs, and creeping materials.

A hillside planting must appear to flow gracefully from the house level down to the street, or to lower garden sections. Use lines, balance, scale, and proportion to create unity throughout the design, paying special attention to the selection and arrangement of shrubs and trees.

On the house elevation, apply the same guidelines used with level properties. The extent of landscaping depends upon the size of the lot. Do not overcrowd a small area with secondary structures.

Consider your hillside property an opportunity to develop an especially natural and attractive landscape by means of appropriate trees and shrubs, open spaces, meandering paths, and strategically located seats for viewing local and distant vistas.

HOW TO DRESS YOUR GARDEN WITH PLANTS

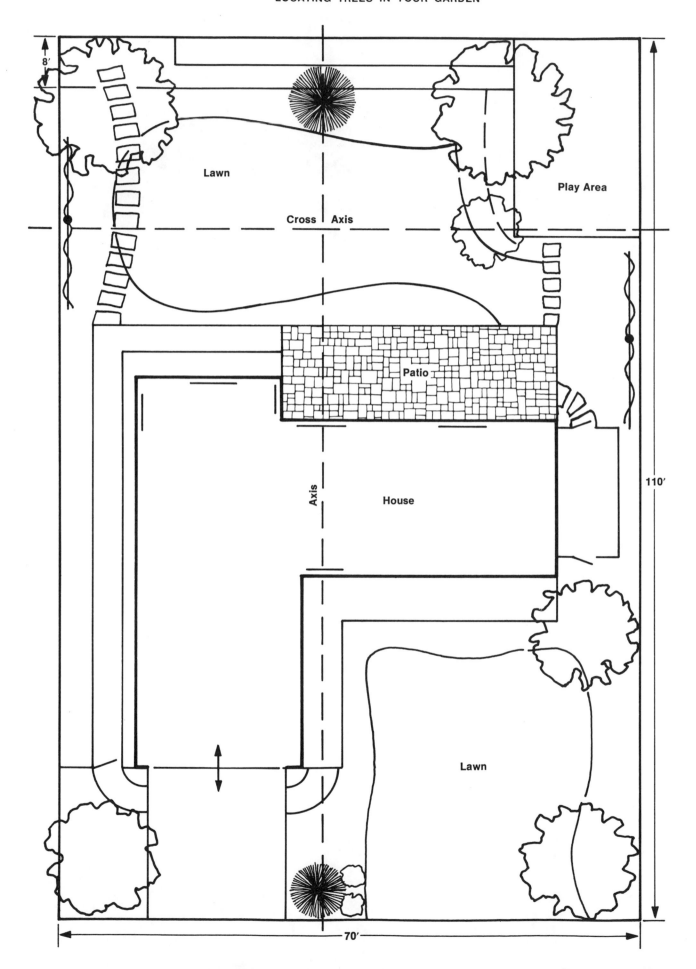

Figure 4.1 **DRESSING YOUR GARDEN WITH PLANTS: LOCATING TREES IN YOUR GARDEN**

Placement of Plants
in Your Garden

You have now reached the most pleasurable and creative phase of garden design, that of dressing your garden with plants. How do you proceed? The first step is to familiarize yourself with the functions of plants in design. Understanding the design functions of various plants will enable you to visualize the proper tree, shrub, flower groupings for each part of your garden. You will then be ready to indicate these plantings, by use of symbols, on your design paper. The final step, which we will discuss in subsequent chapters, is the selection of specific plants to fit the individual requirements of your garden.

FUNCTION OF TREES
IN DESIGN

Trees perform many important functions in the landscape. Each dominates its individual area, while collectively they seem to control the garden and either enhance its aesthetic qualities or depreciate them. Furthermore, type, size, and location of trees influence the character of your house, making it appear broader, taller, or in some other way visually changing its proportions.

Balance

Both house and garden require aesthetic balance. Notice the placement of trees in Figure 4.1. Viewed from the front, the house appears excessively heavy on the garage side of the lot. Two broadleaf trees of similar specie are located on the opposite side, one near the sidewalk and property line, the other near the house. The combined bulk of the two trees brings the weaker side of the house into balance with the heavier portion. On the heavy side, one broadleaf tree is located

reasonably near the sidewalk and property line to create an illusion of distance.

Balance is an equally important factor in the back garden where the right side appears heavier than the left. This permits us to place the right broadleaf tree a little nearer the central axis than the left. Yet balance is maintained, and the play area receives the correct amount of sun and shade. Figure 1.1 clearly illustrates the balancing qualities of broadleaf trees and conifer groupings.

Conifers, or needle-leaf trees, are strong and impressive. A group of two or three relatively small ones will easily balance one large broadleaf tree. Since balance between individuals and groups of trees is imperative throughout your entire design, you should take time to observe coniferous trees and their association with broadleaf trees and shrubs in other gardens.

Effect

Judiciously selected and located trees do more than balance: they establish moods that affect the house, garden, and any other unit within their sphere of influence. For example, a tight series of tall, columnar Italian cypress in a small to medium garden might suggest a melancholy mood, or at least produce a monotonous effect, through excessive repetition of strong vertical lines and lack of animation. See Sketch 4.1. On the other hand, species of broadleaf maples, beech, liquidambars, and crabapples, as examples, establish a merry mood. The foliage reflects light and shadow and moves with the breeze, creating an effect of aliveness and pleasant appeal.

The choice and placement of trees in your design will go a long way toward establishing a harmonious composition and a pleasurable garden atmosphere. This is particularly true with the newer trend toward natural gardens that rely heavily upon tree and shrub association for privacy and woodsy effect.

Shade

It is usually possible to conform to the rules of
plant arrangement and yet locate a tree or trees
to provide shade where needed. Decide where you
want shade—patio or play area, perhaps—the
extent of shade desired, and general position of
the sun at the time of day shade is needed. Will
your play area, for instance, require partial shade
in mid-afternoon? If so, place a broadleaf tree
where it will not interfere with play apparatus but
will provide adequate shade at that particular
time of day.

Photo 4.1

Sycamore (*Platanus occidentalis*) offers bold form, shade,
and sturdiness.

Sketch 4.1   **GARDEN MOODS: MELANCHOLY**

A series columnar conifers in a small to medium garden
may produce a melancholy mood and a feeling of disturbing monotony.

Photo 4.2

Colorado blue spruce (*Picea pungens glauca*)—strong, bold, and beautiful—in front of a *Myrtus communis* hedge.

Photo 4.3

A filmy screen of clipped *Viburnum tinus*—excellent for wind protection.

Wind Protection

Many of the heavily foliaged broadleaf trees can persistently resist winds of considerable force without becoming distorted: ash, beech, catalpa, Chinese elm, several varieties of eucalyptus, fruitless mulberry, horse-chestnut, liquidambar, magnolia, maple, plane, and poplar, are examples. Their resilient branches and heavy foliage make them ideal where wind protection is needed. Combine such trees with group arrangements of appropriate shrubs to form an effective wind barrier. Buckthorn, dogwood, escallonia, holly, lilac, melaleuca, pittosporum, privet permitted to grow naturally, strawberry bush, and xylosma are generally successful.

Groups of conifer trees are equally or even more effective as wind retardants. It is not necessary to plant them tightly in a wind-shield row. Instead, arrange them in groupings that follow the patterns of nature.

Decoration

Specimen Trees

A specimen tree is one of distinctive form, foliage, character, and color. It is usually placed in a strategic location for the specific purpose of attracting attention to a particular part of the garden and increasing its interest. A specimen need not necessarily stand alone, but may be accompanied by subordinate plants, usually of similar specie. Colorado blue spruce, dogwood, flowering cherry, flowering peach, golden-chain, golden-shower, Hinoki cypress, jacaranda, liquidambar, mountain hemlock, purple beech, and redbud are typical specimen trees.

Flowering Trees

Happily, there is a wide selection of magnificent flowering trees, beauties capable of turning your garden into an exciting floral display. Flowering apricot, cherry, crabapple, peach, and plum are just the beginning of a long and diversified list of species, sizes, and colors.

Every garden can benefit from one or more of these elegant trees, and there is no problem in finding a suitable location. Figure 1.1 shows four excellent spots for flowering tree displays—two at either end of the patio. These are typical locations that you may want to consider in your garden design.

Seasonal Interest

Autumn Foliage

Do not allow your garden to become drab and uninteresting as summer fades. Fall easily can be made as beautiful as spring by using impressive trees that change their foliage to glamorous autumn colorations of gold, orange, and red. A little projection of your imagination into the fall landscape will open avenues of thought for selection and location of appropriate species. Fortunately, there are types and sizes of color-producing species for almost every temperature zone.

Winter Appeal

Trees do not lose their identity in winter, although their image may change. Conifers stand out more dramatically, and snow serves to enhance their deep green beauty. On the other hand, the bare branches of deciduous trees silhouetted against the sky form interesting compositions. Structural elements in a garden appear bolder in winter, and their aesthetic image blends upward with the vertical lines of the trees. A careful review of your developing design will reveal opportunities for impressive garden effects during the winter months.

PLACING TREES AND SHRUBS ON YOUR DESIGN

To locate trees and shrubs on your design paper, begin with on-the-spot analysis of your property. For example, you probably need a tree at the right and left sides of your front yard. Why? To frame and balance the house and lot. Where should they be located? Forward and toward the lot lines to frame and widen the house and lot and to create the illusion of greater distance from the sidewalk to the house. Next, add some shrub groupings near the trees to balance the vertical lines and dress up the front yard.

If a rather persistent wind blows across your patio, consider a grouping of wind-resistant trees and shrubs. Where should they be located? Near the lot line, perhaps. But the location of the patio and the direction of the wind are the deciding factors here. Does the children's play area need to be shaded from afternoon sun? Place an appropriate tree at a logical point.

It is obvious, then, that the placement of trees and shrubs is a matter of visualizing *what* you need and *where* you need it. Then you are ready to indicate your choices on your design paper by use of symbols. Figure 4.2 illustrates the placement of generalized plant groupings, such as

shade trees, conifers, and flowers. Note the symbolic representation of broadleaf trees, conifers, and shrubs in Figure 4.2: large circles for broadleaf trees, smaller circles for shrubs, and pointed circles for conifers. Don't concern yourself now with plant names. We will come to that after the symbols are in place.

As you add plantings to your design, bear in mind that every tree, shrub, vine, and flower unit has a particular function to perform in its special location. If a planting has no specific purpose, it should not be there.

Unit Arrangement

The nonprofessional gardener is inclined to plant trees and shrubs as a series of isolated items, somewhat like striking single notes on a piano. Instead, make your goal a pleasing composition. This is most easily achieved by developing unit arrangements and then tying the units together with blending plants, as suggested by Figure 4.3, which illustrates unit planting. Let's take a look at it. Broadleaf tree, shrub, and conifer symbols mark the principal units, which are smoothly tied together with blenders. Each unit is circled and labeled for easy identification. Note the size, arrangement, location, and functional reason for each grouping.

Moving clockwise from the front left corner, each plant unit performs a definite function— framing the house, softening the fence line, shielding the patio from wind, forming a backdrop for flowers, promoting continuity, providing shade, and so on. As examples, the arrangement of conifers in unit G retards the wind; tall shrubs behind the pergola soften its structural lines and assist the trees in making it less noticeable; the small conifer and broadleaf units at either end of the rose and flower panels soften, balance, frame, and naturalize the whole area; tree number 4 produces shade for the play area.

Continuing clockwise, the smaller tree number 6 helps balance the conifer grouping opposite. Flowering shrubs 4 to 6 feet high in units K and L make the side garden lively and colorful and form an important screen. The conifer grouping M creates interest and helps frame the house. In addition, conifers balance the large unit on the left. The two units, A and B, in front of the house are simple, strong, and effective in enhancing the charm of the entrance.

→ Indicate the location of major tree and shrub units on your design paper.

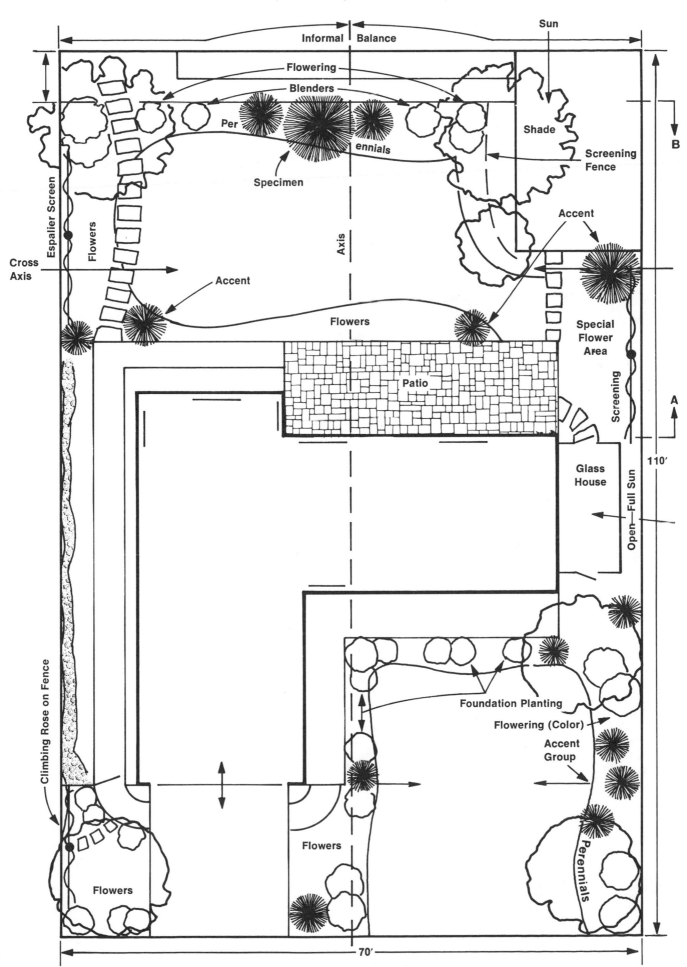

Figure 4.2   DRESSING YOUR GARDEN WITH PLANTS:
BACKGROUND, BLENDERS, ACCENT PLANTS, FOUNDATION PLANTING

Sketch 4.2

Unit arrangement of shrubs and trees, units tied together with *blender* shrubs.

Photo 4.5

Unit composition.

Photo 4.6

At either side of the front yard, a grouping that expresses variety, related form, texture, color, and character. Left to right: daisies, *Chamaecyparis pisifera squarrosa minima, Pinus mugo,* Australian fuchsia. Front: *Juniperus chinensis procumbens.*

Figure 4.3   **DRESSING YOUR GARDEN WITH PLANTS:
UNIT METHOD OF ARRANGING TREES AND SHRUBS**

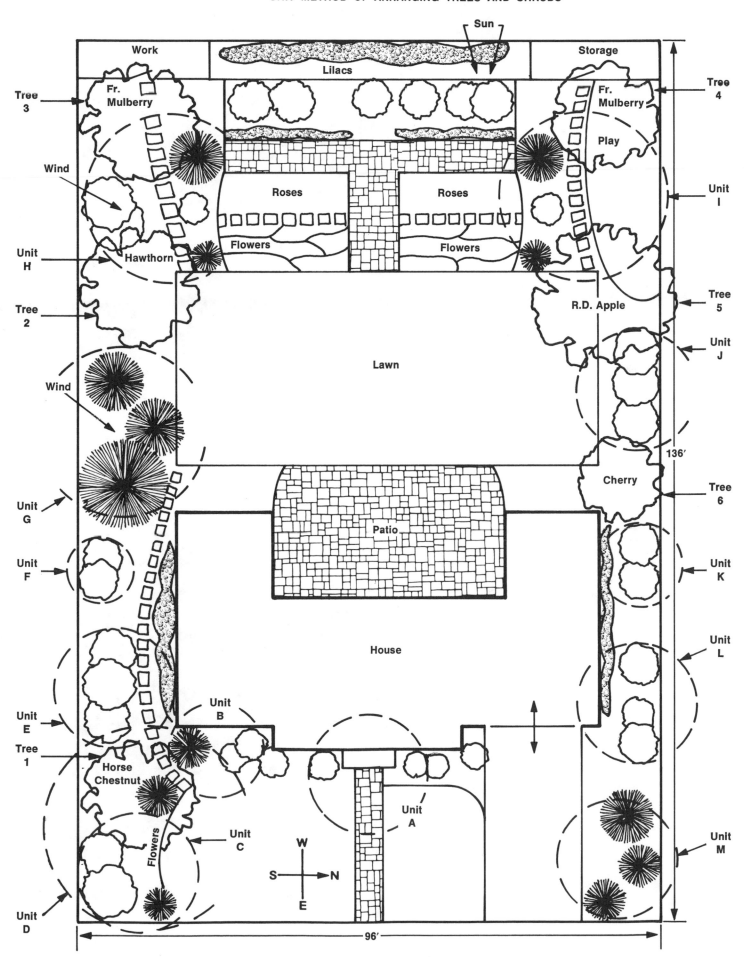

Plant Blenders

The blending plants that tie units together are usually somewhat subordinate in size, and should have foliage similar to that of the plant groups they are uniting. You will probably need only one or two plants between units.

→ Add blender shrubs to your design.

The Garden Background

Walk into a garden. Your first impression is probably formed by the quality of its background. Your eye jumps to the distant trees and then returns through a conifer grouping, shrubs, flower foreground, and forward into the body of the garden, in just about that order.

Background comprises a complete and delicately balanced composition of trees, shrubs, and flowers that must associate harmoniously in every respect. In an effective background, four seasons of interest are represented. Every segment of the composition performs one or more functions. Together they form a natural picture with clean, flowing lines—simple, well balanced, and artistic. Ideal qualifications include aliveness, a feeling of motion, and a happy mood.

Tree-Shrub Balance

Trees form the vertical lines in the background, but vertical lines usually need a horizontal balance. In the very simple background in Sketch 4.3, the strong vertical line of the central coniferous evergreen is balanced by two adjacent shrub-type conifers. Similarly, broadleaf shrubs are associated with each of the broadleaf trees. With compatible blending shrubs to unite the three units, the background becomes an interesting composition.

In some cases, a shelter or pergola is used in the background to protect and feature valuable plants, such as azaleas, camellias, or rhododendrons. Adjacent broadleaf trees and their respective broadleaf and conifer shrub arrangements will act to widen and frame the floral displays, producing a background well balanced with seasonal color and interest.

→ Complete your background design of trees and shrubs.

Photo 4.7

A mound of soft elegance, *Chamaecyparis pisifera squarrosa minima* is an excellent unit blender.

Photo 4.8

Juniperus squamata meyeri (background) has a gracefully awkward habit of growth and beautiful blue-green foliage—an excellent accent shrub. *Chamaecyparis pisifera squarrosa nana* (foreground) acts as a unit blender.

(Home of Dr. and Mrs. Bolderick)

Photo 4.9

A useful and picturesque background—coniferous and broadleaf trees and shrubs for interesting effect, screening, and wind protection.

Sketch 4.3 **PLEASING LINES AND BALANCE IN THE BACKGROUND**

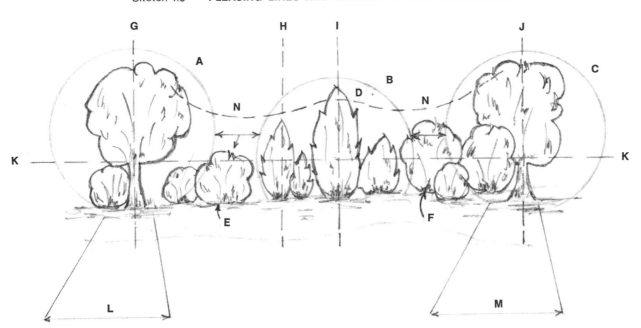

ABC—Combined tree and shrub units
D—Accent unit—usually terminates the central axis
EF—Blenders, used to tie units together
GHIJ—Major vertical lines in the background
K—Horizontal line, to balance the vertical lines
LM—Shadow of shade paths (if the garden faces east)
N—Skyline—an impression of graceful curves against the sky
Plant for a harmonious association of form, foliage, and color to create interest and prevent monotony.

Flowers

The extent of flower planting in this section of
your garden is determined somewhat by the
natural delineation of the border strip. However,
you should strive for free-flowing runs and a
progressive seasonal display of blossoms. Consider using medium to tall perennials, because
of their height and effective balance, with large
background shrubs.
→ Add flowers to your background design.

Side and Structure Planting

The Garden Frame

Plantings along property lines are as important as
the background arrangement because they join
background and house to frame the garden.
Where do you begin this part of design? Most
garden plans have an obvious cross axis or at
least a semblance of one, and the beginning or
termination of this cross axis is a good place for
the nonprofessional to begin work. Follow the
design principles discussed earlier as you plan
property-line planting: balanced vertical and
horizontal lines, pleasing association of plants
within each major grouping or composition,
related texture in associated plants, shrubs and
trees in scale with the house and lot. Arrangement for seasonal color in shrubs and trees will
increase interest throughout the year.
→ Locate the trees on both sides of your plan if
you have not done so, and then place the accom-
panying shrub groupings.

Foundation Plantings

Give considerable thought to the selection and
arrangement of plants along the base of your
house. They must be in scale, interesting in
appearance, strong in character, and alive with
richly colored foliage. The tendency is to over-
plant, to form a hedge. Pull the units farther
apart and allow some of the wall to show through.
Don't block your windows or obstruct doorways.
Trees must not be jammed against the building.

Carefully designed and well-composed foundation plantings can be used to change the proportions of your house. If the house appears too wide
for its height, place a strong and relatively tall
conifer 2 or 3 feet *in* from each outside corner.
This will have a narrowing effect. If the house
seems excessively tall for its width, place relatively tall conifers, or medium height broadleaf
trees, a little way *out* from the outside corners.

Photo 4.10

Conifer background on a sloping lot.

This arrangement will give the illusion of
lowering and broadening the structure. If the
house is excessively long and low, break the horizontal line by locating a tall shrub or small tree
about one-third *in* from one side.
→ Sketch the foundation plantings on your
design paper. Position trees first, then frame the
entrance, and finally locate shrub units.

Garden Structure Planting

Garden buildings require a type of planting that
will frame, balance, and animate them. In addition, the plants should unite the structure with
the garden to form a naturally integrated composition. In hot climates, structure plantings are
often species that will provide sufficient density
for shade in summer. Deciduous trees and vines
are preferable because they admit maximum light
during winter months.
→ Add plantings around any garden structures
in your design.

Finishing Touches

Accent Plants

Place a few individuals or groups of unusually
attractive plants at vantage points in your design
to increase the beauty of the respective areas,

prevent monotony, and draw attention to particular parts of your garden. In a large garden, accent plants are often used to promote continuity in design. They help make the landscape lively and effect a sense of motion by drawing the eye rapidly from one part of the garden to another.
→ Place accent plants at strategic points in your design.

Color—Character Units

All planting sections in your garden will benefit considerably from flowering shrubs. If climate and the size of your garden permit, include several flowering species, particularly for spring and summer display. They greatly assist in maintaining aesthetic interest from the standpoint of both color and natural variation.
→ Study your developing design with placement of flowering shrubs in mind, indicating possible locations.

FLOWERS IN THE TOTAL DESIGN

Color is a major factor in your garden and appears everywhere in the landscape. Every element— tree, shrub, stone—possesses a degree of color. Although variations of green predominate, the composition should include considerable flower color. A limited number of trees and shrubs assist with blossoms in spring and with autumn tones in fall. However, most gardens rely upon flowers for multi-season color.

Flower areas must be meticulously planned as an integral part of the whole color scheme. Avoid indicating clumps of flowers wherever an open space permits a little planting. Locate and shape flower areas so that they seem to flow naturally from one to the other, in harmony with the entire garden.

Observe the flower areas in Figure 4.2. Beginning with the special flower unit at the right, they move upward in an expanding border, appear intermittently across the background, form a special feature between the espaliered screen and path, and then swing gracefully across the garden in a free-flowing curve. These flower areas are designed explicitly for effective continuity. Spotting of the design is carefully avoided, and areas are shaped to induce a feeling of movement

around the garden. The quantity of flowers is adequate but not overpowering.

In the front yard, proportionally fewer flowers are used. The runs appear to swing gracefully through the design and relate harmoniously to the shrub units.
→ Indicate a free-flowing series of flower units on your design paper.

Color Harmony Everywhere

Harmonious blending of colors within flower units is essential to pleasurable response. Bold, aggressive colors side by side seem to compete for individual superiority and should be separated by lighter pastels. To promote continuity, have flower groupings end with colors that blend into adjacent units. A brief study of similar, contrasting, and triad color harmonies as applied to flowers will help you with this part of your design.

Four Seasons of Color Annually

No phase in the development of your garden is more intriguing than providing attractive and well-balanced aesthetic values throughout the year. Let your imagination move from season to season, considering the special beauty of each. Spring brings deciduous broadleaf trees and shrubs into new-green foliage. Flowering species burst into bloom. Fresh shoots increase the luxurious beauty of conifers, and perennials offer their delights. Summer experiences a maturing and natural blending of foliage, forms, color, and effect. Fall rivals spring in beauty as autumn hues take over in deciduous trees and many species of shrubs. Winter expresses her beauty in impressionistic tones, silhouetted forms of deciduous trees, and the velvety sheen of conifer groupings.

Design and arrange your garden's flower areas to express and identify the beauty of each season: soft pastel blossoms in the spring, stronger colors in annuals and perennials through summer, brilliant chrysanthemum displays in fall, holly bushes to enliven the winter landscape. In gardens carefully designed to follow the rhythms of nature, each season has its predominant and harmonious subordinate colors, and one season moves smoothly into the next to produce a color composition entirely different from the preceding one with very little additional planting. The garden in Figure 4.4 is well designed for continuous seasonal interest.

Figure 4.4   **THREE SEASONS OF BLOOM AUTOMATICALLY**

Symbols: Spring blooming,● Summer blooming,■ Fall blooming ▲

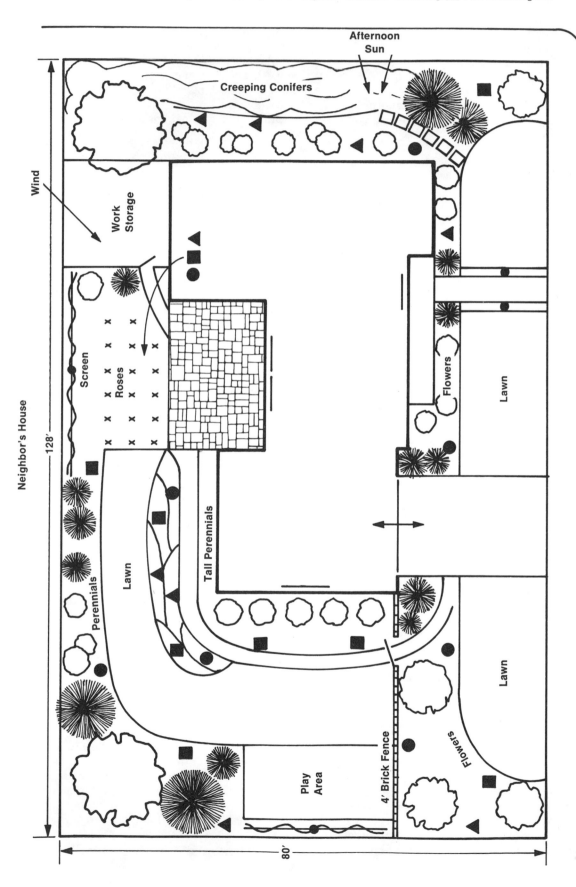

Typical flowers for three-season bloom:

Spring—Candytuft, Bulbs, Delphinium, Pansies, Primrose, Snapdragons

Summer—Coreopsis, Daisies, Gladiolus, Lilies, Marigolds, Petunias, Phlox

Fall—Ageratum, Asters, Chrysanthemums, Dahlias, Day-Lilies, Zinnias

Perennials, Annuals, and Bulbs

Perennials are the flower garden stabilizers. They are strong growers, produce richly colored flowers, are obtainable in heights to suit almost any requirement, and are long lived. They fit gracefully into shrub bays in the background, and add color and interest to side plantings.

Annuals make quick changes in landscape appearance possible and provide interim color during periods of temporary decline in garden interest. Since they bloom within a few weeks after planting, annuals are easily timed to fill a particular need or produce a special effect. For a summer party, for example, you might decorate the patio with annuals growing in containers.

Annuals are appropriate in the front yard too. An entrance walk is made more inviting by successive plantings along its borders.

Bulbs are the true openers of spring and are so informal that they fit naturally into the border of practically any flower area. In a good garden environment, moreover, bulbs are almost self-sustaining. Try blending long runs and graceful groupings into your design to enhance its spring display of color.

Detailed discussions of these three plant categories, together with lists and Selection Charts, appear in Chapter 9.

→ Mark locations for perennials, annuals, and bulbs on your plan.

Plant Selection:
Broadleaf Trees

By use of plant symbols, you have completed the arrangement of your landscape design. Now, the big question: What tree, shrub, or vine does each symbol represent?

A major factor in selecting appropriate plants for your garden is climate. The Agricultural Research Service, U.S. Department of Agriculture, has established temperature zones for the continental United States. These are graphically represented in Figure 1.5, Plant Hardiness Zones. You can quickly determine your zone by referring to this map, which is on page 24.

The influencing factors related to each zone are generally known, and the range of plants adaptable to them has been generally determined. Remember, however, that fractional or mini-climates exist within each major temperature zone. These may be due to sharp changes in altitude, the presence of modifying air currents, or a variation in sectional rainfall. You must therefore familiarize yourself with seasonal temperatures in your particular locality as a guide toward safe selection of plants for your garden.

plants that are appropriate for the location in question.

The general procedure for plant selection, which we will explain in greater detail and with examples, is as follows:

1. Determine the requirements for a particular plant—the height, type, temperature zone, and use.
2. Use the appropriate Selection Chart (Broadleaf Tree, Conifer, Shrub, etc.) to find the names of several plants that meet your requirements fairly closely.
3. Turn to the alphabetical plant descriptions and select the particular plant that seems best suited to your needs.

On the Selection Charts, the zone range of each plant begins with the coldest zone that is considered safe for the plant. Thus you can easily determine whether a given plant will grow well in your particular zone. For example, if you live in zone 5 and the plant requires zone 7 or warmer, you immediately know that it would be unwise to use it in your colder zone.

HOW TO SELECT PLANTS FOR YOUR GARDEN

The homeowner who has little knowledge of plant use is faced with the most frustrating of all landscape problems: *what should I plant here?* A long list of plants is of little consequence without some means of identification and selection. This book offers a unique method.

1. Plant descriptions suggest typical locations for their use in your garden.
2. Plant names and pertinent data are so arranged on Plant Selection Charts that, if you know your temperature zone and the several plant-use requirements for a specific location, you can easily find the names of

BROADLEAF TREES

Because of their size, height, and habit of growth, trees exert tremendous influence upon a landscape, and we will discuss their selection first. Each specie and variety has individual form and characteristics. Their structure and foliage compositions express varying degrees of strength and interest to influence the moods of a garden. The range of their uses is as wide as the garden's requirements. They will widen the house, balance the design, silhouette against the skyline, terminate an axis, retard the wind, provide shade for the patio. The list goes on and on.

Choosing the Right Tree

Let's now see how you can easily select a tree to meet specified functional requirements with confidence that your choice is readily adaptable to your environment. Assume Figure 4.3 (page 87) is your garden design. We will begin with tree number 1 and work clockwise around the property.

Because the house has a relatively shallow setback, about 28 feet from the street, and is one story high, we visualize tree number 1 as a medium-size tree that can be held to 25 to 35 feet high, round-headed, deciduous, with strong trunk and branches and medium to large foliage. Its principal function is to frame your house and lot, increasing the interest of the house and helping unite it with the garden. You live in zone 5, and winters get pretty cold. Therefore all trees must be fairly hardy.

Now that we know what sort of tree is needed, we are ready to begin the selection process. Turn to the Broadleaf Tree Selection Chart on page 97. There you will find:

1. The names of 75 broadleaf trees (their chart numbers are references to their descriptions, which follow).
2. The appropriate controlled height of each tree (the average *pruned* height at which it looks and functions well on a small to medium size property). Note: many will grow taller if permitted.
3. Whether a tree is deciduous or evergreen.
4. Whether it is flowering.
5. Whether it bears noticeable fruit.
6. The zoning range within which a named tree and its varieties may be safely grown.
7. Landscape uses in the garden.
8. Whether a tree displays autumn color in its foliage.
9. Whether it is considered drought resistant.

To find the names of trees that would be suitable as your tree number 1, first place the edge of a piece of paper along the *example strip* at the bottom of the chart and mark your basic requirements on it in the proper columns.

25–35′—D (deciduous)—Zone 5—Fr (framing)

Then slowly move the paper up the chart and match. Sketch 5.1 is illustrative. Reasonable closeness in height is acceptable. Five trees are quickly matched: numbers 8, European white birch; 20, Chinese elm; 33, hornbeam; 34, horse-chestnut; 69, sweet gum. Turn to these numbers in the alphabetical descriptions of broadleaf trees, beginning on page 100, decide which tree you like

best. We will assume your decision is number 34, horse-chestnut.

The form and function of tree 2 are similarly analyzed: medium large, 25 to 35 feet high, *deciduous*, broad habit of growth to blend the lawn and background areas, *flowering*, assists in retarding winds, and is useful in *screening* and for *shade*. Mark these requirements on a selection strip in the proper chart columns.

25–35′—D—Zone 5—Fl (flowering)—
Sc (screening)—SH (shade)

We find at least six trees that qualify: numbers 17, crabapple; 29, hawthorn; 33, hornbeam; 34, horse-chestnut; 44, mayday; 66, silver-bell. Assume that, after reading the descriptions of these trees, you decide upon hawthorn. It will associate well with the nearby conifer grouping and give a bonus of autumn foliage.

Tree 3 is medium large, 30 to 40 feet high, *deciduous*, strong branched, with medium to large leaves, and wind-resistant. It is a *background* tree and helps *frame* the property. Mark the selection strip.

30–40′—D—Zone 5—Fr—B (background)

Three trees are quickly noted: numbers 33, hornbeam; 34, horse-chestnut; 46, fruitless mulberry. Let's say the corresponding descriptions influence your decision to select fruitless mulberry.

Tree 4 has similar functions, but, in addition, must supply shade for the play area. Fruitless mulberry again meets all your requirements and matches tree 3. Therefore it is logical to repeat tree 3, if you so desire.

Tree 5 is of extra importance. It is the framing counterpart of tree 2, 25 to 35 *feet high*, it competes with tree 4, is *deciduous*, falls within the line of vision between the house and play area, provides some afternoon *shade*, and you would like it to be *flowering*. Let's look for it on the selection chart.

25–35′—D—Fl (flowering)—Zone 5—
Fr (framing)—Sh (shade)

Five trees are immediately noticeable: numbers 15, flowering cherry; 18, dogwood; 29, hawthorn; 33, hornbeam; 34, horse-chestnut. Their descriptions indicate that any one of these would serve well in this location. However, this is an excellent point in your design to use one of the hardier fruiting trees. Red delicious apple would provide spring flowers, interesting foliage, the character and interest of fall fruit, autumn color, and winter structural interest. Let's assume that's your choice.

Tree 6 is smaller, 15 to 25 feet high, and must

Sketch 5.1 **USING THE PLANT SELECTION CHARTS**

1—What is the name of this tree? ——————————▶

Lot

2—What kind and size tree do you wish? What is its function? Example: You visualize it as a broadleaf tree, *20 to 30* feet high, *deciduous, flowering.* It is in the *background,* and your garden is in *zone 5.*

3—Turn to the Broadleaf Tree Selection Chart. Mark these requirements on a strip of paper to exactly fit the proper columns (as is done on the example strip at the bottom of the chart).

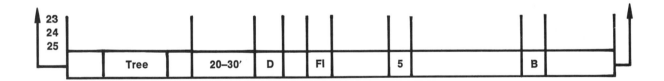

| 23 24 25 | | Tree | | 20–30′ | D | | Fl | | 5 | | | B | |

4—Carefully move the marked strip up over the chart. With reasonable closeness, match your requirements with those on the chart. Note each matching tree's number and name.
Trees located—numbers 15, 18, 29, 33, 34, 66, 70.

5—Turn to each number and name in the alphabetical description list of trees. Read about each and make your choice.

6—Go to a reputable plant nursery and buy the tree by name. It will look well in that location on your lot.

BROADLEAF TREE SELECTION CHART

No.	Name of Tree	Controlled height (feet)	Deciduous	Evergreen	Flowering	Fruits	Zone 2 3 4 5 6 7 8 9 10	Hawaii	Accent	Specimen	Framing	Screening	For shade	Windbreak	Side	Front yard	Background	Lawn tree	Autumn foliage	Drought resistant
1	Apple (Malus)	20–30	+		+	+	+———		+	+	+		+			+	+	+	+	
2	Apricot, flowering	20–30	+		+		+—		+	+	+					+	+	+	+	
3	Ash, Arizona	30–40	+				+—				+	+	+			+	+	+	+	
4	Ash, Modesto	30–40	+				+—				+	+	+			+	+	+	+	
5	Ash, white	40–60	+				+———		+		+					+	+	+	+	+
6	Beech, European	40–50	+				+—		+	+	+	+	+	+	+	+	+			
7	Beech, purple	45–55	+				+—		+	+	+	+			+	+	+	+		
8	Birch, European white	25–50	+				+———		+	+		+			+	+	+	+		
9	Birch, paper	35–60	+				+————		+	+						+	+			
10	Bombax	40–50	+	+			+—										+			
11	Camphor	25–35		+			+—		+	+	+	+	+	+	+	+			+	
12	Caragana	15–20	+		+		+———		+		+	+	+	+			+		+	
13	Catalpa	40–65	+		+	+	+———				+	+	+			+	+	+	+	+
14	Chaste-tree	10–15	+		+		+—		+	+	+	+			+	+	+			
15	Cherry, flowering	20–30	+		+		+—		+	+	+				+	+	+	+		
16	Coral-tree	20–30	+		+		+—		+	+	+			+		+	+			
17	Crabapple	15–25	+		+	+	+———		+	+	+				+	+		+		
18	Dogwood	20–30	+		+	+	+—		+	+					+	+	+	+	+	
19	Elm, American	40–50	+				+———		+	+	+	+	+			+	+	+		+
20	Elm, Chinese	25–35	+				+—		+	+	+	+	+			+	+	+		+
21	Eucalyptus	25–35		+	+		+—		+		+	+	+	+	+				+	
22	Franklinia	15–25	+		+		+—		+		+				+		+	+	+	
23	Frangipani	15–18	+		+		+—		+	+						+	+	+	+	
24	Ginkgo	40–60	+				+—			+		+	+				+	+	+	+
25	Golden-chain	20–30	+		+		+—		+	+	+				+	+	+			
	Example Tree	20–30′ D		Fl			5				B										

Example tree: Requirements are 20–30 feet high, deciduous, flowering, for the background, in zone 5. Mark your zone and requirements on a strip of paper. Move it up over the chart. Match reasonably closely. Find several.

See numbered descriptions for selection. Trees located— numbers 15, 18, 29, 33, 34, 66, 70.
Zoning: Estimated zone-temperature range of each tree's hardiness. Some species may fall within this range.

possess good conformation and four-season interest because it is near the house and opposite a strong conifer tree. It *frames, balances,* serves as an *accent,* and must be particularly attractive. You would like it to be *flowering* and *deciduous.* Mark the selection strip.

15–25′—D—Fl—Zone 5—Ac (accent)—
Fr (framing)

Nine trees qualify: numbers 12, caragana; 15, flowering cherry; 17, crabapple; 18, dogwood; 44, mayday; 45, mountain-ash; 56, flowering plum; 63, redbud; 66, silver-bell. With a little shaping and pruning, you would be happy with any one of this group, but we will assume your selection is flowering cherry. A little annual pruning will control its size.

Study your selections for a moment and you will be delighted with the many phases of four-season interest and service these fine trees offer. Other choices (from among suitable species matched on the Selection Chart) would create a different, yet equally harmonious, landscape. The purpose of the Selection Charts is to allow *you* to

BROADLEAF TREE SELECTION CHART

No.	Name of Tree	Controlled height (feet)	Deciduous	Evergreen	Flowering	Fruits	Zone 2 3 4 5 6 7 8 9 10	Hawaii	Accent	Specimen	Framing	Screening	For shade	Windbreak	Side	Front yard	Background	Lawn tree	Autumn foliage	Drought resistant
26	Goldenrain	25–40	+		+		+ ———		+	+	+					+	+	+	+		+
27	Golden-shower	20–30	+		+			+ —	+	+	+	+				+	+	+			
28	Hackberry	40–60	+			+	+ ———		+	+	+	+				+	+				
29	Hawthorn	20–30	+		+	+	+ ———		+		+		+	+	+	+	+	+		+	
30	Hickory-Carya pecan	60–70	+		+	+	+ ———		+	+						+	+				
31	Holly	20–40		+		+	+ ———		+	+	+			+	+	+	+	+			
32	Honeylocust	50–75	+		+		+ ———————			+		+				+			+		+
33	Hornbeam	25–40	+		+		+ ———		+	+	+	+	+			+	+				
34	Horse-chestnut	25–40	+		+	+	+ ———		+	+	+	+	+			+	+	+	+	+	
35	Indian-cherry	15–30	+			+	+ ——			+	+					+	+	+			
36	Jacaranda	25–30	+		+			+ —	+	+	+					+	+	+	+		
37	Linden, American	40–50	+				+ ———			+	+	+	+			+			+		+
38	Linden, little-leaf	40–65	+				+ ———			+	+		+			+					
39	Loquat	25–30		+		+		+ ——	+	+	+	+	+	+	+	+	+	+	+		
40	Magnolia	25–50	+	+	+		+ ——		+	+	+	+	+			+	+	+			
41	Maple, Norway	35–50	+				+ ———				+	+				+	+	+	+		
42	Maple, red	35–50	+				+ ———————			+	+	+	+			+	+	+	+		
43	Maple, silver	35–50	+				+ ———				+	+	+			+	+	+	+		
44	Mayday	20–35	+		+		+ ———————		+		+	+				+		+	+		
45	Mountain-ash	25–30	+		+	+	+ ———		+	+	+					+	+	+	+	+	+
46	Mulberry, fruitless	30–45	+				+ ——			+	+	+	+			+	+				
47	Oak, holly	35–50		+			+ —					+					+		+	+		
48	Oak, live	40–60		+			+ —					+					+		+	+		
49	Oak, pin	40–60	+				+ ——					+					+		+			
50	Oak, red	35–50	+				+ ——			+	+		+				+		+	+	+	
	Example Tree	20–30′	D		Fl		5											B			

Example tree: Requirements are 20–30 feet high, deciduous, flowering, for the background, in zone 5. Mark your zone and requirements on a strip of paper. Move it up over the chart. Match reasonably closely. Find several.

See numbered descriptions for selection. Trees located—numbers 15, 18, 29, 33, 34, 66, 70.

Zoning: Estimated zone-temperature range of each tree's hardiness. Some species may fall within this range.

choose the particular tree (or plant) you most like, within a range appropriate to your climate and garden design.

Having used the Broadleaf Tree Selection Chart and corresponding descriptions to select trees for Figure 4.3, you may with confidence apply the same method to choosing trees for your own property. The Selection Chart will tell you which trees can be planted successfully in a particular area of your garden and grow well in your climate, and the descriptions will help you make the final choice—one that reflects your own taste and aesthetic values. We have also included lists of trees suitable to the various sections of the country, beginning on page 120. Use these tools to begin developing your own personalized landscape compositions.

In the next chapter, we will follow the same procedure to add shrubs to the garden in Figure 4.3. Selection Charts and plant descriptions in subsequent chapters will similarly assist you in dressing your garden with other plants—conifers, vines, groundcovers, perennials, annuals, and bulbs.

BROADLEAF TREE SELECTION CHART

No.	Name of Tree	Controlled height (feet)	Deciduous	Evergreen	Flowering	Fruits	Zone 2 3 4 5 6 7 8 9 10	Hawaii	Accent	Specimen	Framing	Screening	For shade	Windbreak	Side	Front yard	Background	Lawn tree	Autumn foliage	Drought resistant
51	Oak, scarlet	45–60	+				+———		+	+	+		+			+	+	+	+	+
52	Oak, willow	35–45	+				+———			+	+					+	+			
53	Orchid-tree	20–35	+		+		+—		+	+	+	+				+	+	+		
54	Peach, flowering	20–35	+		+		+———		+	+	+		+			+	+	+	+	
55	Pepper-tree	20–30		+	+		+—		+	+	+	+	+	+		+	+			
56	Plum, flowering	15–20	+		+	+	+———		+	+	+		+			+	+	+	+	
57	Pistacia	35–50	+		+		+—		+		+		+			+	+	+	+	
58	Plane, buttonwood	40–60	+				+———				+				+	+	+		+	+
59	Plane, London	40–60	+				+———				+				+	+	+		+	+
60	Plane, Oriental	40–60	+				+—				+				+	+	+		+	+
61	Poplar	35–60	+				+———					+	+			+	+		+	+
62	Poinciana	25–35	+		+		+—		+	+	+					+	+	+	+	
63	Redbud	12–20	+		+		+———		+	+	+	+				+	+	+	+	+
64	Service-berry	15–20	+				+———		+		+					+	+	+	+	
65	Silk-tree	20–35	+		+		+———		+	+	+					+	+	+		
66	Silver-bell	20–30	+		+		+———		+		+	+				+	+	+		
67	Stewartia	10–15	+		+		+———		+	+	+	+				+	+	+	+	
68	Strawberry-tree	15–20		+	+		+—		+	+	+	+	+		+	+	+	+		+
69	Sweet gum	30–35	+				+———		+	+	+	+				+	+	+	+	
70	Styrax	20–35	+		+		+———		+	+	+	+	+	+	+					
71	Tulip-tree	40–60	+		+		+———			+	+		+	+		+	+	+		
72	Tupelo	35–45	+				+———		+		+					+			+	
73	Walnut	35–65	+			+	+———		+	+	+	+	+			+	+	+	+	
74	Willow	25–35	+				+———			+					+	+		+	+	
75	Zelkova	45–65	+				+———		+	+	+					+				
	Example Tree	20–30'	D		Fl		5									B				

Example tree: Requirements are 20–30 feet high, deciduous, flowering, for the background, in zone 5. Mark your zone and requirements on a strip of paper. Move it up over the chart. Match reasonably closely. Find several.

See numbered descriptions for selection. Trees located—numbers 15, 18, 29, 33, 34, 66, 70.
Zoning: Estimated zone-temperature range of each tree's hardiness. Some species may fall within this range.

ALPHABETICAL DESCRIPTION OF BROADLEAF TREES

Information on tree species and varieties is important to proper selection. After you have matched your requirements with two or more trees on the Broadleaf Tree Selection Chart, read their descriptions below and select the one that best suits your particular need and personal taste. The numbers correspond to those on the Selection Chart. Heights mentioned are controlled heights.

1. APPLE (*Malus*): This widely adapted deciduous fruit tree can be used as an important and very versatile ornamental in gardens of any size. Its spring flowers are beautiful, the form and foliage are pleasing, and the late summer or fall fruit is impressive. Use apples in your landscaping wherever trees 20 to 30 feet high are desired.

2. APRICOT, FLOWERING (*Prunus mume*): This is the Japanese flowering apricot—a 20- to 30-foot, upright, round-headed, deciduous tree that produces quantities of beautiful, fragrant flowers in early spring. Some varieties have double flowers in pink, red, and white. The tree size and shape is controlled by annual pruning.

Plant them in your front yard, near the patio or garden structure units, to begin or terminate a cross axis, or as an accent tree.

3, 4, 5. ASH (*Fraxinus*): The following three species and varieties are among the best for general landscape use.

ARIZONA ASH (*Fraxinus velutina*) is an attractive, open-headed, deciduous tree, easily held at 30 to 40 feet high. The limbs spread and are well dressed with pleasing foliage that turns to deep yellow in autumn. See Sketch 5.2. In mild to warm climates, these trees are very durable and

Sketch 5.2

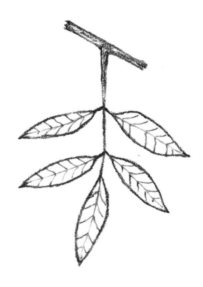

TREE 3,
ARIZONA ASH (*FRAXINUS VELUTINA*)

A deciduous, broadleaf tree—may be held to 30 or 40 feet by careful pruning, has spreading limbs and pleasing foliage that turns yellow to gold in autumn. Use it for balancing, shade, screening, general interest, and large lawn plantings.

Sketch 5.3

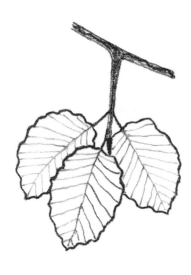

TREE 6,

EUROPEAN BEECH (FAGUS SYLVATICA)

A hardy, deciduous, and ornamental broadleaf tree with attractive form and 2 to 4 inch long, dark green leaves that turn bronzy-red in autumn. Excellent for shade, retarding wind, and framing. Use it in the front yard, with side plantings, in the background, or as a specimen.

will provide an abundance of shade. When placed in the proper locations, they will assist in retarding winds.

MODESTO ASH (*Fraxinus velutina modesto*) is similar to Arizona ash in form, but smaller and more attractive. Spring and summer effects are good, and in autumn the leaves turn to yellow and gold. A street lined with Modesto ash is magnificent in fall. Not hardy in the north.

WHITE ASH (*Fraxinus americana*) is larger, 40 to 60 feet (controlled height), and very hardy in the north. It has pleasing form and foliage and is adaptable to large landscapes.

6, 7. BEECH (*Fagus*): These are hardy, decidu-

ous, ornamental trees with excellent form and foliage.

EUROPEAN BEECH (*Fagus sylvatica*) grows upright with graceful, slender branches. See Sketch 5.3. The bark is light gray, and the foliage is dense and dark green, turning bronzy-red in autumn. The monoecious flowers result in burry nuts that give the tree a decorative aspect.

PURPLE BEECH (*Fagus sylvativa atropunicea*) is the most familiar variety of European beech. It is similar to sylvatica in form and size and very ornamental. In spring the new leaves are bright purplish-red and become dark bronzy-purple as they mature. There are several color variations in

Sketch 5.4

TREE 8,
EUROPEAN WHITE BIRCH (*BETULA PENDULA*)

A rapid growing, medium-size, deciduous, broadleaf tree that is relatively open and has many small pendulous branches. Excellent for framing garden structures, for open lawn or street-side plantings, as an accent or specimen, and for screening.

purple beech, making it advisable to purchase trees after the foliage is well formed.

Both European and purple beech are excellent as specimens, for shade, windbreaks, and framing, in the front yard, side plantings, or background.

AMERICAN BEECH (*Fagus grandifolia*) is similar to European beech in general appearance and use in the landscape. The leaves are larger and slightly bluish-green. It is a hardier tree and very striking in autumn, when its foliage turns golden yellow.

8, 9. BIRCH (*Betula*): There are several important varieties of this deciduous tree.

EUROPEAN WHITE BIRCH (*Betula pendula*) is a rapid growing tree, 25 to 50 feet high, narrow and pyramidal, with slender branches that are gracefully pendulous. See Sketch 5.4. It is relatively open, exposing its dark-lined, artistically patched white bark. The thin, dark green leaves are unevenly toothed. The tree is widely distributed, hardy well into the north, and has many uses—to frame garden structures, for light screening, as an accent or specimen tree.

CUTLEAF WEEPING BIRCH (*Betula pendula dalecarlica*) is an excellent ornamental tree at 25 or 30 feet high. It has deep-cut leaves and is noticeably drooping in growth habit. A good tree for special uses in your design, particularly as an accent or specimen.

PAPER BIRCH (*Betula papyrifera*) is tall, 45 to 60 feet, wider, and has larger ovate leaves 3 or 4 inches long. The bark is white and flakes off in patches. Hardy into the far north. Landscape uses are about the same as *Betula pendula*.

10. BOMBAX (*Bombax malabaricum*): This is a large, wide, and open tropical tree that produces big red flowers in early spring before the leaves appear. The plume-like flower clusters develop near the ends of branches all over the tree. Although it can be maintained at 40 to 50 feet in height, its uses are best limited to the more distant parts of large properties.

11. CAMPHOR (*Cinnamomum camphora*): These are attractive, compact, and round-headed evergreen trees of much landscape value in temperate climates. Their foliage is aromatic, having the scent of camphor when crushed. The small flowers are yellow. Careful pruning will maintain these trees at 25 to 30 feet high. See Sketch 5.5. Use them for shade, wind protection, accents, as specimens, or for framing a garden unit.

12. CARAGANA (*Caragana aborescens*): Because of their yellow pea-like flowers, these are known in some sections of the country as pea-trees. They prefer full sun, are 15 to 20 feet high, densely spreading, and very hardy far north. The compound leaves are small, each composed of four or five pairs of very small leaflets, arranged feather-like. These trees are valuable as large or medium hedges, windbreaks, and in side plantings.

13. CATALPA: Known in some sections as common catalpa, Indian bean tree, or cigar tree.

Sketch 5.5

**TREE 11,
CAMPHOR (*CINNAMOMUM CAMPHORA*)**

Quite compact, round-headed, broadleaf evergreen tree. Useful as an accent tree or specimen, for framing house or garden, for shade, and as a wind retardant.

Sketch 5.6

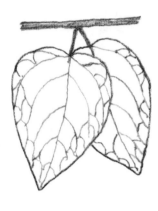

TREE 13,
CATALPA (*CATALPA BIGNONIOIDES*)

An irregularly formed, spreading, 40 to 65 feet high, broadleaf deciduous tree with large heart-shaped leaves. Excellent as a specimen, for balancing effects, shade, retarding wind, and in large lawn areas.

COMMON CATALPA (*Catalpa bignonioides*) is a round-headed, irregularly formed tree, 40 to 65 feet high, and wide spreading with dense foliage. See Sketch 5.6. The yellowish-green, heart-shaped leaves are 7 to 10 inches long. The 1- to 2-inch wide flowers are white with yellow stripes and brown spots and appear in terminal clusters on small branches. The 8- to 12-inch slender pods that result hang most of the winter. This vigorous growing tree prefers moist areas but will tolerate considerable warmth and drought.

WESTERN CATALPA (*Catalpa speciosa*) is very similar to common catalpa in general appearance, except that it is larger. It has the same hardiness. These trees are excellent for shade, in large lawn areas, as specimens, in the distant parts of medium to large landscapes, on estates, and in public parks.

14. CHASTE-TREE (*Vitex agnus-castus*): This cold-tolerant, deciduous ornamental is easily formed into an attractive small tree 10 to 15 feet high, much needed in designing small properties. It has grayish branches and slender leaves. The summer blooming flowers are lilac to lavender spikes that resemble lilac blooms.

Try it in your design behind or toward the sides of a shrub grouping, at a special location in the side plantings, to begin or terminate a cross axis, or as a background filler in plant groupings.

15. CHERRY, FLOWERING (*Prunus species*): There are many varieties: the *serrulata* group includes the ones most widely planted. These are upright, wide spreading, open-headed, deciduous ornamentals, 20 to 30 feet high, of great beauty and use for properties of any size. The 3- to 5-inch long, light green leaves have finely toothed edges. In early spring, cherries produce great quantities of beautiful single or double flowers in delicate tints and shades of pink or in snowy-white, according to variety. Some standard varieties are Akebono, light pink; Amanogawa, light pink; Mount Fuji, snowy-white; Shirofugen, light pink; Yoshino, light pink or white.

Flowering cherries create cheerfulness in any spring garden and are sufficiently hardy to grow well where the temperature does not fall much below zero. Allow them full sun and provide some protection against strong winds. They may be indicated in several locations on your garden plan: appropriately related to pool or patio areas, in the front yard, as specimen or accent trees, at either or both ends of a cross axis, in street-side plantings.

16. CORAL-TREE (*Erythrina poeppigiana*): This is a deciduous, ornamental, warm climate tree that may be held at 20 or 30 feet by pruning. The effective red flowers, which precede the foliage, are almost pea-like and grow in short ra-

cemes. Use trees as accents, or specimens, in the side and background plantings.

17. CRABAPPLE (*Malus* species): These deciduous, open-headed, and wide-spreading trees, are easily held to 15 to 25 feet high by some yearly pruning. They are very cold-hardy, growing well into the north and upper midwest temperature zones. The massive display of flowers in spring usually precedes the foliage. The flowers are either single or double according to variety and are in shades of pink, red, and white. Crabapples prefer good, well-drained soil, deep moisture, and a sunny location that is protected from strong winds. Tone up your garden by using them in the front yard, with side plantings, to frame a garden unit, or as accent or specimen trees.

18. DOGWOOD (*Cornus florida*): This is a cheerful, well-formed, deciduous tree that may be held to 20 to 30 feet by pruning. It is easily grown, hardy, and native to the eastern and southern sections of the country. It produces an abundance of white flowers in spring, followed by scarlet fruits. The handsome foliage turns a rich yellow-brown and red in autumn.

Cornus florida rubra is equally good and has flowers that are pink to deep rose.

Cornus nuttallii has beautiful white flowers and is taller growing but less cold-hardy, most reliable in mild to warm temperature zones. This is the variety generally seen in the west.

Dogwoods grow best among taller trees that filter the sunlight or where they will receive morning sunlight and afternoon protection. Indicate them on your design in the front yard, side plantings, background, as accent or specimen trees.

19. AMERICAN ELM (*Ulmus americana*): These are very hardy and elegant deciduous trees with sturdy trunks, and large structural limbs. The leaves are 3 to 6 inches long and attractively distributed. Elms tolerate considerable pruning and can be held to 40 or 50 feet, if desired. They impart a feeling of stability to the landscape and are used in street-side plantings, large landscapes, parks, and industrial developments. Distribution is wide: east to west and well into the north. However, their use in the eastern United States is limited because of Dutch elm disease, which is reportedly spreading to the midwest and west. Ask your county or state agricultural agent for advice.

20. CHINESE ELM (*Ulmus parvifolia*): This tree is smaller than American elm, 25 to 35 feet controlled height, with spreading and gracefully pendulous branches. It is well formed, with dense and attractive foliage. The glossy, dark green leaves are 1 to 2½ inches long. See Sketch 5.7.

Sketch 5.7

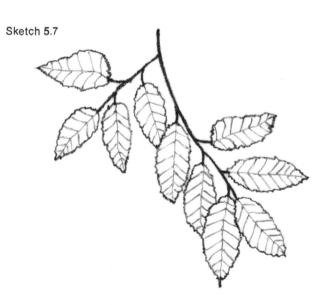

**TREE 20,
CHINESE ELM (*ULMUS PARVIFOLIA*)**

An attractive, round-headed, broadleaf evergreen tree with densely arranged leaves, dark green and glossy. Very useful for background planting, framing house or garden and garden structures, screening, shade, and as a wind retardant.

Hardy well into the north. Although it is considered half-evergreen, it drops its leaves in cold temperatures.

Chinese elms are useful for street-side plantings, to frame your house and garden structures, for screening, as wind retardants, specimens, or in the background.

21. EUCALYPTUS (*Eucalyptus ficifolia*): This is a relatively slow-growing, open-headed, strong structured, flowering evergreen, 30 to 35 feet high. It is not reliably grown in temperatures at or below freezing. The leaves are ovate or narrow, and the clusters of white, salmon, or scarlet flowers are very attractive. These trees are best planted for ornamental purposes on large properties, parks, and parkways.

Eucalyptus sideroxylon rosea is a slender, medium-size, tree. See Sketch 5.8. It has narrow leaves and rose-colored flowers in late spring and summer. Artistically located, these trees enhance the rich simplicity of modern glass and expansive wood-wall houses. Use one or two in side plantings to increase interest. They are excellent for screening and as wind retardants.

22. FRANKLINIA (*Gordonia alatamaha*): This mild to warm climate, mostly deciduous tree grows 15 to 25 feet high and has bright green foliage that turns orange-red in autumn. Its large white flowers appear in late summer and early fall. Give it rather important locations in the garden—to frame a large patio or garden structure, in the side plantings, or in the forepart of the background. Protect it from cold, strong winds.

23. FRANGIPANI (*Plumeria acutifolia*): This is a beautiful, open-headed, warm climate tree, 15 to 18 feet high. It produces quantities of enchantingly fragrant white flowers.

Plumeria rubra is about the same height and size, and has very fragrant pink, red, or purple flowers. These trees are grown in the deep south and in Hawaii, where the flowers are often used in leis. If your climate will permit, use plumerias to bring fragrance into your garden—near lounging areas, seats, garden structures. Try them in movable containers for the patio.

24. GINKGO (*Ginkgo biloba*): Often called maidenhair, this is a deciduous tree, 40 to 65 feet high, upright and rather open in habit of growth. Its 3- to 4-inch wide, fan-shaped leaves impart a sense of elegance. See Sketch 5.9. The foliage turns a rich yellow in autumn. Male and female flowers grow on separate trees. Plant only male trees to avoid ill-smelling fruit. There is a diversity of shape and color of foliage in the horticultural forms: *aurea* has yellowish leaves, *laciniata* has divided leaves, and the leaves of *variegata*

are mottled with yellow. Because they are large trees, restrict ginkgos to appropriate locations on large landscapes, in parks, industrial areas, and farm gardens.

25. GOLDEN-CHAIN (*Laburnum anagyroides*): This ornamental tree is deciduous, 20 to 25 feet high, with an upright and spreading habit of growth. Flowers appear in 8- to 12-inch long, yellow, wisteria-like racemes generally distributed over the entire tree in May and June. These trees are easy to grow and are hardy well into the north. Some pruning increases beauty and performance. In warm climates, they should have some afternoon protection.

Laburnum vossii is very similar in size, shape, and appearance.

Laburnum watereri is 20 to 30 feet high, open-growing and upright, with 8- to 12-inch racemes of light yellow flowers.

These are very colorful trees that merit use in gardens of any size. Consider locating them near garden structures, in property-line plantings, as accent trees, and in the background of medium to large properties.

26. GOLDENRAIN TREE (*Koelreuteria paniculata*): This 25 to 40 foot, rather compact, ornamental tree produces clusters of golden-yellow flowers in summer. The lacy leaves are compound, each composed of up to twelve or fourteen irregularly lobed leaflets. See Sketch 5.10. This is a very attractive tree that is easily held to 15 or 20 feet by pruning. It prefers full sun.

Koelreuteria formosana is a little taller and requires a warmer climate. Its blossoms are similar to *paniculata*. Appropriate locations in your garden include: front yard, near patio and structures, as a specimen or accent tree, to begin or terminate a cross axis.

27. GOLDEN-SHOWER (*Cassia fistula*): This tree requires a warm to tropical climate. It grows 20 to 30 feet high, is deciduous, and has feathery foliage. It blooms profusely through most of the spring. Quantities of flowers are born in yellow racemes.

Cassia javanica is deciduous and displays pinkish-white blossoms.

Cassia grandis (Pink shower) is tall and produces long racemes of rosy-pink flowers.

All three varieties grow well in southern California, Florida, and Hawaii. Try them as accents, or specimens, in the front yard, among side plantings, near garden structures, adjacent to the patio, or keep them low and broad in a large tub.

28. HACKBERRY (*Celtis*): This is a large, mostly deciduous, well-rounded tree that has elm-like foliage and appearance, 40 to 50 feet high if controlled by pruning.

Sketch 5.8

TREE 21,
EUCALYPTUS (*EUCALYPTUS SIDEROXYLON ROSEA*)

A gracefully slender, medium-size tree with long, narrow leaves and rose-colored flowers in late spring. Enhances the rich simplicity of modern glass and wood wall homes. Use one or two as accent trees in side plantings, for screening and as wind retardants.

Sketch 5.9

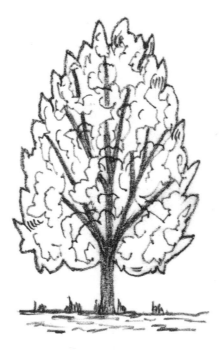

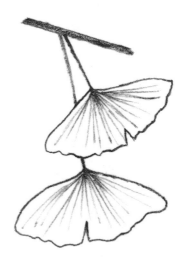

TREE 24,
GINKGO (*GINKGO BILOBA*)

An upright, rather open growing, deciduous tree with fan-shaped leaves that turn yellow to gold in autumn. Most useful in background and lawn plantings on large landscapes, in parks and industrial areas, and in country (farm) plantings.

Sketch 5.10

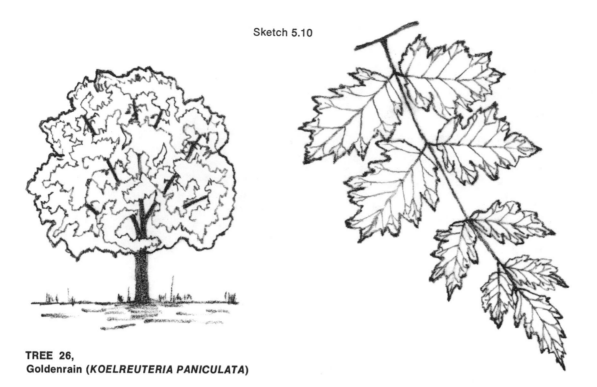

TREE 26,
Goldenrain (*KOELREUTERIA PANICULATA*)

An attractive deciduous tree with compound, lacy leaves and hanging clusters of golden-yellow flowers in summer. Its uses include: front yard, near patio and garden structures, as an accent or specimen, to begin or terminate an axis.

Sketch 5.11

TREE 32,
HONEYLOCUST, THORNLESS (*GLEDITSIA TRIACANTHOS INERMIS*)

A strongly upright, deciduous, slender-branched tree with compound leaves that turn bronzy-yellow in autumn. Twelve to 15 inch long pods mature in the fall. Tolerates unusual droughts, excessive heat, adverse soil conditions, and strong winds. Useful for shade, open plantings for distant effects, and as wind retardants.

Celtis australis is abundantly grown along the California coast and in similar mild climates. It withstands considerable drought.

Celtis laevigata is tall. Its fruit is orange-red and turns to deep purple when mature.

Celtis occidentalis is very hardy in the east, midwest, and into the north.

When used in medium to large landscapes, these trees may be located as windbreaks, for shade, screening, large framing, or in the background.

29. HAWTHORN (*Crataegus*): These very attractive, deciduous trees are hardy well into the north and east. They are well formed, open-headed, upright, and spreading, and are easily held to 20 or 30 feet. Masses of small flowers appear in clusters in spring in pink, red, or white, according to variety, and are followed by red fruits in fall. The foliage changes color in autumn.

Hawthorns are useful to frame structures and areas, in side plantings, as accent or specimen trees, or in the background. They grow best in reasonably fertile soil, with good drainage and adequate moisture. Some pruning increases interest and encourages heavy flowering.

30. HICKORY—*Carya pecan*: This is a large, upright, open-growing deciduous tree with strong trunk and main branches. The bark is interestingly furrowed. The 12- to 16-inch long compound leaves are composed of ten to fifteen yellowish-green leaflets with toothed margins. Altogether, these structural characteristics compose a beautiful tree for the large landscape. To keep its height at 50 to 60 feet, begin pruning when the tree is young.

The edible nuts are delicious, and tree varieties are available for various climates and conditions. Ask your nursery dealer or agricultural agent for advice. Carya pecan trees prefer moist, well-drained soil and considerable warmth. They are appropriate for extensive lawn, estate, and park plantings. Indicate these strong and impressive trees where broad shade is desirable, to assist in retarding winds, or in the distance to frame a property. They may also frame a large house or serve as accent trees.

31. HOLLY (*Ilex*): These very attractive small trees are grown principally for their beauty of form, foliage, and handsome berries. The following evergreen kinds are extremely valuable in a garden of any size. The flowers are inconspicuous, the sexes are on separate plants, and the female plants produce the berries. Be sure there is a male plant nearby to assure berries.

AMERICAN HOLLY (*Ilex opaca*) has evergreen, spiny margined leaves, grows 20 to 30 feet high, and has red berries. This one spreads and requires considerable room for growth. It has smooth gray bark.

Ilex cornuta is an excellent Chinese relative of English holly, growing 12 to 15 feet high, with large, dark green, and shiny leaves that have little spines at the tip and two or three along the sides. The berries are scarlet.

ENGLISH HOLLY (*Ilex aquifolium*) is a luxurious, strongly upright, compact evergreen with glossy, dark green leaves. Its pea-size berries are red and appear in well distributed clusters.

There are many locations on your plan where hollies may be indicated: in the front yard, near garden structures, as accent or specimen trees.

32. HONEYLOCUST, THORNLESS (*Gleditsia triacanthos inermis*): This handsome deciduous tree is 50 to 75 feet high, strongly upright, and open in habit of growth. See Sketch 5.11. The small branches are gracefully slender and support 6- to 12-inch long compound leaves composed of numerous 1- to 2-inch long leaflets that turn bronzy-yellow in autumn. Their twisted pods, 12 to 15 inches long, mature in the fall.

MORAINE LOCUST is an excellent variety that has no thorns or pods and is very cold-tolerant.

Honeylocusts are very valuable anywhere within their range of cold tolerance but especially in areas of unusual heat, wind, drought, and adverse soil conditions. On large properties, they are useful as windbreaks, shade trees, in open plantings, and for distant effects.

33. HORNBEAM (*Carpinus betulus*): European hornbeam is a handsome, 25 to 40 feet high, dense and round-headed tree with many small branches. The light green leaves are 2 to 4 inches long, thin and ovalish in form. They turn shades of yellow in autumn. See Sketch 5.12.

Hornbeams may be used on either side of the front yard, in areas where shade is required, for windbreaks, as accent or specimen trees, for screening, or in the background.

34. HORSE-CHESTNUT (*Aesculus*): These beautiful ornamentals have many possible uses in any landscape plan.

COMMON HORSE-CHESTNUT (*Aesculus hippocastanum*) is naturally a tall and spreading tree, but can be held within 25 to 40 feet by pruning. It is strongly upright, round-headed and thickly covered with digitally compound leaves uniquely composed of five to seven green leaflets that are 5 to 8 inches long. It is deciduous and presents an interesting form and structure. White flowers lightly tinted with red appear in 6- to 12-inch long panicles, followed in fall by walnut-size seeds within a prickly pod.

RED HORSE-CHESTNUT (*Aesculus carnea*) is similar to *hippocastanum* in general appearance and characteristics. See Sketch 5.13. Height and

Sketch 5.12

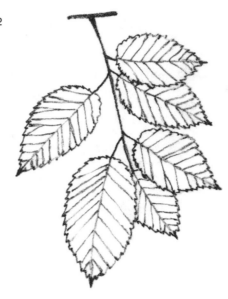

TREE 33,
HORNBEAM (*CARPINUS BETULUS*):

European hornbeam is a medium size, round headed and rather densely foliaged tree that is deciduous. The 2 to 4 inch ovalish leaves turn shades of yellow in autumn. Among its landscape uses are—accent, background and front yard plantings, screening, shade, specimen, wind retardant.

Sketch 5.13

TREE 34,
RED HORSE-CHESTNUT (*AESCULUS CARNEA*)

A medium-size, deciduous, spreading, and densely foliaged tree with digitally compound leaves 5 to 8 inches long. Produces magnificent panicles of red flowers. Many uses in the average garden: front yards, large lawn tree, accent or specimen, to frame the house, shade near patio or childen's play area, background or side plantings, street-side tree.

size are easily controlled to conform to location and desired use. Its spring display of flowers in red panicles is magnificent.

Horse-chestnuts may be used in front yards and on large lawns, as accent or specimen trees, to frame the house, for shade near patio or play area, at either end of an axis, or as street-side planting.

35. INDIAN-CHERRY (*Rhamnus caroliniana*): This is a small, deciduous tree 15 to 30 feet high. The 4- to 6-inch long, oblong leaves have toothed margins. Small greenish flowers appear in umbels in spring and are followed by red, pea-size fruit that turns black when mature.

It is best used in miscellaneous small-tree and large-shrub groupings, in side plantings, for framing small areas, for screening, or in the forepart of the background.

36. JACARANDA (*Jacaranda acutifolia*): This beautiful open growing tree is 25 to 30 feet high, with 15- to 18-inch long, doubly compound, fern-like leaves. The display of 8- to 10-inch long, loose panicles of brilliant blue, tubular flowers is spectacular in early summer. It is a warm climate tree and will not resist frost. Use it in any prominent location that has full sun and protection from wind and cold.

37. LINDEN, AMERICAN (*Tilia americana*): This tree is often called basswood. It is an upright, symmetrical, and heavily foliaged tree, 40 to 50 feet high, with heart-shaped leaves, 3 to 5 inches long. They turn shades of yellow in autumn. The small, fragrant, nearly white flowers hang in little clusters from special leaf units and result in small nut-like fruits. The tree is very hardy and grows well into the north. Use it for large-scale framing, for shade, with miscellaneous plantings in large lawns, and in the background.

38. LITTLE-LEAF LINDEN (*Tilia cordata*): This linden is similar to *americana* in general structure but has small leaves, 2 to 3 inches long, which give it a somewhat different appearance. See Sketch 5.14. *Cordata* can easily be controlled by pruning. It is very cold-hardy, and its uses are the same as *americana*.

39. LOQUAT (*Eriobotrya japonica*): This is a very attractive, large leafed, symmetrical evergreen tree, 25 to 30 feet high with considerable spread. It grows well in warm climates. It is not wise to include it in your garden if temperatures drop below a few degrees of frost—the citrus temperatures are usually safe. It produces edible fruit.

Loquats may be used in many parts of the landscape—on either side of the front yard if the house is set well back, for shade near the patio, and in side plantings.

40. MAGNOLIA (*Magnolia grandiflora*): This stately broadleaf evergreen has excellent proportions and grows 30 to 50 feet high. Its dark green, glossy leaves are 5 to 8 inches long, and the fragrant, cup-shaped flowers are 6 to 8 inches across. This tree grows east to west and into the deep south, but is not hardy far north.

Magnolia denudata is generally smaller, 25 to 40 feet high, but is similar to *grandiflora* in form. Its leaves are oval, and the flowers a little smaller.

Magnolia virginiana (Sweet bay) is half evergreen except in the north, where it is deciduous. Its leaves are nearly oblong, 4 or 5 inches long, and the fragrant white flowers average 3 inches across.

Magnolias impart a feeling of strength and dignity to a garden. If your climate permits, indicate them on your plan—in the front yard, for large lawn planting, to frame the garden, for shade, as specimens, or in the background for special effect.

41, 42, 43. MAPLE (*Acer*): These are cold-hardy deciduous trees of great beauty and interesting variation in foliage: from light and medium greens to reddish-purples in the Japanese cutleaf kinds. The foliage of most species turns beautiful colors in fall—yellow, gold, bronze, reds. The autumn effect is amazing. Each variety has its own characteristic appearance and landscape uses. They tolerate pruning and can be held within the heights suggested here.

NORWAY MAPLE (*Acer platanoides*) is upright, relatively wide, and 35 to 50 feet high. The bright green, five lobed leaves are 4 to 6 inches across. Its variety *Schwedleri* has reddish young foliage that soon turns green. Both are hardy well up into the north.

RED MAPLE (*Acer rubrum*) is well formed and dense, 35 to 50 feet high, with 3- or 4-inch leaves that turn brilliant gold and scarlet in autumn. See Sketch 5.15. These trees are very cold-hardy and widely distributed.

SILVER MAPLE (*Acer saccharinum*) is open and spreading in growth habit and 35 to 50 feet high. The leaves are five lobed, 4 to 6 inches across, bright green above and silvery beneath. Its variety *Wieri* (Wier's cutleaf maple) has deeply dissected leaves.

Locate maples on either side of your front yard to frame the house, for shade near the patio, or in the background to frame the property. They are excellent for industrial park landscaping, large mobile home parks, and housing developments.

44. MAYDAY (*Prunus padus*): Sometimes known as European bird-cherries, these trees are 20 to 35 feet high, hardy, and deciduous, with quantities of fragrant white flowers in thin

Sketch 5.14

**TREE 38,
LITTLE-LEAF LINDEN (*TILIA CORDATA*)**

An upright, symmetrical, and heavily foliaged tree with 2 or 3 inch long, heart-shaped leaves that turn shades of yellow in autumn.
Use it for framing, shade, miscellaneous plantings in large lawns, and in the background. Excellent for mall and street-side plantings in wide parkways.

Sketch 5.15

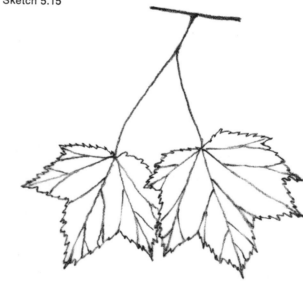

**TREE 42,
RED MAPLE (*ACER RUBRUM*)**

A strong, well formed, and densely foliaged deciduous tree with 3 or 4 inch lobed leaves that turn brilliant gold and scarlet in autumn.
Use to frame your house or garden, for shade, as an accent, in the background, or with large lawn or street-side plantings.

Sketch 5.16

**TREE 45,
EUROPEAN MOUNTAIN-ASH (*SORBUS AUCUPARIA*)**

A medium-size, upright and loosely open, deciduous tree with compound leaves that turn reddish in autumn. Clusters of scarlet berries develop and are spectacular. Useful in the front yard, in side plantings, in the background, as an accent, specimen, or street-side planting.

clusters. The trees are well formed and have small leaves. They are useful as blenders to unite tree groupings, for screening in large side plantings, for framing garden units, as accent trees, or for general use in the background.

45. MOUNTAIN-ASH (*Sorbus americana*): This tree is deciduous, upright, and loosely open in growth habit, 20 to 30 feet high. The fern-like compound leaves are composed of twelve to fourteen narrow leaflets, imparting an airy effect. See Sketch 5.16. The small, white, spring-blooming flowers grow in terminal clusters and in the fall are followed by clusters of shiny red berries. These are cold-hardy trees growing north into Manitoba.

EUROPEAN MOUNTAIN-ASH (*Sorbus aucuparia*) is very cold-hardy, 25 to 30 feet high, and deciduous, with compound leaves composed of small leaflets along a center stem. In fall the leaves turn a reddish color and the clusters of scarlet-red berries become spectacular.

These two kinds of mountain-ash are excellent for your front yard, as side plantings, in the back-

ground, or as accent or specimen trees.

46. MULBERRY, FRUITLESS (*Morus alba*, fruitless): This hardy, open-headed, deciduous tree grows 30 or 45 feet high (controlled), and has large, bright green leaves 3 to 5 inches long. There are several good varieties, such as Kingan and Stribling. Because of their non-fruiting habit, they are valuable in the landscape in locations where shade is needed, near the house, patio, or lawn areas, for protection against summer winds, and in the background planting.

47, 48, 49, 50, 51, 52. OAKS (*Quercus*): These hardy trees are used in the landscape for beauty, character, and shade. They bring a feeling of sturdiness to a garden. Much of their beauty lies in the form and changing color of their spring, summer, and fall foliage. Several are discussed in order that you may have an adequate selection for your plan.

HOLLY OAK (*Quercus ilex*) is a strong, open evergreen, 35 to 50 feet high. It has 2- to 3-inch long, holly-like leaves and prefers medium to warm temperatures. See Sketch 5.17.

Sketch 5.17

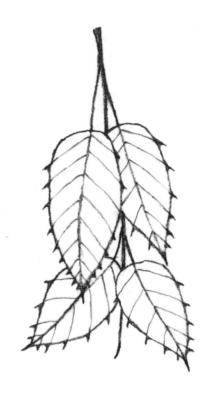

**TREE 47,
HOLLY OAK (*QUERCUS ILEX*)**

A strong, attractive, evergreen, round-headed tree with 2 or 3 inch long, spiny-margined, holly-like leaves. Excellent for shade and as wind retardants, for large lawn plantings, parks, estates, industrial parks, and country (farm) plantings.

LIVE OAK (*Quercus virginiana*) is evergreen, very strong, 40 to 60 feet high, and wide-growing with heavy main branches. The oblong leaves are 3 to 5 inches long. Sturdy and picturesque, this tree prefers a mild to warm climate.

PIN OAK (*Quercus palustris*) is deciduous and cold tolerant, 40 to 60 feet high, with wide-spreading branches and deeply lobed leaves that turn brilliant scarlet in autumn. The five to seven lobes are sharp at the tips.

RED OAK (*Quercus borealis, Quercus rubra*): While both forms are widely considered red oak, *quercus borealis* is a more nothern tree (Northern red oak), growing naturally from Nova Scotia to Pennsylvania and westward. It is sturdy, broad, and open, 35 to 50 feet high (controlled height), with leaves that are 7 or 8 inches long and deeply lobed. *Quercus rubra* (Spanish red oak) is also a large deciduous tree that grows naturally from New Jersey westward and south. The leaves are 7 or 8 inches long with irregular lobes. The foliage of both turns to beautiful red in autumn.

SCARLET OAK (*Quercus coccinea*) is deciduous, 45 to 60 feet high, and upright in habit of growth. It has 5- to 6-inch long leaves with deep, sharply tipped lobes. It is very cold resistant, and the foliage turns a brilliant scarlet in autumn.

WILLOW OAK (*Quercus phellos*) is smaller, 35 to 40 feet high, and deciduous. The 3- to 5-inch, rather narrow leaves are smooth and light green. It grows naturally from New York westward and south.

Oaks are magnificent trees. If your garden will accommodate their size, use them for plantings in extensive lawn areas, in locations for shade, to frame the property, or in the background.

53. ORCHID-TREE (*Bauhinia*): This is a small, well-proportioned tropical tree, 20 to 35 feet high, with double lobed leaves and attractive five-petaled flowers that resemble orchids. Seed pods develop that are 9 or 10 inches long. Bauhinias may be grown in full sun or partial shade.

Bauhinia blakeana has fragrant 4- to 6-inch, scarlet-purple flowers that bloom in early spring.

Bauhinia variegata has broadly lobed leaves and very showy lavender-to-purple flowers.

These small trees are grown in such climates as southern California, Florida, and Hawaii. Use them as accent and specimen trees, near the patio or pool, or in side plantings.

54. PEACH, FLOWERING (*Prunus persica*): These medium-cold hardy, deciduous trees are very similar to fruiting peach in shape, size, and habit of growth. However, the flowers are more exuberant and they bear little if any fruit. In the spring they produce masses of double flowers in pink, red, or white, according to variety. The flowers appear on new wood, requiring that the tree be given an annual pruning. Prune carefully as good shape and size enhance the beauty of this elegant tree.

Indicate flowering peaches on your plan in the front yard, near the patio, pool area, or garden structures, as an accent or specimen tree, to begin or terminate an axis.

55. PEPPER-TREE (*Schinus molle*): California pepper-trees are open, light and airy in appearance, and well covered with feathery foliage that is evergreen and hangs gracefully from long pendulous branches. Long, loose clusters of small, shiny, deep-rose fruits decorate the tree in fall. This pepper-tree requires a mild to warm climate.

BRAZILIAN PEPPER-TREE (*Schinus terebinthifolius*) grows upright, strong, and broadly round-headed, with 6- or 7-inch long compound leaves composed of seven to nine deep green leaflets. This evergreen tree is 20 to 30 feet high and presents a trim and heavily foliaged effect. Its panicles of white flowers in spring are followed by loose clusters of shiny red fruits.

Use pepper-trees in large lawn plantings, near garden structures, as windbreaks, or in the background.

56. PLUM, FLOWERING (*Prunus*): This is a deciduous, upright, open, round-headed, and thickly branched ornamental, 15 to 20 feet high. Its pink or white flowers massively cover all branches in early spring. The 3- or 4-inch long leaves that follow are in varying degrees of reddish-purple, according to variety. The fruit is sparse and small and of no real aesthetic importance.

Prunus blireana is a pink, double-flowered variety.

Prunus pissardii (a variety of *cerasifera*) produces masses of white single flowers.

Prune flowering plums annually for size and shape and to improve flowering. Use them wherever a bold change of foliage color is desired, choosing locations in a way that will avoid spotting your garden. Consider them at either side of the front yard, near garden structures, or in side plantings.

57. PISTACE, CHINESE (*Pistacia chinensis*): This well-formed, deciduous, densely round-headed tree is broadly spreading and 35 to 50 feet high. See Sketch 5.18. Its compound leaves are composed of five or six pairs of light green, sharp-pointed leaflets that turn orange to red in autumn. The loose clusters of nut-like fruits turn from scarlet to purplish. *Pistacias* prefer mild to warm climates. Include a male tree for fruiting. *Pistacia vera* is the nut tree, 25 to 30 feet high, and deciduous.

Use these excellent trees for shade, in the front yard, adjacent to the patio or garden structures, for framing the property or large garden areas, as specimens, and in street-side plantings.

58, 59, 60. PLANE (*Platanus*): Plane-trees are strong, hardy, and deciduous, with large main limbs and maple-like leaves. The bark is patterned in variations of gray and peels off in plate-like patches. Most species are hardy well into the north. They tolerate pruning and can be maintained at the height and size desired.

BUTTONWOOD (*Platanus occidentalis*) is also referred to as American sycamore. It is 40 to 60 feet high and open growing with strong, wide spreading limbs. Its large leaves have three to five triangular lobes.

CALIFORNIA PLANE (*Platanus racemosa*) gracefully twists its heavy main trunk up and outward to form an irregularly shaped body. The light green leaves of three to five lobes are 5 to 10 inches long and 6 to 10 inches wide.

LONDON PLANE (*Platanus acerifolia*) is 35 to 60 feet high and has wide-spreading limbs that form a relatively round head. Its three to five lobed leaves are 5 to 8 inches wide and generously distributed over the tree. It is very hardy and widely used wherever temperature will permit.

ORIENTAL PLANE (*Platanus orientalis*) is 30 to 40 feet high and round-headed. Its leaves are 4 to 7 inches wide and have five to seven lobes. This tree requires a mild to warm climate.

Although plane trees can be maintained at desirable heights for small properties, it is usually advisable to restrict their use to large properties—estates, parks, farms, housing developments, shopping complexes, industrial parks, and parkways. They are valuable for shade, as wind retardants and natural sound barriers, and for screening.

61. POPLAR (*Populus*): These tall deciduous trees are rapid growing and widely distributed over the country. They will grow almost anywhere and are extensively used in the midwest for shade and windbreaks.

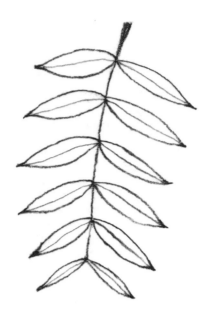

TREE 57,
PISTACE, CHINESE (*PISTACIA CHINENSIS*):

A well formed, deciduous, broadly spreading, round-headed tree with compound leaves consisting of five or six pairs of sharp pointed leaflets that turn brilliant orange to red in autumn. The nut-like fruits that develop turn from scarlet to purplish. Excellent for shade, in the front yard, adjacent to the patio or garden structures, for framing, as an accent or specimen, in the background, and for street-side plantings.

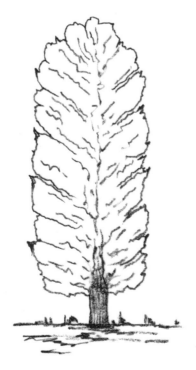

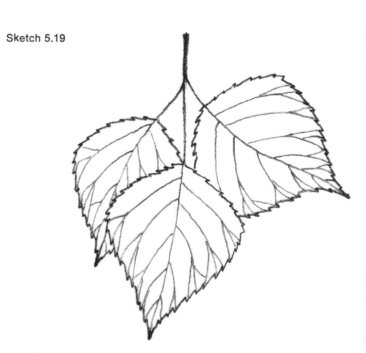

TREE 61,
LOMBARDY POPLAR (*POPULUS NIGRA ITALICA*)

A thinly columnar and densely foliaged deciduous tree with innumerable small branches growing upright and out from the central trunk. Its foliage becomes a magnificent spectacle of golden-yellow in autumn.

Because of extensive root systems, use this and other poplars on large landscapes, estates, or country (farm) properties, for tall wind retardants, screening, and distant autumn color.

CAROLINA POPLAR (*Populus canadensis eugenei*) is upright and relatively narrow, with a pyramidal habit of growth. It is 40 to 60 feet high and heavily foliaged. The 3- or 4-inch leaves are rather oval and move easily in the breeze.

COTTONWOOD (*Populus balsamifera*) is a sturdy upright, and open growing tree, 45 to 60 feet high, with foliage of medium density. Its leaves are 5 to 6 inches long, slightly heart-shaped at the base, medium green above and silvery white below. They quake with the slightest breeze. Cottonwoods are widely distributed and hardy almost anywhere. The fruit is encased in silky fibers often referred to as cotton.

LOMBARDY POPLAR (*Populus nigra italica*) is a thinly columnar and densely foliaged tree, 30 to 50 feet high. Innumerable small branches grow upright and out from the central trunk, from the base to the tip. See Sketch 5.19. The 3- or 4-inch long, light green leaves are nearly triangular and quake in the breeze. These trees turn to golden-yellow in autumn and are spectacular in the distance.

WHITE POPLAR (*Populus alba*) is sturdy, 35 to 60 feet high, and grows in an open, upright, and erratic manner. The 3- to 5-inch long, ovate leaves are lobed, brilliant green above and silvery gray beneath. These trees are very cold-hardy and have wide distribution.

Because of their extensive root systems, it is advisable to restrict the use of poplars to large landscapes—estates, parks, farm properties—where they are excellent for shade, windbreaks, screening, and fall color effects.

62. POINCIANA, ROYAL (*Delonix regia*): This is a mostly deciduous, warm climate tree that grows 25 to 35 feet high and is wide-spreading. Its foliage is fern-like, and the scarlet or orange flowers are spectacular through spring and into summer. These are especially beautiful trees in Hawaii.

63. REDBUD (*Cercis*): These small deciduous trees are particularly valuable for their good form, attractive foliage, and masses of pea-shaped flowers in spring before foliage appears. The leaves turn yellow and red in autumn. Redbud adapts to full sun or partial shade and readily grows in average, well-drained soil.

Cercis canadensis grows from Ontario south and west. It is usually 15 to 20 feet high and open-headed. The flowers are rose-pink.

Cercis chinensis is not as cold-tolerant as *canadensis*. It is similar in form, but its leaves are a little larger and the flowers are rose-purple.

Redbuds may be included in gardens of almost any size, and can be held to the desired height by careful pruning. Plant them on either side of the front yard, near a garden structure, in the side plantings, or to liven up the background.

64. SERVICE-BERRY (*Amelanchier*): These small trees are also known as June-berry. They are deciduous and hardy, growing well into the north. The terminal clusters of white flowers in early spring are very attractive. The small fruits turn from red to dark blue or black when mature. These trees are excellent for fall foliage effects as the leaves turn to gold and orange.

Amelanchier canadensis is 15 or 20 feet high, very hardy and easy to grow. Its 2-inch long flower clusters precede the leaves in an effective spring display.

Amelanchier grandiflora grows to 15 or 20 feet high and is also very hardy. It is especially showy because of its large flowers.

Indicate these trees on your garden design wherever small deciduous trees are appropriate, as side plantings, in the forepart of the background, near the house or patio, in the front yard planting.

65. SILK-TREE (*Albizzia julibrissin*): This is a mild to warm climate, deciduous tree with fern-like foliage and an open and spreading crown. It is 20 to 35 feet high and bears fragrant pink flowers through the summer. Seasonal pruning will control form and height.

Silk-trees fit well into the design of most properties as accent or specimen tres, for screening, and as wind retardants.

66. SILVER-BELL (*Halesia carolina*): This very showy deciduous tree is open and round-headed, growing 30 feet high. See Sketch 5.20. Around May, quantities of ¾-inch-long, white, bell-shaped flowers hang from its branches in small clusters. The oval leaves are 3 or 4 inches long. These trees are hardy into the north. Use them near patio or pool areas, for screening, as an accent, or to back a shrub grouping.

67. STEWARTIA: These attractive trees are well formed, open structured, deciduous, and quite hardy. They bear white flowers and prefer partial shade and moist, fertile soil.

Stewartia japonica grandiflora (*Pseudo-camellia*) can be maintained at 15 to 25 feet high. It produces showy 2-inch flowers with white stamens and orange anthers. In fall the foliage turns to yellow, orange, and crimson.

Stewartia sinensis can be held to 18 or 20 feet high by annual pruning. If permitted, it will grow to 30 feet.

Use stewartias at strategic points along property-line plantings in front or back yards, for limited shade or framing, as an accent or specimen tree.

68. STRAWBERRY-TREE (*Arbutus unedo*): This is an excellent evergreen tree, 15 to 20 feet high,

Sketch 5.20

**TREE 66,
SILVER-BELL (*HALESIA CAROLINA*)**

A rather open and round-headed, deciduous tree that produces clusters of hanging, white, bell-shaped flowers in spring. The informally grouped, 3 or 4 inch oval leaves are very attractive. Use near your patio or pool, for screening, as an accent, or to back a shrub grouping.

Sketch 5.21

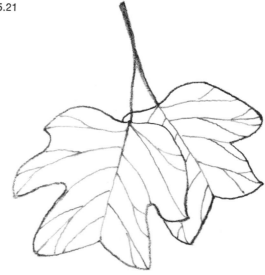

**TREE 71,
TULIP–TREE (*LIRIODENDRON TULIPIFERA*)**

A fast growing, well formed, deciduous tree. Its 4 or 5 inch long leaves are widely oval and its greenish-yellow flowers resemble a tulip.

Because of its size—40 to 60 feet—best used in large landscapes, estates, parks, industrial areas, and for country (farm) plantings.

preferring mild to warm climate. With some pruning it can easily be trained into a graceful, upright, and open-growing tree of exceptional versatility. It has 3- to 4-inch long, medium green, oblong leaves and 2-inch long panicles of small flowers, white to light pink, followed by orange-red fruits that resemble strawberries.

Use strawberry trees almost anywhere in your garden—near the patio, pool, or garden structures; in the side plantings; for windbreaks or screening; at the corners of your house; as an accent or specimen. With training and control, they are also good for special points in foundation plantings.

69. SWEET GUM (*Liquidambar styraciflua*): This stately deciduous ornamental, 30 to 35 feet high, possesses exceptional attributes. It is upright in a loosely pyramidal form with quantities of light green, five-to-seven lobed, maple-like leaves that are 5 to 6 inches wide. This remarkable foliage turns to a blaze of crimson, scarlet, and golden yellow in autumn.

Consider sweet gum for at least one or two special locations—at the sides of the front yard, near the front corners of the house for framing, as an accent or specimen, in large lawn plantings, in the background, or for street-side trees.

70. STYRAX JAPONICA: These are fine, rather slender, deciduous trees, 20 to 30 feet high, requiring mild to warm climates. They have 2- or 3-inch long, oval leaves and fragrant white flowers in pendulous clusters in late spring. They prefer open sunlight and, being slender in growth habit, are excellent in important small areas of the garden.

71. TULIP-TREE (*Liriodendron tulipifera*): This is a fast-growing, hardy, deciduous relative of the magnolia family. It is strong, 40 to 60 feet high, stately in appearance, and openly columnar in habit of growth. See Sketch 5.21. Its 4- or 5-inch long leaves are widely oval, and the 2- to 3-inch, greenish-yellow flowers are tulip-shaped. The tree's large size restricts its general use to extensive landscapes, estates, and parks.

72. TUPELO (*Nyssa sylvatica*): This pyramidal deciduous tree grows 35 to 45 feet high, is very hardy, and boasts distinctive horizontal branches that droop a little at the ends. It has 4-inch long, dark green leaves and small greenish-white flowers. The foliage turns to brilliant scarlet in autumn.

Tupelos are appropriate for large lawn plantings, parks, shopping and rural apartment developments, and industrial park complexes, in the background, for shade, and as specimen trees.

73. WALNUT (*Juglans*): These attractive nut trees are of great value to landscapes of average size. Some species tolerate extremes of heat and cold if located in areas that have good, deep soil and are at least partially protected from freezing winds. Walnuts are deciduous and vary in size, form, and foliage.

BLACK WALNUT (*Juglans nigra*) is tall, open, and wide, reaching heights of 50 to 60 feet within a few years. They have compound leaves 10 to 12 inches long, are hardy, and grow into the far north. The hard shell nuts are rich and tasty.

BUTTERNUT (*Juglans cinerea*) is a tall, very hardy, round-headed tree of excellent proportions and elegant appearance. The egg-shaped nuts are delicious. Both *nigra* and *cinerea* are appropriate on large landscapes and farm properties.

ENGLISH WALNUT (*Juglans regia*) is an impressive, open-headed tree with strong and gracefully spreading main branches. Its 10- to 15-inch long, compound leaves are composed of light green leaflets 3 to 5 inches long. Held to 30 or 35 feet high by annual pruning, it becomes an excellent landscape tree for properties of any size. It is not as cold resistant as black walnut. The delicious nuts from its several varieties are justly famous. Consider locating an English walnut in the front yard, to shade the patio, to frame the house or garden, or as a lawn specimen. However, if the tree is planted in the lawn, drainage should be established from its base. Excessive water is injurious.

74. WEEPING WILLOW (*Salix babylonica*): This tree has an uncommon form with strong, upright main limbs, 25 to 35 feet high, and a dense arrangement of long, slender branches that appear to fountain over from the top and flow downward almost to the ground. The light green leaves are 4 to 6 inches long, thin and lance-like. Tiny flowers are in catkins, which appear with the leaves in spring. This tree has an aggressive root system, which should be borne in mind when selecting its location. Weeping willow is a beautiful tree, particularly if judiciously pruned toward some openness, and is very attractive along a stream to form a background, for heavy screening, or as a specimen. However, some people feel that it imparts a melancholy mood to the garden. Therefore, before including it in your plan, it is advisable to test your own reaction to its pendulous characteristics.

75. *Zelkova serrata*: This is a globe-shaped deciduous tree, 40 to 60 feet high, structurally composed of great numbers of slender limbs supported by a short, heavy trunk and strong, spreading main branches. The dark green, elm-like leaves range from 2 to 6 inches in length and turn scarlet-yellow in autumn. These trees are especially useful for large properties—estates, parks, shopping complexes, industrial park landscaping, and rural developments.

BROADLEAF TREES—EASTERN SECTIONS (ZONES 5–6–7)

The following are some broadleaf trees for the eastern sections of the country—zone 5–6–7. There are species and varieties of listed trees adaptable to the favorable growing areas of the zones indicated. Refer to them in the preceding numbered tree description list and in the Broadleaf Tree Selection Chart on page 97.

Plant number	Plant name	Controlled height	Zone
5	Ash, white (*Fraxinus americana*)	40–60'	5–6–7
6	Beech (*Fagus*)	40–50'	5–6–7
8	Birch, European white (*Betula pendula*)	25–50'	5–6–7
9	Birch, paper (*Betula papyrifera*)	35–60'	5–6–7
12	Caragana (*Caragana arborescens*)	5–20'	5–6–7
14	Chaste-tree (*Vitex agnus-castus*)	10–15'	6–7
15	Cherry, flowering (*Prunus* species)	20–30'	5–6–7
17	Crabapple (*Malus* species)	15–25'	5–6–7
18	Dogwood (*Cornus*)	20–30'	5–6–7
19	Elm, American (*Ulmus americana*)	40–50'	5–6–7
28	Hackberry (*Celtis*)	40–60'	5–6–7
30	Hickory (*Carya pecan*)	60–70'	5–6–7
31	Holly (*Ilex*)	20–40'	5–6–7
33	Hornbeam (*Carpinus betulus*)	25–40'	5–6–7
34	Horse-chestnut (*Aesculus*)	25–40'	5–6–7
37	Linden, American (*Tilia americana*)	40–50'	5–6–7
38	Linden, little leaf (*Tilia cordata*)	40–65'	5–6–7
41	Maple, Norway (*Acer platanoides*)	35–50'	5–6–7
42	Maple, red (*Acer rubrum*)	35–50'	5–6–7
43	Maple, silver (*Acer saccharinum*)	35–50'	5–6–7
44	Mayday (*Prunus padus*)	20–35'	5–6–7
45	Mountain-ash (*Sorbus americana*)	25–30'	5–6–7
49	Oak, pin (*Quercus palustris*)	40–60'	5–6–7
50	Oak, red (*Quercus borealis, Q. rubra*)	35–50'	5–6–7
51	Oak, scarlet (*Quercus coccinea*)	45–60'	5–6–7
59	Plane, London (*Platanus acerifolia*)	40–60'	5–6–7
61	Poplar (*Populus*)	35–60'	5–6–7
63	Redbud (*Cercis*)	12–20'	5–6–7
64	Service-berry (*Amelanchier*)	15–20'	5–6–7
66	Silver-bell (*Halesia carolina*)	20–30'	5–6–7
70	Styrax (*Styrax japonica*)	20–30'	5–6–7
72	Tupelo (*Nyssa sylvatica*)	35–45'	5–6–7

BROADLEAF TREES—CENTRAL SECTIONS (ZONES 5–6–7)

The following are some broadleaf trees for the central sections of the country—zones 5–6–7. There are species and varieties of listed trees adaptable to the favorable growing areas of the zones indicated. Refer to them in the preceding numbered tree description list and in the Broadleaf Tree Selection Chart on page 97.

Plant Number	Plant Name	Controlled Height	Zone
5	Ash, white (*Fraxinus americana*)	40–60'	5–6–7
6	Beech (*Fagus*)	40–50'	5–6–7
8	Birch (*Betula*)	25–50'	5–6–7
12	Caragana (*Caragana arborescens*)	15–20'	5–6–7
13	Catalpa (*Catalpa speciosa*)	40–65'	5–6–7
14	Chaste-tree (*Vitex agnus-castus*)	15–20'	5–6–7
17	Crabapple (*Malus* species)	15–25'	5–6–7
18	Dogwood (*Cornus*)	20–30'	5–6–7
19	Elm, American (*Ulmus americana*)	40–50'	5–6–7
28	Hackberry (*Celtis*)	40–60'	5–6–7
29	Hawthorn (*Crataegus*)	20–30'	5–6–7
32	Honeylocust (*Gleditsia*)	50–75'	5–6–7
34	Horse-chestnut (*Aesculus*)	25–40'	5–6–7
37	Linden (*Tilia*)	40–50'	5–6–7
41	Maple (*Acer*)	35–50'	5–6–7
45	Mountain-ash (*Sorbus*)	25–50'	5–6–7
46	Mulberry (*Morus*)	30–45'	5–6–7
49	Oak (*Quercus*)	20–60'	5–6–7
58	Plane (*Platanus*)	40–60'	5–6–7
61	Poplar (*Populus*)	35–60'	5–6–7
63	Redbud (*Cercis*)	12–20'	5–6–7
64	Service-berry (*Amelanchier*)	15–20'	5–6–7
69	Sweet gum (*Liquidambar*)	30–35'	5–6–7
70	Styrax (*Styrax japonica*)	20–35'	5–6–7
72	Tupelo (*Nyssa sylvatica*)	35–45'	5–6–7
73	Walnut, black (*Juglans nigra*)	35–65'	5–6–7
75	Zelkova (*Zelkova serrata*)	45–65'	5–6–7

BROADLEAF TREES—WESTERN SECTIONS (ZONES 3–10)

The following are some broadleaf trees for the western sections of the country—zones 3–4–5–6–7–8–9–10. There are species and varieties of listed trees adaptable to the favorable growing areas of the zones indicated. Refer to them in the preceding numbered tree description list and in the Broadleaf Tree Selection Chart on page 97.

Plant Number	Plant Name	Controlled Height	Zone
2	Apricot, flowering (*Prunus mume*)	20–30'	7–8–9
3	Ash (*Fraxinus*)	30–40'	7–8–9
6	Beech (*Fagus*)	40–50'	5–6–7–8
8	Birch (*Betula*)	25–50'	4–5–6–7–8–9
11	Camphor (*Cinnamomum camphora*)	25–35'	9–10
13	Catalpa (*Catalpa speciosa*)	40–65'	5–6–7–8–9
15	Cherry, flowering (*Prunus species*)	20–30'	5–6–7–8–9
17	Crabapple (*Malus species*)	15–25'	4–5–6–7–8–9
18	Dogwood (*Cornus*)	20–30'	5–6–7–8–9
19	Elm (*Ulmus*)	25–50'	4–5–6–7–8–9
21	Eucalyptus (*Eucalyptus species*)	25–35'	9–10
24	Ginkgo (*Ginkgo biloba*)	40–60'	5–6–7–8–9
25	Golden-chain (*Laburnum anagyroides*)	20–30'	6–7–8–9
29	Hawthorn (*Crataegus*)	20–30'	5–6–7–8–9
31	Holly (*Ilex*)	20–40'	5–6–7–8–9–10
32	Honeylocust (*Gleditsia*)	50–75	4–5–6–7–8–9–10
34	Horse-chestnut (*Aesculus*)	25–40'	4–5–6–7–8–9
36	Jacaranda (*Jacaranda acutifolia*)	25–30'	10
39	Loquat (*Eriobotrya japonica*)	25–30'	10
40	Magnolia (*Magnolia species*)	25–50'	7–8–9
41	Maple (*Acer*)	35–50'	4–5–6–7–8–9
46	Mulberry, fruitless (*Morus alba, fruitless*)	30–45	5–6–7–8–9
47	Oak (*Quercus species*)	35–50'	5–6–7–8–9–10
54	Peach, flowering (*Prunus persica*)	20–35'	6–7–8–9
56	Plum, flowering (*Prunus species*)	15–20'	5–6–7–8–9–10
58	Plane (*Platanus*)	40–60'	5–6–7–8–9
61	Poplar (*Populus*)	35–60'	3–4–5–6–7–8
63	Redbud (*Cercis*)	12–20'	5–6–7–8–9
69	Sweet gum (*Liquidambar*)	30–35'	6–7–8–9–10
73	Walnut (*Juglans*)	35–65'	5–6–7–8–9
74	Willow (*Salix*)	25–35'	4–5–6–7–8–9
75	Zelkova (*Zelkova serrata*)	40–65'	5–6–7–8–9

BROADLEAF TREES—NORTHERN SECTIONS (ZONES 2–3–4)

The following are some broadleaf trees for the northern sections of the country—zones 2–3–4. There are species and varieties of listed trees adaptable to the favorable growing areas of the zones indicated. Refer to them in the preceding numbered tree description list and in the Broadleaf Tree Selection Chart on page 97.

Plant Number	Plant Name	Controlled Height	Zone
5	Ash, white (*Fraxinus americana*)	40–50'	4
8	Birch, European white (*Betula pendula*)	25–50'	4
9	Birch, paper (*Betula papyrifera*)	35–50'	2–3–4
12	Caragana (*Caragana arborescens*)	15–20'	3–4
17	Crabapple (*Malus species*)	15–25'	3–4
19	Elm, American (*Ulmus americana*)	40–50'	4
28	Hackberry (*Celtis occidentalis*)	40–60'	4
29	Hawthorn (*Crataegus*)	20–30'	4
32	Honeylocust (*Gleditsia*)	50–75'	4
34	Horse-chestnut (*Aesculus*)	25–40'	4
37	Linden, American (*Tilia americana*)	40–50'	4
38	Linden, little-leaf (*Tilia cordata*)	40–60'	4
41	Maple, Norway (*Acer platenoides*)	35–50'	4
42	Maple, red (*Acer rubrum*)	35–50'	3–4

43	Maple, silver		
	(*Acer saccharinum*)	35–50'	4
44	Mayday (*Prunus padus*)	20–35'	2–3–4
45	Mountain-ash		
	(*Sorbus americana*)	25–30'	3–4
50	Oak, northern red		
	(*Quercus borealis*)	35–50'	4
56	Plum, flowering		
	(*Prunus blireana*)	15–20'	4
61	Poplar (*Populus*)	35–60'	3–4
72	Tupelo (*Nyssa sylvatica*)	36–45'	4

BROADLEAF TREES—SOUTHERN SECTIONS (ZONES 8–9–10)

The following are some broadleaf trees for the southern sections of the country—zones 8–9–10. There are species and varieties of listed trees adaptable to the favorable growing areas of the zones indicated. Refer to them in the preceding numbered tree description list and in the Broadleaf Tree Selection Chart on page 97.

Plant Number	Plant Name	Controlled Height	Zone
5	Ash, white		
	(*Fraxinus americana*)	40–60'	8–9
8	Birch (*Betula*)	25–50'	8–9
11	Camphor		
	(*Cinnamomum camphora*)	25–35'	9–10
13	Catalpa		
	(*Catalpa bignonioides*)	40–65'	8–9
15	Cherry, flowering		
	(*Prunus* species)	20–30'	8–9
16	Coral-tree		
	(*Erythrina poeppigiana*)	20–30'	10
17	Crabapple (*Malus* species)	15–25'	8–9
18	Dogwood (*Cornus florida*)	20–30'	8–9
19	Elm (*Ulmus*)	25–50'	8–9
22	Franklinia (*Gordonia*)	15–25'	8–9
23	Frangipani		
	(*Plumeria acutifolia*)	15–18'	10
25	Golden-chain (*Laburnum*)	20–30'	8–9
26	Goldenrain		
	(*Koelreuteria paniculata*)	25–40'	8–9
27	Golden-shower		
	(*Cassia fistula*)	20–30'	10
29	Hawthorn (*Crataegus*)	20–30'	8–9
32	Honeylocust, thornless		
	(*Gleditsia triancanthos inermis*)	50–75'	8–9–10

34	Horse-chestnut (*Aesculus*)	25–40'	8–9
36	Jacaranda		
	(*Jacaranda acutifolia*)	25–30'	10
37	Linden (*Tilia*)	40–50'	8–9
39	Loquat		
	(*Eriobotrya japonica*)	25–30'	10
40	Magnolia		
	(*Magnolia grandiflora*)	25–50'	8–9
43	Maple (*Acer saccharinum*)	35–50'	8–9
46	Mulberry, fruitless		
	(*Morus alba*, fruitless)	30–45'	8–9
47	Oak (*Quercus virginiana*)	35–50'	8–9–10
55	Pepper-tree (*Schinus molle*)	20–30'	9–10
56	Plum, flowering		
	(*Prunus* species)	15–20'	8–9–10
57	Pistace, Chinese		
	(*Pistacia chinensis*)	35–50'	8–9–10
58	Plane (*Platanus orientalis*)	30–40'	8–9–10
62	Poinciana, royal		
	(*Delonix regia*)	25–35'	10
63	Redbud (*Cercis chinensis*)	12–20'	8–9
65	Silk-tree (*Albizzia julibrissin*)	20–35'	8–9–10
68	Strawberry-tree		
	(*Arbutus unedo*)	15–20'	9–10
69	Sweet gum (*Liquidambar*)	30–35'	8–9–10
70	Styrax (*Styrax japonica*)	20–35'	8–9–10
71	Tulip-tree		
	(*Liriodendron tulipifera*)	40–60'	8–9
73	Walnut, black		
	(*Juglans nigra*)	35–65'	8–9
74	Willow, weeping		
	(*Salix babylonica*)	25–35'	8–9

BROADLEAF TREES—HAWAII

The following are some broadleaf trees that grow in Hawaii. Refer to them in the preceding numbered tree description list and in the Broadleaf Tree Selection Chart on page 97.

Plant Number	Plant Name	Controlled Height
10	Bombax (*Bombax malabaricum*)	40–50'
16	Coral-tree (*Erythrina poeppigiana*)	20–30'
23	Frangipani (*Plumeria acutifolia*)	15–18'
27	Golden-shower (*Cassia fistula*)	20–30'
36	Jacaranda (*Jacaranda acutifolia*)	25–30'
53	Orchid-tree (*Bauhinia variegata*)	20–35'
62	Poinciana, royal (*Delonix regia*)	25–35'

Shrubs for Your Garden

Broadleaf shrubs comprise the large volume of plant materials with which to dress your garden. To a great extent, they represent the horizontal plane in design and balance the vertical lines of trees, house, and garden structures. Equally important is their ornamental and decorative function in the landscape.

Shrubs tie house and garden together, unify the several component parts of a design into one smooth landscape composition, and frame garden structures. They create an inviting atmosphere that sets your garden's mood for outdoor living. These are the reasons for thoughtfully selecting each shrub for a specific purpose.

ARRANGING AND SELECTING SHRUBS

Shrubs are best arranged in groupings or *units*, which are then blended or tied together in a graceful manner. The units may consist of two, three, or a half dozen closely related shrubs. Some shrubs within a unit may be evergreen and others deciduous. The completed units must not alternate deciduous and evergreen, however. This would spot the plantings and produce a tone of monotony. Strive for a smoothly harmonious and interesting seasonal pattern by having shrub plantings flow naturally from one to another. Include shrubs that give spring, summer, and fall color, create a sense of motion, and appeal to several senses. Don't crowd the units. Keep them far enough apart so they may grow toward each other and their blenders in a natural manner and yet retain their identity, displaying their individual beauty and characteristics.

The Broadleaf Shrub Selection Chart on page 126 will assist you in creating an enjoyable composition. It includes:

1. The names of 75 broadleaf shrubs and some specific data on each.

2. The approximate *controlled* height of each shrub, the average *pruned* height at which it looks and functions well on small and medium-size properties.
3. The zoning range within which a named shrub and its varieties grow. (Species and varieties may vary in hardiness.)
4. Whether partial shade or full sun is best for a given shrub.
5. Whether it is deciduous or evergreen.
6. Whether it bears flowers or berries or is fragrant.
7. Landscape uses in your garden.
8. Whether a shrub displays autumn color in its foliage.
9. Whether it is considered drought resistant.

A description of each numbered and named broadleaf shrub follows the Selection Chart. Remember: listed heights are *controlled* heights.

Shrubs for a Sample Plan

Let us now return to Figure 4.3 (on page 87) and choose shrubs for the sample garden depicted there. We will follow the same procedure we used in Chapter 5 to select broadleaf trees for that landscape. However, we will be dealing with two types of shrubs—broadleaf and conifer—and will therefore use two Selection Charts, the Broadleaf Shrub Selection Chart in this chapter and the Conifer Selection Chart in the following chapter, page 148. We will also refer to the numbered description list in this chapter, beginning on page 129, and the one on conifers, which begins on page 151 in the next chapter.

Units A and B, in Figure 4.3 are possibly the most difficult to select and arrange. They are foundation plants and must relate to the front of the house and the garden. They should be strong, interesting, and inviting and must *frame* and enhance the entrance rather than compete with it. We visualize relatively small—*2 to 3 feet*—*evergreens* that are generally medium-textured and possess rich variations of green. The two on either side of the entrance (unit A) may match—be the same specie and variety—or closely resemble each other. They may be either broadleaf or conifer shrubs, but let's assume we want broadleaf plants here.

Following the same procedure we used to select broadleaf trees, we place a strip of paper (our selection strip) along the *example strip* at the bottom of the Broadleaf Shrub Selection Chart and indicate our basic requirements in the appropriate columns.

2–3′—Zone 5—Ev (evergreen)—
Fo (foundation)—Fr (frame)

As we move our selection strip up the chart, we find six shrubs that qualify: numbers 3, andromeda; 5, azalea; 6, barberry; 9, boxwood; 21, daphne; 37, hypericum. We next turn to these numbers in the shrub descriptions for more information on each plant. Because the doorway faces east and has protection from afternoon sun, we decide to place an azalea on either side of the entrance.

The two *foundation* plants in unit B may be a little taller, *4 to 5 feet* high, and again we want *broadleaf evergreens*.

4–5′—Zone 5—Ev—Fo

Twelve shrubs qualify: numbers 1, abelia; 3, andromeda; 5, azalea; 6, barberry; 9, boxwood; 26, euonymus; 35, holly; 37, hypericum; 47, mountain laurel; 57, privet; 61, rhododendron. Our choice is two barberries—*Berberis darwinii* and *Berberis julianae*—with andromeda (*Pieris floribunda*) as a blender.

The corner *foundation* conifer is visualized as *6 or 7 feet* high, *upright*, medium to dark green, rather loosely growing, and suitable for *framing* the house. To choose this shrub, we use the Conifer Selection Chart, page 148. The procedure is the same. We mark our selection strip in the correct columns and move it up the chart.

6–7′—Up (upright)—Zone 5—Fo
(foundation)—Fr (framing)

We find that seven plants qualify: numbers 4, *Chamaecyparis obtusa;* 5, *Chamaecyparis obtusa aurea;* 10, *Chamaecyparis pisifera filifera;* 11, *Chamaecyparis pisifera filifera aurea;* 13, *Chamaecyparis pisifera plumosa;* 59, *Taxus cuspidata;* 65, *Thuja occidentalis fastigiata.*

Because of the elegance of these conifers, a decision is difficult. However, we are most attracted by the richly graceful and rather open growing habit of number 4, *Chamaecyparis obtusa.*

For the broadleaf evergreen shrub near the driveway, *Viburnum burkwoodii* is an excellent selection, although under cold winter conditions, it is only half-evergreen. It will produce fragrant flowers each spring.

Unit C is a part of the large unit D. For the two shrubs in unit C, we want fairly small evergreens, about 2 feet high, which will assist the horsechestnuts in framing the front yard and house. Our selection is *Kalmia latifolias*. These shrubs will also act as a backdrop for the flower border, which is framed by two, low (*1 to 2 feet* high), *compact,* and slightly *spreading* conifers suitable as little *accent* plants. Let's find their names on the Conifer Selection Chart.

1–2′—Co (compact)—Sp
(spreading)—Zone 5—Ac (accent)

Seven are quickly noticeable: numbers 9, *Chamaecyparis obtusa pygmaea;* 14, *Chamaecyparis pisifera squarrosa minima;* 22, *Juniperus chinensis sargentii;* 33, *Juniperus sabina tamariscifolia;* 38, *Picea abies procumbens;* 46, *Pinus mughus prostrata;* 62, *Taxus cuspidata minima.* Our choice is number 38.

Unit E is composed of larger shrubs. Our selections are a 7-foot snowball as the central plant, a 5-foot evergreen *Cotoneaster parneyii* on one side, and a *Euonymus japonicus*, held to 5 feet by pruning, on the other side.

For unit F, we choose a pair of lilacs. Units E and F provide this side of the house with interesting form, foliage, and color and lead pleasantly to the conifer grouping comprising unit G, which is located to help protect the patio from wind. Let's select the conifers in this group.

The main tree should be *15 to 25 feet* high with a maximum spread of 10 to 12 feet. In line with the flower-patio panel, it must have both aesthetic and functional qualities. We visualize it as an informal *accent* with sufficient density to have *screening* potential. Use the Conifer Selection Chart.

15–25′—Zone 5—Ac—Sc—Wr
(wind retardant)

Six appear to qualify: numbers 15, *Juniperus chinensis;* 42, *Picea pungens* (Colorado spruce); 43, *Picea pungens glauca* (Colorado blue spruce); 52, *Pinus sylvestris* (Scotch pine); 54, *Taxus baccata* (English yew); 75, *Tsuga mertensiana* (mountain hemlock). Although it will eventually require some control pruning, our choice is number 75, *Tsuga mertensiana.* The second conifer, near the fence, should also be rather large, and we decide on number 15, *Juniperus chinensis*, although this tree, too, will require future control.

The forward conifer is necessarily smaller, 7 *or 8 feet* high, *upright,* and *wind retardant.*

7–8′—Up—Zone 5—Wr

Seven are noted: numbers 4, *Chamaecyparis obtusa;* 5, *Chamaecyparis obtusa aurea;* 10, *Chamaecyparis pisifera filifera;* 11, *Chamaecyparis pisifera filifera aurea;* 13, *Chamaecyparis pisifera plumosa;* 59, *Taxus cuspidata;* 65, *Thuja occidentalis fastigiata.* After reading their descriptions, we decide upon number 10, *Chamaecyparis pisifera filifera,* because of the interesting informality of its growth habit and its pleasing association with the two companion conifers.

The border shrubs in unit H should be 6 *or 7 feet* high, *evergreen,* and *wind resistant.* A good choice is *Ligustrum japonicum* permitted to grow naturally and spread out a little, merely held to the desired height.

Behind the pergola, which protects rhododendrons, is an excellent location for a continuous planting of top-quality lilacs. They are 8 feet high, have good foliage, and will provide an abundance of flowers for cutting.

The twin conifers at either end of the pergola walk should be 2 *or 3 feet* high and rather *compact,* with *accent* qualities.

2–3′—Co—Zone 5—Ac

Eleven conifers qualify: numbers 8, 14, 28, 33, 37, 38, 46, 62, 67, 68, 74. Here we select number 14, *Chamaecyparis pisifera squarrosa minima.* Its form, foliage, and color are impressive, and it associates pleasantly with everything around it.

Unit I might well be a replica of the inner part of unit H.

Unit J, being opposite the strong conifer grouping, requires interest, color, and strong vertical and horizontal lines. After some thought, we decide on this composition: an English holly in the center and two flanking barberries—evergreen *Berberis julianae* near tree 5 and *Berberis thunbergii atropurpurea* on the opposite side.

Unit K is actually associated with tree 6 and can well be bold in flower color. A good broadleaf shrub would be number 29, golden-bells in the variety *Forsythia intermedia spectabilis.*

Unit L contains two plants near the corner of the house and one at a little distance to unite units K and L. The plant nearest the house corner should have height—10 or 12 feet—and be in the form of a small tree. We would like an *evergreen* with *accent* qualities, and find it by using the Broadleaf Tree Selection Chart and tree descrip-tions in the preceding chapter. Our choice is tree number 31, *Ilex cornuta,* a Chinese relative of English holly. With an occasional pruning, it will perform perfectly in this limited space. It is strong, impressive, and has dark green, shiny leaves and red berries.

Visualize the other shrubs in this side planting unit as strong, interesting, *evergreen, flowering,* and around 5 *to 6 feet* in height. For practice, try selecting these two yourself.

Because plantings along the side of a house seem more or less out of direct sight, the tendency is to cheapen their quality and consequently lessen their interest. Actually, the opposite should be practiced—increase quality and interest to brighten and enliven the sides of your house.

Unit N is a grouping of conifers that must have sufficient strength and attractiveness to balance the opposite side of the front yard. The larger symbol represents a conifer tree 10 or 12 feet high with accent qualities. This brings to mind the very beautiful *Picea pungens glauca* (Colorado blue spruce), which may be held at this height for a long time.

The conifer shrub nearest the tree should be 4 *to 6 feet* high, *upright,* and *spreading* a little in growth habit. Again, we also want *accent* qualities. Let's look for it on the Conifer Selection Chart.

4–6′—Sp (spreading)—Up—Zone 5—Ac

Five are noted: numbers 19, *Juniperus chinensis japonica;* 31, *Juniperus sabina;* 35, *Juniperus squamata meyeri;* 45, *Pinus mugo;* 51, *Pinus strobus nana.* Their descriptions lead us to choose number 19, *Juniperus chinensis japonica.* We also find that *Pinus mugo* will do nicely as the conifer near the street, completing the shrub plantings for Figure 4.3.

We used the unit system of locating shrubs to reduce the complexity of grouping plants for a maximum of aesthetic and service values. It is meant to be a very flexible guide in plant organization. Be sure to remember—the groupings must be smoothly tied together so that the entire planting will appear continuous and free-flowing.

Now, return to your own garden design and, following the procedures we have demonstrated here, select the shrubs for your property. The Broadleaf Shrub and Conifer Selection Charts are the places to begin, and the corresponding description lists will guide your final choices. In addition, broadleaf shrubs suitable for various sections of the country are listed at the end of this chapter, and there are similar sectional lists for conifers at the end of the next chapter.

BROADLEAF SHRUB SELECTION CHART

No.	Name of Shrub	1–4 feet	4–6 feet	6–8 feet	8–10 feet	10–15 feet	Zone	Hawaii	Part shade	Full sun	Deciduous	Evergreen	Flowering	Bold berries	Fragrant	Accent	Background	Blender	Foundation	Framing	Hedge	Screening	Side	Support	Shrub group	Autumn foliage	Drought resistant
1	Abelia	+	+	+					+	+	+		+			+	+	+	+	+			+	+	+		
2	Almond, flowering	+	+	+						+	+		+			+	+	+	+				+	+	+		
3	Andromeda	+	+	+					+			+	+				+		+	+			+	+	+		
4	Aucuba	+	+	+					+			+	+				+	+	+	+			+	+		+	+
5	Azalea	+	+						+			+	+			+	+	+	+	+	+		+	+	+		
6	Barberry	+	+	+					+	+	+	+	+	+		+	+	+	+	+		+	+	+	+		+
7	Beauty-bush			+						+	+		+			+							+	+			
8	Bottle-brush		+	+						+		+	+			+						+	+	+			+
9	Boxwood	+								+		+									+		+	+			
10	Buckthorn			+	+					+	+								+	+	+	+	+	+		+ +
11	Butterfly-bush	+	+	+					+	+	+		+		+							+	+	+		+
12	Camellia	+	+	+					+			+	+			+			+	+	+	+	+	+	+		+
13	Ceanothus			+	+					+		+	+		+		+	+	+	+	+	+	+		+		
14	Cherry-laurel			+	+							+	+		+					+							
15	Coral-berry		+						+	+			+						+	+	+						
16	Clerodendrum	+							+	+	+	+	+			+				+			+	+	+		+ +
17	Cotoneaster	+	+		+					+	+	+	+	+			+		+	+	+	+	+	+	+		
18	Crape-myrtle			+	+					+		+	+			+							+	+	+		+ +
19	Crataegus			+	+					+	+					+				+	+		+	+	+		
20	Currant	+	+	+					+	+	+		+			+	+	+	+	+			+	+	+		
21	Daphne	+							+	+		+	+		+	+	+		+				+	+	+		
22	Dogwood			+	+	+			+	+	+		+				+	+	+	+		+	+	+	+	+	
23	Elaeagnus			+	+				+	+	+	+			+		+	+	+		+		+	+	+	+	+
24	Enkianthus			+	+				+		+	+							+				+		+	+	
25	Escallonia			+					+		+	+	+			+	+	+	+		+		+	+	+	+	+
	Example Shrub	X					5		Fs			Ev	Fl						Fo								

Example shrub: Requirements—4 to 6' high, sun, evergreen, flowering, foundation planting, zone 5. Mark your zone and requirements on edge of paper. Move it up the chart. Match reasonably close. Find several plants. Match several plants close. Read numbered descriptions for selection. Shrubs located: numbers 3, 6, 9, 35, 37, 47, 57, 72. Zoning: The above is the estimated zone-temperature range of each shrub's hardiness. (See the zone map for your zone.)

BROADLEAF SHRUB SELECTION CHART

No.	Name of Shrub	Height Range 1–4 feet	4–6 feet	6–8 feet	8–10 feet	10–15 feet	Zone 2–10	Hawaii	Part shade	Full sun	Deciduous	Evergreen	Flowering	Bold berries	Fragrant	Accent	Background	Blender	Foundation	Framing	Hedge	Screening	Side	Support	Shrub group	Autumn foliage	Drought resistant
26	Euonymus	+	+	+	+					+	+					+	+		+	+		+	+		+	+	+
27	Eurya	+	+						+		+	+				+	+	+	+	+		+	+	+	+		
28	Flame-of-the-woods		+	+					+			+	+			+	+	+	+	+			+	+	+	+	
29	Forsythia	+	+	+						+	+		+			+	+	+	+	+			+	+	+		
30	Fuchsia	+	+						+		+		+			+	+	+	+	+			+		+		
31	Gardenia	+	+							+		+	+		+	+	+	+	+	+		+	+	+	+		+
32	Hakea		+	+						+		+					+	+	+						+		
33	Heath	+	+	+	+					+		+	+		+	+	+	+	+	+	+	+	+		+		
34	Hibiscus	+	+	+	+					+	+		+		+	+	+	+	+	+	+	+	+	+	+		
35	Holly		+	+					+	+		+	+	+		+	+	+	+	+	+	+	+	+	+	+	
36	Hydrangea		+	+					+	+	+		+			+	+	+	+	+			+		+		
37	Hypericum	+	+						+	+	+	+	+		+	+	+	+	+	+		+	+	+	+		+
38	Illicium		+	+					+	+		+			+	+	+	+	+	+		+	+	+	+		
39	Jetbead		+							+	+		+	+		+	+	+	+	+			+	+	+		+
40	Kerria		+							+	+		+			+	+	+	+	+			+	+	+		+
41	Lead-plant	+	+							+	+		+		+	+	+	+	+	+			+	+	+		
42	Lilac		+	+	+					+	+		+		+	+	+	+	+	+	+		+	+	+		
43	Lime-berry	+	+	+					+	+	+		+	+	+	+	+	+	+	+	+	+	+	+	+		
44	Mahonia	+		+					+	+		+	+	+		+	+	+	+				+		+		
45	Mexican-orange		+						+	+		+	+		+	+	+	+	+	+		+	+	+	+		
46	Mock-orange	+	+	+	+				+	+	+		+		+	+	+	+	+	+			+	+	+		
47	Mountain-laurel	+	+	+					+	+		+	+			+	+	+	+	+		+	+	+	+		
48	Myrtle	+	+						+	+		+			+		+	+	+	+		+	+	+	+		
49	Ninebark	+	+							+	+					+	+	+	+	+		+	+	+	+	+	
50	Oleander		+	+	+				+	+		+	+			+	+	+	+	+	+	+	+	+	+		+
	Example Shrub	X					5			Fs		Ev Fl				Fo											

Example shrub: Requirements—4 to 6' high, sun, evergreen, flowering, foundation planting, zone 5. Mark your zone and requirements on edge of paper. Move it up the chart. Find several plants. Match reasonably close. Read numbered descriptions for selection. Shrubs located: numbers 3, 6, 9, 35, 37, 47, 57, 72. Zoning: The above is the estimated zone-temperature range of each shrub's hardiness. (See the zone map for your zone.)

BROADLEAF SHRUB SELECTION CHART

Column groups (read across): **Height Range** (1–4 feet, 4–6 feet, 6–8 feet, 8–10 feet, 10–15 feet); **Zone** (2 3 4 5 6 7 8 9 10); Hawaii; Part shade; Full sun; Deciduous; Evergreen; Flowering; Bold berries; Fragrant; **Landscape Uses** (Accent, Background, Blender, Foundation, Framing, Hedge, Screening, Side, Support, Shrub group); Autumn foliage; Drought resistant.

No.	Name of Shrub	1–4 ft	4–6 ft	6–8 ft	8–10 ft	10–15 ft	Part shade	Full sun	Decid.	Everg.	Flowering	Bold berries	Fragrant	Accent	Background	Blender	Foundation	Framing	Hedge	Screening	Side	Support	Shrub group	Autumn foliage	Drought resistant
51	Osmanthus	+	+	+	+		+	+		+	+		+	+	+		+	+	+	+	+	+	+		
52	Pea-shrub	+	+	+	+	+		+	+		+		+	+	+			+	+	+	+	+	+		+
53	Pernettya	+						+		+	+			+	+	+	+	+	+	+	+		+		+
54	Pittosporum		+	+	+	+		+		+	+			+	+	+	+	+	+	+	+	+	+		
55	Pomegranate		+	+				+	+		+	fr	+	+	+	+	+	+		+	+	+	+	+	
56	Potentilla	+	+					+	+		+			+	+	+	+	+	+	+	+	+	+		
57	Privet	+	+	+	+		+	+	+	+	+		+	+	+	+	+	+	+	+	+	+	+		+
58	Pyracantha	+	+	+	+		+	+		+	+	+	+	+	+	+	+	+	+	+	+	+	+		+
59	Quince	+	+	+				+	+		+			+	+		+	+	+	+	+	+	+		
60	Raphiolepis	+	+				+	+		+	+			+	+		+	+	+	+	+	+			
61	Rhododendron	+	+	+	+		+	+		+	+			+	+		+	+	+	+	+	+			
62	Rose	+	+	+				+	+		+		+	+	+	+	+	+		+	+	+			+
63	Rosemary	+	+					+	+	+	+		+	+	+	+	+	+		+	+	+	+		
64	Sarcococca	+	+				+	+		+	+		+	+	+	+	+	+	+	+	+	+	+	+	
65	Skimmia	+		+			+	+		+	+	+	+	+	+		+	+		+	+	+	+	+	
66	Snowball				+	+		+	+		+			+	+	+	+	+	+	+	+	+	+		
67	Snowberry	+	+				+	+	+		+	+		+	+	+	+	+	+	+	+	+	+		+
68	Spiraea	+	+				+	+	+		+		+	+	+	+	+	+	+	+	+	+	+	+	
69	Sumac	+	+	+		+	+	+	+		+	+	+	+		+	+	+	+	+	+		+	+	
70	Surinam-cherry					+	+	+		+	+	+	+	+		+	+	+	+	+	+				
71	Tea-tree	+			+			+	+	+	+		+	+	+	+	+	+	+	+	+	+	+		+
72	Viburnum	+	+	+	+	+	+	+	+	+	+	+	+	+	+	+	+	+	+	+	+	+	+		+
73	Wax-myrtle				+	+		+		+	+		+	+	+	+	+	+	+	+	+	+	+		
74	Weigela	+	+					+	+		+		+	+	+		+			+	+		+		
75	Xylosma	+	+	+			+	+		+	+		+	+	+		+	+	+	+	+	+	+		
	Example Shrub		X					Fs		Ev	Fl						Fo								

Example shrub: Requirements—4 to 6' high, sun, evergreen, flowering, foundation planting, zone 5. Mark your zone and requirements on edge of paper. Move it up the chart. Find several plants. Match reasonably close. Read numbered descriptions for selection. Shrubs located: numbers 3, 6, 9, 35, 37, 47, 57, 72. Zoning: The above is the estimated zone-temperature range of each shrub's hardiness. (See the zone map for your zone.)

ALPHABETICAL DESCRIPTIONS OF BROADLEAF SHRUBS

The following are descriptions and appropriate uses of the shrubs listed on the Broadleaf Shrub Selection Chart. (Numbers match those on Selection Chart).

1. ABELIA (*Abelia grandiflora*): This upright and thickly spreading half-evergreen shrub is 4 or 5 feet high with small shiny leaves. Pink or pinkish-white, bell-shaped flowers appear in late spring and summer. There are several good abelias. Some are comparable to *grandiflora* in size but with rose-pink flowers, others are nearly dwarf in form.

They are useful in many locations—shrub groupings, foundation plantings, as blenders, and associated with small trees.

2. ALMOND, FLOWERING: These are very showy deciduous shrubs.

Prunus glandulosa, called dwarf flowering almond, is 3 to 5 feet high and has 2- to 4-inch ovalish leaves and masses of small pink or white flowers before the leaves appear.

Prunus triloba is taller, 4 to 8 feet high, with 2- or 3-inch oval leaves and pink flowers that precede the leaves in spring. Some varieties have double flowers resembling tiny roses. Both varieties are hardy in medium-cold winter climates.

Use them in accent points, shrub groupings, front yard plantings, and in front of taller shrubs.

3. ANDROMEDA (*Pieris*): These handsome, broadleaf evergreen, sun- or shade-tolerant shrubs are relatively slow growing, require moist acid soil, and are hardy in medium-cold climates.

Photo 6.1

India-Hawthorn (*Raphiolepis indica*), springtime.

White flowers that resemble lily-of-the-valley appear in terminal clusters in spring. Careful pruning will hold these shrubs to desired heights.

Pieris floribunda is an erect grower, 3 to 5 feet high. It has shiny leaves, 2 to 4 inches long, and the flower clusters grow upright.

Pieris japonica grows 4 to 6 feet high and taller if permitted, and has shiny, dark green leaves. The flower clusters hang downward.

Consider using andromedas as accent plants, in foundation plantings, near patio, pool, garden structures, and seats, in the front yard plantings, and at strategic points along paths.

4. AUCUBA (*Aucuba japonica*): This attractive evergreen shrub has dark green, glossy leaves that are 5 to 7 inches long and sparsely toothed. Small purplish-red flowers result in shiny scarlet berries. Male and female flowers are on separate plants. The variety *variegata*, known as gold-dust plant, has yellowish spotted areas on the leaves.

Aubucas require afternoon shade and considerable moisture and are therefore useful in shaded areas of your garden, in boundary-line shrub groupings, in the background, and as foundation plantings.

5. AZALEA: The extensive azalea-rhododendron family contains magnificent flowering shrubs with significant variation in size, form, color, and distribution of flowers. There are both evergreen and deciduous types with foliage that changes color to give delightful effects in autumn. Most species require well-drained, acid soil, though the degree of acidity varies. Some are considered sun-tolerant, but most kinds prefer filtered sunlight. Several species are hardy in cold zones. In this bewildering abundance, homeowners may experience some difficulty in selection. Therefore it is advisable to consult your nursery dealer as to kind, color, and cold hardiness for your specific need.

Use azaleas in groups of the same variety or similar varieties in harmonious colors. They are appropriate in foundation plantings, around the patio, pool, or special feature units, near seats, and in tubs on surfaced areas. In warm climates, grow them under lath structures.

6. BARBERRY (*Berberis*): This widely diverse group of deciduous or evergreen thorny shrubs is of much value in the landscape, principally because of attractive foliage. Barberries grow in sun or shade and have various degrees of hardiness.

Berberis darwinii is a mild climate evergreen, upright in habit of growth, 3 to 5 feet high, with small, holly-like leaves. The drooping clusters are deep golden-yellow and are followed by dark purple fruit.

Berberis julianae is a medium-hardy evergreen,

upright growing and 4 to 5 feet high. It is densely covered with spiny, dark green leaves 2 or 3 inches long and clusters of yellow flowers, which are followed by bluish-black fruit.

Berberis mentoriensis is a very cold-hardy, densely foliaged shrub that is evergreen in mild to warm climates. It is 4 or 5 feet high and the flowers are yellow.

Berberis thunbergii is a very cold-tolerant, deciduous, spiny-leaf shrub that is best at 3 to 5 feet high. The flowers are yellow and the fruit is bright red at maturity. The foliage turns scarlet in autumn. Variety *atropurpurea* has purplish-red foliage.

Berberis triacanthophora is a medium-hardy, low-growing evergreen, 2 or 3 feet high. Its 1- to 2-inch, bristle-margined leaves are bright green above and bluish-gray beneath, and turn scarlet in autumn. The flowers are whitish and the fruit is blue-black.

Berberis verruculosa is a medium-hardy, low-growing evergreen, 1½ to 3 feet high and about the same width, with small, oval, bright green leaves that are spiny margined. The large flowers are bright golden-yellow, and the fruit is bluish-black.

There is a barberry of height, size, and appearance for almost any place in your garden— foundation plantings, tall, medium, or low shrub groupings, background, screening, and hedges. If not controlled by pruning, some of the taller ones will grow to 8 or 10 feet high.

7. BEAUTY-BUSH (*Kolkwitzia*): This is an upright and rather spreading, deciduous shrub, 6 to 8 feet high, with nearly oval leaves 2 or 3 inches long. The very attractive bell-shaped flowers are pink with yellow throats and appear in flat-topped clusters 2 or 3 inches across in late spring. Medium-hardy and easy to grow, *Kolkwitzia* is useful in the background, as an accent plant, and at special locations in side plantings.

8. BOTTLE-BRUSH (*Melaleuca*): There are several species of *Melaleuca* that are of great value to sunny areas of the garden in mild to warm sections of the country. They are evergreen, easy to grow, very colorful, and they tolerate extensive pruning. The flowers are arranged in spikes or heads resembling a bottle-brush.

Melaleuca decussata is by nature a tall grower —attractive even as a 15 or 20 foot tree—but can easily be held to 7 or 8 feet high with a proportionate width by an occasional pruning. It has short, slender, sharp-pointed leaves, and its lilac flowers grow in short spikes.

Melaleuca hypericifolia is upright and spreading, thickly branched, and has slender leaves 1 to 2 inches long, and dense spikes of brilliant red

Photo 6.2

Bottle-brush (*Melaleuca hypericifolia*) supported by Shasta daisies.

Photo 6.3

Coleonema pulchrum.

flowers. This naturally tall shrub is easily held to 7 or 8 feet high.

Melaleuca nesophila is smaller, 6 to 8 feet high, with short slender leaves and compact heads of pink to rose flowers—a very showy shrub.

Use these attractive and long-blooming shrubs in the background for screening, as an informal hedge, or to add interest to garden structures. They are especially effective as informal espaliers or trained flat against fences or walls.

9. BOXWOOD (*Buxus*): Members of this group of widely distributed evergreen shrubs range from dwarf to several feet in height and grow well in sun or shade, in medium-cold to warm sections of the country.

Buxus microphylla is a densely branched and fine-foliaged little shrub around 2 to 3 feet high. Its leaves are light green, smooth, and 1 to 1½ inches long. Variety *japonica* is taller, and variety *koreana* is a little smaller, 18 to 24 inches high. *Koreana* is also much hardier.

Buxus sempervirens (common box) ranges in form from a shrub to a 15-foot tree. It tolerates heavy pruning, which permits control of its size and shape to meet your requirements. The dark green leaves are nearly elliptic and average an inch long. Variety *suffruticosa* is a dwarf form used for low, clipped hedges.

Boxwood's great range in height provides selection for various uses—low, medium, or tall clipped hedges, open or dense screening, a well-formed individual shrub for the background, foundation, or side plantings.

10. BUCKTHORN (*Rhamnus*): Although not exceptionally attractive, this group of medium to extremely hardy shrubs has an important function in gardens with poor soil and other adverse growing conditions.

Rhamnus alternus is a warm climate, upright and spreading shrub, mostly evergreen, 12 to 15 feet high, with 2-inch long, dark green leaves and blue-black fruits.

Rhamnus cathartica is a very cold-hardy, deciduous shrub 10 to 15 feet high with thorny branches. The leaves are 2 or 3 inches long and nearly oval. It has small clusters of greenish flowers and the fruit is black.

Rhamnus frangula is hardy far north, deciduous, upright and spreading, 6 to 12 feet high, with 2- or 3-inch long, nearly oval leaves. The fruit is black when mature.

These shrubs may be used in the background, for screening, as hedges, or in shrub groupings on medium to large properties.

11. BUTTERFLY-BUSH (*Buddleia*): These strongly upright and somewhat spreading shrubs grow well in medium to warm climates and are of landscape value in large gardens, parks, and industrial landscaping.

Buddleia alternifolia is deciduous, upright and open, with pendulous branches. The short lance-like leaves are medium green above and fuzzy-gray beneath. The fragrant flowers, deep lavender, appear in short dense clusters in spring.

Buddleia davidii (often referred to as orange-eye butterfly-bush or, sometimes, as summer lilac) is an upright and attractively branched shrub, 5 to 10 feet high, with 6- to 8-inch long leaves that are green above and fuzzy-white beneath. Its fragrant flowers are lilac with an orange splotch at the throat and are borne on 8 to 10 inch spikes in summer.

Buddleia lindleyana is 5 to 6 feet high and has medium green leaves that are 3 or 4 inches long. It produces 7- or 8-inch spikes of fragrant, purplish-violet flowers in summer.

Associate buddleias with mixed shrub groupings or to support background plantings.

12. CAMELLIA: These elegant ornamentals are unsurpassed in conformation and ability to create an atmosphere of splendor in a garden. They are beautiful evergreens that prefer moderately mild to warm climates and are extensively grown in southern gardens. They are 4 to 10 feet high, and their dark green, glossy foliage forms a perfect background for their floral display. They grow well in good, friable, well-drained soil, with considerable moisture and partial shade. Flowers are in a wide variety of sizes, forms, and colors. The list of named species and varieties provides types and colors for any garden. Because the list is so extensive, it is advisable to see a plant in bloom before purchasing.

Use camellias in partially shaded parts of foundation plantings, in shrub groupings, under large trees and lath structures, or in special camellia gardens.

13. CEANOTHUS: This is a group of mild to warm climate plants of various sizes and shapes with masses of flowers predominantly blue or white.

Ceanothus arboreus is an evergreen, tree-like shrub, 12 to 15 feet high. It has nearly oval leaves and dense clusters of light blue, fragrant flowers in spring.

Ceanothus cyaneus, an evergreen shrub 10 to 15 feet high, with short, medium green leaves and clusters of dark blue flowers in spring.

Ceanothus prostratus (Mahala mat) is an evergreen, mat-like ground cover. The small leaves have spiny-toothed margins and the flowers are medium blue. This is an excellent plant for spreading over banks, slopes, stony areas, and large walls.

Ceanothus spinosus, 8 or 9 feet high, has white flowers.

Ceanothus thyrsiflorus, often called California lilac, is an outstanding evergreen shrub, upright and spreading. It has 2-inch long leaves and great quantities of rich blue flowers in impressive clusters. It may attempt to grow into a shrub-tree 20 feet high, but can be held to 6 or 8 feet.

The taller ceanothus are of value for screening, as background shrubs, wind retardants, and tall clipped hedges.

14. CHERRY-LAUREL or ENGLISH LAUREL (*Prunus laurocerasus*): This is an evergreen shrub that can easily be held to 6 or 8 feet high for extensive landscape use. It has shiny oblong leaves 4 to 6 inches long and and fragrant white flowers in slender clusters. The fruit is small and dark purple. These shrubs are grown principally for their foliage and are not reliably hardy in cold sections of the country. They grow rapidly, tolerate extensive pruning, and have many uses—as foundation plantings, shrub groupings, hedges, side and background arrangements, and screening.

15. CORAL-BERRY (*Symphoricarpos orbiculatus*): This is a hardy, deciduous, upright shrub, 4 to 6 feet high, with nearly oval leaves that average 2 inches long. The small bell-shaped flowers are white in late spring and are followed by reddish-purple fruit. Consider coral-berry for side plantings, in mixed shrub groupings, near the patio or pool, as an accent plant, or as a shrub blender to unify two shrub units.

16. CLERODENDRUM SPECIOSISSIMUM: This is a warm climate shrub and must be protected from inclement weather. It is 3 to 4 feet high, with nearly oval leaves that are 10 to 12 inches long and heart-shaped at the base. The 2-inch wide flowers are scarlet, and appear in attractive panicles 10 to 15 inches long. Use these shrubs in special places; for example, adjacent to the pool, near the patio, close to doorways, seats, and garden structures, and in movable tubs.

17. COTONEASTER: These shrubs vary widely in size, height, and use, and are of particular value in landscaping the small to medium-size property.

Cotoneaster acutifolia is upright, hardy, and deciduous, 6 to 8 feet high, with medium green leaves 1½ to 2 inches long. The flowers are pink, in small clusters, and the berries are black.

Cotoneaster adpressa is a very low spreading type, hardy and deciduous. It has small leaves and produces tiny, light pink flowers and quantities of shiny red berries.

Cotoneaster apiculata is nearly deciduous, hardy from moderately cold winter climates

Photo 6.4

Cherry laurel or English laurel (*Laurocerasus officinalis*) is a many purpose shrub—background, side plantings, shrub groupings, screening, informal hedges.

Photo 6.5

Cotoneaster harroviana.

southward, and 4 or 5 feet high. It has small, light green leaves, pale pink flowers, and bright red berries.

Cotoneaster divaricata is noticeably upright in growth habit, 4 to 6 feet high, deciduous, and fairly cold-hardy. It has glossy, dark green leaves that are ½ to ¾ inch long, light pink flowers, and masses of red berries.

Cotoneaster microphylla is evergreen, low-growing and spreading, and hardy in medium-cold winter areas southward. It has small leaves, white flowers, and red berries.

Cotoneaster integerrima is 4 to 6 feet high, deciduous, and hardy into the far north. The leaves are 1½ to 2 inches long; the flowers are light pink, and followed by red berries.

Cotoneaster multiflora is 4 to 6 feet high, deciduous, upright in growth habit, and cold-hardy. Its medium green leaves are 1½ to 2 inches long. The flowers are white and the berries are red.

Cotoneaster parneyii (Lactea) is a handsome, well-formed, evergreen shrub, 5 to 6 feet high, that prefers a mild to warm climate. Its berries are red.

There are other low, medium, and tall-growing cotoneasters worthy of a place in your garden. Use the low-growing ones in rock gardens, along the driveway, as a ground cover, or to trail over retaining walls. Taller cotoneasters may be used anywhere that non-specialty shrubs are appropriate.

18. CRAPE-MYRTLE (*Lagerstroemia indica*): This is an upright shrub to small tree, 8 to 15 feet high. It is deciduous and grows well in mild to warm climates. Its principal attraction is a fabulous display of 1½-inch wide, fringe-petaled flowers in pink, purple, red, or white, according to variety. Because flowers are produced on new branches, prune the shrub each winter to the size and shape desired. Give crape-myrtle special locations that are adjacent to or in view of your house, patio, pool, or garden structures.

19. CRATAEGUS: This group of deciduous plants varies in size and height and is popularly known as hawthorn. Some of the low-growing hawthorns can be formed into attractive, upright, and open-headed shrubs by starting judicious pruning when they are young. Included in this group that may be held to 10 or 12 feet high are:

Crataegus intricata, which produces reddish-brown fruit.
Crataegus laneyii, with orange-red fruit.
Crataegus oxyacantha (English hawthorn), with scarlet fruit. Its variety *paulii* has scarlet flowers, and variety *plena* has white flowers.
Crataegus rotundifolia, which flowers profusely and has red fruit.

The several hawthorns are hardy, easy to grow, tolerate drastic pruning, and produce beautiful displays of flowers and fruit. Consider using the shrub forms in side or border plantings, for screening, hedges, or accent, or in the background.

20. CURRANT (*Ribes*): Some of the species are ornamental. They are easy to grow, flower in spring, and have many uses in most gardens.

Ribes alpinum, or mountain currant, is a dense bushy shrub 3 to 5 feet high. It has small, lobed leaves, clusters of greenish-yellow flowers, and small, scarlet fruit. It is hardy far north.

Ribes sanguineum, or flowering currant, is deciduous, upright in growth habit, and grows to a height of 6 to 8 feet or more. The leaves are lobed; the pink flowers hang in multiple clusters; and the fruit is blue-black. This is a very attractive garden shrub.

These two species of currant may be used in several ways. *Alpinum* makes a nice clipped hedge and is also attractive in small shrub groupings. *Sanguineum* is excellent in peripheral plantings, such as side or boundary-line units, and in the background.

21. DAPHNE: These are grown primarily for their handsome form, pleasing foliage, and delightfully fragrant flowers. It is a special shrub for a special location.

Daphne cneorum is a compact, hardy, trailing evergreen, 10 to 12 inches high. It has nearly oblong leaves and produces small, mildly fragrant, pink flowers in clusters during spring.

Daphne odora is a mild to warm climate, compact evergreen, 3 or 4 feet high, with nearly oblong leaves 2 to 3 inches long. Its flowers—purplish-rose, pink, red, or white, according to variety—are deliciously fragrant and appear in compact clusters in very early spring.

Daphne mezereum is a hardy, deciduous, upright-growing shrub, 3 to 4 feet high, with oblong leaves 2 or 3 inches long. Very fragrant, purple flowers appear in small clusters before the leaves.

Place these shrubs on your garden plan at points where their fragrance will be appreciated —near the patio, seats, or garden furniture, adjacent to a pool or other water feature, by a frequently used doorway or lounging area. *Daphne cneorum* may be used as a special ground cover and to cascade a little over walls.

22. DOGWOOD (*Cornus*): Several species of dogwood are showy shrubs that supplement dogwood trees or brighten a subdued area of the garden.

Cornus alternifolia, or pagoda dogwood, is a very hardy, deciduous shrub, 10 to 15 feet high, with an attractive horizontal branching habit. Its

Photo 6.6

Dogwood (*Cornus florida rubra*) is a shrub-tree of unusual quality, form, and character and is particularly beautiful when flowering. Use as an accent or specimen.

leaves are nearly oval and 3 or 4 inches long. Flowers are cream-white in small clusters, and the fruit is dark blue. The foliage turns purplish-scarlet in autumn.

Cornus racemosa is very hardy, deciduous, and tolerates either sun or shade. It is 6 to 8 feet high and has slender oval leaves 3 or 4 inches long. Clusters of white flowers are followed by white fruit.

Cornus sanguinea, or red dogwood, is very hardy, deciduous, and 6 to 8 feet high. It has reddish branches, nearly oval leaves, clusters of white flowers, and black fruit.

Cornus stolonifera, called red-osier, is a very hardy, sun-tolerant, deciduous, upright growing shrub, 5 or 6 feet high, with reddish branches and oval leaves 3 to 5 inches long. Small clusters of off-white flowers are followed by blue-white fruit.

These dogwoods tolerate reasonable pruning, which qualifies them for use in many locations— in shrub groupings, associated with dogwood trees, as an accent shrub, or near garden structures.

23. ELAEAGNUS: Several species qualify as good garden shrubs and are especially useful where winds and drought are factors. They tolerate pruning for height control.

Elaeagnus fruitlandii is a very hardy, upright growing evergreen shrub, 8 to 10 feet high, with

brownish splotches on the silvery underside of its leaves.

Elaeagnus pungens can be held to 8 or 10 feet high. It is a well-formed, upright evergreen and spreading shrub that prefers mild to warm climates. Its nearly oblong, 3- or 4-inch long, wavy-margined leaves are silvery on the underside and speckled with small brown spots. The small, hanging, fall-blooming flowers are silvery white and mildly fragrant. The brownish fruit turns red when mature.

Use these two shrubs in heavy shrub groupings and background arrangements, for screening, or as wind retardants.

24. ENKIANTHUS CAMPANULATUS: This is a well-formed, deciduous shrub, 8 feet high (more if you like), with 2- or 3-inch long leaves that are ovalish-oblong. The small bell-shaped flowers are pale yellowish-orange with reddish veins and hang in small clusters. In autumn the foliage becomes crimson.

Enkianthus perulatus is an attractive and hardy shrub, 4 to 7 feet high, with light green, oblong leaves that average 2 inches long. Its small white flowers are in little, flat-topped clusters. The foliage turns golden-yellow and scarlet in autumn.

Locate these shrubs in strategic places for fall foliage effect, particularly in side or background shrub and tree arrangements.

25. ESCALLONIA: These are strong-growing, evergreen shrubs that tolerate enough pruning to make them useful for varied garden purposes in mild to warm climates.

Escallonia montevidensis is a thick-foliaged, upright shrub, 8 or 9 feet high (higher if you wish), with nearly oblong leaves 2 to 4 inches long and white flowers in clusters.

Escallonia organensis is an upright, densely foliaged shrub, 7 or 8 feet high (or more), with medium green leaves 2 or 3 inches long and rosy pink flowers in small thick clusters.

Escallonia rubra grows dense and erect, 8 or 9 feet high (more if required) and has 2-inch long, shiny, dark green leaves and red flowers.

These durable shrubs are usable for screening, as wind breaks or tall hedges, and in large shrub arrangements in the background.

26. EUONYMUS: These are excellent shrubs, and the species have a wide range of temperature tolerance and garden use.

Euonymus alatus, or winged euonymus, is a very hardy, deciduous shrub, 5 to 10 feet high. It has ovalish, medium green leaves 2 or 3 inches long, creamy-yellow flowers, and light purple fruits. The leaves turn pinkish-rose in autumn.

Euonymus alatus compactus is a smaller form,

4 to 6 feet high, and its foliage turns one or two shades of red in autumn.

Euonymus japonicus is an upright and spreading, medium-hardy, evergreen shrub, 5 to 10 feet high, with glossy ovalish leaves 2 or 3 inches long, and greenish-white flowers, followed by pink fruit. Its variety *microphyllus* is hardy, low growing, 1 to 2 feet high, and has small leaves. Its compactness makes it a good low hedge plant.

Euonymus fortunei is a hardy, vine-like, evergreen shrub, excellent for trailing, climbing, or cascading. It has oval leaves 1 or 2 inches long, greenish-white flowers, and pale pink fruits.

Use the taller euonymus in foundation plantings, against wood or brick walls (try pruning for an informal flat and spreading effect), or as a very attractive conventional-type shrub.

27. EURYA JAPONICA: This is a mild to warm climate, evergreen shrub, 3 to 5 feet high, with shiny and nearly oval leaves. The flowers are small and white with a slight tint of green. It requires culture and environment similar to that of camellias. Indicate it on your garden plan in protected parts of foundation plantings, or in the patio, pool, or other water feature areas. It is useful as an accent or to blend shrub groupings together.

28. FLAME-OF-THE-WOODS (*Ixora coccinea*): This warm climate, evergreen shrub can be held at the desired height by pruning. Its shiny oblong leaves are 4 or 5 inches long. The small, red, tubular flowers grow in showy compact clusters.

Ixora macrothyrsa has 8- to 10-inch leaves and large, dark red flowers. It is very attractive.

These shrubs are useful in accent locations or to increase the color in side and background shrub arrangements.

29. FORSYTHIA, commonly known as goldenbells. These are excellent shrubs for a garden of any size. They are hardy, deciduous, and easy to grow, and they have beautiful form, foliage, and flowers.

Forsythia intermedia is 6 to 8 feet high with upright, and gracefully spreading branches, and medium green, nearly oval leaves 3 or 4 inches long. Masses of golden bell-shaped flowers seem to cover the entire shrub before the leaves appear. Its variety *spectabilis* has larger flowers and is more graceful in growth habit.

Forsythia suspensa grows upright and has arching branches with slightly pendulous tips. It is 5 to 8 feet high with ovalish leaves 3 or 4 inches long. Masses of golden-yellow flowers precede the leaves.

There are other species and varieties of forsythia that are perfect for your garden if winter temperatures will permit. They are suitable in any

reasonable location for accent, specimen, foundation, shrub groupings, framing, screening, or hedges.

30. FUCHSIA: These mild to warm climate shrubs are specialty plants of great beauty and wide selection. There are relatively tall and upright species that grow well in open gardens in locations that have some protection from hot afternoon sun. They bloom more or less continuously through spring, summer, and fall, and are available in many pleasing colors. Low-growing shrub types 3 or 4 feet high have long flowering ranges and are elegant when used at the base of buildings, as accents, in mixed shrub arrangements, or in sizable fuchsia garden units. The hanging or cascading forms are spectacular and are available in variable tints and shades of blue, purple, red, and white. These species and varieties have special culture requirements—rich organic soil, occasional mulching, frequent light feeding, constant moisture, periodic tipping of the branches, removal of seed heads, and so on. Discuss the care of specific plants with your nursery dealer before purchase.

31. GARDENIA: These mild to warm climate, evergreen shrubs are popular for their shiny foliage, informal growth habit, and deliciously fragrant flowers.

Gardenia jasminoides (Cape-jasmine) is upright, open and spreading, 3 to 5 feet high, with lance-like or slender, ovalish, deep green leaves 3 or 4 inches long. The flowers are a rich waxy white.

This fine shrub prefers full, moderately warm sun and therefore may be used in many locations—for fragrance near the patio, bordering a lounging area, adjacent to garden seats, in featured shrub groupings, or as a foundation shrub.

32. HAKEA SUAVEOLENS: This is an evergreen, mild to warm climate shrub (will not tolerate much frost). It is upright and spreads a little, 6 to 8 feet high, with needle-like and sharp-tipped leaves 2 to 4 inches long and clusters of fragrant white flowers in the fall. In addition to the conventional garden environment, this shrub responds to near desert conditions and is useful in any shrub planting, as a windbreak, for screening, or to form a tall unclipped hedge.

33. HEATH (*Erica*): These evergreen and richly flowering ornamental shrubs are mainly medium-hardy to warm climate plants. They vary considerably in size and form.

Erica carnea is low and spreading, 10 to 12 inches high and 2 or 3 feet wide. It has short narrow leaves and bears small, rosy red, bell-shaped flowers in early spring. It is medium-hardy. Use it along driveways, for patio edging, in a rock garden, or as a ground cover. Its variety *alba* has white flowers, and variety *rosea* has rose-colored flowers.

Erica mediterranea is an upright and bushy shrub, 5 to 10 feet high, with typical *Erica* leaves and masses of lilac-red flowers in spring. It is medium-hardy. This one may be used in the background, in an accent or specimen location, or as a hedge.

Erica melanthera is a low shrub that grows to a height of 2 feet; it is quite compact. The flowers are rosy red and appear in late fall and winter. Use this plant in the forepart of shrub groupings, in special accent units, for a wide edging along the driveway, on gentle slopes, in shrub panels, or in a rock garden.

Erica stricta (Corsican heath) is 5 to 8 feet high and and has rose-purple flowers in summer and early fall. Its uses are similar to those of *mediterranea*.

ERICA VAGANS (Cornish heath) is a mild climate, low-growing and spreading shrub, 10 to 12 inches high, with light purplish-pink flowers in summer. Its uses are similar to those of *carnea*. It is often planted as a ground cover.

34. HIBISCUS: The average hibiscus is a warm climate evergreen exceptionally attractive in form, foliage, and flower.

Hibiscus rosa-sinensis (Chinese hibiscus) is a loosely upright and spreading shrub, 8 to 10 feet high. It is heavily foliaged with shiny ovalish leaves 3 or 4 inches long, and it bears spectacular flowers in pink, purple, red, rose, or white. The flowers are either single or double and up to 6 inches in diameter. This hibiscus may be used in any tall shrub arrangement but requires a warm location, protection from strong winds, and considerable moisture.

Hibiscus syriacus (Rose-of-Sharon) is a hardy deciduous shrub, upright and spreading, 6 to 10 feet high. It has oval leaves 3 to 5 inches long and bell-shaped flowers in red, violet, or white, according to variety. Plant it against a fence, in the background, or in a distant accent location.

35. HOLLY (*Ilex*): Several species of holly are of great value because of their beauty of form, foliage, and berries. The berries are on the female plant, and there must be a male plant nearby to assure pollination.

Ilex cornuta is a Chinese relative of English holly. Although listed under trees, there are low-growing varieties of much landscape value. *Ilex cornuta rotunda* averages 2 feet in height. The 4 or 5 foot *Cornuta burfordii* varieties are evergreen shrub forms that are particularly attractive. They prefer mild to warm climates.

Ilex crenata (Japanese holly) is a small, hardy,

evergreen shrub-tree, but is included here because of its use as an elegant hedge plant. There are also several very fine, low-growing varieties that are 4 or 5 feet high.

Ilex vomitoria nana (Dwarf yaupon) is a mild to warm climate holly, 4 or 5 feet high, with small glossy leaves and bright scarlet berries.

Hollies are among the plant aristocrats. They contribute character, dignity, and beauty to your garden and are worthy of special locations—in foundation plantings, to frame your doorway, in patio and pool areas, to frame garden structures, in accent or specimen locations.

36. HYDRANGEA: These shrubs are grown principally for their huge clusters of flowers through summer and into fall.

Hydrangea arborescens is a hardy, deciduous, upright and open-appearing shrub, 4 to 8 feet high, with thick and nearly oval leaves 4 to 6 inches long. Its white flowers grow in clusters 5 or 6 inches across.

Hydrangea arborescens grandiflora (Hills-of-snow) has larger ball-shaped clusters of white flowers that begin appearing in late spring.

Hydrangea macrophylla is a mild to warm climate, deciduous, upright, and irregularly spreading shrub, 6 to 8 feet high. It has widely oval leaves 5 or 6 inches long, and blue, pink, or white

Photo 6.7

Chinese holly (*Ilex cornuta*) trimmed to force spreading.

flowers in nearly flat topped large clusters.

Hydrangea paniculata grandiflora is hardy and deciduous. It grows upright and a little straggly, is 6 to 8 feet high (more if desired), and has large leaves and huge clusters of white flowers that become deep pink at late maturity.

Give these showy shrubs room to develop properly in partially shaded locations.

37. HYPERICUM (St. Johns-wort): Several species are dependable growers and of value in the more difficult parts of the garden. They have attractive, fluffy-stamened flowers that vary from light yellow to golden yellow, according to variety.

Hypericum densiflorum is a hardy evergreen, 3 to 5 feet high, with slender leaves 1 or 2 inches long and dense clusters of small flowers.

Hypericum kalmianum is a very hardy evergreen, 2 to 3 feet high, with narrow leaves that average 2 inches long. It has fewer flowers than some species but is an attractive shrub.

Hypericum moserianum (Gold-flower)is a mild to warm climate, bushy shrub, 1½ to 2 feet high. Its leaves are nearly oval, about 2 inches long, and the showy flowers are large —2½ inches wide.

Hypericum patulum also prefers mild to warm climates. It is an evergreen around 3 to 5 feet high, with ovalish leaves 2 inches long, and 2-inch wide flowers. Its variety *henryii* is a larger evergreen that grows to a height of 4 feet. It is hardier, more adaptable to cold winter temperatres, and has larger flowers.

These several species and varieties of *Hypericum* offer vigorous-growing and attractive shrubs for many garden locations—to edge the driveway, for a shrub planting in a rough part of the garden or to cover a slope, as a blender shrub to tie two groupings together, or as a single shrub used as an accent.

38. ILLICIUM ANISATUM: This is a warm climate, aromatic, evergreen shrub, 5 to 8 feet high (more if desired). The leaves average 2½ inches long and are narrowly oval. Use it in the shrub border, near the patio or lounging area, or in the background.

39. JETBEAD (*Rhodotypos tetrapetala*): This deciduous shrub is hardy, upright, and somewhat spreading. It grows 4 to 6 feet high and has nearly oblong leaves 3 or 4 inches long. White flowers 2 inches across are followed by jet-black berries. This is an excellent shrub for foundation or boundary-line plantings.

40. KERRIA JAPONICA: This is a medium-hardy, deciduous shrub, 3 to 6 feet high, and upright with multiple slender branches. Its golden yellow flowers are 2 inches wide and appear toward the end of the lateral branches. Use this shrub in an accent location, in foundation and property-line groupings, or to brighten shrub arrangements anywhere.

41. LEAD-PLANT (*Amorpha canescens*): Sometimes called false-indigo, this is a hardy, deciduous, densely branched shrub, 2 to 4 feet high, with slightly grayish foliage and 4- or 5-inch long clusters of blue pea-like flowers. It is useful in side plantings, in front of background groups, as a blender, or at the base of garden structures.

42. LILAC (*Syringa*): The common lilacs, *Syringa vulgaris*, are garden favorites everywhere. These very hardy, deciduous ornamentals are strongly upright in growth habit, have pleasing foliage, and produce magnificent panicles of fragrant flowers in springtime. There are superior French hybrids in shades of blue, lilac, pink, purple, violet, and white.

The landscape uses of lilac are limitless. Use it as a single accent shrub, in groupings, for screening or hedges, in the side or background plantings.

43. LIME-BERRY (*Triphasia trifolia*): This is a mild to warm climate, thorny, evergreen shrub, 3 to 8 feet high, with compound leaves and fragrant white flowers followed by red berries. It tolerates clipping and is often used as an armoured hedge.

44. MAHONIA: These are low-growing evergreens with attractive holly-like leaves.

Mahonia aquifolium (Holly grape) is a hardy shrub 2 to 4 feet high (or more), with nearly oval, spiny-margined leaves, and clusters of yellow flowers on the ends of the branches.

Mahonia nervosa (Oregon grape) is also a hardy shrub. It grows 1½ to 3 feet high and has shiny, narrowly oval leaflets 2½ to 3 inches long and light yellow flowers in clusters 6 to 8 inches long.

Mahonia repens is a hardy creeper, 10 to 12 inches high, with ovalish leaflets that average 2 inches long. The clusters of yellow flowers are on the ends of the branches.

Use mahonias in filtered shade and in areas of the garden that are partially protected from hot sun, hard winds, and heavy winter snow.

45. MEXICAN-ORANGE (*Choisya ternata*): This is a mild to warm climate, evergreen shrub. It grows upright, 4 to 6 feet high, and has handsome, medium green foliage, and fragrant white flowers from spring into summer. Use this fine shrub in the border, near garden structures or a water feature, as a foundation plant, or near the children's play area.

46. MOCK-ORANGE (*Philadelphus*): These hardy deciduous shrubs are usually grown for their masses of fragrant flowers.

Photo 6.8

Mexican orange (*Choisya ternata*).

Philadelphus coronarius is 6 to 12 feet high with numerous upright and arching branches that bear great quantities of fragrant white flowers in spring. Among the good varieties are *aureus*, with yellowish foliage; *dianthiflorus*, which has double flowers; *pumilus nanus*, a low-growing variety.

Philadelphus microphyllus is low-growing, 2 to 4 feet high, with small oblong leaves and quantities of very fragrant flowers.

Use the taller *Philadelphus* in the background of tall shrub groupings and near trees to lighten the area, or adjacent to structures for color and fragrance. The low-growing ones are valuable for color and fragrance near the patio or pool, beside the garden furniture area, or near seats.

47. MOUNTAIN-LAUREL (*Kalmia latifolia*): This is a hardy, rather bushy shrub, 3 to 8 feet high, with oval leaves 3 to 5 inches long. Its flowers vary from rose to white and appear in showy terminal clusters. Variety *alba* has white flowers, and *myrtifolia* is a dwarf form.

These fine shrubs are widely distributed, prefer partial shade, and are often used around a patio or pool area, in foundation and special shrub plantings, in shrub sections of the front yard, and among trees.

48. MYRTLE (*Myrtus communis*): This densely foliaged evergreen shrub is 3 to 6 feet high and has oval aromatic leaves 1 or 2 inches long and small white to pale pink flowers. Variety *compacta* is around 2 feet high; *microphylla* has very small leaves and is 3 to 3½ feet high.

Use common myrtle in shrub groupings, for large clipped or unclipped hedges, or to frame small structures or garden features. The varieties

compacta and *microphylla* are valuable as low clipped hedges, edgings, and informal groupings of low-growing shrubs.

49. NINEBARK (*Physocarpus*): These are very hardy deciduous shrubs that resemble spiraea in form, and the foliage changes color in autumn.

Physocarpus intermedius grows 4 or 5 feet high, has nearly oval leaves about 2 inches long, and bears clusters of small whitish flowers in spring.

Physocarpus monogynus is smaller—2 to 3 feet high—and has fewer clusters of white to very light pink flowers.

These showy shrubs are useful in the usual low to medium shrub locations in your design.

50. OLEANDER (*Nerium oleander*): These evergreen shrubs are usually grown for their outstanding flower displays and long season of bloom. They are upright and multi-branched, 6 to 10 feet high (or more), and the several varieties offer beautiful single or double flowers in shades of pink, red, salmon, yellow, white, and intermediate tints and shades.

Oleanders are strong growers and are usually used in peripheral plantings for distant long-flowering effect. Note: The leaves are poisonous if eaten.

51. OSMANTHUS: These striking evergreen shrubs are particularly attractive because of their holly-like foliage.

Osmanthus delavayii is upright, 4 to 6 feet high, and has slightly pendulous branches, small ovalish leaves, and fragrant white flowers.

Osmanthus ilicifolius is gracefully upright, 8 to 12 feet high, with handsome dark green foliage. The oval leaves average 2 inches long and have a few spines on the margins. The flowers are fragrant and white.

Use these excellent shrubs for foundation plantings, for framing, as specimens, in accent locations in your design, and for fragrance.

52. PEA-SHRUB (*Caragana*): These deciduous shrubs are hardy, easy to grow, and produce quantities of pea-shaped flowers.

Caragana arborescens resists extreme cold, is generally upright in growth habit, 7 to 10 feet high (or more), and has feathery foliage and yellow flowers in spring.

Caragana microphylla, 5 or 6 feet high and spreading to a comparable width, has feathery foliage and yellow flowers in spring.

Caragana pygmaea is low growing, 2 or 3 feet high, with drooping branches, feathery foliage, and yellow flowers in spring.

These attractive shrubs have a place in the garden plan, especially in cold regions, as windbreaks, for screening, and as tall, protective shrubs around buildings. The low-growing types are excellent in shrub groupings and foundation plantings or as hedges.

53. PERNETTYA MUCRONATA: This is a low-growing evergreen shrub, 2 or 3 feet high, with shiny, nearly oval leaves about ¾ inch long. A profusion of small bell-shaped flowers, white to faded pink, appears in spring. The subsequent berries are red. Variety *alba* has white berries; *coccinea*, red berries; *lilacina*, lilac-colored berries, *purpurea*, purple berries, and *rosea*, deep pink to rose berries.

Pernettyas are very useful little shrubs along a driveway, as part of the foundation planting, near the patio and special garden units, in a rock garden, as support plants, and in containers.

54. PITTOSPORUM: These very attractive evergreen shrubs are grown principally for their good foliage effect and many landscape uses.

Pittosporum eugenioides is upright and open in growth habit. It has light green, wavy-margined leaves 3 or 4 inches long and clusters of small, fragrant, yellowish flowers. It is inclined toward growing into a 20- to 25-foot tree, but is easily held at 10 or 12 feet.

Pittosporum tobira is a Japanese pittosporum that is strongly upright, 6 or 8 feet high (or higher), with thick, nearly oval leaves 3 or 4 inches long and clusters of small white flowers with a fragrance reminiscent of orange blossoms.

Pittosporum undulatum (Victorian box) grows naturally into a globular tree 30 to 40 feet high, but if restrained by pruning, it becomes a shrub of great merit, easily held to 8 or 10 feet. The leaves are narrowly oblong, 4 to 6 inches long, with wavy margins.

Consider using *eugenioides* and *undulatum* for screening, as windbreaks, and in the background or side plantings on large properties. *Tobira* is useful in large shrub locations on large properties —in the background, among boundary-line plantings, behind secondary structures, or as a coarse unclipped hedge.

55. POMEGRANATE (*Punica granatum*): This is a showy, upright, deciduous, and medium-hardy shrub, 6 to 10 feet high, with shiny slender leaves 3 or 4 inches long. Clusters of brilliant orange-red flowers are followed by orange-size rusty-red fruits. This pomegranate is very useful as a specimen shrub, an accent related to shrub groupings, in the foundation plantings, and to frame secondary buildings.

Punica granatum nana is a dwarf, compact type, 2 or 3 feet high, with small leaves and many yellowish-orange flowers. It is very useful in front yard plantings, especially near the doorway or in adjacent shrub units, beside the patio or pool, in

Photo 6.9

Japanese pittosporum (*Pittosporum tobira*).

Photo 6.10

Victorian box (*Pittosporum undulatum*) held to a large shrub by pruning.

lawn areas, at proper points along a path, and in rock gardens.

56. POTENTILLA FRUTICOSA (*Shrub cinquefoil*): This is an extremely hardy, deciduous, multi-branched shrub. It grows quite wide and 3 or 4 feet high, with tiny leaves and small clusters of yellow flowers in summer.

Potentilla nepalensis, around 2 feet high, has clusters of rose-red flowers an inch in diameter.

These two species are representative of a long list of prostrate to upright shrubs that are of value to gardens of any size. Use them in foundation plantings, to brighten mixed shrub arrangements in the front or back yard, as ground covers, or in a rock garden.

57. PRIVET (*Ligustrum*): These versatile shrubs are grown principally for their foliage and for more difficult uses in the landscape.

Ligustrum japonicum is an evergreen, medium-hardy, upright, and spreading shrub. It has shiny, medium green, ovalish-oblong leaves 3 to 5 inches long and produces clusters of small white flowers in summer.

Ligustrum obtusifolium, with oblong leaves averaging 2 inches long and 1½ inches wide, displays clusters of small white flowers in summer. It is deciduous.

Ligustrum ovalifolium (California privet) is a medium-hardy, half-evergreen, many-branched shrub. It is 5 to 10 feet high (or higher), with deep green, glossy leaves 2 inches long and clusters of small white flowers in summer.

Ligustrum sinense is deciduous, upright, spreading, and 6 to 10 feet high. The ovalish leaves are about 3 inches long, and small flowers grow in 4 or 5 inch clusters in summer. Not hardy in the very cold zones.

Ligustrum vulgare (Common privet) is a hardy, deciduous, upright, and multi-branched shrub, 6 to 8 feet high, with nearly oval, dark green leaves averaging 2 inches in length. Small flower clusters appear in late spring and early summer. There are several interesting varieties of *vulgare*.

These shrubs are excellent used individually for screening, as windbreaks, and in the background. *Ovalifolium* and *vulgare* are extensively grown for use as clipped hedges.

58. PYRACANTHA: The firethorns are strong growers with irregularly formed branches and are grown principally for their masses of berries in late fall and through winter.

Pyracantha coccinea is a hardy, evergreen, sharply thorned shrub, 6 to 10 feet high. Its habit of growth is upward and wide spreading. The leaves are oval and about an inch long. Clusters of small white flowers in spring are followed by masses of shiny red berries. The variety *lalandii* is smaller—5 to 6 feet—with orange-red berries.

Pyracantha crenulata, 6 to 10 feet high and spreading, prefers a mild winter climate. Its berries are orange-red.

Pyracantha gibbsii yunnanensis is a hardy shrub 6 to 8 feet high, or it may be trained as a creeping groundcover 2 feet high. The masses of large berries are coral-red.

The majority of pyracanthas are used as espaliered plants or tied to walls and structures so that they spread thinly for a more effective display of their massive show of berries in deep fall and winter. Held in this manner, they also provide an effective screen and windbreak. Some species are used as heavy groundcovers for rocky areas or rough slopes.

59. QUINCE, FLOWERING (*Chaenomeles*): These are among the earliest of spring flowering shrubs and usually bloom before the leaves appear.

Chaenomeles japonica (Dwarf Japanese quince) is a hardy deciduous shrub, 2 or 3 feet high, with oval leaves 2 inches long and crimson flowers. Variety *alpina* is lower and grows about 1 foot high.

Chaenomeles lagenaria is hardy and deciduous, grows to 6 or 8 feet high, has ovalish leaves 2 or 3 inches long, and produces deep scarlet flowers. Some varieties bear apricot, pink, red, or white flowers.

Uses for flowering quince include accents, side or background plantings, and espaliers. The dwarf varieties may be included in front yard plantings near doorways, walks, and driveways, in patio and pool areas, near garden seats, and in tubs.

60. RAPHIOLEPIS: These evergreen shrubs are valuable to the garden designer because of their handsome appearance and wide range of usage. If shrub selection seems impossible, try *Raphiolepis*.

Raphiolepis indica (India-hawthorn) is a medium-hardy and widely upright shrub, 3 to 5 feet

Photo 6.11

Andromeda (*Pieris floribunda*) deserves special locations —accent; foundation plantings; near the patio, pool, garden structures, and seats; beside paths.

Photo 6.12

The elegance of dwarf rhododendrons is seldom equalled.

high, with nearly oblong leaves 2 or 3 inches long and clusters of small, light pink flowers in spring. Variety *rosea* has rose-pink flowers.

Raphiolepis umbellata (Yeddo-hawthorn) is 5 feet high (8 or 10 if desired), or it may be held low and spreading. The flowers are white. Variety *ovata* is around 5 feet high, compact, and has fragrant white flowers. Growers periodically offer new varieties of *Raphiolepis* with impressive form, foliage, and flowers, as variety *springtime*.

Use these fine shrubs in foundation plantings or shrub groupings, to help frame a doorway, gate, or garden structure, in special design units, to curve a path, in a rock garden, or near a water feature.

61. RHODODENDRON: These magnificent broadleaf shrubs are available in many sizes and shapes—from dwarfs 2 or 3 feet high to an average garden height of 8 or 10 feet. In many older gardens, they are 15 feet high and 25 feet in circumference. Their general form is quite open, graceful, and usually slightly pendulous. The foliage is excellent in shape and quality, smooth and glossy, and the huge flower clusters in late spring range through shades of lavender, pink, red, and white. The cinnamon scent of the *fragrantissimum* varieties permeates the atmosphere for some distance.

With all their grace and splendor, rhododendrons are not difficult to grow in moist climates where winter temperatures are only reasonably cold. In severely cold areas, some species can be grown in tubs and winter protected. When the temperature permits, they can be moved to parts of the garden where they will receive filtered sunlight in the afternoon. Check the adaptability of selected varieties before purchasing.

Plant rhododendrons under trees, in shaded areas around the house, or under lath structures.

Rhododendrons are so important to the garden that something should be said about their culture. The soil mixture and method of planting are vital to their normal growth and good health. They require a natural woodsy growing media that is slightly acid and constantly cool and moist. This media consists of sandy loam with a preponderance of decomposed organic material, preferably treated leaf mold and coarse peat moss. Good drainage is essential. Investigate by digging several feet into the existing soil. If evidence points toward good drainage, set the root ball three-fourths into an oversize planting hole. Then fill the hole and cover the plant ball broadly with planting mixture. If there is evidence of improper drainage (as might be the case in heavy clay or adobe soils), set the root ball one half above the existing soil level and mound the soil mixture over and widely around it. This raised position will provide a natural root-run for the near surface feeder-root system and protect it from an over-abundance of water.

Because of their shallow feeder-root characteristic, rhododendrons require frequent spring, summer, and fall watering. Occasional overhead sprinkling of the foliage is highly beneficial. To conserve moisture and maintain a cool soil surface environment, mulch the area with a mixture of coarse peat moss and leaf mold. Provide rhododendrons with these few simple requirements and each will become a garden showpiece.

62. ROSES: Roses play an important part in a garden's color program. They are hardy and vigorous growers. With a little cultural attention, they respond with unequaled multi-season color. From the extensive groups of teas, hybrid teas, hybrid perpetuals, polyanthas, floribundas, climbers, pillars, and miniatures, it is not difficult to select roses specifically suited to individual parts of any garden aynwhere. Fences, walls, gates, borders, and shrub bays welcome appropriate kinds of roses. If room permits, an especially designed rose garden is a continuously interesting landscape feature. Groupings can be cleverly merged into peripheral borders.

63. ROSEMARY (*Rosmarinus officinalis*): This is a medium-hardy, evergreen, upright and spreading shrub, 3 or 4 feet high, with small,

slender, dark green leaves and little clusters of light blue flowers in spring and into summer. Variety *prostratus* is 1 or 2 feet high and has a habit of spreading 4 or 5 feet wide. Its leaves are pleasantly aromatic and its flowers are blue.

Use *Rosmarinus officinalis* in informal framing, as an accent plant, adjacent to the patio or pool, at the approach to doorways, as a blender or support plant. The variety *prostratus* may be used as a limited ground cover, or as a walk or driveway edging.

64. SARCOCOCCA HOOKERIANA: This medium-hardy evergreen is 4 or 5 feet high. Its slender leaves are 2 or 3 inches long. Variety *humilis* is about 2 feet high and spreads 6 or 7 feet. Its small fragrant flowers are nearly white.

Sarcococca ruscifolia is a medium-hardy, evergreen, 3 or 4 feet high, with glossy, narrowly oval leaves 2 or 3 inches long and small fragrant white flowers in early spring. It enjoys shade and has a tendency to spread.

These fine shrubs are excellent to cover shady banks, among foundation plantings, in shrub arrangements in the front yard, and in a special shade garden.

65. SKIMMIA JAPONICA: These attractive evergreen shrubs prefer temperate climates. They grow rather compact and wide, 2 to 4 feet high, and have smooth, light green, oval leaves 3 to 5 inches long. Clusters of small, fragrant, white flowers in spring are followed by shiny red berries.

Skimmia reevesiana is similar to *japonica* in form but is smaller. The leaves are smaller and the flowers are nearly white.

Use these fine shrubs in the more important locations in your garden design—near the front doorway or adjacent to the driveway, patio, or lounging area.

66. SNOWBALL (*Viburnum opulus roseum sterile*), also referred to as *Viburnum opulus roseum*: This is a very hardy deciduous shrub. It grows 6 to 9 feet high, is upright and open, with long branches that bend gracefully under its load of flowers. The thin leaves are lobed, average 3 inches wide, and resemble small maple leaves. Nearly white flowers appear in large ball-shaped clusters 4 or 5 inches in diameter in late spring. The foliage turns bronzy-red in autumn.

These beautiful shrubs are particularly valuable as accents to brighten background and side plantings, to grow tall against a fence or behind and to the side of a garden structure, to begin or terminate a cross axis.

67. SNOWBERRY (*Symphoricarpos albus*): This is a very hardy and deciduous shrub, 2½ to 3 feet high. It is upright and open with flexible branches. The leaves are light green, oval, and 1 or 2 inches long. Its clusters of small tubular flowers are light pink and the berries are shiny white.

Symphoricarpos albus laevigatus is similar except that it is 4 to 6 feet high and has larger leaves.

Use snowberries in shady areas, under trees, to tone up shrub groupings in the fall, or around a weekend cottage in the woods.

68. SPIRAEA: An important group of deciduous shrubs that vary considerably in size, shape, and flower. Each has a valuable function in the landscape.

Spiraea billiardii is very hardy and grows upright to 5 feet. Its oblong leaves average 3 inches in length, and it produces dense plumes of rosy pink flowers in summer.

Spiraea bumalda is a hardy, low-growing shrub about 2 feet high, with summer flowers ranging from dark pink to white. Variety *anthony waterer* is widely grown and is rather densely foliaged. Light crimson flowers appear in late spring and summer. Variety *froebeli* grows 2 to 4 feet in height and displays 4- or 5-inch-wide clusters of deep pink flowers.

Spiraea prunifolia (Bridal wreath) is an upright, wide, and somewhat arching shrub. It is thickly foliaged and bears great numbers of white flowers in little clusters along the arching branches in spring.

Spiraea vanhouttei grows 5 feet high (or more) and has numerous gracefully arching branches and bluish-green foliage. Its white flowers appear in spring in dense clusters. *Vanhouttei* is also referred to as bridal wreath in some sections of the country.

Spiraeas brighten background and general shrub groupings. Also use them as accent plants, blenders, or to frame a garden structure.

69. SUMAC (*Rhus*): These hardy, deciduous or evergreen shrubs are especially valuable for autumn foliage effects. Certain species—such as *Rhus toxicodendron* (Poison ivy), *Rhus diversiloba* (Poison oak), and *Rhus vernix* (Poison sumac)—are skin irritants and must *not* be planted.

Rhus aromatica or *canadensis* (fragrant sumac) is an upright and deciduous shrub, 4 to 6 feet high, with nearly oval leaves that are fragrant. Clusters of light yellow flowers appear in early spring and are followed by red berries.

Rhus typhina (Staghorn sumac) is a large and very hardy deciduous shrub that grows to a height of 8 feet (or more). Its large leaves are comprised of many 3- to 5-inch long leaflets; dense clusters of yellowish-green flowers bloom in summer.*Rhus typhina dissecta* and *laciniata* differ principally in the form of foliage.

The autumn foliage of deciduous sumacs is brilliant red and gold, making these shrubs quite valuable for keeping the fall garden colorful and alive.

70. SURINAM-CHERRY (*Eugenia uniflora*): This is a temperate climate evergreen, 10 to 20 feet high and densely foliaged with shiny, nearly oval leaves 1 or 2 inches long. Its small, fragrant white flowers are followed by crimson fruit. Use surinam cherry for screening, windbreaks, or tall hedges.

71. TEA-TREE (*Leptospermum laevigatum*): The Australian tea-tree is a temperate to warm climate, evergreen shrub, upright and gracefully distorted in growth habit, 8 or 9 feet high (more if permitted). Its numerous branches are slender and somewhat pendulous. It has small gray-green leaves and a generous distribution of white flowers. This shrub is useful on medium to large properties for screening, background, and general side plantings. It is also very effective in stabilizing sandy areas in semi-desert gardens.

72. VIBURNUM: This is a valuable group of garden favorites that vary in size, shape, and flower according to specie and variety.

Viburnum burkwoodii is a hardy, half evergreen shrub, 5 to 8 feet high, with shiny leaves. In early spring, before leaves appear, there are clusters of attractive and very fragrant pinkish-white flowers. The foliage turns to autumn colors.

Viburnum carlesii is a hardy deciduous shrub, 5 or 6 feet high, with oval leaves averaging 3 inches in length. It produces clusters of intensely fragrant white flowers in spring.

Viburnum dentatum (Arrow-wood) is very hardy, deciduous, 8 to 12 feet high, and densely covered with ovalish leaves 2 or 3 inches long. It shows clusters of white flowers in late spring and will grow well in filtered shade.

Viburnum lantana (Wayfaring-tree) is hardy, upright, and deciduous. It grows to around 8 to 12 feet high, has nearly oval and rather coarse leaves 3 to 5 inches long, and bears clusters of white flowers in late spring.

Viburnum lentago (Nanny-berry) is extremely hardy, deciduous, 10 to 12 feet high (to 25 feet if permitted), with oval leaves 3 or 4 inches long and large clusters of white flowers in late spring. The fruit is black.

Viburnum odoratissimum is a temperate climate evergreen, 7 to 9 feet high, with nearly oval, glossy leaves 3 to 6 inches long. It displays 4-inch wide clusters of fragrant white flowers in late spring. The fruit is red and turns black when mature.

Viburnum seiboldii is hardy and deciduous,

Photo 6.13

Graceful patterns of *Viburnum tinus.*

7 or 8 feet high. It has ovalish and coarsely dentate leaves 4 or 5 inches long and produces clusters of white flowers in late spring. The fruit is pink and turns black at maturity.

Viburnum suspensum is a moderate to warm climate evergreen, 4 to 6 feet high. The oval leaves are 3 or 4 inches long, and small clusters of light pink flowers appear in early summer. Its fruit is red.

Viburnum tinus (*Laurestinus*) prefers temperate climates, is evergreen, and grows 6 to 10 feet high with some spread. It has nearly oblong leaves that are 2 or 3 inches long and displays dense clusters of fragrant pinkish-white flowers in the springtime. The fruit is black.

Viburnum tomentosum is a hardy deciduous shrub, 6 to 9 feet high, with oval leaves 3 or 4 inches long and clusters of white flowers in spring. The fruit is red, but turns blue-black at maturity. *Tomentosum* has several very attractive varieties.

This list of viburnums offers shrubs of exceptional landscape value for almost any location and purpose in any garden—as foundation plantings, shrub groupings, accent plants, blenders, and screening. *Viburnum tinus* can be fanned out against a wall to create impressive patterns. The intensely fragrant varieties should be located in close proximity to the patio, lounging and outdoor furniture areas, and garden seats.

73. WAX-MYRTLE (*Myrica cerifera*): This shrub is relatively cold hardy, evergreen, and 8 to 15 feet high (to 30 feet if desired), with narrow leaves 2 or 3 inches long. It has unimpressive flowers but aromatic gray-white fruit, and is particularly useful as a windbreak or screen.

74. WEIGELA: This group comprises several

mostly hardy and deciduous species of good garden shrubs, 3 to 6 feet in height with an upright and spreading growth habit. They produce an excellent display of pink, red, or white flowers in spring and early summer and are valuable in side plantings, general shrub groupings, foundation plantings, and against walls and fences.

75. XYLOSMA RACEMOSA: This temperate climate evergreen is gracefully upright, 6 or 8 feet high and somewhat spreading. The light green, ovalish leaves are 3 or 4 inches long.

Xylosma senticosum is similar but smaller—4 or 5 feet high—with glossy foliage and small fragrant flowers. It tolerates rather intense heat.

Use *racemosa* for background, side plantings, screening, or closely pruned hedges. *Senticosum* is good as a foundation shrub, near garden structures, against walls, in low shrub arrangements, as an accent plant, or as a blender to tie shrub units together.

BROADLEAF SHRUBS—EASTERN AND CENTRAL SECTIONS (ZONES 5–6–7)

The following are some broadleaf shrubs for the eastern and central sections of the country—zones 5-6-7. There are species and varieties of listed shrubs adaptable to the favorable growing areas of the zones indicated. Refer to them in the preceding numbered shrub description list and in the Broadleaf Shrub Selection Chart on page 126.

Plant Number	Plant Name	Zone
1	Abelia	6–7
2	Almond, flowering (*Prunus glandulosa*)	5–6–7
3	Andromeda (*Pieris*)	5–6–7
5	Azalea	5–6–7
6	Barberry (*Berberis*)	5–6–7
7	Beauty-bush (*Kolkwitzia amabilis*)	6–7
9	Boxwood (*Buxus*)	6–7
11	Butterfly-bush (*Buddleia alternifolia*)	7
15	Coral-berry (*Symphoricarpos orbiculatus*)	5–6–7
17	Cotoneaster	5–6–7
19	Crataegus	5–6–7
21	Daphne	5–6–7
22	Dogwood (*Cornus*)	5–6–7
23	Elaeagnus	5–6–7
26	Euonymus	5–6–7
29	Forsythia	5–6–7
33	Heath (*Erica*)	6–7
35	Holly (*Ilex*)	5–6–7
37	Hypericum	5–6–7
39	Jetbead (*Rhodotypos*)	5–6–7
40	Kerria	5–6–7
41	Lead-plant (*Amorpha canescens*)	5–6–7
42	Lilac (*Syringa*)	5–6–7
46	Mock-orange (*Philadelphus*)	5–6–7
47	Mountain-laurel (*Kalmia latifolia*)	5–6–7
49	Ninebark (*Physocarpus*)	5–6–7
52	Pea-shrub (*Caragana arborescens*)	5–6–7
56	Potentilla	5–6–7
57	Privet (*Ligustrum*)	5–6–7
58	Pyracantha	5–6–7
59	Quince, flowering (*Chaenomeles*)	5–6–7
61	Rhododendron	5–6–7
62	Rose	5–6–7
66	Snowball (*Viburnum opulus roseum sterile*)	5–6–7
67	Snowberry (*Symphoricarpos albus*)	5–6–7
68	Spiraea	5–6–7
69	Sumac (*Rhus*)	5–6–7
72	Viburnum	5–6–7
73	Wax-myrtle (*Myrica cerifera*)	5–6–7
74	Weigela	5–6–7

BROADLEAF SHRUBS—WESTERN SECTIONS (ZONES 4–5–6–7–8–9–10)

The following are some broadleaf shrubs for the western sections of the country—zones 4-5-6-7-8-9-10. There are species and varieties of listed shrubs adaptable to the favorable growing areas of the zones indicated. Refer to them in the preceding numbered shrub description list and in the Broadleaf Shrub Selection Chart on page 126.

Plant Number	Plant Name	Zone
1	Abelia	6–7–8–9
2	Almond, flowering (*Prunus glandulosa*)	5–6–7–8–9
3	Andromeda (*Pieris*)	5–6–7–8–9
4	Aucuba (*Aucuba japonica*)	7–8–9–10
5	Azalea	4–5–6–7–8–9–10
6	Barberry (*Berberis*)	4–5–6–7–8–9
7	Beauty-bush (*Kolkwitzia amabilis*)	6–7–8–9
8	Bottle-brush (*Melaleuca*)	8–9–10
9	Boxwood (*Buxus*)	6–7–8–9
12	Camellia	7–8–9–10
13	Ceanothus	8–9–10
17	Cotoneaster	4–5–6–7–8–9
21	Daphne	5–6–7–8–9–10
22	Dogwood (*Cornus*)	4–5–6–7–8–9–10
25	Escallonia	8–9–10
26	Euonymus	4–5–6–7–8–9–10
29	Forsythia	5–6–7–8–9
30	Fuchsia	8–9–10

33	Heath (Erica)	6–7–8–9–10
34	Hibiscus	9–10
35	Holly (Ilex)	5–6–7–8–9
36	Hydrangea	5–6–7–8–9–10
37	Hypericum	5–6–7–8–9–10
40	Kerria	5–6–7–8
42	Lilac (Syringa)	4–5–6–7–8
44	Mahonia	5–6–7–8–9
48	Myrtle (Myrtus)	8–9–10
51	Osmanthus	7–8–9
53	Pernettya	7–8–9–10
54	Pittosporum	8–9–10
56	Potentilla	4–5–6–7–8
57	Privet (Ligustrum)	5–6–7–8–9
58	Pyracantha	5–6–7–8–9
60	Raphiolepis	8–9–10
61	Rhododendron	5–6–7–8–9–10
64	Sarcococca	7–8–9–10
68	Spiraea	4–5–6–7–8
72	Viburnum	4–5–6–7–8
75	Xylosma	8–9–10

BROADLEAF SHRUBS—NORTHERN SECTIONS (ZONES 2–3–4)

The following are some broadleaf shrubs for the northern sections of the country—zones 2–3–4. There are species and varieties of listed shrubs adaptable to the favorable growing areas of the zones indicated. Refer to them in the preceding numbered shrub description list and in the Broadleaf Shrub Selection Chart on page 126.

Plant Number	Plant Name	Zone
5	Azalea	4
6	Barberry (Berberis)	3–4
10	Buckthorn (Rhamnus)	2–3–4
15	Coral-berry (Symphoricarpos orbiculatus)	4
17	Cotoneaster	4
20	Currant (Ribes)	2–3–4
22	Dogwood (Cornus)	2–3–4
23	Elaeagnus	3–4
26	Euonymus	4
36	Hydrangea	4
39	Jetbead (Rhodotypos tetrapetala)	4
41	Lead-plant (Amorpha canescens)	3–4
42	Lilac (Syringa)	3–4
49	Ninebark (Physocarpus)	3–4
52	Pea-shrub (Caragana arborescens)	2–3–4
56	Potentilla	2–3–4
62	Rose	3–4
66	Snowball (Viburnum opulus roseum sterile)	4

67	Snowberry (Symphoricarpos albus)	3–4
68	Spiraea	4
69	Sumac (Rhus)	4
72	Viburnum	4

BROADLEAF SHRUBS—SOUTHERN SECTIONS (ZONES 8–9–10)

The following are some broadleaf shrubs for the southern sections of the country—zones 8–9–10. There are species and varieties of listed shrubs adaptable to the favorable growing areas of the zones indicated. Refer to them in the preceding numbered shrub description list and in the Broadleaf Shrub Selection Chart on page 126.

Plant Number	Plant Name	Zone
1	Abelia	8–9–10
4	Aucuba	8–9–10
5	Azalea	8–9–10
8	Bottle-brush (Melaleuca)	8–9–10
12	Camellia	8–9–10
13	Ceanothus	8–9–10
14	Cherry-laurel (Prunus laurocerasus)	8–9–10
16	Clerodendron	9–10
18	Crape-myrtle (Lagerstroemia indica)	8–9–10
21	Daphne	8–9–10
25	Escallonia	8–9–10
26	Euonymus	8–9–10
30	Fuchsia	8–9–10
31	Gardenia	8–9–10
33	Heath (Erica)	8–9–10
34	Hibiscus	9–10
35	Holly (Ilex)	8–9–10
36	Hydrangea	8–9–10
37	Hypericum	8–9–10
43	Lime-berry (Triphasia trifolia)	9–10
45	Mexican-orange (Choisya ternata)	8–9–10
48	Myrtle (Myrtus)	8–9–10
50	Oleander	8–9–10
53	Pernettya	8–9–10
54	Pittosporum	8–9–10
55	Pomegranate (Punica)	8–9–10
58	Pyracantha	8–9–10
60	Raphiolepis	8–9–10
63	Rosemary (Rosmarinus)	8–9–10
64	Sarcococca	8–9–10
65	Skimmia	8–9–10
70	Surinam-cherry (Eugenia uniflora)	8–9–10
71	Tea-tree (Leptospermum laevigatum)	9–10
74	Weigela	8–9–10
75	Xylosma	8–9–10

Coniferous Evergreens

Conifers are recognized by their narrow or needle-like leaves and distinctive characteristics in form and foliage. They bear seed-producing cones of varying sizes and shapes. All but a few kinds, such as bald cypress and larches, are evergreen. With a few exceptions, conifers are cold-hardy and perform well in reasonably moist climates. Most species, however, do not adapt well to the hot, dry areas of the country.

THE MANY USES OF CONIFERS

The coniferous genera form a versatile plant reservoir from which you may select shrubs and trees of immense beauty and function for almost any location in the garden—in the background, along property lines, in foundation plantings, as specimens, and so on. Conifers are particularly valuable in providing winter interest while deciduous trees and shrubs are bare.

One important functional characteristic of conifers is their ability to *retard winds*. If you need a wind-screen in your garden, try an irregular grouping of harmonious conifers. It will effectively shield the patio from the winds without the wall-like appearance of most garden windbreaks. Conifers are also exceptionally versatile in *framing*. Your house, for example, can easily be made to appear wider or narrower, taller or lower, by judicious selection and calculated placement of appropriate conifers. (The various design functions of trees are discussed in detail in Chapter V). Smaller conifers are valuable garden shrubs. For example, your *foundation* planting might contain a predominance of conifers—there are species compatible with any architectural style.

Coniferous shrubs and trees are available with so many interesting characteristics and foliage colorations that they can help you achieve virtually any landscape effect you desire. In general,

their luxurious foliage imparts a feeling of richness to the garden.

The majority of conifers tolerate considerable wind and fluctuations of climate. They adapt to reasonable ecological factors and accept a wide range of soil conditions. However, they do best in a moist, woodsy environment and in fertile, well-drained soil that is conducive to unrestricted root development.

Enjoy the beauty of conifers during the several years they stay within the height and size suitable to your garden. If some become overly large, remove them and replant with young and perhaps more appropriate ones. Don't hesitate to replace them, for occasional renewal of plants—like redecorating a room—refreshes the aesthetic values of your garden. One note of warning: resist the temptation to overuse golden or yellow colored conifers. They are excellent, but too many may upset the foliage color balance.

SELECTING CONIFERS

The key to success with conifers, like all other plants in your garden, lies in selecting the right one for a specific location. The Conifer Selection Chart on page 148 will help you choose appropriate plants for the conifer locations you have indicated on your design paper. The chart includes:

1. The names of 75 conifers and some specific data on each.
2. Numbered references to the conifer description list.
3. The approximate height of each conifer.
4. Whether each is compact, spreading, or upright in growth habit.
5. The approximate zoning range in which each conifer may be safely grown.
6. Several prominent landscape uses for each conifer.

Use this Selection Chart exactly as you used those in the two preceding chapters. For review, let's set up an example. You wish a *low-growing* conifer with *spreading* growth habit for a *front-yard shrub grouping*, and you live in zone 5. Mark these requirements on the edge of a sheet of paper, exactly in the proper columns.

Lo—Sp—Zone 5—Fy (Front yard)—
Sg (Shrub group)

Move the paper up the chart. Note that several conifers qualify; they match the requirements on your selection strip. By reading the descriptions of these plants in the alphabetical description list, which begins on page 151, you can easily make your decision.

NOTE: Conifers: You will notice non-consistency in this chapter by the listing of scientific names first. I was persuaded to do this because I found the great majority of homeowners know very few,

if any common or scientific names of conifers and that they are more interested in the scientific names than in the common. Chamaecyparis obtusa nana whets their interest but Hinoki cypress falls rather flat.

The common names of a great many conifers are not consistent across the country anyway. I also notice that recognized authorities on conifers do not relate common names to a sizeable percentage of conifers and in many cases they disagree, which could subject a long list of common names to considerable criticism.

In addition, I refer many of the plants in this category to a particular Figure (Plot plan) to illustrate their use in design. People are impressively befuddled by conifers and in teaching, I found this to be an important visual aid in clarifying the perplexing *use* problem of these valuable plants. This procedure does not seem necessary in the other better known plant categories.

CONIFERS—NEEDLE-LEAF EVERGREENS—SELECTION CHART

No.	Name of Conifer	Low shrub	Medium shrub	Tall shrub	Compact	Spreading	Upright	Tree	Zone (2–10)	Accent	Background	Foundation	Framing	Front yard	Ground cover	Rock garden	Screening	Shrub group	Side	Slopes	Specimen	Wind retardant
1	Cedrus deodara						+	30'	6–9	+	+		+	+			+					+
2	Cedrus deodara aurea						+	30'	6–9	+	+		+	+			+	+	+		+	+
3	Chamaecyparis lawsoniana elwoodi			6'			+		5–9	+		+	+	+				+	+		+	+
4	Chamaecyparis obtusa			7'			+		4–9	+		+	+	+				+	+		+	+
5	Chamaecyparis obtusa aurea			7'			+		4–9	+		+	+	+				+	+		+	
6	Chamaecyparis obtusa compacta		4'		+				4–9		+	+	+	+		+		+				
7	Chamaecyparis obtusa gracilis		5'		+		+		4–9	+	+	+	+	+				+	+		+	
8	Chamaecyparis obtusa nana	3'			+				4–9	+		+	+	+				+				
9	Chamaecyparis obtusa pygmaea	1'			+	+			4–9	+	+		+	+		+		+	+			
10	Chamaecyparis pisifera filifera			8'		+	+		3–9	+	+	+	+	+				+	+		+	+
11	Chamaecyparis pisifera filifera aurea			7'		+	+		3–9	+		+	+	+		+	+	+	+			+
12	Chamaecyparis pisifera filifera nana	3'							3–9	+			+	+				+	+			
13	Chamaecyparis pisifera plumosa			8'			+		4–9	+	+	+	+	+		+	+	+	+		+	+
14	Chamaecyparis pisifera squarrosa minima	2'			+	+			4–9	+	+		+	+				+	+			
15	Juniperus chinensis						+	25'	3–9	+			+				+					+
16	Juniperus chinensis armstrongii	3'				+			4–9			+		+	+			+		+		
17	Juniperus chinensis columnaris glauca			12'			+		5–9	+	+	+	+	+			+	+	+		+	+
18	Juniperus chinensis globosa	3'			+				5–9		+	+	+	+		+		+	+		+	
19	Juniperus chinensis japonica		4'		+	+			5–9			+		+	+			+	+			
20	Juniperus chinensis pfitzeriana		4'			+			4–9			+	+	+	+			+	+	+		
21	Juniperus chinensis pfitzeriana aurea	3'				+			4–9			+	+	+	+			+	+	+		
22	Juniperus chinensis sargentii	1'			+	+			4–9	+	+	+	+	+	+	+		+	+	+	+	
23	Juniperus chinensis torulosa			8'			+		5–9	+	+	+	+	+		+	+	+	+		+	+
24	Juniperus communis compressa		4'		+	+	+		2–9	+		+	+	+	+	+			+			
25	Juniperus conferta	2'			+	+			5–9					+	+	+				+		

| Example | Conifer | lo | | | | sp | | | 5 | | | | | fy | | | | sg | | | | |

Example conifer: Requirements—a low (1'–3'), spreading shrub for a front-yard shrub group in zone 5. Mark your zone and requirements on a strip of paper. Move it up over chart. Match reasonably closely. Find several. Turn to descriptions for decision. Conifers located—numbers 9, 14, 21, 22, 26, 27, 28, 30, 33, 36, 38, 58, 73. Zoning: Estimated zone-temperature range of each conifer's hardiness. See zone map on page 24.

CONIFERS—NEEDLE-LEAF EVERGREENS—SELECTION CHART

No.	Name of Conifer	Low shrub	Medium shrub	Tall shrub	Compact	Spreading	Upright	Tree	Zone 2	3	4	5	6	7	8	9	10	Accent	Background	Foundation	Framing	Front yard	Ground cover	Rock garden	Screening	Shrub group	Side	Slopes	Specimen	Wind retardant
26	Juniperus horizontalis	1'				+				+												+	+	+		+		+		
27	Juniperus horizontalis douglasii	1'				+				+												+	+	+		+		+		
28	Juniperus horizontalis plumosa	2'			+	+				+											+	+	+	+		+	+	+		
29	Juniperus occidentalis						+	30'			+							+	+	+		+			+	+	+		+	+
30	Juniperus procumbens	1'				+				+												+	+	+		+		+		
31	Juniperus sabina		5'			+	+			+								+	+	+	+	+				+	+		+	
32	Juniperus sabina fastigiata		5'				+		+									+	+	+	+	+				+	+		+	
33	Juniperus sabina tamariscifolia	2'			+	+				+								+	+	+	+	+	+			+	+	+		
34	Juniperus scopulorum						+	35'		+								+	+	+	+	+			+	+	+		+	+
35	Juniperus squamata meyeri		4'			+	+			+								+		+	+	+		+		+	+		+	
36	Juniperus virginiana reptans	2'				+	+			+										+	+	+		+		+	+			
37	Picea abies nidiformis	3'			+					+								+		+	+	+		+		+	+	+		
38	Picea abies procumbens	2'			+	+				+										+	+	+	+	+		+	+	+		
39	Picea abies pygmaea	1'			+					+										+	+	+		+		+	+	+		
40	Picea abies remontii		4'		+		+			+								+		+	+	+	+	+		+	+		+	+
41	Picea glauca conica		5'		+		+			+								+	+	+	+	+		+		+	+		+	+
42	Picea pungens						+	20'		+								+	+	+	+	+	+	+	+	+	+	+	+	+
43	Picea pungens glauca						+	15'		+								+	+	+	+	+	+	+	+	+	+	+	+	+
44	Pinus halepensis				+		+	30'					+						+		+				+	+	+		+	+
45	Pinus mugo		4'			+	+			+								+	+	+	+	+		+		+	−			
46	Pinus mugo mughus prostrata	2'			+	+				+								+		+	+	+		+		+				
47	Pinus parviflora						+	35'				+						+	+	+	+	+			+	+	+		+	+
48	Pinus pinea						+	45'				+							+	+	+	+				+	+		+	+
49	Pinus resinosa						+	50'	+										+							+	+		+	+
50	Pinus strobus						+	50'		+									+		+	+				+	+		+	+
	Example Conifer	lo				sp			5													fy				sg				

Example conifer: Requirements—a low (1'–3'), spreading shrub for a front-yard shrub group in zone 5. Mark your zone and requirements on a strip of paper. Move it up over chart. Match reasonably closely. Find several. Turn to descriptions for decision. Conifers located—numbers 9, 14, 21, 22, 26, 27, 28, 30, 33, 36, 38, 58, 73. Zoning: Estimated zone-temperature range of each conifer's hardiness. See zone map on page 24.

CONIFERS—NEEDLE-LEAF EVERGREENS—SELECTION CHART

No.	Name of Conifer	Size and Growth Habit — Low shrub	Medium shrub	Tall shrub	Compact	Spreading	Upright	Tree	Zone (2–10)	Accent	Background	Foundation	Framing	Front yard	Ground cover	Rock garden	Screening	Shrub group	Side	Slopes	Specimen	Wind retardant
51	Pinus strobus nana		6'			+			2–7	+	+	+	+	+			+	+	+			
52	Pinus sylvestris		5'				+	25'	2–7	+	+	+	+	+			+	+	+		+	+
53	Pinus sylvestris nana glauca		5'				+		2–8	+	+	+	+	+			+	+	+		+	+
54	Taxus baccata						+	15'	5–8	+	+	+	+	+			+	+	+		+	
55	Taxus baccata adpressa		5'		+		+		5–8	+	+	+	+	+				+	+			
56	Taxus baccata fastigiata			8'	+		+		6–8	+	+	+	+	+		+	+	+	+		+	
57	Taxus baccata repandens		4'		+		+		6–8	+	+	+	+	+		+		+	+			
58	Taxus canadensis	3'				+			3–7	+	+	+	+	+	+	+		+	+	+		+
59	Taxus cuspidata			7'		+	+	30'	3–7	+	+	+	+	+			+	+	+		+	+
60	Taxus cuspidata densa		4'		+		+		4–7	+	+	+	+	+				+	+			
61	Taxus cuspidata nana		4'		+		+		4–7	+	+	+	+	+		+		+	+			
62	Taxus cuspidata minima	2'			+	+			4–7	+	+	+	+	+		+		+	+	+		
63	Thuja koraiensis		4'		+		+		5–8	+	+	+	+	+		+		+	+	+	+	+
64	Thuja occidentalis ellwangeriana aurea		4'		+		+		3–8	+	+	+	+	+			+	+	+		+	+
65	Thuja occidentalis fastigiata			8'	+		+		3–8	+	+	+	+	+			+	+	+		+	+
66	Thuja occidentalis globosa		4'		+		+		5–8	+	+	+	+	+		+		+	+		+	
67	Thuja occidentalis pumila	2'			+		+		5–8	+	+	+	+	+		+		+	+			
68	Thuja occidentalis recurva nana	3'			+		+		5–8	+	+	+	+	+				+	+		+	
69	Thuja orientalis aurea nana	2'			+		+		6–9	+	+	+	+	+		+		+	+			
70	Thuja orientalis beverleyensis			7'			+		6–9	+	+	+	+	+				+	+		+	
71	Thuja orientalis conspicua		4'		+		+		6–9	+	+	+	+	+		+		+	+			
72	Thuja orientalis elegantissima			6'	+		+		6–9	+	+	+	+	+				+	+		+	
73	Tsuga canadensis nana	2'				+			4–7	+	+	+	+	+	+	+		+	+	+		
74	Tsuga canadensis pendula	2'			+		+		5–7	+	+	+	+	+	+	+		+	+	+		
75	Tsuga mertensiana						+	25'	5–8	+	+	+	+	+	+		+	+	+		+	+
	Example Conifer	lo				sp			5					fy				sg				

Example conifer: Requirements—a low (1'–3'), spreading shrub for a front-yard shrub group in zone 5. Mark your zone and requirements on a strip of paper. Move it up over chart. Match reasonably closely. Find several. Turn to descriptions for decision. Conifers located—numbers 9, 14, 21, 22, 26, 27, 28, 30, 33, 36, 38, 58, 73. Zoning: Estimated zone-temperature range of each conifer's hardiness. See zone map on page 24.

Photo 7.1

Cedrus deodara brings a soft elegance to the landscape.

Photo 7.2

Chamaecyparis obtusa increases character and interest in a foundation planting.

ALPHABETICAL DESCRIPTIONS OF CONIFEROUS SHRUBS AND TREES

Following are descriptions and typical uses of the coniferous shrubs and trees that appear on the Conifer Selection Chart. (Numbers match those on the Selection Chart).

1. CEDRUS DEODARA (Deodar cedar): This is a very handsome, mild climate evergreen, 25 to 40 feet high (more if uncontrolled), with bluish-green foliage on horizontally spreading and slightly pendulous branches. It is useful in the background, as a specimen, in the front yard, or for a screening and windbreak grouping, as in Figure 3.12.

2. CEDRUS DEODARA AUREA: This tree is similar to *Cedrus deodara* in description and uses but is lightly golden in appearance.

3. CHAMAECYPARIS LAWSONIANA ELWOODI: Columnar and rather compact in growth habit, this shrub has rich bluish-green foliage and at 5 to 8 feet in height is useful to frame doorways, as an accent or specimen, particularly in formal designs, and for vertical interest in a low shrub grouping. This is an ideal conifer to terminate the parallel walks in Figure 3.9, for example.

4. CHAMAECYPARIS OBTUSA (Hinoki cypress): This conifer is beautifully structured with an abundance of dark green, scale-leaved, and rather flat foliage. It is relatively slow-growing and prefers a moist, temperate environment with some protection from afternoon sun in hot areas. It may be held to 7 or 8 feet for many years by careful pruning. Use it in the more distinctive parts of foreground and side plantings. It is a superb specimen, accent in foundation plantings, or near the corners of your house.

5. CHAMAECYPARIS OBTUSA AUREA: This plant is similar in form, characteristics, and uses to CHAMAECYPARIS OBTUSA. Its foliage has a golden yellow sheen when young.

6. CHAMAECYPARIS OBTUSA COMPACTA: This is a low-growing variety that is relatively broad and somewhat conical in appearance. At 3 or 4 feet in height, it is excellent for foundation plantings, shrub groupings, and accent locations. It might be used, for example, at the juncture of the back walk and path in Figure 4.2, or in a special grouping, as a substitute for flowers, near the end of the pool in Figure 3.8.

7. CHAMAECYPARIS OBTUSA GRACILIS: This excellent conifer assumes a pyramidal form and, although rather compact, has an attractive unevenness that makes it uniquely distinctive in appearance. It is a slow grower with dark green, scale-like leaves. Use it in shrub groupings where

Photo 7.3

Chamaecyparis obtusa nana is outstanding in beauty and character.

Photo 7.4

Shrub association with form, color, and texture. Front to back and left: *Chamaecyparis obtusa nana*, rosemary, *Cryptomeria compacta*, *Chamaecyparis pisifera squarrosa nana*, azalea.

(Author's home)

Photo 7.5

A front entrance enhanced by dwarf conifers (*Cryptomeria*), rock, and used brick.

you need 5 or 6 feet of height. Beside the driveway or at the ends of the pergola walk in Figure 4.3 are typical locations.

8. CHAMAECYPARIS OBTUSA NANA: This is a very striking conifer at 2 or 3 feet high with a similar width. It is informally roundish in shape and has dark green foliage of excellent quality. Use it in low shrub groupings, to frame a driveway, in special or featured parts of the garden, or in a rock garden.

9. CHAMAECYPARIS OBTUSA PYGMAEA: This is a very small, thick foliaged, irregularly formed, and almost creeping little plant. It is exceptionally interesting at an entrance or in a special unit arrangement, in a rock garden, and in small retirement gardens (see Figure 3.13).

10. CHAMAECYPARIS PISIFERA FILIFERA: This is a variety of sawara cypress that has slightly ascending, then loosely cascading, thread-like branches with bright green foliage that imparts a feeling of motion. It fits perfectly into the locations in your garden where 6 or 8 feet of height is required, such as at the sides of the patio near the hedge in Figure 3.8.

11. CHAMAECYPARIS PISIFERA FILIFERA AUREA: This false-cypress is similar to FILIFERA in size, form, and thread-like branches, but it has golden yellow foliage, which makes it exceptional as an accent conifer.

12. CHAMAECYPARIS PISIFERA FILIFERA NANA: This conifer is very similar to FILIFERA in open, gracefully cascading effect, but it is smaller. It has the same general characteristics—arching and long, loosely descending, thread-like branches—and, with a little pruning, will stay within 3 or 4 feet high for many years. Use it in such typical locations as the front-yard corner plantings in Figure 2.1, or between the patio and house in Figure 1.1.

13. CHAMAECYPARIS PISIFERA PLUMOSA: This hardy conifer has gray-green, soft-textured, feathery foliage and an informally conical form with frond-like branches. If held to a height of 8 or 10 feet, it is very effective in background or side plantings to provide a change in color and texture. It is also excellent as a wind retardant.

14. CHAMAECYPARIS PISIFERA SQUARROSA MINIMA: This very slow grower gradually develops into a feathery, gray-green mound-like shrub, which a little pruning will maintain at a height of 2 or 3 feet for a long time. It has many uses in the landscape—as a foundation planting, near the patio or play area, in a rock garden, or to give a change of color and texture in a low shrub unit. It would be appropriate at the ends of the patio flower border in Figure 2.1, or to frame the patio entrance in Figure 1.1.

15. JUNIPERUS CHINENSIS (Chinese juniper):
Under cultivation this naturally tall, slender-branched conifer can be maintained as a medium-size tree, 20 to 25 feet high, rather compact and pyramidal. It is of value in the background, for screening, and for wind protection. To use it as a shrub, begin pruning it to form and size when it is 7 or 8 feet high.

16. JUNIPERUS CHINENSIS ARMSTRONGII (Armstrong juniper): This is an elegant, medium-hardy, procumbent-type conifer with golden yellow foliage. It grows 2 or 3 feet high and has a spread of 3 or 4 feet. Use it as an individual shrub, in shrub groupings, or as a ground cover.

17. JUNIPERUS CHINENSIS COLUMNARIS GLAUCA: This conifer is upright in growth habit, 12 to 15 feet high, and usable in side or background plantings, in a house-corner grouping, as part of a screening or wind-retardant unit, or as a tall, loosely trimmed hedge.

18. JUNIPERUS CHINENSIS GLOBOSA: This hardy conifer is rather dense and globe-like in growth habit and is attractive for low framing and in small or restricted areas.

19. JUNIPERUS CHINENSIS JAPONICA: This is a low-growing coniferous shrub of exceptional beauty. Its branches are spreading and often gracefully procumbent. At 4 or 5 feet, it is useful as a foundation shrub, in side plantings, or in a general shrub grouping.

20. JUNIPERUS CHINENSIS PFITZERIANA (Pfitzers juniper): This shrub is a rapid and continuous grower, particularly from the standpoint of spread—6 or 8 feet if uncontrolled by pruning. Its massive, plume-like, slightly drooping branches are irregularly placed, and the foliage is gray-green. Although this is a valuable plant, caution must be exercised in its location because of its relentless spread. For best effect, keep it pruned to a height of 3 or 4 feet. Use it to cover slopes, in front of the background corner conifer (as in Figure 1.1), or in the planting strip beside the driveway (as in Figure 2.1).

21. JUNIPERUS CHINENSIS PFITZERIANA AUREA: This juniper is similar to PFITZERIANA except that the foliage toward the ends of the branches is golden yellow.

JUNIPERUS CHINENSIS PFITZERIANA COMPACTA is a small version of PFITZERIANA—about half its size—and is more usable in a small garden.

22. JUNIPERUS CHINENSIS SARGENTII: This is a very hardy, low, creeping juniper, 1 foot high with a 5 or 6 foot spread. It will cover banks and slopes, and it associates well with all low-growing conifers or broadleaf shrubs. Use it in a rock garden.

23. JUNIPERUS CHINENSIS TORULOSA: This

Photo 7.6

Juniperus chinensis pfitzeriana turns the walkway, informalizes the clipped hedge, and increases the interest and quiet beauty of the unit.

Photo 7.7

Beside the driveway, a thick golden carpet of *Juniperus chinensis pfitzeriana aurea* edged with deep green *Juniperus sabina*.

juniper grows upright with branches uniquely tortuous and gracefully curving. It is very attractive and a rapid grower, but careful pruning will hold it to 8 or 9 feet for several years. It's useful as a foundation conifer, for framing, or in a screening wind-retardant group, as in Figure 3.12.

24. JUNIPERUS COMMUNIS COMPRESSA: This is a medium-hardy, dwarf, conical, and quite compact conifer that is slow growing. At 3 or 4 feet in height, it may be only 9 or 10 inches in diameter. The slender, upright branches are closely compressed, and the foliage is an impressive gray-green. There are many landscape uses for this plant—in the front foundation planting, near the driveway walk (as in Figure 3.12), or in any small retirement garden (see Figure 3.13).

25. JUNIPERUS CONFERTA (Shore juniper): This juniper requires a cool, moist environment such as that which prevails along sea shores. It grows into a 1- or 2-foot, mat-like ground cover for banks, slopes, and panels, and will work its way over and around rocks, softening the local landscape.

26. JUNIPERUS HORIZONTALIS (Creeping juniper): This creeping juniper is very hardy, grows rapidly, and spreads out in a mat. HORIZONTALIS is 1 to 2 feet high and will completely cover slopes or become a level ground cover. It is excellent for narrow parkways and for edging strips.

27. JUNIPERUS HORIZONTALIS DOUGLASII (Waukegan juniper): This is a hardy, prostrate variety with bluish-green foliage that turns purplish in fall. Being drought resistant, it is one of the best creeping junipers for covering dry slopes or rocky areas. Under favorable growing conditions, it spreads rapidly and becomes 12 to 18 inches high. This creeper might be used to cover the parallel panels in Figure 3.9.

28. JUNIPERUS HORIZONTALIS PLUMOSA: This creeper has light green foliage that is feathery and soft to touch. It turns bronzy in winter, creating a valuable accent color in the garden. This juniper spreads wide and grows from 18 inches to 2 feet high. It may be used as an individual creeper in a special area, to cover slopes, to confine a flower bed (as at the end of the front lawn in Figure 4.3), or between the driveway and lawn (as in Figure 4.2).

29. JUNIPERUS OCCIDENTALIS (Western juniper): This round-headed tree may reach an uncontrolled height of 40 or 45 feet (or more) and is used effectively in western landscape work, particularly on medium to large properties. Its shape and height can be controlled if judicious pruning is started when it is young. Use it for framing the lot, as a background specimen, or as a large lawn tree.

30. JUNIPERUS PROCUMBENS: Although this hardy conifer is primarily a low, dense, slow-growing mat 1 foot high, it can be staked, control-pruned, and trained into a very attractive shrub 4 or 5 feet high. Or it can be attached to a wall and fanned out to form interesting natural patterns. As a ground cover, it might be used in a narrow planting strip (see Figure 3.12) or in conifer panels (see Figure 3.9).

31. JUNIPERUS SABINA (Savin juniper): This hardy conifer has a tendency to grow upright, but it is easily held to a height of 5 or 6 feet. It has dark green foliage. Use it in shrub groups, foundation planting, or near the children's play area (as in Figure 2.1).

32. JUNIPERUS SABINA FASTIGIATA: This hardy shrub grows upright and columnar. It has attractive, dark green leaves that are short and almost scale-like. In the 5- or 6-foot height range, use this one as a foundation plant, an accent, or to form a vertical line in a conifer grouping.

33. JUNIPERUS SABINA TAMARISCIFOLIA: This is one of the most useful of the low-growing conifers. Several grown together form a dense, light green mat, 1 or 2 feet thick, that seems to flow over the area. When planted in the foreground, it becomes an excellent blender unifying two shrub units. It will cover slopes, and it is not uncommon to see small front yards substitute TAMARISCIFOLIA for lawn. It could replace flowers at the end of the pool in Figure 3.7, or be planted on both sides of the front yard near the sidewalk in Figure 2.1.

34. JUNIPERUS SCOPULORUM (Rocky mountain juniper): This is a round-headed tree, 30 to 45 feet in height. Its trunk is relatively short, and its bark is reddish-brown. It is principally a background or large lawn tree for medium to large properties.

35. JUNIPERUS SQUAMATA MEYERI: This beautifully awkward shrub has silvery blue-green foliage on its branches that grow crazily to a height of 4 or 5 feet; in time the plant may have a 5- or 6-foot spread. Control by pruning is not difficult, but requires removal of entire branches to avoid a stubby effect. This variety contributes aliveness and interest to a shrub grouping.

36. JUNIPERUS VIRGINIANA REPTANS: This is a hardy, low growing shrub, in the 2- to 4-foot range, with bright green foliage on slender and spreading branches. Use it in a rock garden, as a ground cover, in front of the foundation planting, or near a water feature.

37. PICEA ABIES NIDIFORMIS (Bird's nest spruce): This is a very hardy and slow-growing

Photo 7.8

Juniperus procumbens controlled-pruned and staked to form a beautiful shrub.

Photo 7.9

Juniperus sabina tamariscifolia and Japanese black pine dress a slope.

Photo 7.10

Juniperus squamata meyeri.

conifer with bold grassy-green foliage. It has mound-like compactness and will stay within the 3- or 4-foot range for a long time. It may be used in such typical locations as the special planting well at the end of the patio in Figure 1.1, or on both sides of the front yard in Figure 3.9.

38. PICEA ABIES PROCUMBENS: This is a hardy, prostrate, but irregularly mounding shrub with dark green leaves on slender branches. It is slow-growing and will eventually grow to a height of 1½ to 2 feet and a width of 4 or 5 feet. It could be planted in the conifer strip beside the driveway in Figure 3.12, for example.

39. PICEA ABIES PYGMAEA: This small spruce is dense and grows slowly into a ragged, rounded pyramid 10 to 12 inches high. It is excellent in small areas of special interest—for example, at a curve in a walk, beside steps, or in a rock garden.

40. PICEA ABIES REMONTII: This is a compact, conical conifer with a uniquely ragged type of growth, which is its principal and charming characteristic. The yellowish reflection of its foliage increases in interest. At 3 or 4 feet in height, it is particularly valuable in the forepart of a conifer grouping, to frame a driveway, in a foundation planting, adjacent to a patio, or as an accent. Visualize this plant terminating the parallel walks in Figure 3.9.

PICEA ABIES CAPITATA is an intriguing miniature tree of exceptional interest. It is cone-shaped and when 3 feet high will be 2 feet wide at the base.

Photo 7.11

Picea abies nidiformis is an excellent low-growing conifer for such special uses as in a rock arrangement.

41. PICEA GLAUCA CONICA: This dwarf spruce is 4 or 5 feet high, and typically quite narrow. Its dense foliage is soft and bright green. It is a slow grower and prefers good soil and considerable moisture, with some protection from hot sun and strong wind. Use it in a rock garden, in formal designs, or at the end of a back flower panel (as in Figure 4.3).

42. PICEA PUNGENS (Colorado spruce): This is a very hardy, upright tree of excellent proportions and appearance, with stiff, radially arranged leaves 1½ inches long. It can be held within 20 to 30 feet for many years, but eventually it will become quite large. Replace it with a young plant if space is limited.

Use PICEA PUNGENS to frame the house, in the background, as a large lawn tree, or in a large screening and windbreak grouping.

43. PICEA PUNGENS GLAUCA (Colorado blue spruce): This magnificent variety of PICEA PUNGENS is similar in stately conformation, but its foliage is boldly bluish. It grows slowly and will remain in the 15- to 20-foot range for years. Use it as a lawn specimen, to begin or terminate an axis, in the front yard (as in Figure 1.1) or as a background specimen (as in Figure 4.2).

PICEA PUNGENS KOSTERIANA has slightly pendulous branches.

PICEA ENGELMANNII is more pyramidal, with softer foliage.

44. PINUS HALEPENSIS (Aleppo pine): This mild to warm climate pine is round-headed and quite open in growth habit. Although it can be held to a height of 30 to 35 feet for a long time, it is essentially a large tree, best used in the background on large properties. It tolerates heat, strong winds, and considerable drought.

45. PINUS MUGO (Swiss mountain pine): This hardy little conifer is almost a *must* for small and medium-size gardens. It is shrub-like in form and unpredictable in size if allowed to grow freely. However, a little careful pruning will easily maintain it at 3 or 4 feet in height, with a similar width. It is roundish with several slender vertical trunks, and the leaves are dark green. PINUS MUGO has many uses, such as at the end of the patio in Figure 1.1 and at the right of the front lawn in Figure 2.1.

46. PINUS MUGO MUGHUS PROSTRATA: This is a beautiful little conifer, 16 or 18 inches high with a 20-inch spread. It is perfect for rock gardens, beside a short path, in a patio planting well, near a water feature, or as a tub plant.

47. PINUS PARVIFLORA (Japanese white pine): This is a medium-hardy tree with bluish-green needles and relatively dense growth. Although it can be held within the 30 to 35 foot range for

several years, it will eventually grow to 60 or 65 feet. Therefore, it is best used on larger landscapes as a background, framing, or large lawn tree.

48. PINUS PINEA (Italian stone pine): This mild to warm climate conifer becomes massive at ground level and branches upward to form a spreading crown. It has long, light green needles that give it a dense appearance. Because of its 25- to 45-foot height range and its wide spread at the base, this pine should be restricted to large landscapes—parks, industrial designing, campuses, estates—and used as a distant specimen or accent tree.

49. PINUS RESINOSA (Red pine): This is a hardy, rapid-growing, pyramidal tree with glossy needles 5 or 6 inches long. It will reach 45 or 50 feet in a few years and grow taller if permitted, making it useful on medium to large properties for framing, background, and shade.

50. PINUS STROBUS (White pine): This hardy pine has blue-green, soft-appearing needles that are attractively distributed. It can be held within a 45 foot height range for a long time but, if uncontrolled, will eventually reach 75 or 80 feet. It may be used in locations such as the background corner in Figure 1.1.

51. PINUS STROBUS NANA: This is a hardy shrub form with bluish-green, soft-textured needles. When 5 or 6 feet in height, it is 5 or 6 feet in width. It is easily controlled by careful pruning and is usable in many locations—to frame the pool area surfacing in Figure 3.7, for example.

Photo 7.12

Pinus mugo is strong and effective in any shrub grouping.

52. PINUS SYLVESTRIS (Scotch pine): This fine conifer is a hardy and strong-charactered tree that can be held within the 25-foot range for many years and within 40 feet indefinitely, thus permitting its use in medium-size gardens. The needles are twisted, quite stiff, and slightly bluish-green. Use Scotch pine as a background specimen (as in Figure 1.2), to terminate a cross axis, or along vista lines (as in Figure 3.14).

53. PINUS SYLVESTRIS NANA GLAUCA (Dwarf blue Scot): This hardy dwarf has a bushy form and bluish-green needles. It is particularly attractive in the 5- to 7-foot height range. Use it as a foundation plant, in a coniferous shrub grouping, near the patio or pool, or in the back part of the rock garden.

54. TAXUS BACCATA (English yew): Hardy, densely branched, and heavily foliaged, this conifer grows upright and forms a broad head. Pruning will keep it within a 15- to 20-foot height range for several years. The leaves are about an inch long and dark green. Use English yew in the background, in screening and wind-retardant groupings, near the corner of the house, or in the front yard as indicated in Figure 1.1.

55. TAXUS BACCATA ADPRESSA: This hardy shrub is densely covered with very short, dark green leaves. At a height of 4 or 5 feet, it is excellent as a foundation plant or in a conifer grouping; for example, in the strip beside the driveway in Figure 3.7.

56. TAXUS BACCATA FASTIGIATA (Irish yew): This is a beautiful, medium-hardy, upright, and densely columnar shrub to small tree with short, dark green leaves and closely arranged vertical branches. It is relatively slow-growing and will stay in the 7- to 10-foot height range for many years. Eventually, it will develop into a small tree. Irish yews form strong vertical lines and must be used wisely in the garden—principally as accents or prominent plants in a conifer grouping (as in Figure 3.12).

57. TAXUS BACCATA REPANDENS: This shrub is informally sprawling and densely foliaged, 2 to 4 feet high, with an 8- or 10-foot spread. It is ideal where large rocks are used in the design on prominent slopes, or picturesquely trailing along and over walls.

TAXUS BACCATA PYGMAEA is an elegant little mound-like yew for the rock garden. Use it at a turn in a stepping-stone path or in a planting beside a patio.

58. TAXUS CANADENSIS (Ground hemlock): This one is a hardy, straggly, low-growing shrub with relatively long, dark green leaves. It ranges around 3 or 4 feet in height. Use it in locations similar to that near the driveway in Figure 3.7.

59. TAXUS CUSPIDATA (Japanese yew): This is a very hardy, upright-growing, tall shrub or tree that has many uses in the landscape because it can easily be controlled by pruning. CUSPIDATA and its varieties are probably the Japanese yews most widely used. CUSPIDATA can be maintained as 6- to 8-foot shrub. Uncontrolled, it will eventually grow into a 30- or 35-foot tree. Use it principally in background or side groupings where some size is permitted. It is an excellent hedge plant.

60. TAXUS CUSPIDATA DENSA: This variety has a compact form, is 3 or 4 feet high, and has rich, dark green leaves densely arranged on upright branches. It has many uses—as foundation planting, to frame an entrance, as an accent, or in conifer groupings. There are several appropriate places in the three small gardens in Figure 3.13.

61. TAXUS CUSPIDATA NANA: This excellent variety of Japanese yew is an irregularly growing shrubby form with 3 or 4 feet of height and some spread. Use it in locations similar to those suggested for TAXUS BACCATA REPANDENS.

62. TAXUS CUSPIDATA MINIMA: This fine creeping variety is 12 to 18 inches high and has a 5- or 6-foot spread. Use it over walls, on small slopes, and in rock gardens.

63. THUJA KORAIENSIS: This shrub-type arborvitae is usually low-growing, with branches close to the ground. It will be 4 or 5 feet high for several years. Occasionally one will assume an excellent 6- to 10-foot pyramidal form. These plants are useful at the sides of the front yard or in a background setting of importance.

64. THUJA OCCIDENTALIS ELLWANGERIANA AUREA: This is a striking, somewhat pyramidal, and compact conifer with a golden sheen to its foliage. The heavily foliaged branches form flat sprays that grow at irregular angles, giving it a vibrant effect. It is a hardy grower and, at 3 or 4 feet, it has many uses in the garden, such as at the right side of the back lawn in Figure 3.12, or to frame a flower panel.

65. THUJA OCCIDENTALIS FASTIGIATA: This columnar arborvitae has bright green foliage, and its clean, 8- to 18-foot, vertical lines fit beautifully into the background of any large shrub grouping. Planted closely together, this variety has few equals as a clipped or unclipped hedge and, if allowed to grow tall, a screen or windbreak.

66. THUGA OCCIDENTALIS GLOBOSA (Globe arborvitae): This is an old-time dwarf American arborvitae that is still widely used. It forms a dense globe 3 or 4 feet high (eventually more). Use it as an accent plant, in a large rock garden, to change the lines of a conifer grouping, or to frame a structural feature. It is very effective in formal design.

Photo 7.13

Two *thuja orientalis aurea nana* frame a doorway.

67. THUJA OCCIDENTALIS PUMILA: This is a dwarf, dense form of arborvitae with deep green leaves. At 1 or 2 feet in height, it is excellent for use in small areas of special interest.

68. THUJA OCCIDENTALIS RECURVA NANA: This dwarf arborvitae has attractively recurved branches. It will stay within the 3- to 4-foot range almost indefinitely. Use this conifer adjacent to a driveway, near a patio or pool, or in a rock garden.

69. THUJA ORIENTALS AUREA NANA: This hardy arborvitae is a small, modified oval of golden foliage arranged in consecutive vertical sprays laid tightly together. It is an intriguing little accent or special purpose plant. It will remain in the 2- or 3-foot range for a long time. Use it in places similar to the patio planting well in Figure 3.8, in patio edging strips, to help frame a doorway or in small retirement gardens (see Figure 3.13).

70. THUJA ORIENTALIS BEVERLEYENSIS: This is a medium-hardy, columnar, and quite compact shrub. The tips of the small branches have a light golden sheen. At 6 or 7 feet, it is very attractive near the corners of a house, to frame a garden structure, to form a vertical line in a conifer grouping, or in an accent location in your garden.

71. THUJA ORIENTALIS CONSPICUA: An upright and compact conifer of strong character, this arborvitae has a delicate tone of gold in its foliage. In the 4-foot range, it brightens any shrub group.

72. THUJA ORIENTALIS ELEGANTISSIMA: This is a slow-growing and somewhat columnar arborvitae with dense and casually arranged yellowish-green foliage sprays in erratically arranged vertical planes—an unusually elegant variety. It will remain in the 4- to 7-foot range for several years. Use it in side plantings, in the front yard, for framing, foundation planting, or in accent locations.

73. TSUGA CANADENSIS NANA: This plant is a very hardy, low-growing, and convexly spreading form of hemlock. The branches and branchlets arch down a little and carry what appears to be an over-abundance of short leaves. This attractive shrub can be maintained within an 18- to 24-inch height range with a 2-foot spread. It is excellent in rock gardens or areas that will accommodate spreading plants of some height.

74. TSUGA CANADENSIS PENDULA: This is a fine little hemlock that is slow-growing and well-formed with ascending branches that droop at the tips. Heavily covered with attractive foliage, it is 1 to 3 feet high and has a 2- or 3-foot spread. Trail this one over walls or down short slopes; use it in a rock garden, or to turn a stepping-stone path.

75. TSUGA MERTENSIANA (Mountain hemlock): This gracefully formed tree can be held within a 25- to 40-foot height range for several years by pruning. Eventually it becomes taller. Its leaves, a brilliant bluish-green, are arranged in a unique spiral around the slightly pendulous branches. This variety prefers cool, moist parts of the country. Use it principally for framing, background, and screening, or in country (farm) landscaping (see Figure 3.14).

CONIFERS—EASTERN SECTIONS (ZONES 5–6–7)

The following are some conifer shrubs and trees for the eastern sections of the country—zones 5–6–7. There are species and varieties of listed conifers adaptable to the favorable growing areas of the zones indicated. Refer to them in the preceding numbered conifer description list and in the Conifer Selection Chart on page 148.

Plant Number	Plant Name	Controlled Height	Zone
1	Cedrus deodara	30′	7
3	Chamaecyparis lawsoniana elwoodii	6′	6–7
4	Chamaecyparis obtusa	7′	5–6–7
6	Chamaecyparis obtusa compacta	4′	5–6–7
7	Chamaecyparis obtusa		

	gracilis	5'	5–6–7
8	Chamaecyparis obtusa nana	3'	5–6–7
9	Chamaecyparis obtusa pygmaea	1'	5–6–7
10	Chamaecyparis pisifera filifera	8'	5–6–7
12	Chamaecyparis pisifera filifera nana	3'	5–6–7
13	Chamaecyparis pisifera plumosa	8'	5–6–7
14	Chamaecyparis pisifera squarrosa minima	2'	5–6–7
15	Juniperus chinensis	25'	5–6–7
16	Juniperus chinensis armstrongii	3'	6–7
17	Juniperus chinensis columnaris glauca	12'	5–6–7
18	Juniperus chinensis globosa	3'	5–6–7
19	Juniperus chinensis japonica	4'	5–6–7
20	Juniperus chinensis pfitzeriana	4'	5–6–7
22	Juniperus chinensis sargentii	1'	5–6–7
23	Juniperus chinensis torulosa	8'	7
24	Juniperus communis compressa	4'	5–6–7
25	Juniperus conferta	2'	6–7
26	Juniperus horizontalis	1'	5–6–7
27	Juniperus horizontalis douglasii	1'	5–6–7
28	Juniperus horizontalis plumosa	2'	5–6–7
29	Juniperus occidentalis	30'	6–7
30	Juniperus procumbens	1'	5–6–7
31	Juniperus sabina	5'	5–6–7
32	Juniperus sabina fastigiata	5'	5–6–7
33	Juniperus sabina tamariscifolia	2'	5–6–7
34	Juniperus scopulorum	35'	5–6–7
35	Juniperus squamata meyeri	4'	5–6–7
36	Juniperus virginiana reptans	2'	5–6–7
37	Picea abies nidiformis	3'	5–6–7
38	Picea abies procumbens	2'	5–6–7
39	Picea abies pygmaea	1'	5–6–7
40	Picea abies remontii	4'	5–6–7
41	Picea glauca conica	5'	5–6–7
42	Picea pungens	20'	5–6–7
45	Pinus mugo	4'	5–6–7
46	Pinus mugo mughus prostrata	2'	5–6–7
47	Pinus parviflora	35'	5–6–7
48	Pinus pinea	45'	7
49	Pinus resinosa	50'	5–6–7
50	Pinus strobus	50'	5–6–7
51	Pinus strobus nana	6'	5–6–7
52	Pinus sylvestris	25'	5–6–7
54	Taxus baccata	15'	5–6–7
55	Taxus baccata adpressa	5'	5–6–7
56	Taxus baccata fastigiata	8'	6–7
57	Taxus baccata repandens	4'	6–7
58	Taxus canadensis	3'	5–6–7
59	Taxus cuspidata	7'	5–6–7
60	Taxus cuspidata densa	4'	5–6–7
62	Taxus cuspidata minima	2'	5–6–7

63	Thuja koraiensis	4'	5–6–7
64	Thuja occidentalis ellwangeriana aurea	4'	5–6–7
65	Thuja occidentalis fastigiata	8'	5–6–7
66	Thuja occidentalis globosa	4'	5–6–7
67	Thuja occidentalis pumila	2'	5–6–7
68	Thuja occidentalis recurva nana	3'	5–6–7
69	Thuja orientalis aurea nana	2'	6–7
71	Thuja orientalis conspicua	4'	6–7
72	Thuja orientalis elegantissima	6'	6–7
73	Tsuga canadensis nana	2'	5–6–7
74	Tsuga canadensis pendula	2'	5–6–7
75	Tsuga mertensiana	25'	5–6–7

CONIFERS—CENTRAL SECTIONS (ZONES 5–6–7)

The following are some conifer shrubs and trees for the central sections of the country—zones 5–6–7. There are species and varieties of listed conifers adaptable to the favorable growing areas of the zones indicated. Refer to them in the preceding numbered conifer description list and in the Conifer Selection Chart on page 148.

Plant Number	Plant Name	Controlled Height	Zone
10	Chamaecyparis pisifera filifera	8'	5–6–7
11	Chamaecyparis pisifera filifera aurea	7'	5–6–7
12	Chamaecyparis pisifera filifera nana	3'	5–6–7
15	Juniperus chinensis	25'	5–6–7
18	Juniperus chinensis globosa	3'	5–6–7
19	Juniperus chinensis japonica	4'	5–6–7
20	Juniperus chinensis pfitzeriana	4'	5–6–7
24	Juniperus communis compressa	4'	5–6–7
26	Juniperus horizontalis	1'	5–6–7
27	Juniperus horizontalis douglasii	1'	5–6–7
28	Juniperus horizontalis plumosa	2'	5–6–7
30	Juniperus procumbens	1'	5–6–7
31	Juniperus sabina	5'	5–6–7
33	Juniperus sabina tamariscifolia	2'	5–6–7
34	Juniperus scopulorum	35'	5–6–7
37	Picea abies nidiformis	3'	5–6–7
38	Picea abies procumbens	2'	5–6–7
39	Picea abies pygmaea	1'	5–6–7

40	Picea abies remontii	4'	5–6–7
41	Picea glauca conica	5'	5–6–7
42	Picea pungens	20'	5–6–7
43	Picea pungens glauca	15'	5–6–7
45	Pinus mugo	4'	5–6–7
46	Pinus mugo mughus prostrata	2'	5–6–7
49	Pinus resinosa	50'	5–6–7
50	Pinus strobus	50'	5–6–7
52	Pinus sylvestris	25'	5–6–7
53	Pinus sylvestris nana glauca	5'	5–6–7
58	Taxus canadensis	3'	5–6–7
63	Thuja koraiensis	4'	5–6–7
65	Thuja occidentalis fastigiata	8'	5–6–7
73	Tsuga canadensis nana	2'	5–6–7
74	Tsuga canadensis pendula	2'	5–6–7
75	Tsuga mertensiana	25'	5–6–7

CONIFERS—WESTERN SECTIONS (ZONES 2 THROUGH 10)

The following are some conifer shrubs and trees for the western sections of the country—zones 2–3–4–5–6–7–8–9–10. There are species and varieties of listed conifers adaptable to the favorable growing areas of the zones indicated. Refer to them in the preceding numbered conifer description list and in the Conifer Selection Chart on page 148.

Plant Number	Plant Name	Controlled Height	Zone
1	Cedrus deodara	30'	7–8–9–10
4	Chamaecyparis obtusa	7'	5–6–7–8–9
6	Chamaecyparis obtusa compacta	4'	5–6–7–8–9
9	Chamaecyparis obtusa pygmaea	1'	5–6–7–8–9
10	Chamaecyparis pisifera filifera	8'	4–5–6–7–8–9
12	Chamaecyparis pisifera filifera nana	3'	4–5–6–7–8–9
13	Chamaecyparis pisifera plumosa	8'	5–6–7–8–9
14	Chamaecyparis pisifera squarrosa minima	2'	5–6–7–8–9
15	Juniperus chinensis	25'	4–5–6–7–8–9
16	Juniperus chinensis armstrongii	3'	6–7–8–9–10
18	Juniperus chinensis globosa	3'	5–6–7–8–9
20	Juniperus chinensis pfitzeriana	4'	4–5–6–7–8–9
22	Juniperus chinensis sargentii	1'	4–5–6–7–8–9
23	Juniperus chinensis torulosa	8'	7–8–9–10
24	Juniperus communis compressa	4'	2–3–4–5–6–7–8
25	Juniperus conferta	2'	6–7–8–9–10
26	Juniperus horizontalis	1'	3–4–5–6–7–8–9
27	Juniperus horizontalis douglasii	1'	3–4–5–6–7–8–9
29	Juniperus occidentalis	30'	6–7–8–9–10
30	Juniperus procumbens	1'	4–5–6–7–8–9
33	Juniperus sabina tamariscifolia	2'	5–6–7–8–9–10
34	Juniperus scopulorum	35'	4–5–6–7–8–9–10
35	Juniperus squamata meyeri	4'	4–5–6–7–8–9–10
37	Picea abies nidiformis	3'	4–5–6–7–8–9
40	Picea abies remontii	4'	4–5–6–7–8–9
43	Picea pungens glauca	15'	2–3–4–5–6–7–8
45	Pinus mugo	4'	3–4–5–6–7–8–9
47	Pinus parviflora	35'	5–6–7–8–9
50	Pinus strobus	50'	4–5–6–7–8–9
52	Pinus sylvestris	25'	2–3–4–5–6–7–8
53	Pinus sylvestris nana glauca	5'	4–5–6–7–8
54	Taxus baccata	15'	5–6–7–8–9
56	Taxus baccata fastigiata	8'	6–7–8–9
58	Taxus canadensis	3'	3–4–5–6–7–8–9
59	Taxus cuspidata	30'	5–6–7–8–9
61	Taxus cuspidata nana	4'	5–6–7–8–9
62	Taxus cuspidata minima	2'	5–6–7–8–9

66	Thuja occidentalis globosa	4'	5–6–7–8–9
67	Thuja occidentalis pumila	2'	5–6–7–8–9
69	Thuja orientalis aurea nana	2'	6–7–8–9–10
70	Thuja orientalis beverleyensis	7'	6–7–8–9–10
72	Thuja orientalis elegantissima	6'	6–7–8–9–10
73	Tsuga canadensis pendula	2'	3–4–5–6–7–8
75	Tsuga mertensiana	25'	4–5–6–7–8

43	Picea pungens glauca	15'	2–3–4
45	Pinus mugo	4'	3–4
46	Pinus mugo mughus prostrata	2'	3–4
49	Pinus resinosa	50'	3–4
50	Pinus strobus	50'	4
51	Pinus strobus nana	6'	3–4
52	Pinus sylvestris	25'	2–3–4
53	Pinus sylvestris nana glauca	5'	4
58	Taxus canadensis	3'	3–4
63	Thuja koraiensis	4'	4
64	Thuja occidentalis ellwangeriana aurea	4'	4
65	Thuja occidentalis fastigiata	8'	4
73	Tsuga canadensis nana	2'	3–4
74	Tsuga canadensis pendula	2'	4
75	Tsuga mertensiana	25'	4

CONIFERS—NORTHERN SECTIONS (ZONES 2–3–4)

The following are some conifer shrubs and trees for the northern sections of the country—zones 2–3–4. There are species and varieties of listed conifers adaptable to the favorable growing areas of the zones indicated. Refer to them in the preceding numbered conifer description list and in the Conifer Selection Chart on page 148.

CONIFERS—SOUTHERN SECTIONS (ZONES 8–9–10)

The following are some conifer shrubs and trees for the southern sections of the country—zones 8–9–10. There are species and varieties of listed conifers adaptable to the favorable growing areas of the zones indicated. Refer to them in the preceding numbered conifer description list and in the Conifer Selection Chart on page 148.

Plant Number	Plant Name	Controlled Height	Zone
10	Chamaecyparis pisifera filifera	8'	4
11	Chamaecyparis pisifera filifera aurea	7'	4
12	Chamaecyparis pisifera filifera nana	3'	4
15	Juniperus chinensis	25'	4
20	Juniperus chinensis pfitzeriana	4'	4
21	Juniperus chinensis pfitzeriana aurea	3'	4
22	Juniperus chinensis sargentii	1'	4
24	Juniperus communis compressa	4'	2–3–4
26	Juniperus horizontalis	1'	3–4
27	Juniperus horizontalis douglasii	1'	3–4
28	Juniperus horizontalis plumosa	2'	3–4
30	Juniperus procumbens	1'	4
31	Juniperus sabina	5'	4
34	Juniperus scopulorum	35'	4
37	Picea abies nidiformis	3'	4
38	Picea abies procumbens	2'	4
39	Picea abies pygmaea	1'	4
40	Picea abies remontii	4'	4
41	Picea glauca conica	5'	3–4
42	Picea pungens	20'	2–3–4

Plant Number	Plant Name	Controlled Height	Zone
1	Cedrus deodara	30'	8–9–10
3	Chamaecyparis lawsoniana elwoodii	6'	8–9
4	Chamaecyparis obtusa	7'	8–9
10	Chamaecyparis pisifera filifera	8'	8–9
13	Chamaecyparis pisifera plumosa	8'	8–9
14	Chamaecyparis pisifera squarrosa minima	2'	8–9
15	Juniperus chinensis	25'	8–9
16	Juniperus chinensis armstrongii	3'	8–9–10
18	Juniperus chinensis globosa	3'	8–9
19	Juniperus chinensis japonica	4'	8–9
20	Juniperus chinensis pfitzeriana	4'	8–9
22	Juniperus chinensis sargentii	1'	8–9
23	Juniperus chinensis torulosa	8'	8–9–10
24	Juniperus communis compressa	4'	8–9
25	Juniperus conferta	2'	8–9–10
26	Juniperus horizontalis	1'	8–9
29	Juniperus occidentalis	30'	8–9–10
31	Juniperus sabina	5'	8–9
33	Juniperus sabina tamariscifolia	2'	8–9–10

34	Juniperus scopulorum	35'	8–9–10
35	Juniperus squamata meyeri	4'	8–9–10
37	Picea abies nidiformis	3'	8–9
38	Picea abies procumbens	2'	8–9
44	Pinus halepensis	30'	8–9–10
45	Pinus mugo	4'	8–9
47	Pinus parviflora	35'	8–9
50	Pinus strobus	50'	8–9

54	Taxus baccata	15'	8–9
56	Taxus baccata fastigiata	8'	8–9
59	Taxus cuspidata	30'	8–9
66	Thuja occidentalis globosa	4'	8–9
69	Thuja orientalis aurea nana	2'	8–9–10
70	Thuja orientalis beverleyensis	7'	8–9–10
71	Thuja orientalis conspicua	4'	8–9–10

8

Vines and Ground Covers

VINES FOR YOUR GARDEN

There are a number of garden situations in which trees and shrubs are not adequate to meet landscape demands. A rough bank, the wall of a garden structure, a pergola or similar lath structure are but a few.

Vines often are the answer. In very warm areas, a vine-covered garden structure offers cool and relaxing comfort. Some vines—*Ficus pumila,* for example—create interesting patterns as they creep up and along a wall. Clematis delicately twines itself around and up a pillar to soften the structure and display beautiful flowers. Many vines present brilliant autumn foliage effects, and there is great variety in form, foliage, and color. Some vines, such as Boston ivy, have self-clinging devices, but the majority require means of attachment to walls and other vertical structures.

Like all other plants in your garden, the vines you select must be adaptable to your particular climate. They must also be suitable for their locations and perform prescribed functions.

Selecting Vines

Study your garden design carefully to determine where you might like to use vines, and what sort of vine (flowering, climbing, evergreen or deciduous, etc.) would be appropriate in these various situations. To choose the right vine for each location, consult the Vine Selection Chart and then read the descriptions of suitable vines in the following alphabetical list.

The Vine Selection Chart is used in exactly the same way as earlier Selection Charts. For review, let's work through the example at the bottom of the chart. Assume you live in *zone 5* and want a vine to *climb up a fence* in a location that receives *full sun.* You want an *evergreen* vine of *medium spread* that bears *flowers.*

> M (medium)--zone 5—Fs (full sun)— Fl (flowers)—Fe (fence)

By moving your selection strip up the chart, you find five vines that meet your basic requirements: numbers 1, 16, 18, 26, 31. To make your final selection, read the descriptions of these plants in the alphabetical description list.

VINE SELECTION CHART

No.	Name of Vine	Low 5–15'	Medium 15–25'	Tall 25–50'	Zone 2	3	4	5	6	7	8	9	10	Hawaii	Part shade	Full sun	Deciduous	Evergreen	Flowering	Fragrant	Over structures	Up high walls	Along low walls	Along fences	On trellises	On rock walls	Ground covers	Banks—slopes	Up pillars
1	Akebia quinata	+	+				+								+	+		+	+	+			+	+	−	+		+	+
2	Allamanda		+	+								+	+			+		+	+	+	+		+	+	−	+			+
3	Beaumontia		+	+								+		+		+		+	+	+		+	+	+	+	+			
4	Boston ivy		+	+			+									+	+					+	+						
5	Bougainvillaea	+	+									+	+			+			+		+	+	+	+	+				
6	Bower actinidia	+	+	+					+						+	+	+	+				+	+	+				+	+
7	Cape-honeysuckle	+	+									+			+	+	+	+	+	+		+	+	+	+	+			+
8	Clematis, evergreen	+	+							+					+	+	+	+	+	+			+	+	+	+			+
9	Clematis, deciduous	+	+					+								+	+		+			+	+	+	+			+
10	Climbing hydrangea		+	+				+							+		+	+		+	+	+	+	+			+
11	Climbing roses	+	+	+		+									+	+	+		+	+	+	+	+				+
12	Creeping fig	+	+	+								+			+			+						+			
13	Cup-of-gold or chalice vine	+	+										+	+	+		+	+	+	+		+	+	+			
14	Dutchman's pipe			+					+						+	+	+		+			+	+	+			
15	English ivy	+	+	+					+						+	+		+	+			+		+		+	+	+
16	Honeysuckle, trumpet	+	+	+				+							+	+		+	+	+	+	+	+	+	+		+	+
17	Jade vine	+										+	+	+	+		+	+	+			+	+	+		
	Example Vine		M					5							S		Ev	Fl				Fe					

Example vine: Requirements—medium spread, full sun, evergreen, flowering, to climb over fence, zone 5. Mark your zone and requirements on paper strip.

Move it up over the chart. Match reasonably closely. Find several. Turn to numbered descriptions for decision. Vines located—numbers 1, 16, 18, 26, 31.

Zoning: Estimated zone-temperature range of each plant's hardiness.

VINE SELECTION CHART

No.	Name of Vine	Height Range: Low 5-15'	Medium 15-25'	Tall 25-50'	Zone (2-10, Hawaii)	Part shade	Full sun	Deciduous	Evergreen	Flowering	Fragrant	Over structures	Up high walls	Along low walls	Along fences	On trellises	On rock walls	Ground covers	Banks—slopes	Up pillars
18	Japanese honeysuckle	+	+		4—Hawaii	+	+		+	+	+	+	+	+	+	+		+	+	
19	Jasmine, Arabian	+			9—Hawaii		+		+	+	+	+		+	+	+	+			+
20	Jessamine, Carolina yellow		+		8—Hawaii		+	+		+	+	+		+	+	+	+		+	+
21	Madagascar jasmine	+	+		10—Hawaii	+			+	+	+	+	+	+	+	+	+			+
22	Mexican creeper			+	9—Hawaii	+	+		+	+				+	+	+	+			+
23	Morning glory	+			7—		+			+			+	+	+	+				+
24	Passion-vine		+		8—		+	+		+	+	+		+	+	+	+	+	+	+
25	Periwinkle	+			4—	+	+		+	+	+	+	+	+	+	+	+	+	+	+
26	Silver lace-vine	+	+		4—		+	+		+		+		+	+	+	+	+	+	+
27	Star-jasmine	+			8—	+	+		+	+	+	+	+		+	+	+	+	+	+
28	Sweet pea	+			5—		+	+		+	+	+			+	+				
29	Trumpet-vine		+	+	5—	+	+	+		+		+	+	+	+	+				
30	Wax plant	+			9—				+	+	+	+		+	+	+				
31	Winter-creeper	+	+		4—		+		+	+			+	+	+	+	+		+	+
32	Wisteria, Chinese		+	+	4—		+	+		+	+		+	+	+	+				+
33	Wisteria, Japanese		+	+	4—		+	+		+	+	+	+	+	+	+				+
34	Wooden rose	+			10—Hawaii		+	+		+		+		+	+	+	+			+
	Example Vine	M			5		Fs		Ev	Fl					Fe					

Example vine: Requirements—medium spread, full sun, evergreen, flowering, to climb over fences, zone 5. Mark your zone and requirements on paper strip.

Move it up over the chart. Match reasonably closely. Find several. Turn to numbered descriptions for decision. Vines located—numbers 1, 16, 18, 26, 31.

Zoning: Estimated zone-temperature range of each plant's hardiness.

Alphabetical Descriptions of Vines

Following are descriptions and typical uses of the vines listed on the Vine Selection Chart. (Numbers match those on the Selection Chart).

1. AKEBIA QUINATA: This five-leaf akebia is a hardy, half-evergreen, vigorously growing vine, 10 to 25 feet, with compound leaves, each composed of five leaflets. The small fragrant flowers are rose-purple and appear in spring. Plant akebias in full sun or partial shade to climb walls and pillars, along fences, or on trellises. Although trim in appearance, this variety can be used as ground covers for banks and limited slopes. Prune in the fall.

2. ALLAMANDA CATHARTICA: This is a warm climate, vigorously growing evergreen, 15 to 30 feet high, with nearly oval leaves 4 to 6 inches long. It produces large, deep yellow, bell-shaped flowers in summer. These vines are elegant in the deep south and in Hawaii. Use them on garden structures, to trail along fences, on large trellises, and to meander along low walls. Pinch out growths for constant control.

3. BEAUMONTIA GRANDIFLORA: This evergreen vine grows best in warm climates, is 12 to 25 feet high, and boasts 6- or 8-inch long leaves and fragrant, white, trumpet-shaped flowers that are 4 or 5 inches long and bloom in spring. Main pruning should be done after flowering. Use it against walls, over lath structures, or along fences. It is very effective on trellises or twining up pillars.

4. BOSTON IVY (*Parthenocissus tricuspidata*): This hardy vine is tightly clinging and 15 to 50 feet long. The leaves are usually three lobed, glossy, and 6 or 7 inches long. The foliage turns to pleasing colors in autumn. This self-attaching vine will evenly cover walls of any height and size or spread up and over structures. It is especially good on hard-surface buildings, but can become a problem on houses with shingle siding. Do main pruning in late fall or winter.

5. BOUGAINVILLAEA SPECTABILIS: This tender, partially deciduous, temperate climate vine is a heavy grower, 10 to 25 feet high, with nearly oval leaves 2 or 3 inches long. It produces a massive display of pink, purple, red, or salmon-pink flowers (bracts), according to variety. They bloom in late spring and summer. Some varieties are hardier than *spectabilis*. Prune after flowering. Bougainvillaea is useful on large screening-trellises, attached to the sides of buildings, along tall fences, and over arbors and pergolas.

6. BOWER ACTINIDIA (*Actinidia arguta*): This is a hardy, rapid growing, deciduous vine, 12 to 25 feet in spread, with dense and attractive foliage. The leaves are broadly oval, 3 to 5 inches long. Clusters of nearly white flowers are followed by small plum-like fruits that are edible. These vines grow well in sun or shade and are excellent for covering shade structures, such as arbors or lath lounging shelters. They may be progressively attached to walls or grown on fences. Pinch and thin to control size.

7. CAPE-HONEYSUCKLE (*Tecomaria capensis*): This shrubby evergreen requires a warm climate. It spreads 8 to 20 feet and has compound leaves. The leaflets are nearly oval and 1 or 2 inches long. Orange-red to scarlet flowers grow in small clusters and have a long blooming season. Prune after flowering. Grow this vine on trellises or wall supports, along fences, on banks and slopes of limited size.

8. CLEMATIS, EVERGREEN (*Clematis armandii*): This is a fairly hardy and rather soft-textured vine that climbs 10 to 25 feet. It has narrow, glossy leaves 4 or 5 inches long and showy clusters of fragrant white or light pink flowers 2 inches wide. It blooms in spring and early summer. Prune after flowering. Remove old branches. Grow these vines over garden walls and along fences. They are particularly effective on trellises, on wall supports, or twining up pillars.

9. CLEMATIS, DECIDUOUS (*Clematis jackmanii*): This is a hardy and very popular clematis, 10 to 18 feet high, with pleasing foliage and elegant, 4- to 6-inch wide, violet-purple flowers. This clematis prefers full sun, but will adapt to partial shade. Its uses are similar to those of *armandii*.

Photo 8.1

Bougainvillaea valances a window.

(Home of Mr. and Mrs. Ben Irons)

Photo 8.2

English ivy (*Hedera helix*) forms patterns on a wall.

There are several magnificent and closely related hybrids—*lanuginosa, lawsoniana, lawsoniana henryii,* for example—that have larger flowers in blue, pink, purple, and white.

10. CLIMBING HYDRANGEA (*Hydrangea petiolaris*): This is a hardy, deciduous, and vigorous climber that will go up 15 to 40 feet. It progresses by means of aerial roots and is self-attaching. Its 3- or 4-inch long leaves are oval to heart-shaped, and the clusters of white flowers are 7 to 10 inches in diameter. The blooms appear in late spring. Prune in the fall for control. Use this vine on strong supports, attached to walls, along tall fences, or to cover an arbor or patio structure.

11. CLIMBING ROSES: These have world-wide popularity and find use in any garden. New innovations are offered each year. Include several in your design to adorn fences, walls, fireplace chimneys, and porches. Prune them in winter, their dormant season.

12. CREEPING FIG (*Ficus pumila*): This is a tender, mild-to-warm climate, self-attaching evergreen creeper, 10 to 30 feet, with 1- to 4-inch long leaves. The larger mature leaves are on branches that have a tendency to extend outward. An occasional trimming to remove these extended branches gives this vine a thin blanketing effect as it climbs up and spreads over walls, fences, or rock structures. If kept quite thin, it will fan out to create fascinating patterns. Prune in the fall.

13. CUP-OF-GOLD OR CHALICE VINE (*Solandra nitida*): This evergreen, warm climate vine climbs 10 to 20 feet. It has nearly oval leaves 4 to 6 inches long and bears golden, fragrant, tubular flowers 6 to 8 inches long in winter. Spectacular in Hawaii, it is excellent for porches, garden structures, fences, trellises, and pillars,

to display beautiful floral effects. Often sold as *Solandra guttata.*

14. DUTCHMAN'S-PIPE (*Aristolochia durior*): This is a hardy, vigorously growing, deciduous vine with a 15- to 30-foot spread. It has broad leaves 8 to 15 inches long, and its yellowish-brown flowers resemble a curved pipe. This vine provides dense shade when trained over arbors. Along fences and low walls, its unique flowers attract attention. Prune in winter.

15. ENGLISH IVY (*Hedera helix*): This hardy evergreen vine extends 10 to 35 feet or more and is self-attaching to ordinary surfaces. Its smooth, medium green, lobed leaves vary from 1 to 4 inches long, according to variety. Do the main pruning in the fall, but shear it anytime. English ivy has two major uses: as a quality climber and an excellent and widely used ground cover.

16. HONEYSUCKLE, TRUMPET (*Lonicera sempervirens*): This is a hardy evergreen climber suitable for temperate climates. It has a spread of 10 to 30 feet, ovalish leaves 2 or 3 inches long, and clusters of 2-inch long, trumpet-shaped flowers that are orange-red outside and yellow inside. They bloom in late spring and summer and are followed by scarlet fruit. This plant prefers sun but will tolerate shade. Use it to climb up wall supports, over arbors, along fences, and on trellises. It lends a relaxing fragrance to the atmosphere around a lounging shelter. Main pruning and thinning should be done in the fall.

17. JADE VINE (*Strongylodon macrobotrys*): This warm climate, strong-growing vine spreads 5 to 15 feet and produces unique jade-green, pea-like flowers on long clusters from late spring into summer. It blooms profusely in Hawaii. Use it on trellises, for ornamental effect on garden structures and fences, or to cascade over a rock wall. Tip or thin when necessary.

18. JAPANESE HONEYSUCKLE (*Lonicera japonica*): This is a hardy, half-evergreen vine that grows rapidly and spreads 10 to 25 feet. It has nearly oval leaves 2 or 3 inches long. The fragrant tubular flowers are purplish-white and bloom in late spring, followed by black fruit. Main pruning should be done in fall.

Lonicera japonica halliana is a vigorously spreading vine often used as a coarse ground cover in addition to supported climbing. Its flowers are white.

19. JASMINE, ARABIAN (*Jasminum sambac*): This everygreen climber requires a temperate climate, spreads 6 or 8 feet, and has nearly oval leaves 2 or 3 inches long. Its clusters of intensely fragrant flowers are white. It will not tolerate frost. This jasmine is excellent climbing over lath structures or on low walls. Grow in full sun.

20. JESSAMINE, CAROLINA (*Gelsemium sempervirens*): This is a mild to warm climate, evergreen climber, 15 to 20 feet high, with narrow leaves 3 or 4 inches long and fragrant, trumpet-shaped, yellow flowers 1 to 2 inches long. It blooms in early spring and prefers filtered shade. Prune after flowering. Plant it on trellises or train it to creep along fences. Its delightful fragrance is advantageous around arbors, covered patios, or near a water feature.

21. MADAGASCAR JASMINE (*Stephanotis floribunda*): This is a tender evergreen vine, 8 to 12 feet high, with a twining growth pattern. Its leaves are nearly oval, 3 or 4 inches long, dark green, and shiny, and it has little clusters of fragrant, waxy-white, tubular flowers 1 or 2 inches long. Stephanotis requires a no-frost climate. Do main pruning in fall. Let these exquisite vines twine up porch pillars or up supports near a doorway, on a trellis, or beside the patio. Their delicate fragrance can be detected for a considerable distance. Grow them in a greenhouse in cool climates.

22. MEXICAN CREEPER (*Antigonon leptopus*): Often called coral-vine, this warm-climate, usually deciduous vine climbs 15 to 30 feet. It has heart-shaped leaves 2 or 3 inches long and a profusion of small pink flowers in late spring and summer. The vine attaches itself by means of tendrils. Grow it on fences, arbors, and trellises or in a greenhouse in cold climates. Prune it heavily each winter.

23. MORNING GLORY (*Ipomoea*): This is a group of annual and perennial twining vines with variable cold tolerances, according to variety. Their main attraction is their beautiful flowers ranging through blue, pink, purple, white, and related combinations. Plant morning glories to twine up pillars, arbors, trellises, and trees, or support them on sides of structures. Prune for control.

24. PASSION-VINE (*Passiflora*): These tender evergreen or deciduous vines spread 10 to 20 feet and are grown principally for the beauty of their unique flowers. Although they are generally considered temperate climate vines, some varieties grow well in the colder north in protected locations. Prune in the fall. Cut unwieldy branches to juncture of shorter branches.

Passiflora alato-caerulea is a hardy evergreen hybrid with pleasing foliage and fragrant flowers. It has 4-inch wide flowers that are white outside, pink within, and blue and purple at the crown. The color blendings are exquisite.

Passiflora caerulea is a little less hardy but will withstand mildly cold climates. Its leaves are five-lobed and 4 to 6 inches wide. The 3- or 4-inch wide flowers are light pink with a blending of white and purple on the crown. The fruit is yellow.

Several varieties of *passiflora* are available, each with its fascinating arrangement of color combinations. Use them to climb along fences, over lath structures, up pillars, and on supports against walls.

25. PERIWINKLE (*Vinca minor*): Although this hardy plant is generally used as a ground cover, it can be trained as a short vine to climb up pillars, trellises, and rock walls very effectively. Its branches are slender and bear oval evergreen leaves about an inch long. Its blue flowers appear in spring. Do main pruning in the fall, but some pruning anytime.

26. SILVER LACE-VINE (*Polygonum aubertii*): This hardy deciduous or evergreen grows in temperate climates. It has a 10- to 25-foot spread, pointed ovalish leaves 2 or 3 inches long, and lace-like clusters of small, fragrant, white flowers in summer. Its slender branches have a twining habit of growth. It prefers full sun. Prune after flowering. Use it on fences, over lath structures, up pillars, or on supports beside the porch.

27. STAR-JASMINE (*Trachelospermum jasminoides*): This cool to warm climate evergreen will creep 5 to 10 feet. It has glossy, medium green leaves 2 or 3 inches long and small, fragrant, white star-like flowers in spring and into summer. It climbs by long, slender, twining stems. Grow it in sun or part shade on pillars, trellises, or along walls, or use it as a ground cover 1½ or 2 feet high. Prune for control of height and density.

Photo 8.3

Star jasmine (*Trachelospermum jasminoides*) is a brilliant many purpose plant.

28. SWEET PEA (*Lathyrus odoratus*): A hardy annual climber, this plant will grow in full sun almost anywhere if soil preparation is right and seed planting is properly timed. Grow them on 10-foot-high supports (such as coarse mesh wire). The delicate fragrance of sweet peas is incomparable, and they are available in shades of blue, lavender, orange, peach, pink, red, purple, and white. They are excellent cut flowers.

29. TRUMPET-VINE (*Campsis radicans*): This is a hardy, densely growing, deciduous, and woody vine that spreads 15 to 30 feet. Its compound leaves are composed of leaflets averaging 2 inches in length. Its clusters of 3-inch long trumpet-like flowers are orange-scarlet and very attractive. Allow trumpet-vine full sun. Use it on large and strong supports, along fences or sizable walls, up and over garden structures for shade, or to completely cover balustrades and uninteresting parts of old buildings. Prune in the fall. Remove root suckers.

30. WAX PLANT (*Hoya carnosa*): This mild to warm climate evergreen climber grows 6 to 12 feet high and has oval to oblong leaves that are 2 to 4 inches long. It produces little clusters of small, waxy, and fragrant, white flowers with pink centers in late spring and summer. Wax plants prefer partial shade. Use them to climb up pillars and small garden structures, or on trellises, shady walls, and fences. They will enhance the aesthetic value of low structures of any kind. Prune for size control.

31. WINTER-CREEPER (*Euonymus fortunei*): This is a hardy evergreen trailing-climber, 10 to 18 feet, with nearly oval leaves to 2 inches long, small greenish-white flowers, and light pink fruit. It has several interesting varieties: *acutus*, a good climber with small leaves; *coloratus*, with 1½- to 2-inch, medium green leaves that turn purplish-red in autumn; *minimus*, which has very small leaves and is relatively slow growing, and *vegetus*, a very hardy and excellent climber with broadly oval leaves around 2 inches long. Use these attractive vines in the smaller climbing locations, on rock or masonry walls, trellises, or fences.

32. WISTERIA, CHINESE (*Wisteria sinensis*): This is a fabulous and versatile deciduous and woody vine with a 15- to 40-foot spread and dense but cool and airy foliage. The compound leaves are composed of 10 or 12 leaflets 3 or 4 inches long. In springtime elegant, 8- to 12-inch long, hanging clusters of fragrant, pea-like flowers appear in lavender, pink, or white, according to variety. The flowers in the entire cluster bloom almost at the same time and usually prior to the appearance of foliage. Use wisteria to climb and spread over arbors and pergolas, along high fences, or up and over lattice-covered patios. Prune in August.

33. WISTERIA, JAPANESE (*Wisteria floribunda*): Hardier than *sinensis* but usually not as large (15 to 20 feet), this vine has large compound leaves composed of 12 to 18 nearly oval leaflets that are 2 or 3 inches long. The hanging clusters of violet flowers are 10 to 18 inches long. Uses are similar to those of *sinensis*.

34. WOODEN ROSE (*Ipomoea tuberosa*): This is a tender, tropical, perennial vine that spreads 8 to 15 feet and has leathery, dark green leaves 4 or 5 inches long and large, yellow, trumpet-like flowers that bloom in the spring. A unique flower-to-seed pod transition results when the petals recede to a wide-open position, exposing a roundish seed pod. The petals and pod dry to a light brown, which gives the flower the appearance of a carved wooden rose. The vine grows along fences and over structures. They are very impressive in Hawaii. Prune in the fall for size and shape.

VINES—NORTHERN, EASTERN, CENTRAL SECTIONS (ZONES 2–3–4–5–6–7)

Here are some vines for the northern, eastern, and central sections of the country—zones 2–3–4–5–6–7. There are species and varieties of listed vines adaptable to the favorable growing areas of the zones indicated. Refer to them in the preceding numbered vine description list and in the Vine Selection Chart on page 164. Height and spread are synonymous.

Plant Number	Plant Name	Controlled Height	Zone
1	Akebia quinata	5–25'	5–6–7
4	Boston ivy (*Parthenocissus tricuspidata*)	15–50'	4–5–6–7
6	Bower actinidia (*Actinidia arguta*)	12–25'	5–6–7
8	Clematis, evergreen (*Clematis armandii*)	10–25'	7
9	Clematis, deciduous (*Clematis jackmanii*)	10–18'	5–6–7
11	Climbing roses	5–25'	4–5–6–7
14	Dutchman's pipe (*Aristolochia durior*)	15–30'	6–7
15	English ivy (*Hedera helix*)	10–35'	6–7
16	Honeysuckle, trumpet (*Lonicera sempervirens*)	10–30'	5–6–7
18	Japanese honeysuckle (*Lonicera japonica*)	10–25'	5–6–7
25	Periwinkle (*Vinca minor*)	5–15'	5–6–7

26	Silver lace-vine (*Polygonum aubertii*)	10–25'	5–6–7
29	Trumpet vine (*Campsis radicans*)	15–30'	5–6–7
31	Winter creeper (*Euonymus radicans*)	10–18'	5–6–7
32	Wisteria, Chinese (*Wisteria sinensis*)	15–40'	5–6–7
33	Wisteria, Japanese (*Wisteria floribunda*)	15–20'	5–6–7

VINES—SOUTHERN SECTIONS (ZONES 8–9–10)

Here are some vines for the southern sections of the country—zones 8–9–10. There are species and varieties of listed vines adaptable to the favorable growing areas of the zones indicated. Refer to them in the preceding numbered vine description list and in the Vine Selection Chart on page 164. Height and spread are synonymous.

Plant Number	Plant Name	Controlled Height	Zone
1	Akebia quinata	10–25'	8–9–10
2	Allamanda cathartica	15–30'	9–10
3	Beaumontia grandiflora	12–25'	9–10
4	Boston ivy (*Parthenocissus tricuspidata*)	15–50'	8–9–10
5	Bougainvillaea spectabilis	10–25'	9–10
7	Cape honeysuckle (*Tecomaria capensis*)	8–20'	9–10
8	Clematis, evergreen (*Clematis armandii*)	10–25'	8–9–10
10	Climbing hydrangea (*Hydrangea petiolaris*)	15–40'	8–9–10
11	Climbing roses	5–25'	8–9–10
12	Creeping fig (*Ficus pumila*)	10–30'	8–9–10
13	Cup-of-gold (*Solandra nitida*)	10–20'	10
14	Dutchman's pipe (*Aristolochia durior*)	15–30'	8–9–10
17	Jade vine (*Strongylodon macrobotrys*)	5–15'	9–10
18	Japanese honeysuckle (*Lonicera japonica*)	10–25'	8–9–10
19	Jasmine, Arabian (*Jasminum sambac*)	6–8'	9–10
20	Jessamine, Carolina (*Gelsemium sempervirens*)	15–20'	8–9–10
21	Madagascar jasmine (*Stephanotis floribunda*)	8–12'	10
22	Mexican creeper (*Antigonon leptopus*)	15–30'	9–10

23	Morning glory (*Ipomoea*)	5–15'	8–9–10
24	Passion-vine (*Passiflora*)	10–20'	8–9–10
26	Silver lace-vine (*Polygonum aubertii*)	10–25'	8–9–10
27	Star jasmine (*Trachelospermum jasminoides*)	5–10'	8–9–10
29	Trumpet vine (*Campsis radicans*)	15–30'	8–9–10
30	Wax plant (*Hoya carnosa*)	6–12'	9–10
32	Wisteria	15–40'	8–9–10
34	Wooden rose (*Ipomoea tuberosa*)	8–15'	10

VINES—WESTERN SECTIONS (ZONES 4 THROUGH 10)

Here are some vines for the western sections of the country—zones 4–5–6–7–8–9–10. There are species and varieties of listed vines adaptable to the favorable growing areas of the zones indicated. Refer to them in the preceding numbered vine description list and in the Vine Selection Chart on page 164.

Plant Number	Plant Name	Controlled Height	Zone
1	Akebia quinata	10–25'	5–6–7–8–9–10
3	Beaumontia cathartica	12–25'	9–10
4	Boston ivy (*Parthenocissus tricuspidata*)	12–25'	4–5–6–7–8–9
5	Bougainvillaea spectabilis	10–25'	9–10
8	Clematis, evergreen (*Clematis armandii*)	10–25'	7–8–9–10
9	Clematis, deciduous (*Clematis jackmanii*)	10–18'	5–6–7–8–9–10
10	Climbing hydrangea (*Hydrangea petiolaris*)	15–40'	5–6–7–8–9–10
11	Climbing roses	5–25'	4–5–6–7–8–9–10
12	Creeping fig (*Ficus pumila*)	10–30'	8–9–10
15	English ivy (*Hedera helix*)	10–35'	6–7–8–9–10
16	Honeysuckle, trumpet (*Lonicera sempervirens*)	10–30'	5–6–7–8–9–10

18	Japanese honey-suckle (*Lonicera japonica*)	10–25'	5–6–7–8–9–10
23	Morning glory (*Ipomoea*)	5–15'	7–8–9–10
24	Passion vine (*Passiflora*)	10–20'	8–9–10
25	Periwinkle (*Vinca minor*)	5–15'	5–6–7–8–9–10
26	Silver lace-vine (*Polygonum aubertii*)	10–25'	5–6–7–8–9–10
27	Star-jasmine (*Trachelospermum jasminoides*)	5–10'	8–9–10
29	Trumpet-vine (*Campsis radicans*)	15–30'	5–6–7–8–9–10
31	Winter-creeper (*Euonymus radicans*)	10–18'	5–6–7–8–9–10
32	Wisteria	15–40'	5–6–7–8–9–10

GROUND COVERS IN LANDSCAPING

Ground covers play an important role in landscaping. They offer plants that not only serve well in the most difficult parts of your garden but pleasantly substitute for conventional plantings here and there as you strive to lower costs and reduce maintenance.

However, remember: ground covers are not just coverups. Each must meet the particular requirements, both functional and aesthetic, of its location. First of all, the ground covers you select must be hardy in your temperature zone. They must also cover well and be strong growers that will persist against moisture difficulties, sun, snow, rain, and erosion. In addition, they must be controllable by pruning and resistant to disease and pests. Equally important is their landscape effect. Their height, density, and color of foliage and flower must associate harmoniously with adjacent plantings.

This sounds like a sizable order for any plant to fill, but actually there are ground covers for almost any place and requirement. Your property may have a steep bank, a gentle wavy slope, or just a smooth incline. Obviously these diverse situations vary greatly in planting requirements,

and yet there are suitable, and attractive, ground covers for each. Ground covers are useful in many places besides banks and slopes. Many owners of small properties decide against lawns in their front yard. They prefer, for instance, a combination of small rock and a ground cover. If this is carefully thought through and well designed, it can be a very attractive treatment for a small front yard. Here, particularly, the ground cover must be wisely selected.

Study your own garden design. Are there areas where ground covers would be appropriate? Perhaps you have a long and narrow strip between the driveway and property line, as in Figure 3.12 on page 72. The indicated combination of shrubs and ground cover supplies the answer. Figure 3.9, on page 68, has two parallel panels, one on either side of the back lawn. A low and attractive ground cover is an excellent landscape solution. Creeping conifers are indicated here, but there are several good and appropriate ground covers that might be used. Let's select some.

Selecting Ground Covers

Begin by asking yourself what is required. In this case (Figure 3.9), it is a ground cover that is *low, carpet-like*, around *4 to 8* inches high, *creeping*, suitable for *edging*, strong charactered, and *evergreen*. It must tolerate *sun*, and we will assume this garden is in *zone 5*.

Mark these requirements on the edge of a sheet of paper under the proper columns of the Ground Cover Selection Chart (see the example at the base of the chart). Move the marked paper up the chart and note which plants match your requirements reasonably closely. Right away several ground covers are located: numbers 5, blueberry; 7, bugle; 11, cinquefoil; 31, periwinkle; 36, snow-in-summer; 39, stonecrop; 44, trailing arbutus; 49, wild strawberry.

Turn to the numbered alphabetical descriptions and read about each of these plants—its habit of growth, color, size, general characteristics, flowers, and degree of attractiveness. This information should make a final selection fairly easy.

Alphabetical Descriptions of Ground Covers

Following are descriptions and typical uses of the plants listed on the Ground Cover Selection Chart. (Numbers match those on the Selection Chart.)

GROUND COVER SELECTION CHART

No.	Name of Ground Cover	Creeping	Carpet-like	Shrubby	5-7 in	7-12 in	12-18 in	18-30 in	Sun	Part shade	Deciduous	Evergreen	Zone 2	3	4	5	6	7	8	9	10	Accent areas	Among trees	Banks	Edging	Gentle slopes	Level plots	Panels	Rock garden	Rocky slopes	Blue	Pink	Purple	Red	Rose	Yellow	White
1	Akebia	+	+			+			+	+		+				+						+	+	+	+	+	+	+					+		+		
2	Alleghany spurge	+	+	+		+			+	+	+					+							+	+	+	+	+	+					+		+		+
3	Bear-berry	+	+	+	+				+	+		+		+								+	+	+	+	+	+	+	+	+				F			+
4	Bellflower	+	+		+				+	+	+				+									+		+	+	+	+								+
5	Blueberry	+	+			+			+	+	+					+						+	+	+	+	+	+	+	+			+					
6	Bog-rosemary			+	+				+	+		+			+							+	+	+	+	+	+	+	+			+					
7	Bugle (Ajuga)	+	+			+			+	+		+			+									+	+	+	+	+	+		+						
8	Carmel creeper	+	+	+				+	+			+								+				+		+	+	+									
9	Carolina jessamine	+		+		+			+	+									+			+		+												+	
10	Chilean pernettya			+			+	+	+	+		+							+			+		+					+	+		+	+				
11	Cinquefoil	+	+		+				+	+		+			+								+	+		+	+	+	+	+						+	
12	Cornish heath	+	+			+			+	+		+					+						+	+	+	+	+	+	+			+	+				
13	Creeping mahonia	+	+	+		+			+	+		+							+			+	+	+			+	+	+	+						+	
14	Creeping juniper	+	+	+		+			+	+		+			+				+			+	+	+			+	+	+	+				F	+		
15	Dwarf rosemary	+	+	+			+		+	+		+								+		+	+	+	+	+	+	+	+	+	+		+				
16	English ivy	+	+	+		+			+	+		+						+					+	+	+	+	+	+	+	+							
17	Gazania	+	+		+				+		+								+	+	+	+		+	+	+	+	+	+	+					+	+	+
18	Geranium, ivy	+	+			+			+	+	+								+	+	+	+	+	+	+	+	+	+	+	+		+	+	+	+		+
19	Ground holly	+	+	+					+	+	+											+	+	+		+	+	+	+	+				+			+
20	Ground ivy	+	+		+				+	+	+	+				+						+		+	+	+	+	+	+	+			+				+
21	Heather, Scotch	+	+	+		+			+	+		+				+						+	+	+	+	+	+	+	+	+		+	+	+	+		+
22	Heath, spring	+	+	+		+			+	+		+				+						+	+	+	+	+	+	+	+	+		+		+	+		
23	Honeysuckle, Hall's	+	+	+		+			+	+	+					+								+		+	+	+	+	+		+		+	+		+
24	Ice plant	+	+	+	+		+		+	+		+						+				+	+	+	+	+	+	+	+	+		+	+	+			+
25	Japanese fleece-flower	+	+	+	+		+		+	+	+	+							+			+	+	+	+	+	+	+	+	+		+	+				+
	Example Ground cover	Cl	+		+				Su			Ev				5									Ed												

Example ground cover: Carpet-like, 5 to 7 inches high, in full sun, evergreen, for edging a driveway, zone 5. Mark your zone and requirements on a paper strip. Move it up over the chart. Match reasonably closely. Find several. See numbered descriptions for decision. Ground covers located—5, 7, 11, 31, 36, 39, 43, 44, 49. Zoning: Estimated zone-temperature range of each plant's hardiness.

GROUND COVER SELECTION CHART

No.	Name of Ground Cover	Creeping	Carpet-like	Shrubby	5-7 inches	7-12 inches	12-18 inches	18-30 inches	Sun	Part shade	Deciduous	Evergreen	Zone (2–10)	Accent areas	Among trees	Banks	Edging	Gentle slopes	Level plots	Panels	Rock garden	Rocky slopes	Blue	Pink	Purple	Red	Rose	Yellow	White
26	Japanese juniper	+	+	+			+		+	+		+	3–	+	+	+	+	+	+	+		+							
27	Japanese spurge	+	+			+	+		+	+		+	4–	+	+	+	+	+	+	+									+
28	Leadwort	+	+			+			+	+	+						+	+	+	+		+	+						
29	Lippia	+	+		+				+	+		+	6–		+	+	+	+	+	+		+		+					
30	Natal plum	+		+		+	+	8	+	+		+		+	+	+	+	+	+	+		+							+
31	Periwinkle	+	+		+	+	+		+	+		+	4–	+	+	+	+	+	+	+		+	+						+
32	Rockspray	+		+	+	+			+	+	+		5–	+	+	+	+	+	+	+	+	+				F			
33	Sarcococca	+	+						+	+		+	3–	+			+	+	+	+	+	+							
34	Sargents juniper	+	+	+		+			+	+		+		+			+	+	+	+	+	+							+
35	Sea-campion	+	+		+				+	+	+			+			+	+	+	+	+								+
36	Snow-in-summer	+	+		+	+			+	+		+	5	+			+	+	+	+	+	+							+
37	Star-jasmine	+		+			7		+	+		+		+	+	+	+	+	+	+		+							
38	St. Johns-wort	+	+	+	+				+	+	+		4–		+	+	+	+	+	+								+	
39	Stonecrop	+	+		+	+			+	+		+	3–		+	+	+	+	+		+	+						+	
40	Sunrose	+		+	+				+	+		+	4–		+		+	+	+		+	+						+	
41	Sweet-fern	+		+		+		+	+	+	+		2–	+		+	+	+	+	+	+	+						+	
42	Tamarix juniper	+	+	+	+	+		+	+	+		+	4–	+		+	+	+	+	+	+	+							
43	Thyme	+	+		+				+	+		+			+		+	+	+	+	+				+				
44	Trailing arbutus	+	+		+	+				+		+	2–	+	+	+	+	+	+			+		+					+
45	Trailing lantana	+	+		+		7		+			+				+	+	+	+		+	+			+				
46	Twin-flower	+		+	+	+	+			+		+	2–	+	+	+	+	+	+	+		+		+			+		
47	Waukegan juniper	+	+	+		+	+		+	+		+	2–	+	+	+	+	+	+	+	+	+			+				
48	Wild ginger	+	+		+				+	+		+	3–		+	+	+	+	+	+	+	+			+				
49	Wild strawberry	+	+	+	+	+			+	+		+	4–		+	+	+	+	+	+	+	+				F			
50	Wintercreeper	+	+		+		+			+	+		4–	+		+	+	+	+	+		+							+
	Example Ground cover		Cl						Su			Ev	5				Ed												

Example ground cover: Carpet-like, 5 to 7 inches high, in full sun, evergreen, for edging a driveway, zone 5. Mark your zone and requirements on a strip of paper. Move it up over the chart. Match reasonably closely. Find several. See numbered descriptions for decision. Ground covers located—5, 7, 11, 31, 36, 39, 43, 44, 49. Zoning: Estimated zone-temperature range of each plant's hardiness.

Photo 8.4

Creeping conifers provide an interesting and permanent ground cover.

1. AKEBIA (*Akebia quinata*): The excellent character and growth habit of this vine qualifies it as a commendable ground cover. See description in section on vines.

2. ALLEGHANY SPURGE (*Pachysandra procumbens*): This is a hardy, low-growing (to 10 inches high), deciduous plant with medium green, oval leaves 3 or 4 inches long, and light purple to nearly white flowers in spring. It spreads by means of trailing branches and is useful for steep or gentle slopes, to cover level areas, or to wander at the base of trees.

3. BEAR-BERRY (*Arctostaphylos uva-ursi*): This is a very hardy evergreen creeper, 8 to 10 inches high, with small ovalish and rather thick leaves and small white to pinkish flowers. Its attractive berries are red, and it grows in sun or partial shade. Use it on most slopes or under trees.

4. BELLFLOWER (*Campanula portenschlagiana*): Often sold as *Campanula muralis*, this 5- or 6-inch high, partially deciduous creeper forms a thin, carpet-like, ground cover with an abundance of lavender-blue bell-shaped flowers in late spring and summer. Use it for edging along the driveway or patio, in small accent areas, in the planting strip along the top of a rock wall, beside an ascending path, or in a rock garden.

5. BLUEBERRY (*Vaccinium angustifolium*): This is a very hardy and spreading plant, 6 or 7 inches high, with small ovalish leaves, white flowers, and blue berries. *Vaccinium* requires acid soil, but will grow well in full sun or partial

shade. It can be used almost anywhere that a low ground cover is indicated.

6. BOG-ROSEMARY (*Andromeda polifolia*): This very hardy, evergreen shrub is low-growing and spreading, 10 to 12 inches high, with 1-inch long leaves and terminal clusters of small pink flowers. Use it in ground covering groups in front of taller shrubs or trees or to cover smooth and gentle slopes.

7. BUGLE (*Ajuga reptans*): This popular creeper is a low-growing, semi-evergreen with narrow ovalish leaves and flowers that grow in dense spikes 5 or 6 inches high. It forms a blanket of blue-purple, pink, or white, according to variety. Bugle does well in sun or partial shade and is appropriate on large or small slopes, on banks or level areas, for edging, or among trees.

8. CARMEL CREEPER (*Ceanothus griseus horizontalis*): This is a beautiful, low-growing, evergreen creeping shrub that flourishes in temperate climates and requires full sun and considerable moisture. It averages 2 feet high and spreads 5 to 10 feet, displaying generous clusters of bright blue flowers. Use it to cover all types of slopes, borders, large and long panels.

9. CAROLINA JESSAMINE (*Gelsemium sempervirens*): Carolina yellow jessamine is a moderately hardy evergreen vine that serves as an excellent ground cover. See description under vines. As a ground cover, use it on rocky and other large sloping areas.

10. CHILEAN PERNETTYA (*Pernettya mucronata*): This low-growing shrub is often planted as a ground cover to edge driveways and to cover gentle slopes or small auxiliary areas. See description in section on shrubs.

11. CINQUEFOIL (*Potentilla verna*): This very hardy and low-matting plant covers by stems that spread. It has a similarity to strawberry. The leaves are palmate, five- to seven-parted, and the flowers are deep yellow and appear in spring. Use cinquefoil on small, smooth and gentle slopes or in ground covered edgings and other limited areas.

12. CORNISH HEATH (*Erica vagans*): This moderately hardy, low-growing evergreen is wide-spreading and has many little, shrubby branches with tiny, slender leaves and small, purplish-pink flowers in summer. Plant it on slopes, to cover narrow panels at the top of walls, in strips along driveways, or for special or accent areas near a garden feature.

13. CREEPING MAHONIA (*Mahonia repens*): This is a hardy shrub-type creeper 10 to 12 inches high that is often planted as a ground cover. See description in section on shrubs. Use it to cover slopes and level areas or under trees.

14. CREEPING JUNIPER (*Juniperus horizontalis*): This very hardy, low-growing and spreading, coniferous evergreen is often used as a ground cover. For a description, see the section on conifers. Consider using creeping juniper to cover slopes or sections of the front or back yard, such as the two parallel panels in Figure 3.9, page 68.

15. DWARF ROSEMARY (*Rosmarinus officinalis prostratus*): This temperate climate shrub is low-growing and spreading, which makes it an excellent ground cover. See section on shrubs for description. It is often used to cover slopes and special garden areas.

16. ENGLISH IVY (*Hedera helix*): Ground covering is a major use for this well-known vine. For description, see the section on vines. Because it tolerates shade, English ivy may be used to cover banks and slopes of any size or shape or any other sizable area where ground coverage is desirable. It requires considerable moisture and fertile soil for good results.

17. GAZANIA: This low-growing, mild to warm climate perennial is one of the most colorful ground covers in use. Planted a foot apart, gazanias spread and produce a thin blanket of orange, red, or yellow daisy-like flowers from late spring to early fall. Use them to cover slopes, edgings, panels, or wherever a blaze of color is permissible.

18. GERANIUM, IVY (*Pelargonium peltatum*): This temperate climate, deciduous, trailing plant grows 8 or 10 inches high and has lobed leaves and great quantities of lavender, pink, red, rose, or white flowers on long-stemmed clusters in late spring, summer, and early fall. Plant ivy geraniums in full sun to cover banks, slopes, level areas, edgings, or use them in accent areas for striking and long-lasting color.

19. GROUND HOLLY (*Gaultheria procumbens*): This hardy evergreen is low-growing and spreading, 4 or 5 inches high, with nearly oval leaves 1 or 2 inches long and tiny white flowers that are followed by red fruit. It is called wintergreen in some sections of the country and teaberry in others. Use it as a ground cover on gentle slopes and small areas within the central parts of the landscape. It prefers partial shade.

20. GROUND IVY (*Nepeta hederacea*): This is a hardy, creeping perennial that forms a dense ground cover 8 or 10 inches high. It has roundish leaves averaging 2 inches across and small clusters of lavender to light blue flowers. It adapts to sun or shade and is useful to cover small, gentle slopes or to partially cover areas of a large rock garden.

21. HEATHER, SCOTCH (*Calluna vulgaris*): Scotch heather comprises a group of low, creeping, evergreen varieties that vary in size, form, and color with flowers in shades of lavender, pink, red, or white. Some are carpet-like, 7 or 8 inches high, and others 15 to 20 inches high. They are exceptionally interesting. Plant them along wide edgings, on banks and slopes, in accent areas near a pool or patio, or beside large rocks and irregular drifts in the rock garden.

22. HEATH, SPRING (*Erica carnea*): Among the many species and varieties of *Erica*, spring heath is one of the very best ground covers for limited areas. It is evergreen, 8 to 12 inches high, with dark green foliage and a profusion of tiny, bright crimson flowers in spring. Use it on small slopes, beside a path, in small accent areas, or in bordering panels.

23. HONEYSUCKLE, HALL'S (*Lonicera japonica halliana*): This is a vigorous and hardy vine with nearly oval leaves 2 or 3 inches long and fragrant white flowers that gradually turn a little yellowish. It is a good cover for steep, rocky, or general slopes.

24. ICE PLANT (*Cryophytum crystallinum*): This annual succulent is prostrate and spreading, 6 or 8 inches high. It has sparkling, narrow, angular, fleshy foliage (resembling slivers of ice), and pinkish-white flowers. Although principally a temperate climate plant, it can be grown in the colder north by starting the plants indoors. Use it to cover warm slopes, rocky areas, and rather dry sandy sections of the landscape.

25. JAPANESE FLEECE-FLOWER (*Polygonum cuspidatum compactum*): This is a hardy and attractive ground cover 12 to 18 inches high that spreads rapidly. Its foliage has a unique characteristic: it is reddish in appearance in spring and fall and medium green through the summer. It dies to the ground in winter. The flowers are pink, and bloom in late summer. This plant is useful on slopes and in peripheral areas of the garden, but is not recommended for central locations because of difficulty in controlling its surface runners.

26. JAPANESE JUNIPER (*Juniperus procumbens*): Hardy and low-growing with thin, sharp-pointed, bluish-green leaves, this coniferous evergreen is an impressive ground cover 18 inches in height. Use it to cover gentle slopes, level plots and panels, edging strips, and special accent areas.

27. JAPANESE SPURGE (*Pachysandra terminalis*): This is a hardy and low-growing evergreen, 8 to 10 inches high, with dark green, narrowly oval leaves 3 or 4 inches long, and white flowers borne on terminal spikes in spring. It spreads nicely and will tolerate sun, but it prefers shade. Use this ground cover on shady banks and

slopes, in level plots and controllable edging strips, or around trees.

28. LEADWORT (*Plumbago larpentae*): This hardy, low-growing, half-evergreen plant is 12 to 14 inches high and has 2- or 3-inch long, ovalish leaves and blue flowers in summer. It grows in sun or partial shade and is useful to cover banks and slopes, for wide edgings along driveways, in panels, and above walls.

29. LIPPIA CANESCENS: This medium-hardy, mat-forming creeper is 3 to 5 inches high with tiny gray-green leaves and whitish-lavender flowers. It grows well in sun or shade and in mild climates is acceptable as a lawn. It tolerates mowing.

30. NATAL PLUM, DWARF (*Carissa grandiflora prostrata*): This is a spreading evergreen with small ovalish leaves and fragrant white flowers. It grows well in sun or partial shade. Consider using it on gentle slopes and in edging strips.

31. PERIWINKLE (*Vinca minor*): This hardy and rapid growing evergreen creeper is of much use in special places such as creek banks, small slopes, edging strips, and panels. For description, see the section on vines.

Vinca major is a little less hardy then *vinca minor*. It is taller (15 to 20 inches), has glossy leaves 1 or 2 inches long, and spreads rapidly. Its flowers are larger (¾-inch wide) and purplish-blue. This variety is useful for covering large and steep slopes, smooth or rough banks, or for wandering among trees.

32. ROCKSPRAY (*Cotoneaster microphylla*): This is a hardy and low-growing evergreen, shrubby plant that is widely used as a ground cover. For description, see the section on shrubs. Use it on small slopes, in edging strips, and to cover panels.

33. SARCOCOCCA, HOOKER (*Sarcococca hookeriana humilis*): This hardy evergreen makes an excellent shrubby ground cover for special places. It is 18 to 24 inches high, has 2- or 3-inch long, narrow oblong leaves and tiny fragrant flowers. It is slow-growing and prefers partial shade. Use it on gentle, shady slopes; to cover prominent areas; in wide edging strips; or for ground covered areas in front of background plantings.

34. SARGENT'S JUNIPER (*Juniperus chinensis sargentii*): This fine, low-growing, coniferous evergreen is an outstanding ground cover. For description, see the section on coniferous evergreens. Consider using it on gentle slopes, as a low accent unit, to cover level plots, panels, or wide edging strips.

35. SEA-CAMPION (*Silene maritima*): This low, dense and spreading perennial grows 10 or 12 inches high and is a relative of the *Pink* family.

Photo 8.5

Rockspray (*Cotoneaster microphylla*) in the foreground, bugle (*Ajuga reptans*) in the background.

Its small gray-green leaves are broadly lance-shaped. Clusters of small white flowers appear in late spring. As a ground cover, use it in the smaller parts of the garden—on slopes beside steps, in panels paralleling a walk, in little accent areas, and for narrow edging.

36. SNOW-IN-SUMMER (*Cerastium tomentosum*): This is a very hardy, low-growing, perennial creeper, 5 or 6 inches high, with gray-green leaves and white flowers in summer. Use it on small slopes or to cover edging strips.

37. STAR-JASMINE (*Trachelospermum jasminoides*): This dense evergreen vine is widely used as a prominent ground cover. For description, see the section on vines. Use star-jasmine to cover gentle slopes or in large edging units in front of shrubs and tree plantings.

38. ST. JOHNS-WORT (*Hypericum calycinum*): This small, hardy, evergreen, spreading plant is a very satisfactory ground cover. It is around 6 to 12 inches high and has oblong leaves to 4 inches long. The yellow, fluffy-stemmed flowers average 2 inches across. Plant it on banks and slopes or in planting srtips between the sidewalk and street.

39. STONECROP (*Sedum acre*): This hardy, low-growing, evergreen, creeping succulent is 4 to 8 inches high. With small angular leaves and attractive yellow flowers, it forms a colorful expanding mat. Stonecrop is an interesting plant to cover the small but important places—an irregulary outlined strip beside a path, the slope at either end of steps, an edging strip in front of a

wide flower border, the area at the base of large rocks.

40. SUNROSE (*Helianthemum nummularium*): This miniature shrub-like plant is a hardy, low-growing and spreading evergreen. It is 6 to 10 inches high and has 1- or 2-inch long, nearly oval leaves and attractive yellow flowers ¾ to 1 inch wide. There are several good varieties: *alboplenum*, with double white flowers; *aureum*, with golden-yellow flowers; *cupreum*, with flowers that are copperish in color; *macranthum*, which has white flowers spotted with yellow; *roseum*, which has light rose flowers. Use these fine little plants to cover small banks and slopes, in specially defined areas in a large rock garden, or for strips and panels in formal design.

41. SWEET-FERN (*Comptonia peregrina*): This is a very hardy, shrubby, deciduous, fern-like plant 25 to 30 inches high (or more). Its 3- to 5-inch leaves have margins cut into rounded lobes similar to ferns. The leaves release a delightful fragrance when crushed. Consider using sweet-fern to cover slopes that are hot and have little available moisture, rocky areas, and sandy locations.

42. TAMARIX JUNIPER (*Juniperus sabina tamariscifolia*): One of the more aristocratic coniferous evergreens, this juniper forms an elegant ground cover from 15 to 36 inches high. For description, see the section on coniferous evergreens. This plant has many uses—to cover appropriate areas in the front yard, slopes, accent

Photo 8.6

Juniperus sabina tamariscifolia covers and holds a slope.

plots, wide edgings, and entire panels in either formal or informal design.

43. THYME (*Thymus serpyllum*): This hardy, rather woody, sprawling creeper forms a durable mat 5 to 8 inches thick. It has little narrowly oval leaves and tiny purplish flowers throughout summer. There are varieties with red, yellow, and white flowers. These mostly evergreen plants are adaptable to warm sunny situations and are resistant to drought. Use them to cover open sections of patio areas, small and warm banks and slopes, narrow edging strips.

44. TRAILING ARBUTUS (*Epigaea repens*): This is a hardy, low-growing and trailing evergreen with ovalish leaves 2 or 3 inches long. It has very fragrant white to light pink flowers in early spring, and is very useful for covering small important areas in the garden, small slopes, and among trees.

45. TRAILING LANTANA (*Lantana montevidensis*): This temperate climate plant is shrubby and trailing, 10 to 18 inches high, with 1 inch long, nearly oval leaves and small clusters of lavender flowers. It adapts to adverse growing conditions and is useful for covering steep and rocky slopes.

46. TWIN-FLOWER (*Linnea borealis*): This is an extremely hardy, very low-growing and spreading, evergreen sub-shrub, 4 to 8 inches high, with nearly round leaves about an inch long. It produces tiny, fragrant, bell-shaped, rose-pink flowers. Use it to cover moist and shady edging strips, small shrub bays, or informal places near a water feature.

47. WAUKEGAN JUNIPER (*Juniperus horizontalis douglasii*): This low-growing, trailing, blue-green coniferous evergreen is one of the most beautiful shrubby ground covers. For description, see the section on coniferous evergreens. Use it to cover areas indicated for low conifers—plots adjacent to lawns in the front yard, accent areas, strips above rock walls, edging or gentle slopes.

48. WILD GINGER (*Asarum*): These very hardy, creeping perennials are 6 to 8 inches high with excellent foliage. They are of particular interest as a ground cover in shady natural sections of the garden. The flowers are purple, slightly shaded with brown.

Asarum canadense is deciduous and has nearly heart-shaped leaves 3 to 6 inches wide on long stalks.

Asarum caudatum is evergreen, and its leaves are 4 or 5 inches wide.

Asarum europaeum is evergreen with leaves 3 to 5 inches wide.

Asarum virginica loses its 2- to 5-inch leaves in winter.

Use wild ginger to cover designated areas in shady parts of the garden.

49. WILD STRAWBERRY (*Fragaria*): These hardy little low-growing plants are widely used as ground covers. They are very easily grown, and they spread by runners.

Fragaria chiloensis is a small, rather bushy plant 6 or 7 inches high. It has glossy leaves, relatively large white flowers about an inch across, and large edible red fruit.

Duchesnea indica, or mock-strawberry, closely resembles true strawberry and is often sold as *Fragaria indica.* It has the typical three-parted leaves and spreads by rooting runners. The flowers are yellow and the fruit is red.

Fragaria vesca is very cold-resistant and a little taller than *chiloensis.* It has white flowers and the fruit is red and edible. Use these little plants to cover strips above walls (the runners will creep over and down the walls), to cover gentle slopes, beside ascending steps or at the curve of an ascending path, to cover open places adjacent to lounging facilities, near a water feature, in edging strips, or other similar situations.

50. WINTERCREEPER (*Euonymus fortunei*): This hardy, evergreen, trailing shrub spreads 10 to 15 feet or more by long, rooting runners that effectively cover large areas of ground.

Euonymus fortunei coloratus has oval leaves 1 or 2 inches long that turn reddish-purple in autumn.

Euonymus fortunei minimus has small, dark green leaves.

Euonymus fortunei vegetus is a low, spreading, bushy variety with nearly round, dull green leaves 1 or 2 inches in diameter.

Select the appropriate type for covering banks and slopes on your property.

Photo 8.7

Petunias—a quick but temporary colorful groundcover.

GROUND COVERS—EASTERN SECTIONS (ZONES 5–6–7)

Here are some ground covers for the eastern sections of the country—zones 5–6–7. There are species and varieties of listed ground covers adaptable to the favorable growing areas of the zones indicated. Refer to them in the preceding numbered ground cover list and in the Ground Cover Selection Chart on page 172.

Plant Number	Plant Name	Controlled Height	Zone
1	Akebia quinata	7–12"	5–6–7
2	Alleghany spurge (*Pachysandra procumbens*)	7–12"	5–6–7
3	Bear-berry (*Arctostaphylos uva-ursi*)	8–10"	5–6–7
4	Bellflower (*Campanula portenschlagiana*)	5–6"	5–6–7
5	Blueberry (*Vaccinium angustifolium*)	6–7"	5–6–7
6	Bog rosemary (*Andromeda polifolia*)	10–12"	5–6–7
7	Bugle (*Ajuga reptans*)	5–6"	5–6–7
11	Cinquefoil (*Potentilla verna*)	5–7"	5–6–7
12	Cornish heath (*Erica vagans*)	7–12"	5–6–7
13	Creeping mahonia (*Mahonia repens*)	7–12"	5–6–7
14	Creeping juniper (*Juniperus horizontalis*)	7–12"	5–6–7
16	English ivy (*Hedera helix*)	6–12"	5–6–7
19	Ground holly (*Gaultheria procumbens*)	4–7"	5–6–7
20	Ground ivy (*Nepeta hederacea*)	8–10"	5–6–7
21	Heather, Scotch (*Calluna vulgaris*)	7–20"	5–6–7
22	Heath, spring (*Erica carnea*)	8–12"	5–6–7
23	Honeysuckle, Hall's (*Lonicera japonica halliana*)	7–12"	5–6–7
25	Japanese fleece-flower (*Polygonum cuspidatum compactum*)	12–18"	5–6–7
26	Japanese juniper (*Juniperus procumbens*)	12–18"	5–6–7
27	Japanese spurge (*Pachysandra terminalis*)	8–10"	5–6–7
31	Periwinkle (*Vinca minor*)	5–18"	5–6–7
32	Rockspray (*Cotoneaster microphylla*)	7–12"	6–7

33	Sarcococca, hooker (*Sarcococca hookeriana humilis*)	18–24″	5–6–7
34	Sargent's juniper (*Juniperus chinensis sargentii*)	12–18″	5–6–7
36	Snow-in-summer (*Cerastium tomentosum*)	5–6″	5–6–7
39	Stonecrop (*Sedum acre*)	4–8″	5–6–7
41	Sweet-fern (*Comptonia peregrina*)	25–30″	5–6–7
42	Tamarix juniper (*Juniperus sabina tamariscifolia*)	15–36″	5–6–7
44	Trailing arbutus (*Epigaea repens*)	5–12″	5–6–7
46	Twin-flower (*Linnaea borealis*)	4–8″	5–6–7
47	Waukegan juniper (*Juniperus horizontalis douglasii*)	7–18″	5–6–7
49	Wild strawberry (*Fragaria*)	6–8″	5–6–7
49	Wild straberry (*Fragaria*)	6–7″	5–6–7
50	Wintercreeper (*Euonymus fortunei*)	12–18″	5–6–7

GROUND COVERS—CENTRAL SECTIONS (ZONES 5–6–7)

Here are some ground covers for the central sections of the country—zones 5–6–7. There are species and varieties of listed ground covers adaptable to the favorable growing areas of the zones indicated. Refer to them in the preceding numbered ground cover description list and in the Ground Cover Selection Chart on page 172.

Plant Number	Plant Name	Controlled Height	Zone
2	Alleghany spurge (*Pachysandra procumbens*)	7–12″	5–6–7
3	Bear-berry (*Arctostaphylos uva-ursi*)	8–10″	5–6–7
5	Blueberry (*Vaccinium angustifolium*)	6–7″	5–6–7
6	Bog rosemary (*Andromeda polifolia*)	10–12″	5–6–7
7	Bugle (*Ajuga reptans*)	5–6″	5–6–7
11	Cinquefoil (*Potentilla verna*)	5–7″	5–6–7
12	Cornish heath (*Erica vagans*)	7–12″	5–6–7
14	Creeping juniper (*Juniperus horizontalis*)	7–12″	5–6–7
19	Ground holly (*Gaultheria procumbens*)	4–7″	5–6–7
20	Ground ivy (*Nepeta hederacea*)	8–10″	5–6–7
21	Heather, Scotch (*Calluna, vulgaris*)	7–20″	5–6–7

22	Heath, spring (*Erica carnea*)	8–12″	5–6–7
26	Japanese juniper (*Juniperus procumbens*)	12–18″	5–6–7
27	Japanese spurge (*Pachysandra terminalis*)	8–10″	5–6–7
32	Rockspray (*Cotoneaster microphylla*)	7–12″	6–7
34	Sargent's juniper (*Juniperus chinensis sargentii*)	12–18″	6–7
39	Stonecrop (*Sedum acre*)	4–8″	5–6–7
41	Sweet-fern (*Comptonia peregrina*)	25–30″	5–6–7
42	Tamarix juniper (*Juniperus sabina tamariscifolia*)	15–36″	5–6–7
44	Trailing arbutus (*Epigaea repens*)	5–12″	5–6–7
46	Twin-flower (*Linnaea borealis*)	4–8″	5–6–7
47	Waukegan juniper (*Juniperus horizontalis douglasii*)	7–18″	5–6–7
49	Wild strawberry (*Fragaria*)	6–7″	5–6–7
50	Wintercreeper (*Euonymus fortunei*)	12–18″	5–6–7

GROUND COVERS—WESTERN SECTIONS (ZONES 2 THROUGH 10)

Here are some ground covers for the western sections of the country—zones 2–3–4–5–6–7–8–9–10. There are species and varieties of listed ground covers adaptable to the favorable growing areas of the zones indicated. Refer to them in the preceding numbered ground cover description list and in the Ground Cover Selection Chart on page 172.

Plant Number	Plant Name	Controlled Height	Zone
1	Akebia quinata	7–12″	5–6–7–8–9–10
2	Bellflower (*Campanula portenschlagiana*)	5–6″	4–5–6–7–8–9–10
6	Bog rosemary (*Andromeda polifolia*)	10–12″	2–3–4–5–6–7–8–9
7	Bugle (*Ajuga reptans*)	5–6″	5–6–7–8–9–10
8	Carmel creeper (*Ceanothus griseus horizontalis*)	18–30″	8–9–10

10	Chilean pernettya (*Pernettya mucronata*)	12–30"	7–8–9–10
11	Cinquefoil (*Potentilla verna*)	5–7"	3–4–5–6–7–8–9
13	Creeping mahonia (*Mahonia repens*)	7–12"	5–6–7–8–9–10
14	Creeping juniper (*Juniperus horizontalis*)	7–12"	3–4–5–6–7–8–9–10
15	Dwarf rosemary (*Rosmarinus officinalis prostratus*)	12–18"	8–9–10
16	English ivy (*Hedera helix*)	6–12"	6–7–8–9–10
17	Gazania	5–7"	8–9–10
18	Geranium, ivy (*Pelargonium peltatum*)	7–12"	8–9–10
21	Heather, Scotch (*Calluna vulgaris*)	7–20"	4–5–6–7–8–9
23	Honeysuckle, Hall's (*Lonicera japonica halliana*)	7–12"	5–6–7–8–9–10
24	Ice-plant (*Cryophytum crystallinum*)	6–8"	9–10
25	Japanese fleece-flower, dwarf (*Polygonum cuspidatum compactum*)	12–18"	5–6–7–8–9–10
26	Japanese juniper (*Juniperus procumbens*)	12–18"	4–5–6–7–8–9
28	Leadwort (*Plumbago larpentae*)	12–14"	7–8–9–10
29	Lippia canescens	3–5"	7–8–9–10
31	Periwinkle (*Vinca minor*)	5–18"	5–6–7–8–9–10
32	Rockspray (*Cotoneaster microphylla*)	7–12"	6–7–8–9
33	Sarcococca, hooker (*Sarcococca hookeriana humilis*)	18–24"	5–6–7–8–9
34	Sargent's juniper (*Juniperus chinensis sargentii*)	12–18"	4–5–6–7–8–9–10
35	Sea-campion (*Silene maritima*)	10–12"	7–8–9–10
37	Star jasmine (*Trachelospermum jasminoides*)	12–24"	8–9–10
38	St. Johns wort (*Hypericum calycinum*)	6–12"	6–7–8–9–10
39	Stonecrop (*Sedum acre*)	4–8"	4–5–6–7–8–9–10
40	Sunrose (*Helianthemum nummularium*)	6–10"	5–6–7–8–9–10
42	Tamarix juniper (*Juniperus sabina tamariscifolia*)	15–36"	4–5–6–7–8–9–10
43	Thyme (*Thymus serpyllum*)	5–8"	5–6–7–8–9–10
45	Trailing lantana (*Lantana montevidensis*)	10–18"	8–9–10
47	Waukegan juniper (*Juniperus horizontalis douglasii*)	7–18"	4–5–6–7–8–9–10
49	Wild strawberry (*Fragaria*)	6–7"	4–5–6–7–8–9
50	Winter creeper (*Euonymus fortunei*)	12–18"	5–6–7–8–9

GROUND COVERS—NORTHERN SECTIONS (ZONES 2–3–4)

Here are some ground covers for the northern sections of the country—zones 2–3–4. There are species and varieties of listed ground covers adaptable to the favorable growing areas of the zones indicated. Refer to them in the preceding numbered ground cover description list and in the Ground Cover Selection Chart on page 172.

Plant Number	Plant Name	Controlled Height	Zone
3	Bear-berry (*Arctostaphylos uva-ursi*)	8–10"	2–3–4
5	Blueberry (*Vaccinium angustifolia*)	6–7"	3–4
6	Bog-rosemary (*Andromeda polifolia*)	10–12"	2–3–4

11	Cinquefoil (*Potentilla verna*)	5–7″	3–4
14	Creeping juniper (*Juniperus horizontalis*)	7–12″	3–4
20	Ground ivy (*Nepeta hederacea*)	8–10″	3–4
21	Heather, Scotch (*Calluna vulgaris*)	7–20″	4
26	Japanese juniper (*Juniperus procumbens*)	12–18″	4
34	Sargent's juniper (*Juniperus chinensis sargentii*)	12–18″	4
36	Snow-in-summer (*Cerastium tomentosum*)	5–6″	4
39	Stonecrop (*Sedum acre*)	4–8″	4
41	Sweet-fern (*Comptonia peregrina*)	25–30″	2–3–4
42	Tamarix juniper (*Juniperus sabina tamariscifolia*)	15–36″	4
44	Trailing arbutus (*Epigaea repens*)	5–12″	3–4
47	Waukegan juniper (*Juniperus horizontalis douglasii*)	7–18″	3–4
49	Wild strawberry (*Fragaria*)	6–7″	4

GROUND COVERS—SOUTHERN SECTIONS (ZONES 8–9–10)

Here are some ground covers for the southern sections of the country—zones 8–9–10. There are species and varieties of listed ground covers adaptable to the favorable growing areas of the zones indicated. Refer to them in the preceding numbered ground cover description list and in the Ground Cover Selection Chart on page 172.

Plant Number	Plant Name	Controlled Height	Zone
1	Akebia quinata	7–12″	8–9–10
2	Alleghany spurge (*Pachysandra procumbens*)	7–12″	8–9
4	Bellflower (*Campanula portenschlagiana*)	5–6″	8–9–10
5	Blueberry (*Vaccinium angustifolia*)	6–7″	8–9
6	Bog rosemary (*Andromeda polifolia*)	10–12″	8–9
7	Bugle (*Ajuga reptans*)	5–6″	8–9–10
9	Carolina jessamine (*Gelsemium sempervirens*)	7–12″	8–9–10
10	Chilean pernettya (*Pernettya mucronata*)	12–30″	8–9–10
12	Cornish heath (*Erica vagans*)	7–12″	8–9–10
14	Creeping juniper (*Juniperus horizontalis*)	7–12″	8–9–10
15	Dwarf rosemary (*Rosmarinus officinalis prostratus*)	7–12″	8–9–10
17	Gazania	5–7″	9–10
18	Geranium, ivy (*Pelargonium peltatum*)	7–12″	8–9–10
22	Heath, spring (*Erica carnea*)	8–12″	8–9–10
23	Honeysuckle, Hall's (*Lonicera japonica halliana*)	7–12″	8–9–10
29	Lippia canescens	3–5″	8–9–10
30	Natal plum, dwarf (*Carissa grandiflora prostrata*)	7–18″	9–10
33	Sarcococca, hooker (*Sarcococca hookeriana humilis*)	18–24″	8–9
34	Sargent's juniper (*Juniperus chinensis sargentii*)	12–18″	8–9–10
37	Star jasmine (*Trachelospermum jasminoides*)	12–24″	8–9–10
40	Sunrose (*Helianthemum nummularium*)	6–10″	8–9–10
42	Tamarix juniper (*Juniperus sabina tamariscifolia*)	15–36″	8–9–10
43	Thyme (*Thymus serpyllum*)	5–8″	8–9–10
45	Trailing lantana (*Lantana montevidensis*)	10–18″	8–9–10
47	Waukegan juniper (*Juniperus horizontalis douglasii*)	7–18″	8–9–10
48	Wild ginger (*Asarum*)	6–8″	8–9–10

Perennials-Annuals-Bulbs

Perennials, annuals, and bulbs constitute a great reservoir of plants from which you may select to color your garden exactly as you wish. They provide the means for seasonal color compositions that change automatically from one flowering period to the next if the blooming time of each planting area is carefully calculated.

Where do you begin in planning this very important aspect of your garden? As always, by considering your overall landscape design. Each flower area must (1) possess harmonious colors, (2) blend smoothly into adjacent flower groups, and (3) be an integral part of your total design scheme.

GARDEN-WIDE FLOWER DISTRIBUTION

Be extravagant but wise with color in your garden. Use some *system* of flower distribution over your entire garden, a border, or even a flower panel to assure a harmonious association of colors. You will find the following method very advantageous:

1. Divide your flower plantings into three seasons of bloom—spring, summer, and fall.
2. For easy distribution over your entire garden, use a system of symbols, such as a circle (○) for spring bloom, a square (□)

to indicate summer bloom, a triangle (△) for fall bloom, as in Figure 9.1.

3. Locate the respective symbols on your garden plan in a well-distributed seasonal pattern and color them according to seasons. Or drive marked (colored) stakes in their proper locations in your open garden, for example, yellow for spring bloom, blue for summer bloom, red for fall bloom.
4. Select flowers for each symbol (or stake), carefully considering height, size, and color combinations. Each seasonal group should predominate in your favorite color. Subordinate colors must be harmonious ones. The Perennial, Annual, and Bulb Selection Charts in this chapter will help you with your selections.

Flowers for a Sample Plan

Let's assume Figure 9.1 is your garden and that you are ready to select plants for the locations you have indicated by symbols on your design.

The All-Perennial Garden

You might decide to use only perennials—many people do. Once planted, they bring seasonal color to your garden automatically. You merely maintain them. Here is an attractive, all-perennial arrangement for Figure 9.1, beginning with the spring-blooming symbols (○).

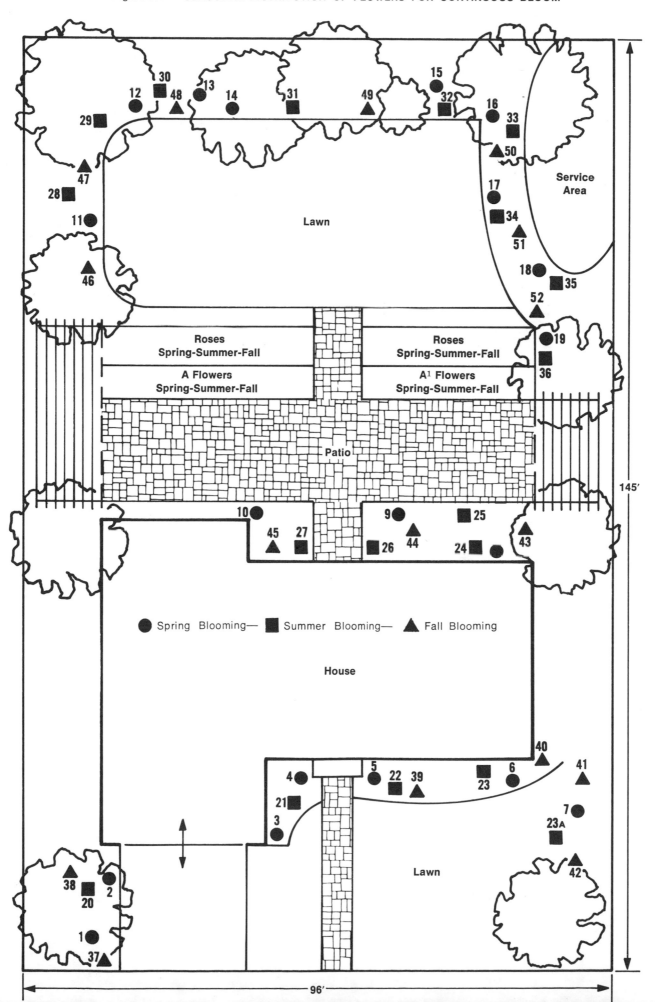

Figure 9.1 SEASONAL DISTRIBUTION OF FLOWERS FOR CONTINUOUS BLOOM

FOR SPRING BLOOM ○

Symbol ○	Plant	Height	Comment
1	Candytuft	8–12″	full sun or partial shade
2	Campanula persicifolia	30–36″	full sun or partial shade
3	Delphinium	40–60″	full sun or some PM shade
4–5	Coreopsis	18–30″	full sun or some PM shade
6	Delphinium	40–60″	full sun or some PM shade
7	Salvia	24–36″	full sun
8	Coreopsis	18–30″	full sun or partial shade
9	Campanula carpatica	5–10″	full sun or partial shade
10	Carnations	12–18″	full sun
11	Delphinium	40–60″	full sun or some PM shade
12	Peony (Tree)	3–6′	filtered sun
13	Peony (Tree)	3–6′	filtered sun
14	Violets	4–8″	filtered sun or shade
15	Delphinium	40–60″	full sun or some PM shade
16	Peony (Tree)	3–6′	filtered sun
17	Coreopsis	18–30″	full sun or some PM shade
18	Iris (Butterfly)	30–45″	full sun
19	Poppies (Oriental)	30–40″	full sun or some PM shade

FOR SUMMER BLOOM □

Symbol □	Plant	Height	Comment
20	Gypsophila	30–40″	full sun or some PM shade
21–22	Campanula carpatica	5–10″	full sun or partial shade
23	Coneflower (*Rudbeckia*)	30–36″	full sun or partial shade
23a	Aster (Michaelmas daisy)	18–30″	full sun or partial shade
24	Phlox paniculata	30–40″	full sun or partial shade
25	Campanula carpatica	5–10″	full sun or partial shade
26–27	Coneflower (*Rudbeckia*)	30–36″	full sun or partial shade
28	Rose-mallow	30–36″	full sun
29	Campanula glomerata	12–18″	full sun or partial shade
30	Campanula pyramidalis	40–50″	full sun or some PM shade
31	Campanula portenschlagiana	5–6″	full sun or partial shade
32	Gaillardia	12–18″	full sun
33	Daylily	18–30″	full sun or partial shade
34–35	Veronica maritima subsessilis	12–24″	full sun
36	Phlox paniculata	30–40″	full sun or partial shade

FOR FALL BLOOM △

Symbol △	Plant	Height	Comment
37–38	Helenium	12–18″	full sun or some PM shade
39	Chrysanthemum, dwarf	8–10″	full sun
40–41	Balloon-flower	24–30″	full sun or partial shade
42	Helenium	12–18″	full sun or some PM shade
43	Aster (Michaelmas daisy)	24–36″	full sun or partial shade
44–45	Chrysanthemum, dwarf	8–12″	full sun
46–47	Helenium	12–18″	full sun or partial shade
48–49	Aster (Michaelmas daisy)	24–36″	full sun or some PM shade
50–51–52	Chrysanthemum	18–30″	full sun

Plant all, or the majority, of perennials at one time—fall or early spring—as your climate permits. They will bloom in their respective seasons and combine with seasonal blooming shrubs, trees, and vines to give your garden the colors you enjoy most. The spring garden will fade smoothly into a completely new color scheme for summer and then move automatically into the beautiful color harmonies of fall.

Including Annuals

Instead of an all-perennial flower planting, you might wish a perennial and annual combination. Merely substitute some of your favorite annuals for the suggested perennials, remembering, of course, that the annuals must associate well with adjacent perennials in size, color, and sun or shade tolerance.

For example, note the flower areas A and A-1 that border the patio in Figure 9.1. Suppose you wanted to combine perennials and annuals in these locations. Sketch 9.1 offers a graceful combination.

Bulbs in the Flower Layout

There is also an impressive selection of magnificent bulbs that bloom in spring, summer, and fall. They are suitable for the front yard, as an edge for the patio, near secondary structures, and in the background at strategic locations. We will not add bulbs to our sample plan, but consider the following for your own garden.

For Spring Bloom: Crocus, daffodils, freesias, fritillary, grape hyacinths, hyacinths, lilies, narcissus, ranunculus, scillas, snowdrops, star-of-Bethlehem, tulips.

For Summer Bloom: Cannas, dahlias, gladiolus, jacobean lilies, montbretia, rain-lilies, scillas, summer hyacinth, tuberose, windflowers, zephyr lilies.

For Fall Bloom: Continue with some amaryllis located near or among low shrubs, autumn crocus, gladiolus, late blooming lilies, and several nerine.

Sketch 9.1

A PERENNIAL AND ANNUAL BORDER

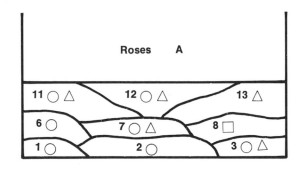
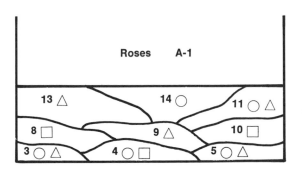

Flowers selected for these two border sections (symbols indicate season of bloom):

1—Alyssum	8—Asters (China)
2—Linum	9—Zinnias
3—Campanula portenschlagiana	10—Phlox drummondii
4—Lobelia	11—Delphinium
5—Pansies	12—Oriental poppies
6—Iceland poppies	13—Chrysanthemums
7—Snapdragons	14—Lupines (Russell strain)

PERENNIALS

Perennials are the reliable stabilizers of all-season color. They fit perfectly into spring, summer, and fall plans and will provide brilliant displays season after season. In addition, perennials provide the attractive form and foliage essential to a balanced picture. They associate harmoniously with shrubs and trees to form a unified garden and create an adequate backdrop for annuals and bulbs.

To reduce the time and labor involved in producing seasonal color, the flower component of many gardens is composed almost entirely of perennials. Plant young perennials over the entire garden in accordance with your seasonal plan, and nature will bring them into bloom on schedule, year after year. Every imaginable size, shape, color, and habit of growth is available—from 5 or 6 foot campanula pyramidalis for the background to impressive little creepers to crawl over walls.

The principal requisite for successful handling of perennials is thoughtful planning to assure harmonious seasonal color. The Perennial Selection Chart and alphabetical descriptions of these fine flowers will assist you. Use this chart exactly as we used those in earlier chapters. Mark your requirements and temperature zone on a strip of paper in the appropriate columns. Move the paper up the chart and find several perennials that closely match your needs. Read about these plants in the alphabetical description list and decide which one you like best.

Alphabetical Descriptions of Perennials

The following are descriptions and typical uses of the plants listed on the Perennial Selection Chart.

1. ACHILLEA (YARROW): These hardy perennials range in height from ground mat to 40 inches. Their aromatic leaves appear in varying forms of fern-like divisions, and their attractive flowers are mostly in dense flat-topped clusters. Yarrows are predominantly yellow. However, some are pink or white.

Achillea ageratifolia is 6 or 8 inches high. The foliage has a silvery sheen, and the flowers are white.

Achillea ageratum is 16 or 18 inches high with toothed leaves and convex clusters of yellow flowers.

Achillea filipendulina is around 40 inches high with large, finely parted leaves and 4- or 5-inch wide clusters of yellow flowers.

Achillea moschata is 4 to 6 inches high with feathery foliage and clusters of white flowers.

Achillea tomentosa grows to 8 or 10 inches high. It is a wooly little spreading plant with yellow flowers.

Occasionally, new varieties appear on the market, particularly in the taller species. Consider using the low growing kinds in edgings beside driveways, paths, and walks, in rock gardens, in level planting areas in the patio, or in irregular beds beside steps and paths. The taller species and varieties are elegant in perennial borders, meandering strips in front of shrub plantings, or unified groupings at the base of fences or walls.

2. ACONITE or MONKSHOOD (*Aconitum*): The plants in this group are mostly hardy, tall-growing, and attractive. *Aconitum napellus* is a common one used in the garden. It grows 30 or 40 inches high and has divided leaves and blue-helmeted flowers. It is poisonous if chewed. These plants are useful in the background of perennial borders, in coves in shrub groupings, and as accent groups in foundation and plot plantings.

3. AJUGA REPTANS (*Bugle*): This is a hardy, ground-carpeting, half-evergreen plant 5 to 8 inches high, with 3- or 4-inch long leaves and spikes of blue flowers in late spring and early summer. Some varieties have rosy-pink or white flowers. Use ajuga to cover edgings, in front of borders, or to cover slopes or level areas. (See "Bugle" under ground covers).

4. ARABIS or ROCK-CRESS: These hardy perennials range from 4 or 5 inches to 2 feet in height. (A few species are taller). The foliage is slightly gray, and the entire plant is generously covered with purple, rose-pink, or white flowers, according to specie or variety.

Arabis albida is 8 to 12 inches high and has fragrant white flowers in spring.

Arabis alpina, or mountain rock-cress, is 6 or 8 inches high and has small white flowers.

Arabis mollis is 12 to 18 inches high and has white flowers.

These are but a few of the species and varieties. Use arabis in rock gardens, to edge paths and walks, in special little open spaces, or in front of a perennial border.

5. ARTEMISIA (Wormwood): These are moderately hardy, low to medium-height plants with attractive gray-green, usually divided leaves and unimportant flowers. They seem to welcome poor and sandy soil.

Artemisia albula, silver king, is 30 to 40 inches high and has ovalish, light-gray, lobed and tomentose leaves 1 or 2 inches long and tiny flowers.

Artemisia canadensis is 18 to 24 inches high with smooth gray-green leaves and tiny greenish-white flowers.

Artemisia frigida, sometimes called mountain sage, is 12 to 14 inches high with silvery-gray foliage and small yellow flowers heads.

Artemisia schmidtiana, commonly known as silver mound, is 8 to 12 inches high with smoothly divided leaves.

These are typical kinds of artemisia useful for rock gardens, edgings, or special accent groupings. Use the taller ones at the inner edge of side and background shrub plantings.

6. ASTER (Michaelmas daisy): These hardy perennial asters are upright, many-branched, and 24 to 60 inches high. They produce great quantities of daisy-like flowers in lavender, blue, pink, rose-pink, and white. In late summer and fall, they are of great value in front of shrubs, in specially located units, or in perennial borders.

7. BABY'S-BREATH (*Gypsophila paniculata*): This is a very cold-hardy and attractive perennial with slender airy branches that give a dainty effect. In summer they display quantities of small pink or white flowers. It is 30 to 36 inches high and wide spreading.

Gypsophila repens is a low, trailing type, 6 or 8 inches high, with blue-green foliage and pink or white flowers. Its variety *rosea* has rose-colored flowers.

The taller ones are excellent for perennial borders or groupings and in mixed, meandering flower strips in front of shrubs. The trailing types are good on slopes, beside steps or walks, bordering paths, in rock gardens, or near water features.

8. BALLOON-FLOWER (*Platycodon grandiflorum*): This is a hardy and upright growing plant 30 to 36 inches high, with 3-inch-long, narrowly oval leaves. The flowers are large and bell-shaped, dark blue or white according to variety. The buds resemble little balloons. These perennials bloom in summer and early fall and are useful in special or perennial borders, to face shrub units, and in plantings at the base of structures.

The variety *mariesii* is a dwarf type, 12 to 18 inches high. Use this one in rock gardens, to cover small slopes, and in small special areas.

9. BAPTISIA: These medium-hardy, lupine-like perennials grow 24 to 60 inches high, according to variety, and are commonly referred to as false-indigo. Their dark green leaves are divided, and the flowers are indigo blue, yellow, or white, and bloom in late spring and summer. They are good for cutting. Use these plants in perennial borders, in planting coves in front of shrub groupings, and in rather small accent units.

10. BEEBALM (*Monarda*): Two species are of considerable interest.

Monarda didyma, or beebalm, is very hardy, 24 to 36 inches high, with 4- to 6-inch long, nearly oval leaves and lavender, pink, red, or white flowers in late spring and summer. It has a mint-like fragrance.

Monarda fistulosa, or wild bergamot, is a hardy perennial 24 to 36 inches high. It has wide lance-like leaves 3 or 4 inches long and produces clusters of lilac or white flowers, according to variety.

These plants are located preferably in single or mixed perennial groupings in front of the side or background shrubs.

11. CAMPANULA (Bellflower): This large and versatile group of hardy, elegant perennials provides a quality selection for almost any part of the garden. There are tall, medium, or low-growing types with beautiful form and color. The following is a cross section of available species and varieties.

Campanula carpatica, or Carpathian harebell, is a low-growing (5 to 10 inches) perennial with large, blue, bell-shaped flowers in summer. Variety *alba* has white flowers.

Campanula glomerata, or clustered bellflower, is 12 to 18 inches high with large leaves and clusters of purplish-blue flowers arranged around the central branch. Variety *acaulis* is 5 or 6 inches high, and variety *superba* displays clusters of dark violet flowers.

Campanula latifolia grows 30 or 40 inches high with clusters of purplish-blue flowers. Variety *alba* has white flowers.

Campanula persicifolia, or peach-leaf bellflower, is 30 to 36 inches high and displays large blue or white flowers. Some varieties have double flowers.

Campanula poscharskyana, or Serbian bellflower, is a 4-inch high, trailing plant with small lavender-blue flowers that bloom in spring.

Campanula portenschlagiana, formerly known as *muralis,* spreads, is 5 to 8 inches high, has toothed leaves, and produces deep blue flowers. It is an excellent ground cover.

Campanula pyramidalis, or chimney bellflower, is delphinium-like in growth habit, 50 or 60 inches high, with quantities of light blue, saucer-shaped flowers. Variety *alba* has white flowers.

Select a campanula for any use in any part of the garden.

12. CANDYTUFT, EVERGREEN (*Iberis sempervirens*): This hardy and rather bushy little perennial grows 6 to 10 inches high and has narrow leaves and elongated clusters of white flowers in spring. It is excellent for rock gardens, beside a driveway, in walk or path edgings, in the front strip of a perennial border, to associate with spring bulb flowers such as late daffodils or tulips, and for special effects.

13. CARDINAL FLOWER (*Lobelia cardinalis*):
This is a hardy and upright plant, 30 to 40 inches high, with nearly oblong leaves 3 to 5 inches long and attractive red flowers in summer. Use it in a perennial border, in mixed annual and perennial flower plantings, for wide edging beside a driveway, or for special feature units.

14. CARNATION, HARDY (*Dianthus caryophyllus*): With winter protection, some varieties of carnation, or clove pink, can be grown as a hardy perennial. Their excellent fragrance and colors make them valuable in edgings, borders, little accent areas, and special plantings near seats or lounging structures.

15. CHRYSANTHEMUM: This is probably one of the most widely used and genuinely satisfactory plants on the list of hardy garden perennials. Chrysanthemums are easy to grow, easy to propagate, and come in an amazing range of heights— 6 to 36 inches. Plant forms include dwarf, slender upright, bushy, and magnificent cascading types. Bunched groupings are dazzling in color and form.

Use them anywhere in the garden that is appropriate for fall blooming perennials—as edging; perennial borders; meandering strips in front of fences, walls, or shrubs; in front of foundation plantings; or as a special chrysanthemum garden.

16. COLUMBINE (*Aquilegia*): This group includes very cold-hardy plants ranging from 12 to 30 inches in height. Columbines have pleasing foliage and beautiful color harmonies in spring. They appear fragile but actually are vigorous growers. Consider using them in perennial borders or strips, near water features or around a bird bath, to assist in edging the driveway or patio, under trees, and in areas for special effects.

17. CONEFLOWER (*Rudbeckia*): Several species and varieties of these fine cold-hardy perennials are worthy of inclusion in your garden plans. Like daisies, these flowers have a central cone-like disc or eye.

Gloriosa daisy is a magnificent summer blooming development of *Rudbeckia hirta*. It is an upright and open plant, 30 to 36 inches high, with 4- to 6-inch wide flowers that are golden-yellow outlined with deep maroon. It prefers full sun and is good for cutting.

Rudbeckia laciniata averages 50 to 60 inches in height and has 4- or 5-inch wide flowers that are yellow with greenish-yellow centers. Variety *hortensia* is the well-known golden glow which has double-yellow flowers.

Rudbeckia speciosa is 30 to 36 inches high with 4-inch wide flowers that are yellow with brownish centers.

Use these valuable perennials in foundation plantings and borders, in front of side or background shrubs, or as accent color.

18. COREOPSIS: These hardy perennials are upright and slender-stemmed, 18 to 30 inches high, with deep yellow, 1½- to 2-inch wide flowers that resemble daisies in form. They bloom in spring and are excellent cut flowers. Use them in borders, wide edgings, meandering flowering strips in the background, and as special accent units.

19. DAYLILY (*Hemerocallis*): These hardy, aggressive plants bloom in late spring and summer and range from 12 to 15 inch dwarfs to hybrids with stems 40 to 50 inches high. The leaves are long and narrow, and arch gracefully from the ground. The flower clusters are at the tips of the stems, and most of these resemble lilies in form, although some kinds are double and somewhat shallowly bell-shaped. They range in exquisite colors from clear yellow through pinks and shades of orange.

Plant daylilies in mixed borders, in side and background shrub coves, adjacent to garden structures, at the base of walls, and in special garden features.

20. DELPHINIUM: This tall aristocrat in the field of garden elegance is a hardy perennial that may grow 5, 6, or 7 feet high, according to variety. Multi-branched shafts of beautiful flowers range in color through shades of blue, lavender, purple, pink, and white. In the more highly hybridized strains—Pacific and Wrexham hybrids, for example—each floret is of particular interest.

Plant delphiniums in full sun, and be sure they are not crowded. The tall varieties are perfect for foundation planting (at the base of your house), at either side of the front yard and associated with shrub units, in front of a wall or fence, or to frame a gateway.

21. DIANTHUS: This group includes pinks, sweet-williams, and carnations. The latter is listed separately (number 14). The perennial *Dianthus* are hardy and easy to grow. They are excellent for cutting.

Pinks (*Dianthus plumarius*) are low-growing, sending up 5- to 8-inch slender flower stems from ground-hugging mats of attractive blue-gray foliage. The flowers are very fragrant, 1 or 2 inches in diameter, and range in color through variations of pink, rose, and white in late spring and summer.

Sweet-williams (*Dianthus barbatus*) are a little more rugged in appearance but equally as beautiful. They send up 12- to 18-inch stems that support dense clusters of non-frgrant flowers in single colors in a harmonious mixture in shades of purple, red, rose, and white. Although sweet-williams are considered perennials, they are best grown as biennials. They bloom in late spring and early summer.

Dianthus are excellent for edging along driveways, walks, paths, and the patio, in accent locations, in the front planting strip of flower borders, in a rock garden, and near water features.

22. DICENTRA SPECTABILIS: This hardy perennial is the widely distributed bleeding-heart. In spring it sends up 12- to 18-inch stems that support small heart-shaped flowers in brilliant rosy-red. There are smaller and equally hardy varieties with 10- to 15-inch flower stems and blooms in variations of pink and white.

When using *Dicentra spectabilis*, consider its color association with neighboring flowers. It has an aggressive color that blends safely with blues, yellows, and white. Plant it in edgings, the forepart of borders, and rock gardens.

23. EVENING PRIMROSE (*Oenothera*): These hardy, summer blooming plants grow to 36 inches high and have long narrow leaves and attractive flowers that open toward evening and may close in the morning. They are most often yellow, but some varieties produce shades of pink, red, rose, and white. *Oenothera youngii* blooms in the daytime. Plant evening primroses in the background as a color accent, in wide borders, and in patio plantings.

24. FEVERFEW (*Chrysanthemum parthenium*): This is a hardy, summer-blooming, bushy-type perennial, 24 to 36 inches high, with partially divided leaves and yellow or white flowers. It prefers sunny locations and requires good drainage. Use it in perennial borders, mixed annual and perennial borders, or flower strips.

25. GAILLARDIA: The perennial species and varieties of Gaillardia are hardy, 15 to 30 inches high, with 4- or 5-inch long lance-like leaves and deep yellow flowers 4 or 5 inches wide. They bloom in summer and are useful in borders, in plots of mixed flowers, or for wide edging.

26. GASPLANT (*Dictamnus*): This is a very hardy, bushy perennial that sends up multiple, loosely flowered spires 30 to 36 inches high. The pink or white flowers emit a slightly volatile vapor that will flash if touched by a lighted match, a phenomenon that may be experienced on a hot night. Gasplant enjoys full sun and, once established, is extremely long-lived. Use it in front of side plantings or in the background, in groupings around garden structures, and in special locations.

27. GLOBE THISTLE (*Echinops ritro*): This plant is hardy and thistle-like in appearance. It grows 24 to 36 inches high and has whitish-gray fuzzy foliage. Large, light blue flowers bloom in thistly heads in summer.

Echinops sphaerocephalus has similar characteristics but is more rugged and grows to a height of 6 or 7 feet.

Some of the new varieties have a more refined appearance, are 40 to 60 inches high, and have 3- or 4-inch wide flower heads in shades of blue. Plant *Echinops* principally in background locations, at the back of wide borders, or at one side of the garden.

28. HELENIUM: These are hardy, bushy plants with a specie and variety height range of 12 to 60 inches. They have 2-inch wide, daisy-like flowers in variations of red and yellow, and bloom profusely in summer and into fall. They prefer full sun, good soil, and considerable moisture.

All are useful in borders. The low ones are excellent in edgings, and the taller ones in special garden features or distant flower units.

29. HIBISCUS MOSCHEUTOS: This is the common summer blooming rose-mallow. It is shrub-like, 30 to 60 inches high, with oval and slightly lobed leaves 3 to 6 inches long. The 5- to 7-inch wide flowers in pink, rose or white resemble hollyhocks. There are elegant hybrids available with larger flowers in richly toned colors. They require full sun, good soil, and considerable moisture.

Consider using rose-mallow on the sunny side of buildings, against warm walls and fences, as an accent, or in front of side or background shrub groupings.

30. HOSTA: These exquisite, shade-loving plantain-lilies (or Funkia) are grown principally for their unique foliage. The leaves are longitudinally ribbed and rather oval, solid green, or green with light margins, and from 2 to 10 inches wide, according to variety. Blue, lilac, or white tubular flowers grow in loose clusters on stems that rise from the leaf stalks.

Use plantain-lilies in partially shaded places where fertile soil and continuous moisture are available. Typical locations are water-feature plantings, damp areas at the base of small spreading trees, and the shady side of a garden structure. They are also appropriate as part of the foundation planting or as a special accent unit.

31. IRIS: This hardy group comprises many species and hybrid varieties with varying forms of foliage and flowers.

Bearded iris are universally known and are planted in gardens of every shape and size. They grow from rhizomes and there are three major height divisions—tall, medium, and dwarf. Varieties of the tall division are 30 to 40 inches high and have long, blade-like leaves arranged in spreading clusters from the rhizome. The *petal, beard,* and *fall* (major parts of the flower structure) combine to rival orchids in their handsome form and elegant color blendings, predominantly in variations of blue, brown, red, yellow, and white.

Irises in the medium-height division are similar in almost every respect except that they are not as tall and they bloom a little earlier than the tall ones.

The low-growing kinds of bearded iris—dwarf iris, 8 to 10 inches high—are a small version of their taller relatives. They bloom earlier than those in the medium-height division. These consecutive blooming periods permit plantings for progressive bloom through the entire spring.

Butterfly iris (*Iris spuria*) are beardless types that grow from 30 to 45 inches high and have long-lasting foliage. Flowers come in a magnificent color range of blue, brown, purple, yellow, and white, and are among the very best for cutting.

Crested iris (*Iris cristata*), an exquisite miniature type, gradually spreads to become increasingly attractive near water features, in rock gardens, or beside an ascending path.

Dutch iris are close relatives of Spanish iris (*Iris xiphium*) and belong to the bulbous group. The flowers are supported on long, straight stems and are unsurpassed for cutting. The color range is wide. Include them in the foundation planting, in a perennial border, in meandering strips in front of side and background shrubs, or in clumps among low shrubs.

English iris (*Iris xiphioides*) are also in the bulbous group. Their flowers are larger than those of Dutch iris and in striking color combinations of blue, pink, red, and white. Plant them in moist sections of the garden with some protection from excessive heat or high winds.

Japanese iris (*Iris kaempferi*) are relatives of the beardless group and possess a magnificent orchid-like beauty. They are very hardy, grow 24 to 36 inches high, and produce large, flattened, and slightly crinkled flowers in rich color combinations of blues, pinks, purples, and white. They are early summer-blooming and require fertile soil, considerable moisture, and some protection from excessive heat.

Siberian iris (*Iris sibirica*), very hardy members of the beardless group, have tall slender leaves and medium-size, butterfly-like flowers on strong, thin stalks 30 to 40 inches high. Colors range through shades of blue, purple, red, and white. They prefer full sun, fertile soil, and ample moisture.

These irises are excellent for borders, at proper locations in the foundation plantings, associated with low informal shrubs, near a water feature, or in drifts in the background.

32. LIATRIS: These are very hardy, multi-branched perennials 18 to 60 inches tall, according to variety, with rather stiff and slender leaves ranging from 4 to 10 inches long. Their purplish or white flower heads are arranged in rather dense spikes and appear in late summer and fall. Use these plants in wide edgings, mixed borders, or side and background flower locations.

33. LILY-OF-THE-VALLEY (*Convallaria majalis*): This hardy, fragrant, low-growing perennial spreads to form a small but dense ground cover. The leaves are nearly oval, and the little white, bell-shaped flowers grow in loose clusters on 6 to 8 inch stems. These plants grow readily in cool, moist, partially shaded locations.

34. LOOSESTRIFE (*Lythrum*): Among the *Lythrum* species, several are hardy perennials 24 to 48 inches high, usually with terminal clusters of small pink, purple, rose, or white flowers in late spring and summer. They grow well in sun or shade and tolerate considerable drought. Plant them in borders, in foundation plantings, near water features, or in unusually wet or dry locations.

35. LUPINE (*Lupinus*): The perennial species and varieties are hardy, 24 to 48 inches high, and have airy, deep-cut foliage and long spikes of thickly arranged pea-like flowers in blue, pink, purple, rose, or white. They bloom in spring and prefer full sun, ample moisture, and good drainage.

Lupines are beautiful in borders, informal plots, meandering strips in the outer areas of the garden, groupings at the base of walls, or along fences.

36. NEPETA (*Catnip*): The several perennial species are attractive and very useful in the garden.

Nepeta cataria is hardy, 24 to 36 inches high, with nearly oval leaves 2 inches long and 4- or 5-inch long dense spires of small, light purple or nearly white flowers.

Nepeta mussini is 12 to 14 inches high and bushy with a somewhat spreading habit of growth and grayish aromatic foliage. The flowers are lavender.

These fine plants prefer full sun and will tolerate a considerable amount of drought. They are useful in edgings, borders, above and over rock walls, in mixed drifts in the background, and in a rock garden.

37. PEONY (Paeonia): These are long-lived and hardy perennials with good form and foliage and extravagantly beautiful flowers that are large, fragrant, and delicately colored.

Herbaceous peonies are the common garden bushy types that die down in winter. They are 36 to 48 inches high with equal width, have attractive foliage, and 5- to 8-inch wide, single or double flowers in shades of pink, red, or white.

Tree peonies are elegantly structured in an open miniature tree-like form with handsome woody branches. These deciduous plants are 3 to 6 feet high, have fascinating foliage, and appear to be thickly decorated with large, single or double flowers in shades of pink, red, or white.

Although peonies are hardy, they have certain culture requirements that must be pretty closely adhered to. Follow these guidelines with herbaceous peonies. *Planting depth:* in northern cold winter zones, plant the woody roots so the growth bud is 2 inches below the soil surface. In milder climates, the growth bud should be 1½ inches below the soil surface. In warm climate zones, merely cover the buds. *Condition of the soil:* a loose, fertile, predominantly humus soil mixture is mandatory and must be well below and wide around the root-stock. *Moisture:* an ample supply of moisture must be constant and reasonably even (not wet today and dry next week). *Winter protection:* in severely cold winter zones, peonies must be winter-protected, particularly young or recently planted ones, by placing several inches of peat moss, fine straw, or soil over the root system. *Fertilizing:* Generously sprinkle a complete fertilizer around each plant early in spring and shortly after flowering. *Disease and pest control:* Watch for attacks by insects and blight, and spray with insecticides or fungicides immediately if either appear on foliage or buds.

The culture requirements of tree peonies are similar to those of herbaceous kinds except for planting depth. The top-growth buds should be 6 or 7 inches below the soil surface. A mulch around the base of the plants will provide a cool and moist soil surface.

Give herbaceous peonies very special locations in full sun. Tree peonies prefer filtered sunlight, such as that found under large trees in the afternoons.

38. PHLOX PANICULATA: This is the hardy perennial phlox, tall (30 to 40 inches high), beautiful, and easy to grow. Its foliage is pleasing, and in summer the upright stalks display large clusters of flowers in lavender, orange, pink, red, or white. A sizable grouping harmoniously fitted into the landscape is an attractive sight. Phlox prefer full sun in cool climates and afternoon protection in hot climates.

Plant perennial phlox in the side plantings of the front yard, in perennial borders, wide edgings, or special plots, in patio plantings, and in distant meandering drifts.

39. PHLOX SUBULATA: Commonly called moss pink, this is a low-growing and spreading little evergreen. It is 5 or 6 inches high and mats out 8 or 10 inches in every direction. It has tiny needle-like leaves and in spring is covered with masses of flowers in pink, purple, red, or white, according to variety.

These phlox are good for edging the front of a mixed border, in a rock garden, beside a walk or path, or in a low accent planting. They require full sun for best results.

40. POPPY, ICELAND (*Papaver nudicaule*): This extremely cold-hardy perennial grows 15 to 20 inches high and has delicately beautiful, 3- or 4-inch wide flowers on slender stems. The colors range through pink, orange, red, yellow, and white. Use Iceland poppies in special flower features, in edgings and patio plantings, along walks and paths, or near water features. An informal clump near a doorway or garden seat is always inviting.

41. POPPY, ORIENTAL (*Papaver orientale*): This is a large and cold-hardy perennial, often 30 to 40 inches high, with 8- to 12-inch long, deeply divided leaves and huge crinkly flowers 6 or 7 inches across in fabulous tones of orange, pink, scarlet, or white, according to variety. They bloom in spring. Grow these poppies in mixed flower plantings, in a perennial border, near garden structures, to color the foundation planting, or to enliven the background.

42. PRIMROSE (*Primula*): Most of the perennial species of primroses are hardy and low-growing, each with a clump of thickly arranged leaves from which rise leafless stems that support flowers in a range of colors. They prefer cool, semishaded locations, ample moisture, and good drainage.

Primula japonica has 4- or 5-inch long, narrowly oval leaves and tight whorls of pink, purple, or white flowers on 10- to 12-inch high stems in late spring.

Primula polyanthus is a hybrid of exceptional beauty with good foliage and tight clusters of flowers. It has an exceptional range of colors and blooms in mid-spring.

Primula sieboldi has 4-inch long, nearly oval leaves and clusters of 2-inch wide, lavender, pink, or white flowers on 8- to 10-inch stems in mid-spring.

Primula vulgaris, the universally distributed English primrose, has 3- to 5-inch long, oblong rippled leaves with wavy margins. Large blue, purple, yellow, or white flowers bloom on 5- or 6-inch stems in early spring.

Grow primroses in walk, driveway, or patio edgings, along paths, as low accent flowers, near shady water features, along stream banks, in the forepart of foundation plantings, in a rock garden, or in containers.

43. SALVIA: This group includes species and varieties of garden perennials with pleasing

foliage and clusters or spikes of flowers on 24- to 36-inch stems and in colors that range through blue, pink, purple, red, rose, scarlet, and white, according to variety. Salvias like full sun. Use them in borders, to face low shrub plantings, or in distant related clumps.

44. SEDUM: Some of these hardy succulent perennials are low-growing and gracefully spreading, others reach 30 to 36 inches high. The low, spreading ones are the kinds usually grown in small gardens. The attractive foliage is from light gray-green to greenish-red combinations, according to variety, and the delightful little flowers range through shades of pink, rose, yellow, and white. These plants prefer full sun but will do well in filtered shade. Use them to create four-season interest above and over walls, crawling over rocks, beside walks and paths, at the base of dwarf trees, or in a rock garden.

45. SUNFLOWER (*Helianthus*): The tall-growing kinds, 7 or 8 feet high, are particularly valuable in the large landscape. Those usually grown in the small and medium-size garden are hybrid varieties that are bush-like, 30 to 45 inches high, with 2- to 4-inch wide flowers in yellow or golden-yellow. They are summer-blooming. Use them in accent areas, in the side plantings of the front yard, and in distant flower bays in front of shrubs.

46. TRITOMA (*Kniphofia*): These hardy perennials are often called poker-plant. They have long, slender leaves clustered near the ground through which strong flower stalks rise 40 to 50 inches, ending in poker-like tubular racemes of flowers in brilliant yellow, yellow-red, orange-red, or scarlet-red combinations. These plants require full sun, ample moisture, and good drainage. Plant them in the distance in front of side or background shrubs. A clump will tone up a colorless section of the garden.

47. TROLLIUS: The several species of globe-flowers are hardy perennials, 12 to 24 inches high, with dark or bronzy-green, deeply divided leaves, and orange or yellow globe-like flowers in spring.

Trollius europaeus (European globe-flower) is a vigorous and massively flowering variety with lemon-yellow blooms.

Trollius ledebouri (Golden queen) produces quantities of golden-yellow, saucer-shaped flowers with tuft-like anthers through late spring and summer. It prefers shady locations.

Use trollius in borders, wide edgings, or small accent areas.

48. TURTLE-HEAD (*Chelone glabra*): Also called snakeheads in some parts of the country, these are very hardy plants that resemble Penstemons and are 18 to 20 inches high with 4- to 6-inch long leaves and white or light pink summer blooming flowers that are said to resemble a turtle's head.

Chelone lyonii, sometimes called red turtlehead, grows to 30 inches high and has 5- or 6-inch long, oval leaves and rose-purple flowers that bloom in summer.

Chelones should be located in partial shade, and they require considerable moisture. Plant them in borders, in drifts in front of shrubs, in wide edgings, or near a water feature.

49. VERONICA: These hardy perennials are often called speedwell. They are excellent multi-branched plants, and some varieties are low creepers. Each of the following kinds bloom in summer and into early fall. They prefer some afternoon shade.

Veronica incana is a creeping type with 2- or 3-inch long leaves and 10- or 12-inch spikes of blue flowers.

Veronica maritima subsessilis is an elegant multi-branched plant with each 2-foot branch terminating in a long, tapering raceme of blue flowers.

Veronica repens is a creeping variety that forms a mat. It has glossy leaves and short-stemmed flowers in light blue or deep pink.

Veronica repens alba has white flowers.

Veronica teucrium prostrata is a superb, densely matted creeper, 3 or 4 inches high, with dark green foliage. It produces an intense display of bright blue flowers in late spring.

There are many standard species and varieties of veronicas to choose from. All are aggressive growers with pleasing foliage and impressive flowers. There are also several very fine, newly developed kinds listed under catalog names, these have flowers in pink, mauve-pink, and rose.

Use the taller veronicas in wide edgings, among the plantings adjacent to the patio, in the foreground drift of a perennial border, to cover a small gentle slope, or beside an ascending walk in a hillside garden. Plant the creeping types in patio planting spaces, rock gardens, and rock placements in a hillside garden.

50. VIOLET (*Viola*): There are many species and varieties of these elegant, fragrant, and rapidly spreading little perennials. There are kinds for every geographical location and for gardens in the mountains, plains, or sea coast. They spread over the ground and produce myriads of exquisite, sweet-scented, single or double flowers in many shades of blue, pink, purple, and white. They grow in full sun or partial shade and are unsurpassed for picking.

Use violets to spread under trees, in little drifts in retirement gardens, in edgings along

PERENNIAL SELECTION CHART

No.	Name of Perennial	Height Ranges: 4–8 in	8–12 in	12–18 in	18–30 in	30–40 in	40–60 in	Blooming Season: Spring	Summer	Fall	Cutting	Fragrant	Zone: 2	3	4	5	6	7	8	9	10	Landscape Uses: Part shade	Full sun	Accent	Background	Borders	Edging	Foundation	Ground cover	Plots	Rock garden	Sides	Special effects
1	Achillea	+		+		+		+	+		+			+									+	+	+		+			+	+	+	+
2	Aconite		+			+			+	+	+			+									+	+	+				+		+	+	+
3	Ajuga	+	+												+							+	+			+	+	+	+	+	+	+	
4	Arabis	+	+	+				+								+							+			+	+	+		+	+	+	+
5	Artemisia	+		+	+	+			+		+				+		+					+	+	+	+	+	+	+		+		+	+
6	Asters (Michaelmas daisy)			+	+	+	+		+	+	+			+	+							+	+	+	+	+	+	+		+		+	+
7	Baby's-breath	+				+			+		+	+		+									+		+	+				+	+	+	+
8	Balloon-flower		+	+		+		+	+		+			+	+							+	+	+	+	+	+			+	+	+	
9	Baptisia			+	+			+	+		+				+								+	+		+		+				+	
10	Beebalm			+	+			+	+		+	+			+		+					+	+	+	+	+	+	+	+	+		+	+
11	Campanula	+	+	+	+	+		+	+		+			+									+	+	+	+	+	+	+	+	+	+	+
12	Candytuft	+	+					+			+					+							+			+	+			+	+	+	
13	Cardinal-flower			+	+	+		+	+	+	+			+								+	+		+	+				+		+	+
14	Carnation	+	+	+		+			+		+	+			+			+				+	+	+		+	+	+		+		+	+
15	Chrysanthemum	+		+	+				+	+	+				+							+	+	+	+	+	+	+		+		+	+
16	Columbine			+		+		+			+				+							+	+		+	+	+			+		+	+
17	Coneflower				+	+			+		+			+								+	+	+	+	+	+	+	+	+		+	+
18	Coreopsis				+			+	+		+				+							+	+	+		+				+		+	+
19	Daylily			+	+	+		+	+	+	+			+		+						+	+	+	+	+		+		+	+	+	+
20	Delphinium					+	+	+	+	+	+	+			+	+						+	+	+	+	+	+	+		+	+	+	+
21	Dianthus			+	+			+	+	+	+				+								+	+		+	+	+		+	+	+	+
22	Dicentra	+	+		+			+							+							+	+		+	+				+			
23	Evening primrose				+			+	+		+					+							+	+	+	+	+	+		+		+	+
24	Feverfew		+		+			+	+		+	+				+						+	+	+	+	+	+	+		+	+	+	+
25	Gaillardia	+			+	+		+	+		+				+							+	+	+	+	+	+	+		+	+	+	+

| | Example Perennial | | | 12 | 18 | | | | Su | | | | | | | 5 | | | | | | | Fs | | | Bo | | | | | | | |

Example: Plant requirements—12 to 18 inches high, summer blooming, full sun, for a border, zone 5. Mark your zone and requirements on a paper strip. Move it up over chart. Match reasonably closely. Find several. Turn to numbered descriptions for selection. Perennials located—numbers 1, 8, 11, 15, 19, 21, 25, 28, 36, 49. Zoning: Estimated zone-temperature range of each plant's hardiness. Heights vary according to variety.

PERENNIAL SELECTION CHART

No.	Name of Perennial	Height Ranges						Blooming Season					Zone (2–10)	Landscape Uses											
		4–8 in	8–12 in	12–18 in	18–30 in	30–40 in	40–60 in	Spring	Summer	Fall	Cutting	Fragrant	Zone	Part shade	Full sun	Accent	Background	Borders	Edging	Foundation	Ground cover	Plots	Rock garden	Sides	Special effects
26	Gasplant				+		+		+			+	4–		+		+	+						+	
27	Globe thistle			+	+		+		+		+		3–	+	+		+	+	+					+	+
28	Helenium				+	+	+		+	+	+		3–	+	+	+	+	+	+	+		+		+	+
29	Hibiscus (Rose-mallow)					+	+	+	+	+	+		5–		+	+	+	+	+	+	+	+		+	+
30	Hosta			+				+	+				4–	+	+	+	+	+	+	+	+	+		+	+
31	Iris	+		+	+	+	+	+	+		+		4–		+	+	+	+	+	+		+	+	+	+
32	Liatris			+	+	+			+		+		3–		+		+	+	+	+				+	+
33	Lily-of-the-valley	+						+			+	+	2–	+		+			+	+	+			+	+
34	Loosestrife			+	+			+					3–	+			+	+		+	+			+	+
35	Lupine			+	+	+		+			+		4–		+	+	+	+				+		+	+
36	Nepeta		+	+	+	+		+	+			+	3–		+	+	+	+	+	+		+		+	+
37	Peony					+	+	+			+	+	2–		+	+	+	+		+		+		+	+
38	Phlox paniculata				+	+			+		+	+	3–	+		+	+	+		+				+	+
39	Phlox subulata	+						+					2–	+	+	+				+	+		+	+	+
40	Poppy, Iceland			+				+			+		2–		+	+	+	+	+	+		+	+	+	+
41	Poppy, oriental			+				+			+		2–		+	+	+	+		+				+	+
42	Primrose	+	+					+	+				4–	+				+	+					+	+
43	Salvia			+	+			+	+		+		4–		+	+	+	+	+	+		+		+	
44	Sedum	+		+	+			+	+				3–		+			+	+			+	+	+	+
45	Sunflower				+	+	+		+				4–		+		+	+				+	+	+	+
46	Tritoma						+			+			6–	+	+	+	+	+	+	+				+	+
47	Trollius		+	+		+		+			+		4–		+	+	+	+	+					+	+
48	Turtle-head		+	+				+					3–	+		+								+	
49	Veronica	+		+	+			+	+		+	+	3–	+	+	+	+	+	+		+	+	+	+	+
50	Violet	+	+					+	+				4–	+	+			+	+	+	+	+	+	+	+
	Example Perennial			12	18				Su				5		Fs			Bo							

Example: Plant requirements—12 to 18 inches high, summer blooming, full sun, for a border, zone 5. Mark your zone and requirements on a paper strip. Move it up over chart. Match reasonably closely. Find several. Turn to numbered descriptions for selection. Perennials located—numbers 1, 8, 11, 15, 19, 21, 25, 28, 36, 49. Zoning: Estimated zone-temperature range of each plant's hardiness. Heights vary according to variety.

walks and paths, near water features, at the base of large rocks, or as a ground cover on gentle slopes. These are just a few typical uses.

PERENNIALS—EASTERN AND CENTRAL SECTIONS (ZONES 5–6–7)

Here are some perennials for the eastern and central sections of the country—zones 5–6–7. There are species and varieties of listed perennials adaptable to the favorable growing areas of the zones indicated. Refer to them in the preceding numbered perennial description list and in the Perennial Selection Chart on page 193.

Plant Number	Plant Name	Height	Zone
1	Achillea (Yarrow)	4–40″	5–6–7
2	Aconite (*Aconitum*)	30–40″	5–6–7
3	Ajuga	4–8″	5–6–7
4	Arabis (Rock-cress)	6–18″	5–6–7
6	Aster (Michaelmas daisy)	24–40″	5–6–7
7	Baby's-breath (*Gypsophila*)	30–36″	5–6–7
8	Balloon-flower (*Platycodon grandiflorum*)	12–30″	5–6–7
10	Beebalm (*Monarda*)	18–36″	5–6–7
11	Campanula	4–60″	5–6–7
12	Candytuft (*Iberis sempervirens*)	6–10″	5–6–7
13	Cardinal flower (*Lobelia cardinalis*)	30–40″	5–6–7
15	Chrysanthemum	6–36″	5–6–7
16	Columbine (*Aquilegia*)	12–30″	5–6–7
17	Coneflower (*Rudbeckia*)	30–36″	5–6–7
20	Delphinium	40–60″	5–6–7
21	Dianthus	4–18″	5–6–7
22	Dicentra (*Dicentra spectabilis*)	12–18″	5–6–7
23	Evening primrose (*Oenothera*)	18–36″	5–6–7
27	Globe thistle (*Echinops ritro*)	18–36″	5–6–7
28	Helenium	12–60″	5–6–7
31	Iris	6–45″	5–6–7
32	Liatris	18–60″	5–6–7
35	Lupine (*Lupinus*)	24–40″	5–6–7
37	Peony (*Paeonia*)	36–60″	5–6–7
38	Phlox (*Phlox paniculata*)	30–40″	5–6–7
39	Phlox (*Phlox subulata*)	5–6″	5–6–7
40	Poppy, Iceland (*Papaver nudicaule*)	15–30″	5–6–7
41	Poppy, oriental (*Papaver orientale*)	30–40″	5–6–7
42	Primrose (*Primula*)	6–10″	5–6–7
43	Salvia	18–36″	5–6–7
47	Trollius	12–24″	5–6–7
49	Veronica	6–24″	5–6–7
50	Violet (*Viola*)	4–8″	5–6–7

PERENNIALS—WESTERN SECTIONS (ZONES 2 THROUGH 10)

Here are some perennials for the western sections of the country—zones 2–3–4–5–6–7–8–9–10. There are species and varieties of listed perennials adaptable to the favorable growing areas of the zones indicated. Refer to them in the preceding numbered perennial description list and in the Perennial Selection Chart on page 193.

Plant Number	Plant Name	Height	Zone
1	Achillea (Yarrow)	4–40″	3–4–5–6–7–8–9
2	Aconite (*Aconitum*)	30–40″	5–6–7–8
3	Ajuga (*Ajuga reptans*)	4–8″	5–6–7–8–9–10
5	Artemisia (*Artemisia albula*)	10–36″	6–7–8
6	Aster (Michaelmas daisy)	24–40″	4–5–6–7–8–9
7	Baby's-breath (*Gypsophila*)	30–36″	3–4–5–6–7–8
9	Baptisia	24–60″	6–7–8
10	Beebalm (*Monarda*)	18–36″	4–5–6–7–8–9
11	Campanula (*Campanula carpatica*)	4–10″	3–4–5–6–7–8–9
12	Candytuft (*Iberis sempervirens*)	6–10″	5–6–7–8–9
14	Carnation (*Dianthus caryophyllus*)	12–15″	7–8–9
15	Chrysanthemum	6–36″	4–5–6–7–8–9
16	Columbine (*Aquilegia*)	12–30″	4–5–6–7–8–9
17	Coneflower (*Rudbeckia*)	30–36″	3–4–5–6–7–8–9
18	Coreopsis	18–30″	4–5–6–7–8–9–10
19	Daylily (*Hemerocallis*)	12–36″	5–6–7–8–9–10
20	Delphinium	40–60″	4–5–6–7–8–9
21	Dianthus	4–18″	5–6–7–8–9
23	Evening primrose (*Oenothera*)	18–36″	5–6–7–8–9
24	Feverfew (*Chrysanthemum parthenium*)	24–36″	5–6–7–8–9
29	Hibiscus (*Hibiscus moscheutos*)	30–36″	6–7–8–9–10
31	Iris	6–40″	4–5–6–7–8–9–10
32	Liatris	18–60″	3–4–5–6–7–8–9
33	Lily-of-the-valley (*Convallaria majalis*)	6–8″	8–9
35	Lupine (*Lupinus*)	24–40″	4–5–6–7–8–9

37	Peony (*Paeonia*)	36–60″	3–4–5–6–7–8
38	Phlox (*Phlox paniculata*)	30–40″	4–5–6–7–8–9
39	Phlox (*Phlox subulata*)	5–6″	4–5–6–7–8–9
40	Poppy, Iceland (*Papaver nudicaule*)	15–30″	3–4–5–6–7–8–9
41	Poppy, oriental (*Papaver orientale*)	30–40″	3–4–5–6–7–8
42	Primrose (*Primula*)	6–10″	5–6–7–8–9
43	Salvia	18–36″	5–6–7–8–9–10
44	Sedum	4–40″	4–5–6–7–8–9–10
45	Sunflower (*Helianthus*)	30–60″	5–6–7–8–9
47	Trollius	12–24″	5–6–7–8–9
49	Veronica (*Veronica maritima subsessilis*)	12–24″	4–5–6–7–8–9
50	Violet (*Viola*)	4–8″	5–6–7–8–9

31	Iris	6–45″	4
32	Liatris	18–60″	3–4
34	Loosestrife (*Lythrum*)	24–48″	3–4
35	Lupine (*Lupinus*)	24–48″	4
37	Peony (*Paeonia*)	36–60″	3–4
38	Phlox (*Phlox paniculata*)	30–40″	4
39	Phlox (*Phlox subulata*)	5–6″	4
40	Poppy, Iceland (*Papaver nudicaule*)	15–30″	3–4
41	Poppy, oriental (*Papaver orientale*)	30–40″	3–4
48	Turtle-head (*Chelone glabra*)	18–20″	4
49	Veronica	6–24″	4

PERENNIALS—NORTHERN SECTIONS (ZONES 2–3–4)

Here are some perennials for the northern sections of the country—zones 2–3–4. There are species and varieties of listed perennials adaptable to the favorable growing areas of the zones indicated. Refer to them in the preceding numbered perennial description list and in the Perennial Selection Chart on page 193.

Plant Number	Plant Name	Height	Zone
1	Achillea (Yarrow)	4–40″	3–4
2	Aconite (*Aconitum*)	30–40″	4
4	Arabis	6–18″	4
6	Aster (Michaelmas daisy)	24–40″	4
7	Baby's-breath (*Gypsophila*)	30–36″	3–4
8	Balloon-flower (*Platycodon*)	12–30″	4
10	Beebalm (*Monarda*)	18–36″	4
11	Campanula	4–60″	3–4
13	Cardinal flower	30–40″	3–4
15	Chrysanthemum	6–36″	4
16	Columbine (*Aquilegia*)	12–30″	4
17	Coneflower (*Rudbeckia*)	30–36″	3–4
18	Coreopsis	18–30″	4
20	Delphinium	40–60″	4
22	Dicentra (*Dicentra spectabilis*)	12–18″	4
25	Gaillardia	15–30″	4
26	Gasplant (*Dictamnus*)	18–36″	4
27	Globe thistle (*Echinops ritro*)	18–60″	4
28	Helenium	12–60″	4

PERENNIALS—SOUTHERN SECTIONS (ZONES 8–9–10)

Here are some perennials for the southern sections of the country—zones 8–9–10. There are species and varieties of listed perennials adaptable to the favorable growing areas of the zones indicated. Refer to them in the preceding numbered perennial description list and in the Perennial Selection Chart on page 193.

Plant Number	Plant Name	Height	Zone
1	Achillea (Yarrow)	4–40″	8–9
3	Ajuga (*Ajuga reptans*)	4–8″	8–9–10
6	Aster (Michaelmas daisy)	24–40″	8–9
11	Campanula	4–60″	8–9–10
12	Candytuft (*Iberis sempervirens*)	6–10″	8–9
13	Cardinal flower (*Lobelia cardinalis*)	30–40″	8–9–10
14	Carnation (*Dianthus caryophyllus*)	12–15″	8–9
15	Chrysanthemum	6–36″	8–9
17	Coneflower (*Rudbeckia*)	30–36″	8–9
18	Coreopsis	18–30″	8–9–10
19	Daylily (*Hemerocallis*)	12–36″	8–9–10
20	Delphinium	40–60″	8–9
29	Hibiscus (*Hibiscus moscheutos*)	30–60″	8–9–10
30	Hosta	8–12″	8–9
31	Iris	6–40″	8–9–10
33	Lily-of-the-valley (*Convallaria majalis*)	6–8″	8–9
35	Lupine (*Lupinus*)	24–40″	8–9
38	Phlox (*Phlox paniculata*)	30–40″	8–9
39	Phlox (*Phlox subulata*)	5–6″	8–9
40	Poppy, Iceland (*Papaver nudicaule*)	16–30″	8–9

42	Primrose (*Primula*)	6–10″	8–9
43	Salvia	18–36″	8–9–10
44	Sedum	4–40″	8–9–10
45	Sunflower (*Helianthus*)	30–60″	8–9–10
46	Tritoma (*Kniphofia*)	40–50″	8–9–10
49	Veronica	6–24″	8–9

ANNUALS

Annuals, which grow from seed, develop, bloom and end their life span in one year, provide quick and vivid splashes of color in spring, summer, and fall. If seed planting or plant setting is done with pre-planned timing, flower blooming can be controlled with amazing accuracy to accommodate specific requirements such as special social functions, garden club tours, vacations, and garden units for special effects.

In the great majority of gardens, perennials, shrubs, and trees provide the main progressive four-season color and interest program through most of the landscape. Periodically, however, there are lulls in the flowering activity that are easily supplemented by quick-growing annuals. Many kinds bloom within a few weeks after their seeds are planted in boxes or flats. Stock, for instance, can bloom in 8 or 10 weeks. The time from seed planting to bloom is usually given on seed packets and in flower catalogs.

Annuals are tender, and most species will tolerate very little frost. This requires careful timing in early spring planting. In cold winter climates, plant the seeds of spring-flowering annuals in boxes well before the final frost, and keep them in a warm place indoors. By the time last frost has occurred, the young plants will be ready for replanting into garden soil.

Although there are annuals to fit almost any requirement in any garden, finding the right ones for a particular situation can be frustrating. For this reason, the Annual Selection Chart is designed specifically to assist you in the selection, timing, and location of these valuable plants. It not only gives the names of sixty spring, summer, and fall blooming annuals but, in addition, answers the question of what to plant in a specific location for flowers with the height and color you want at a particular time of year.

Look at the chart. The example selection strip at its base indicates that you wish *blue* flowers for a *border* in *partial shade* and that they should bloom in *summer*. To find which annuals meet your needs, mark these requirements on a strip of paper in the proper columns and slowly move the paper up the chart.

Ps (part shade)—Su (summer bloom)—
Bo (border)—Bl (blue)

Very quickly you find several plants that closely match your marked strip: numbers 7, 8, 16, 25, 26, 32, 38, 42. To make a final choice, turn to these numbers in the alphabetical description list of annuals.

ANNUAL SELECTION CHART

No.	Name of Annual	Height (inches)	Sun	Part shade	Spring	Summer	Fall	Background	Baskets	Borders	Cutting	Edging	Foundation	Fragrant	Plots	Pots	Rock garden	Shrub area	Special feature	Trailing	Window box	Blue	Orange	Pink	Purple	Red	Rose	Yellow	White
1	African daisy	20–30	+			+	+	+		+			+		+			+	+					+					+
2	Baby's-breath	12–20	+		+	+			+	+	+	+			+	+				+	+						+		+
3	Baby blue-eyes	8–10	+	+	+				+	+					+		+				+	+							+
4	Bachelor's-button	18–30	+	+	+	+		+	+	+	+	+	+		+	+			+		+	+		+	+	+	+		+
5	Balsam, garden	8–20	+	+	+	+				+	+	+	+		+	+	+		+		+	+		+	+	+	+	+	+
6	Blanket flower	14–18	+		+	+		+		+		+			+														
7	Blue lace-flower	15–25	+	+		+	+				+	+					+	+	+										+
8	Browallia	10–24	+	+		+		+	+	+			+		+	+	+				+	+					+	+	+
9	Butterfly-flower	12–18	+	+	+	+		+	+	+	+	+	+		+	+	+		+	+	+			+	+		+	+	+
10	California poppy	10–18	+		+	+	+	+		+	+	+			+	+			+				+		+	+		+	+
11	Calliopsis	10–30	+		+	+	+	+		+	+	+	+		+		+							+	+	+		+	+
12	Candytuft	10–15	+	+	+	+				+	+	+			+	+	+		+		+			+	+				+
13	Canterbury bells	24–30	+	+	+	+		+			+	+	+		+	+		+	+		+	+		+	+		+		+
14	China asters	12–30	+	+		+	+	+			+	+	+		+	+	+		+					+	+		+	+	+
15	China pinks	10–12	+	+	+	+	+				+	+	+		+	+	+				+			+					+
16	Chinese forget-me-not	15–20	+	+		+	+	+			+	+	+		+	+	+	+	+			+		+					+
17	Clarkia	18–30	+	+		+	+	+		+	+	+	+		+	+				+				+	+				+
18	Cockscomb	10–30	+		+	+	+				+	+	+		+	+	+	+	+				+	+	+		+	+	+
19	Corn-marigold	12–20	+			+	+			+	+	+	+		+				+		+			+		+		+	+
20	Corn-poppy	20–30	+		+					+	+	+	+		+		+		+			?	+	+		+			+

| Example Annual | | | | Ps | | Su | | | | Bo | | | | | | | | | | | | Blue | | | | | | | |

Example: Requirements—for part shade, to bloom in summer, good for borders, and having blue flowers. Mark your requirements on a paper strip. Move it up over the chart. Match reasonably closely. Find several. See numbered descriptions for decision. Annuals located—numbers 7, 8, 16, 25, 26, 32, 38, 42.

Several of the listed annuals are available in additional colors and shades. Heights and time of bloom are influenced by altitude, temperature, climate, soil, and moisture.

ANNUAL SELECTION CHART

No.	Name of Annual	Height (inches)	Sun	Part shade	Spring	Summer	Fall	Background	Baskets	Borders	Cutting	Edging	Foundation	Fragrant	Plots	Pots	Rock garden	Shrub area	Special feature	Trailing	Window box	Blue	Orange	Pink	Purple	Red	Rose	Yellow	White
21	Cosmos	30–60	+	+		+	+	+		+	+		+		+			+	+						+	+	+		+
22	Everlasting	12–24	+	+		+	+	+		+	+	+			+	+		+						+			+		+
23	Farewell-to-spring	12–20	+			+	+	+	+	+	+	+	+	+		+	+	+		+				+	+		+		+
24	Flax, flowering	12–20	+	+			+	+		+	+	+	+			+	+	+					+		+					+
25	Floss flower	10–12	+	+	+	+				+	+	+	+			+	+	+		+		+	+		+	+				
26	Forget-me-not	8–10	+	+	+	+		+		+	+	+	+			+	+	+				+	+		+		+			+
27	Four-o'clock (Perennial-annual)	14–30	+			+	+			+	+	+		+		+	+		+		+	+		+		+		+	+
28	French marigold	8–30	+			+	+		+		+	+	+	+		+		+	+					+					+	
29	Globe amaranth	12–20	+	+		+	+	+		+	+	+	+	+		+	+	+	+	+			+		+	+		+		+
30	Honesty	18–30		+		+		+			+	+	+	+	+	+				+			+		+	+				+
31	Larkspur, rocket	12–20	+	+		+	+	+	+	+	+		+			+	+	+				+	+		+	+				+
32	Lobelia	6–10	+	+	+	+				+	+	+	+			+	+	+			+	+	+		+	+		+		+
33	Love-in-a-mist	12–18	+	+	+	+			+	+	+	+	+			+	+	+	+				+			+				
34	Lupine, annual	15–40	+	+	+	+			+		+	+							+										+	
35	Marigold	8–24	+	+		+	+	+	+		+	+	+			+	+	+	+					+					+	+
36	Mentzelia	12–36	+		+	+					+	+	+		+	+													+	
37	Mignonette	12–24		+	+			+	+	+	+	+	+		+	+	+												+	+
38	Morning glory, dwarf	10–12	+	+	+	+	+	+		+	+	+	+		+		+	+			+	+		+						
39	Nasturtium	8–60	+	+	+	+	+	+		+	+	+	+	+	+	+	+	+			+	+		+			+	+		
40	Nemesia	10–20	+	+	+	+	+	+	+	+	+	+	+	+		+	+	+				+	+		+	+		+	+	+
	Example	Annual			Ps		Su		Bo														Blue							

Example: Requirements—for part shade, to bloom in summer, good for borders, and having blue flowers. Mark your requirements on a paper strip. Move it up over the chart. Match reasonably closely. Find several. See numbered descriptions for decision. Annuals located—numbers 7, 8, 16, 25, 26, 32, 38, 42.

Several of the listed annuals are available in additional colors and shades. Heights and time of bloom are influenced by altitude, temperature, climate, soil, and moisture.

ANNUAL SELECTION CHART

No.	Name of Annual	Height (inches)	Sun	Part shade	Spring	Summer	Fall	Background	Baskets	Borders	Cutting	Edging	Foundation	Fragrant	Plots	Pots	Rock garden	Shrub area	Special feature	Trailing	Window box	Blue	Orange	Pink	Purple	Red	Rose	Yellow	White
																									Color Ranges				
41	Painted tongue	24–36	+			+	+	+		+	+				+	+			+				+		+		+			+
42	Pansy (Perennial-annual)	6–8	+	+	+	+	+		+	+	+	+	+	+	+	+	+	+	+				+			+	+		+	+
43	Petunia (Perennial-annual)	8–18	+	+	+	+	+		+	+	+	+	+	+	+	+	+	+	+	+	+	+			+	+	+	+		+
44	Phlox, annual	12–14	+	+	+	+	+		+	+	+	+	+	+	+	+	+	+		+	+					+	+	+		+
45	Pot marigold	12–18	+	+	+	+	+		+	+	+	+	+	+		+	+	+						+			+		+	+
46	Rose-moss	6–9	+			+	+	+	+	+	+	+	+	+		+	+	+	+	+	+	+		+	+	+	+	+	+	+
47	Snapdragon (Perennial-annual)	8–30	+	+	+	+	+	+	+		+	+		+		+	+		+	+					+	+	+	+	+	+
48	Spider-flower	30–40	+	+		+	+	+		+	+	+		+		+		+							+	+	+	+	+	+
49	Stock, annual	12–30	+	+	+	+	+	+	+	+	+	+	+	+	+	+	+	+	+	+						+	+	+	+	+
50	Strawflower	20–30	+			+		+	+	+	+	+			+	+			+	+				+		+	+		+	+
51	Summer-cypress	24–36	+				+	+	+									+		+										
52	Sunflower	60–80	+				+		+											+									+	
53	Sweet alyssum	6–8	+	+	+	+				+	+		+		+	+	+	+				+			+	+		+		+
54	Sweet pea	36–90	+	+	+	+			+		+	+		+	+	+	+					+			+	+	+	+	+	+
55	Sweet scabiosa	24–30	+	+	+	+	+		+		+	+		+		+	+	+	+				+	+	+	+	+	+	+	+
56	Tassel flower	30–45	+	+	+	+	+		+		+			+		+		+	+	+		+					+			
57	Toadflax	10–16	+	+	+	+	+			+	+		+			+	+	+		+		+				+		+	+	+
58	Tobacco, flowering	18–36	+	+	+	+	+		+		+	+		+	+	+	+	+	+	+		+				+	+	+		+
59	Virginian stock	4–6	+	+	+	+			+	+	+		+	+		+	+	+				+			+	+	+	+	+	+
60	Youth-and-old-age	12–36	+	+		+	+	+	+		+		+	+		+				+					+	+	+	+	+	+
	Example Annual		Ps			Su					Bo												Blue							

Example: Requirements—for part shade, to bloom in summer, good for borders, and having blue flowers. Mark your requirements on a paper strip. Move it up over the chart. Match reasonably closely. Find several. See numbered descriptions for decision. Annuals located—numbers 7, 8, 16, 25, 26, 32, 38, 42.

Several of the listed annuals are available in additional colors and shades. Heights and time of bloom are influenced by altitude, temperature, climate, soil, and moisture.

Alphabetical Descriptions of Annuals

The following are descriptions of the plants listed on the Annual Selection Chart. (Numbers match those on the Selection Chart.)

1. AFRICAN DAISY (*Arctotis stoechadifolia*): This is a half hardy and rather open growing annual, 20 to 30 inches high, with light green foliage. The 3- or 4-inch wide daisy-like flowers are white or white tinted with light violet. It blooms in summer and early fall. Give it a sunny location.

2. BABY'S-BREATH (*Gypsophila elegans*): This plant is dainty, open, and airy. It grows 12 to 20 inches high and has tiny light rose or white flowers in spring. It tolerates a sunny location or will do well in partial shade.

3. BABY BLUE-EYES (*Nemophila insignis*): This low-growing and somewhat spreading plant is 8 or 10 inches high by 12 to 18 inches wide and bears small blue cup-shaped flowers in spring. Variety *alba* has white flowers. These annuals grow well in sunny areas in a moderately cool climate, but require some protection in warm sections of the country.

4. BACHELOR'S-BUTTON (*Centaurea cyanus*): This is an upright and long-stemmed plant, 18 to 30 inches high, with light gray-green, slender leaves and small, thistle-like flowers—blue, pink, rose, or white—in late spring and early summer. It prefers full sun.

5. BALSAM, GARDEN (*Impatiens balsamina*): Sometimes known as touch-me-not, this is a compact and bushy plant with glossy foliage. The dwarf kinds are 8 to 10 inches high, and the regular species and varieties average 15 to 20 inches. The small rose-like flowers that bloom in summer range through shades of pink, purple, red, rose, yellow, and white. Plant balsam in sunny locations in mild climates and in partial shade in hot summer regions.

6. BLANKET FLOWER (*Gaillardia pulchella*): This bushy annual is 14 to 18 inches high with medium-dense foliage and predominately dark red or yellow flowers. It blooms in late spring and summer and does best in full sun.

7. BLUE LACE-FLOWER (*Trachymene caerulea*): This is a feathery and tall-stemmed plant, 15 to 25 inches high, with tiny blue flowers in lacy flat clusters similar to Queen Anne's lace. It blooms in summer and fall, and grows well in sun or shade.

8. BROWALLIA (*Browallia grandiflora*): This spreading, multi-stemmed plant grows 10 to 24 inches high and produces light blue or white tubular flowers in summer. Grow it in sun or shade.

9. BUTTERFLY FLOWER (*Schizanthus*): These annuals have dainty cut-leaf foliage. Some grow tall, 4 feet or higher. The kinds generally grown are 12 to 18 inches high with little orchid-like flowers in combinations of lavender, pink, purple, rose, yellow, and white. They like warm locations that are protected from wind.

10. CALIFORNIA POPPY (*Eschscholzia californica*): These are very attractive, loosely erect, multi-branched plants with clumps of short feathery foliage and masses of open, cup-shaped flowers in spring, predominately in brilliant variations of cream, orange, red, and yellow. Although perennials, they are nearly always grown as annuals. They require full sun.

11. CALLIOPSIS (*Coreopsis tinctoria*): These fine annuals are upright and vigorous growers with strong slender stems and feathery foliage. The dwarf varieties are 10 to 12 inches high, and the tall ones reach 24 to 30 inches. Their daisy-shaped flowers have yellow petals and red or reddish-brown centers, that splash color up the petals in rays. They bloom in spring and through summer.

12. CANDYTUFT (*Iberis umbellata*): These low-branching plants are 10 to 15 inches high with slender leaves 2 or 3 inches long. They bear clusters of little hyacinth-like flowers in pink, purple, red, violet, or white. They bloom in spring. Successive plantings will extend their excellent blooms through summer.

13. CANTERBURY BELLS (*Campanula medium*): This biennial is typically grown as an annual. It is a strong and upright grower, 24 to 30 inches high, with small branches from the main stems and a large bell-shaped flower at the end of each branch. The lavender, pink, purple, or white flowers are single or double in a close cup-and-saucer form. Canterbury bells bloom in late spring and into summer. They prefer full sun but will tolerate partial shade.

14. CHINA ASTER (*Callistephus chinensis*): One of the most beautiful and widely grown annuals, this aster has oval, medium green leaves with 12- to 30-inch, erect stems that carry big, single or double, soft-rayed flower heads 4 or 5 inches across in delicate tones of lavender, pink, purple, rose, violet, and white—excellent for cutting. It is summer blooming and prefers full sun.

15. CHINA PINKS (*Dianthus chinensis*): Slender, 10- or 12-inch stems rise from low, tufted plants that bear single or double flowers in shades of pinks, red, rose, or white. These pinks bloom in late spring, summer, and fall and should be planted in sunny locations.

16. CHINESE FORGET-ME-NOT (*Cynoglossum amabile*): These fine plants produce erect leafy stems 15 to 20 inches high and bear loose clusters of flowers resembling forget-me-nots in blue, pink or white. They grow in sun or partial shade, as under large trees. This specie of *Cynoglossum* is a biennial but is generally grown as an annual.

17. CLARKIA: Erect reddish stems display spires of claw-petaled flowers in shades of pink, purple, red, or white. The flowers are in single or double form and are excellent for cutting. These plants grow in sun or partial shade and bloom through summer and into fall.

18. COCKSCOMB (*Celosia argentea cristata*): This is an upright, well-branched plant, 10 to 30 inches high, with uniquely crested flower spikes resembling a cock's comb. The flowers range in color through crimson, orange, red, and yellow, and appear in summer and fall. Plant these annuals in sunny locations.

19. CORN-MARIGOLD (*Chrysanthemum segetum*): This is a good summer chrysanthemum—hardy, long-blooming, multi-branched, 12 to 20 inches high. Yellowish or white daisy-like flowers 2 or 3 inches wide appear in summer to early fall.

20. CORN-POPPY (*Papaver rhoeas*): Wiry stalks 20 to 30 inches high rise irregularly from a wide, leafy base. The flowers bloom in summer on the tips of the stalks and are purple, red, scarlet, or white, according to variety. Give corn-poppies a sunny location.

21. COSMOS (*Cosmos bipinnatus*): These are many branched, open, bush-like plants, 30 to 60 inches high, with feathery foliage and a generous distribution of mostly single, daisy-shaped flowers in lavender, pink, purplish-pink, rose, or white. They nod with a breeze, creating motion in a garden. The blooming period is summer and fall. They grow well in sun or partial shade.

22. EVERLASTING (*Helipterum roseum*): These interesting plants have slender, medium green leaves, and the flower stalks are 12 to 24 inches high. The pink, rose, or white flowers are disc-like heads 2 or 3 inches wide. When cut and dried, they have the feel and appearance of crisp frilled paper and will last indefinitely. These plants, bloom in summer and require full sun.

23. FAREWELL-TO-SPRING (*Godetia amoena*): This upright, open, and bushy plant grows 12 to 20 inches high with slender flower branches that bear masses of single or double flowers in pink, purplish-pink, light-rose, or white in summer and early fall. It will grow in full sun or partial shade.

24. FLAX, FLOWERING (*Linum grandiflorum*): This is an upright plant, 12 to 20 inches high, with slightly drooping branches that bear flat-face flowers 1½ inches wide in deep pink or shades of red. It blooms in summer and prefers sunny locations.

25. FLOSS FLOWER (*Ageratum houstonianum*): This is a widely planted, fluffy little edging plant 10 or 12 inches high. It produces masses of fuzzy-looking clusters of miniature lavender-blue flowers in late spring and summer. It grows best in full sun in mild climates and in partial shade in hot regions.

26. FORGET-ME-NOT (*Myosotis sylvatica*): This dwarf and densely spreading annual grows 8 to 10 inches high. Most varieties have blue flowers, a few have pink or white. Forget-me-nots bloom in late spring and summer and grow well in sun or shade.

27. FOUR-O'CLOCK (*Mirabilis jalapa*): Although this attractive plant is listed as a perennial, it is nearly always grown as an annual and is considered so here because of its wide popularity. It is spreading, 14 to 30 inches high, and well covered with tubular flowers 1 or 2 inches wide and about the same length. The flowers are in shades of red, yellow, and white; some are striped. They open around 4 P.M. These plants bloom in summer and fall and prefer full sun.

28. FRENCH MARIGOLD (*Tagetes patula*): This is a multi-branched and well-foliaged plant with clustered flower heads. Hybrid varieties are available in dwarfs 8 or 10 inches high, mediums 10 to 15 inches high, and talls 24 to 30 inches high. The large flowers are double in most varieties and are in rich orange or yellow. They bloom in summer and into fall. Give these marigolds sunny locations.

29. GLOBE AMARANTH (*Gomphrena globosa*): This is often dried and used as an *everlasting* for winter bouquets. It is a rather stiffly upright and many-branched plant, 12 to 20 inches high, with clover-like flower heads in pink, purple, rose or white. It blooms in summer and early fall and prefers full sun.

30. HONESTY (*Lunaria annua*): This upright and branching plant grows 18 to 30 inches high and produces fragrant purple or white flowers and thin, flat, ovalish pods averaging 1½ inches wide. When these pods (on the stalk) are dried, they become parchment-like and are very decorative. The flowers bloom in spring and should be grown in partial shade.

31. LARKSPUR (*Delphinium ajacis*): These attractive annuals send up slender, erect, and branching stalks 12 to 30 inches high with predominately blue flowers in terminal clusters. There are also larkspurs with lavender, pink, rose, or white flowers. They bloom in spring and require sunny locations.

32. LOBELIA (*Lobelia erinus*): This is a low-

growing and spreading plant with small, dark green leaves and slender little branches that support quantities of brilliant, ½-inch wide flowers in deep blue. Variety *alba* has white flowers; other varieties are lavender or pink. A smaller and more dense form, *compacta*, is excellent for small spots in the garden that need color. Lobelias bloom in summer and early fall. Grow them in sun or partial shade.

33. LOVE-IN-A-MIST (*Nigella damascena*): This upright, branching, and feathery-foliaged plant is 12 to 18 inches high. The light blue or white, 1- to 2-inch wide flowers at the ends of the branches are veiled in thread-like bracts that give them a misty appearance. The resulting seed pod is attractive. They bloom in late spring and summer. Give them sunny, wind-protected locations.

34. LUPINE (*Lupinus*, annual species): This is a branching plant that sends up erect 15 to 40 inch stalks supporting long loose racemes of blue, purple, rose, yellow, or white pea-like flowers in spring and summer. The grayish-green leaves are palmately formed.

Lupinus subcarnosus is the widely known bluebonnet, 6 or 8 inches high. Plant them in full sun.

35. MARIGOLD (*Tagates*): There are several hybrid varieties that are of excellent quality, with large flowers in brilliant gold, orange, and yellow. They range in height from dwarfs 8 inches high to 25 or 30 inches high. These are bold and aggressive flowers. When used in the small landscape they are best subdued by associated blue and white flowers. They bloom from late spring to fall. Plant them in full sun.

36. MENTZELIA LINDLEYI: This is a 12- to 36-inch high plant with 3-inch long, coarsely toothed leaves and 2-inch wide, fragrant, golden-yellow flowers with tufted stamens. It blooms in summer and prefers sunny locations.

37. MIGNONETTE (*Reseda odorata*): This low, bush-type plant is 12 to 24 inches high and has spikes of yellowish-white flowers in spring. Because of its delightful fragrance, give this annual special locations—near garden seats, adjacent to the patio, beside lounging or pool areas.

38. MORNING-GLORY, DWARF (*Convolvulus tricolor*): This is a nearly prostrate and spreading plant, 10 or 12 inches high, with upright stems that bear 1- or 2-inch wide, typical morning-glory flowers—blue with a yellow throat and white margins. It blooms principally in summer and grows in sun or partial shade.

39. NASTURTIUM (*Tropaeolum majus*): These range from 8- or 10-inch high dwarfs to 5- or 6-foot climbing forms. All produce great quantities of flowers—crimson, orange, red, rose, scarlet, or combinations of these colors. Seed planting may be timed for spring, summer, and fall blooming. Plant them in sunny locations.

40. NEMESIA STRUMOSA: This erect plant grows 10 to 20 inches high, and its tubular flowers resemble miniature orchids. They range in color through shades of purple, pink, red, and yellow. There are dwarf varieties that are compact and have blue flowers. They bloom in late spring and will grow in full sun in mild climates, but generally prefer partial shade.

41. PAINTED TONGUE (*Salpiglossis sinuata*): This is an upright and well-branched plant, 24 to 36 inches high, with funnel-like flowers in shades of cream, blue, brown, purple, red, and yellow—excellent for cutting. Many are two-toned and veined. They bloom in summer and early fall. Give them sunny locations.

42. PANSY (*Viola tricolor hortensis*): These well-formed little plants are generally grown as annuals. They are low and sprawling, 6 or 8 inches high, and produce masses of magnificently colored flowers 2 to 4 inches wide. The range of colors is wide—through single shades of blue, purple, red, yellow, and white or various color combinations. Pansies may be planted to bloom in spring, summer, and fall—even in winter in mild climates. They prefer full sun, but will bloom quite well in partial shade.

43. PETUNIA HYBRIDA: This tender perennial is almost always used as an annual. It is a spreading and smartly foliaged plant available in numerous strains, varieties, and forms—from 8 to 18 inches high and form compact to 2 or 3 feet of spread. New hybrids produce magnificent ruffled flowers, both single and double, in crimson, lavender, lilac, pink, purple, red, rose, salmon, and white. Successive plantings will give bloom from mid-spring into fall. Plant them in sunny locations.

44. PHLOX (*Phlox drummondii*): Annual phlox grows 12 to 14 inches high with clusters of 1- to 1½-inch wide flowers in lavender, pink, red, rose, and white. If timing is carefully calculated and feeding and watering are ample, they will bloom from mid-spring into fall. Plant them in full sun.

45. POT MARIGOLD (*Calendula officinalis*): These branched and well-foliaged plants are 12 to 18 inches high with strong stems that terminally support 4- or 5-inch wide, rayed flowers in brilliant orange, cream, or yellow. They bloom in spring and summer and require full sun.

46. ROSE-MOSS (*Portulaca grandiflora*): This is a low-growing, trailing, succulent-foliaged annual, 6 to 9 inches high, with masses of single or double, 1- or 2-inch wide flowers in orange, pur-

ple, red, rose, yellow, or white in summer and fall. Plant rose moss in sunny locations.

47. SNAPDRAGON (*Antirrhinum majus*): This tender perennial is generally grown as an annual. There are two distinct types: dwarfs 8 or 10 inches high, and tall ones 18 to 30 inches high. Both types and their varieties grow strong stalks that support terminal racemes of deep-throated flowers in shades of orange, pink, purple, red, yellow, and white. They bloom in spring and summer and prefer full sun.

48. SPIDER-FLOWER (*Cleome spinosa*): This is an upright and strong-stalked plant, 30 to 40 inches high, with flowers in large spidery clusters in lavender, pink, pinkish-rose, and white. They bloom from late spring into fall. Plant them in sunny areas.

49. STOCK (MATHIOLA INCANA ANNUA): This is the variety known as ten-week stock. It is not as tall and hardy as *Incana* but is very flower-productive and blooms through summer and into fall.

Mathiola incana is biennial or perennial but is generally grown as an annual. These are the 12- to 30-inch high, many-branched Brampton stocks with magnificent spires of closely arranged, fragrant flowers in lavender, mauve, peach, pink, purple, shades of red, whitish-yellow, or white. They are among the best cutting flowers and prefer full sun. Protect them from winds.

50. STRAWFLOWER (*Helichrysum bracteatum*): One of the *everlastings*, which may be dried and used later in bouquets, this is an upright and usually well-branched plant 20 to 30 inches high. The composition of the 2½- to 3-inch wide flower heads is an overlapping disc arrangement. When picked and dried, the discs have a straw-like feel and appearance. There are many colorful varieties appearing in orange, purple, red, rose, yellow, or white and in bicolors. They bloom in summer and require sunny locations.

51. SUMMER-CYPRESS (*Kochia scoparia trichophila*): This annual is grown principally for its colorful foliage. It is an upright, multi-branched, globe-shaped, bushy plant that is quite compact. The flowers are small, greenish, and hardly noticeable. The foliage, which varies in color, is reddish, varying shades of yellow, or light green. It becomes purplish-red in late fall, and the plant is therefore sometimes called burning-bush. Give it full sun.

52. SUNFLOWER (*Helianthus annuus*): This plant sends up a strong central stalk 5 to 8 feet high with 10- or 12-inch long leaves that grow progressively upward from the sides. It produces 10- or 12-inch wide, terminal, rayed, deep yellow flower heads with brownish discs. The different varieties vary considerably in size and color shading. Sunflowers bloom in summer and fall and require full sun.

53. SWEET ALYSSUM (*Lobularia maritima*): This small and spreading, 6- or 8-inch high perennial is nearly always grown as a self-seeding annual. It produces masses of fragrant little flowers in lilac, violet, or white clusters. It blooms in spring and summer, prefers full sun but will adapt to partial shade.

54. SWEET PEA (*Lathyrus odoratus*): This deliciously fragrant annual is a universal favorite for any garden. There are dwarf, rather bushy varieties and tall climbing kinds that, with proper culture, reach 10 feet in height and produce continuing quantities of flowers on 8- to 10-inch stems. The extensive color range includes shades of blue, lavender, peach, purple, red, yellow, and white. Plant sweet peas in a warm, sunny location and attach them to a trellis, mesh wire support, tall fence, or the warm side of a building.

55. SWEET SCABIOSA (*Scabiosa atropurpurea*): This is an upright and branching plant, 24 to 30 inches high, with predominately basal leaves. The branches support terminal, 2-inch-wide, pincushion-like flower heads in lavender, pink, purple, shades of red, rose, and white. There are several good varieties, including dwarfs. They bloom in late spring and summer and prefer full sun.

56. TASSEL FLOWER (*Amaranthus caudatus*): This is an upright and branching plant, 30 to 45 inches high, with drooping, tassel-like flower clusters in dark red. It is often called love-lies-bleeding. It blooms in summer, grows in sunny areas, and will adapt to partial shade.

57. TOADFLAX (*Linaria maroccana*): This low-growing annual is 10 to 16 inches high with slender leaves and terminal racemes of small snapdragon-like flowers in combinations of purple, rose, violet-purple, and yellow. They bloom in late spring and summer. Toadflax will do well in full sun or partial shade.

58. TOBACCO, FLOWERING (*Nicotiana fragrans*): This is an upright and strongly branched plant, 18 to 36 inches high, with a general distribution of fragrant, light purple flowers. Variety *Macrantha* is similar in form and has white flowers.

Nicotiana Alata is a perennial used as an annual. It is a little larger and has lavender, maroon, rose-red, or white trumpet-like flowers.

Because of its fragrance, plant *Nicotiana* in special places—near doorways, beside a patio, adjacent to lounging areas. It blooms in summer and fall, prefers full sun, but will adapt to partial shade.

59. VIRGINIAN STOCK (*Malcomia maritima*): These little plants are 4 to 6 inches high and may be compact or spreading. They produce masses of small flowers—in lavender, shades of red, rose, or white—in late spring and grow in full sun or partial shade.

60. YOUTH-AND-OLD-AGE (*Zinnia elegans*): These erect, central-stemmed plants are available in two height ranges: a medium group 12 to 18 inches high, and a tall group 24 to 36 inches high. The flower heads are 4 or 5 inches across and produce rich tones of crimson, orange, pink, purple, rose, yellow, and white. Zinnias bloom in late summer and fall. Plant them in sunny locations.

BULBS

Bulbs are widely used and familiar to most people. They are a topic for garden conversation around the world, rightfully so, for if given an opportunity, they thread a color pattern throughout the entire garden from early spring to autumn. Their versatility is enormous, and they are brilliantly rewarding.

Cultivation of bulbs is demanding but not complex. Soil requirements, disease and pest control (see Sketch 9.2), and temperature limitations are all related to a bulb's hardiness. Seasonal variations in climate are particularly important, for some species require cold in winter while others demand continued mildness. The Bulb Selection Chart on page 207 lists three hardiness divisions —hardy, half-hardy, and tender. We are using "Hardiness" in a broad and nontechnical sense here to describe a plant's ability to tolerate various levels of winter cold. Bulb plants that are unable to resist any frost are considered *tender*. Those capable of withstanding light frosts to a few degrees below zero are termed *half-hardy*, And those endowed by nature with protective devices that enable them to resist severe cold are referred to as *hardy*.

Although there are bulbs in these three categories to fit almost any requirement in any garden, finding the right ones for a particular location can sometimes be difficult. For this reason, the Bulb Selection Chart is designed to advise you regarding the selection, degree of hardiness, height, sun or shade tolerance, and time of bloom. It also suggests several specific uses and general color ranges of these fine plants.

Determine your winter temperature and relate it to the chart. The example selection strip at the base of the chart indicates that you want a *hardy* bulb, *8 to 15* inches tall, to grow in *full sun* and bloom in *spring*, *edge* your front walkway, and be in the *yellow* color range. To find which bulbs

Sketch 9.2

GOPHERS AND BULBS

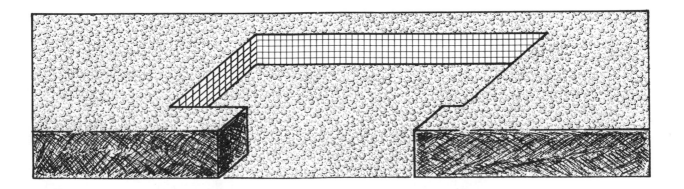

Where gophers are uncontrollable, line the planting area with ½″ mesh galvanized wire to permanently protect special or expensive bulbs.

meet these requirements, mark the requirements on a sheet of paper in the proper columns and slowly move the paper up the chart.

H (hardy)—8–15—Fs (full sun)—Sp (spring)—
Ed (edging)—Y

Very quickly you find seven bulbs that closely match your marked selection strip: numbers 16, 19, 26, 33, 41, 42, 46. To make a final choice, turn to these numbers in the alphabetical description of bulbs.

Alphabetical Descriptions of Bulbs

The following are descriptions and typical uses of the bulbs listed on the Bulb Selection Chart. (Numbers match those on the Selection Chart.)

1. ACIDANTHERA BICOLOR: This tender and fragrant, 14- to 16-inch high, summer-blooming plant (which grows from a corm) has sparse gladiolus-like leaves and 3- or 4-inch long, tubular flowers that are 2 or 2½ inches across with widely separated segments. The flowers droop gracefully and are creamy-white with a bold central splash of dark brown that spreads outward on each segment.

Acidanthera bicolor murieliae is very similar in general conformation but a little taller; the central splash is reddish brown. Both varieties provide excellent cut flowers.

In mild to warm climates, plant *Acidantheras* in early spring in full sun. In cold climates, start them indoors in early spring and replant in the garden when the weather warms. Two or three successive plantings will prolong the seasonal blooming period. In late fall, lift and winter-store the corms.

2. AFRICAN CORN-LILY (*Ixia maculata*): These half-hardy plants have slender leaves and send up thin strong stems 18 to 20 inches high that support clusters of 1½- to 2-inch funnel-like flowers in shades of orange, pink, red, yellow, or creamy-white.

Ixia paniculata is taller—24 to 30 inches high—and has attractive creamy-white flowers.

In mild to warm climates, *Ixias* grow freely and are of much value in the forepart of borders, for edging along walks, paths, or the patio, or in one or two narrow drifts in the foundation area. Plant a few in your rock garden. In cold winter zones, they are more difficult to grow and necessitate spring planting for summer bloom. Lift the corms in fall and winter-store.

3. AMARYLLIS (*Hippeastrum*): There are a number of highly hybridized amaryllis sold under named varieties. They are of magnificent size and color. Strong erect stalks 2 feet high grow from low, clustered leaves and support clusters of beautiful funnel-like flowers that may reach 7 or 8 inches across. The colors are rich in quality and range through shades of pink, red, salmon, and white; some are striped.

Although amaryllis are considered tender plants, use reasonable judgment and do not be afraid to experiment a little. In mild and warm winter climates, plant them in sunny or lightly shaded locations in loose, fertile, well-drained soil with the tip of the neck at, or a little above, soil level. If the soil freezes to a depth of 3 or 4 inches, plant them with the tip 4 or 5 inches below soil level, and apply a thick, protective mulch in winter. In still colder climates, start amaryllis in pots and, when the ground warms in spring, plant the unbroken root ball in the garden. Lift before frost and repot for next spring's garden use or for regular pot-plant display. In tolerant climates, amaryllis bloom in spring, summer, or early fall, according to variety.

4. AUTUMN CROCUS (*Colchicum autumnale*): These hardy cormous plants bloom in the fall after spring foliage has died down. In spring, 10- or 12-inch long leaves develop and die down before summer. In early fall, tubular, 5- or 6-inch long, stemless flowers resembling giant crocus, appear in lavender, lavender-pink, pink, purple, or white.

Because of their long and broad leaves, locate these plants to avoid annoyance. Use them in wide edgings, in plots under large trees, and in rock gardens. Plant them in July or early August. The corm tips should be 3 or 4 inches below the soil surface. Be sure to use winter mulch in cold zones.

5. AUTUMN DAFFODIL (*Sternbergia lutea*): This hardy, fall-blooming bulb plant has narrow, 8- or 10-inch long leaves in fall at the time its flowers appear. The flowers resemble crocus in form, but are larger. They are on 7- or 8-inch stems and are a rich golden-yellow.

Give these plants, like autumn crocus, room to develop properly. They look well in wide edgings, low mixed plantings, open sunny areas, and in rock gardens. In cold winter climates, plant in protected locations and winter-mulch. Plant the bulbs about 4 inches deep in mid-fall, and don't divide them until they appear to be overcrowded.

6. BABIANA STRICTA: This is a low-growing, tender, cormous, spring-blooming plant with sword-shaped leaves and 10- or 12-inch high stems supporting clusters of blooms that resemble freesias and are light or dark blue in color. There are several other interesting kinds of Babiana

BULB SELECTION CHART

No.	Name of Bulb	Hardy	Half Hardy	Tender	Height (inches)	Sun	Shade	Part shade	Spring	Summer	Fall	Background	Borders	Edging	Foundation	Mixed planting	Plots	Pots	Rock garden	Shrub areas	Special feature	Window box	Blue	Orange	Pink	Purple	Red	Yellow	White
1	Acidanthera			+	14–16	+				+		+	+	+	+	+									+				+
2	African corn-lily		+		18–30	+			+	+		+	+	+	+	+	+	+	+	+	+			+	+		+	+	+
3	Amaryllis			+	12–24	+		+	+	+			+	+	+	+	+	+	+						+		+		+
4	Autumn crocus	+			4–6	+		+			+			+					+							+		+	+
5	Autumn daffodil	+			7–8	+					+			+		+			+									+	+
6	Babiana			+	5–12	+			+				+	+		+		+	+				+	+	+		+	+	+
7	Blood-lily			+	18–20	+				+			+	+				+						+			+	+	
8	Caladium			+	18–30			+	Foliage	Foliage	Foliage	+	+	+	+			+		+	+	+		+	+	+	+		+
9	Calla lily		+		10–36	+		+	+	+		+	+	+	+			+			+			+	+		+	+	+
10	Camass	+			24–40	+		+	+			+	+	+		+			+	+	+				+	+	+	+	+
11	Canna		+		18–60	+				+		+	+							+	+			+		+	+	+	+
12	Crinum lily			+	24–36	+	+	+	+	+		+							+	+	+				+	+	+	+	+
13	Crocus	+			3–5	−		+	+				+	+					+		+				+		+	+	+
14	Cyclamen	+		+	4–8			+	+	+	+	+	+	+	+				+		+	+	+	+	+	+	+	+	+
15	Dahlia		+		12–80	+		+		+		+			+					+	+			+	+	+	+	+	+
16	Dog's-tooth violet	+			10–15	+		+	+				+	+	+				+	+			+		+	+	+	+	+
17	Elephants-ear			+	24–60		+	+	Foliage	Foliage	Foliage	+		+	+		+			+	+	+							
18	Freesia			+	10–15	+		+	+	+			+	+	+	+			+		+	+		+	+		+	+	+
19	Fritillary	+			12–40	+		+	+	+		+	+	+	+	+			+	+	+	+		+	+	+	+	+	+
20	Gladiolus		+		18–36	+			+	+		+						+		+	+			+	+		+	+	+
21	Gloxinia			+	12–15		+	+	+												+	+			+	+		+	+
22	Glory-lily			+	60–70	+		+		+											+							+	
23	Glory-of-the-snow	+			5–6	+		+	+				+	+	+	+		+	+		+	+	+		+	+	+	+	+
24	Glory-of-the-sun		+		10–15	+		+	+	+			+	+	+	+		+	+		+	+	+		+	+	+	+	+
25	Grape hyacinth	+			5–10	−		+	+				+	+	+	+		+	+		+	+	+	+	+	+		+	+
	Example Bulb	H			8–15	Fs	Fs		Sp					Ed														Y	

Example Bulb requirements: Hardy bulb, 8–15 inches high, grow in full sun, bloom in spring, for edging and in the yellow color range. To select, mark these requirements on the edge of a sheet of paper in the proper columns, and move the paper up the chart. Seven bulbs closely match the selection strip: numbers 16, 19, 26, 33, 41, 42, 46. Turn to these numbers in the alphabetical description list of bulbs for final selection.

BULB SELECTION CHART

No.	Name of Bulb	Hardy	Half hardy	Tender	Height (inches)	Sun	Shade	Part shade	Spring	Summer	Fall	Background	Borders	Edging	Foundation	Mixed planting	Plots	Pots	Rock garden	Shrub areas	Special feature	Window box	Blue	Orange	Pink	Purple	Red	Yellow	White
26	Hyacinth	+			8–15	+		+	+				+	+	+	+	+	+	+	+	+	+	+		+	+	+	+	+
27	Jacobean lily		+	+	10–12	+		+		+			+	+	+	+	+	+	+	+	+						+	+	+
28	Lily	+	+		15–60	+		+	+	+	+	+	+	+	+	+	+	+	+	+	+				+		+	+	+
29	Lily-of-the-Nile		+	+	12–48	+				+	+	+	+			+	+	+	+	+	+		+		+		+	+	+
30	Lycoris	+	+	+	20–24	+				+	+	+	+		+	+	+	+	+	+	+	+			+		+	+	+
31	Mariposa lily		+		12–24	+		+	+				+	+	+	+	+	+	+		+	+	+					+	+
32	Montbretia		+		20–30	+				+		+	+		+	+		+	+	+				+				+	
33	Narcissus	+	+		12–16	+		+	+				+	+	+	+	+	+	+	+	+	+			+	+	+	+	+
34	Nerine		+		12–20	+		+			+		+	+	+	+	+	+	+	+		+			+		+	+	+
35	Rain-lily		+		7–8	+				+			+	+	+	+	+		+			+			+				+
36	Ranunculus		+		15–20	+		+	+				+	+	+	+	+	+	+	+	+	+	+	+	+		+	+	+
37	Scilla	+			5–18	+		+	+				+	+	+	+	+	+	+		+	+	+		+				+
38	Snowdrop	+			7–12	+		+	+				+	+	+	+	+		+										+
39	Snowflake	+			10–12	+		+	+				+	+	+	+	+		+										+
40	Spider-lily		+		18–24	+				+			+	+	+	+	+	+	+		+							+	+
41	Spring star-flower	+			12–30	+		+	+				+	+	+	+	+	+	+		+		+						+
42	Star-of-Bethlehem	+			12–14	+		+	+	+			+	+	+	+	+	+	+		+			+				+	+
43	Summer hyacinth		+		24–36	+				+		+	+	+	+	+	+		+	+	+	+							+
44	Tiger-flower			+	12–20	+				+		+	+	+	+	+	+	+	+	+	+				+		+	+	+
45	Tuberose			+	20–30	+		+		+	+	+	+	+	+	+	+	+	+	+	+								+
46	Tulip	+			12–30	+			+			+	+	+	+	+	+	+	+	+	+	+		+	+	+	+	+	+
47	Wand-flower		+		16–18	+		+	+	+			+	+	+	+	+	+	+	+	+	+	+		+	+	+	+	+
48	Wind-flower	+	+		5–20	+		+	+	+			+	+	+	+	+	+	+	+	+	+	+		+	+	+	+	+
49	Winter aconite	+			4–8		+	+	+					+			+		+	+	+	+						+	
50	Zephyr-lily		+		8–10	+		+		+	+		+	+	+	+	+	+	+			+			+		+	+	+
	Example Bulb	H			8–15	Fs			Sp					Ed													Y	

Example Bulb requirements: Hardy bulb, 8–15 inches high, grow in full sun, bloom in spring, for edging and in the yellow color range. To select, mark these requirements on the edge of a sheet of paper in the proper columns, and move the paper up the chart. Seven bulbs closely match the selection strip: numbers 16, 19, 26, 33, 41, 42, 46. Turn to these numbers in the alphabetical description list of bulbs for final selection.

including *Hypogea*, which is lower growing with dark blue flowers, and *Plicata*, which is fragrant and only 5 or 6 inches high with lavender flowers. Plant them in low borders, mixed edgings, rock gardens, or pots. They grow freely in mild to warm climates. In cold zones, lift them in fall, store, and replant in spring.

7. BLOOD-LILY (*Haemanthus katharinae*): These tender members of the amaryllis family have wavy basal leaves that are 3 or 4 inches wide and 10 or 12 inches long. The flower stalks rise 18 to 20 inches in summer and support large, round clusters of slender, tube-like, pinkish-red flowers. The colorful cluster is completely pin-cushioned with long thread-thin stamens. Among the several interesting species and varieties are *Haemanthus coccineus*, which has large leaves and red flowers, and *Haemanthus puniceus*, which is 14 or 15 inches high with narrow leaves and scarlet flowers.

Because they are tender, these plants must be treated with care. In warm winter climates, they can be grown outdoors if given some protection from sun and wind. In cold winter areas, they are readily grown indoors in pots or plant tubs and, when in bloom, may be displayed on the warm patio or terrace. Plant the bulbs as early in spring as possible.

8. CALADIUM: These tender summer display plants are grown for their big colorful show-case type leaves that are 8 to 18 inches long. The leaves are heart-shaped at the stalks and the pointed ends angle downward to display lavishly colored patterns in blendings of pink, red, white, and sometimes silvery-green. The small white flowers are of little ornamental value.

In temperate climates, caladiums are easy to grow in wind-protected and partially shaded loca-tions—under lath structures, for example, or open trees, on the shady side of the patio or house. They perform well as pot and tub plants and by this method may be grown in colder sections of the country, where they should be started in a warm room in early spring. When weather and soil warm, plunge the pots into the garden soil or set the plants directly into the soil.

In the fall, when the leaves begin to deteriorate, reduce moisture. When the foliage has died back, dig the tubers, let them dry, and winter-store.

9. CALLA (*Zantedeschia*): A calla lily is uniquely formed by the combination of large, arrow-shaped basal leaves and a thick erect flower stalk terminating in a large wrap-around flower spathe surrounding a central stalk-like spadix, altogether forming a smooth, trumpet-like lily that is colored according to variety. Callas are half-hardy and grow vigorously in temperate

climates if given good growing conditions—moist, fertile, and well-drained soil. In hot climates, they should have afternoon shade. In severe winter zones, start them indoors in fall and dis-play them outside at bloom time.

Zantedeschia aethiopica is the well-known white calla. Under favorable conditions, it grows 2½- to 3-foot stalks that produce 7- or 8-inch long flowers. Plant the rhizomes about 5 inches deep.

Zantedeschia elliottiana is 18 or 20 inches high and has rich golden flowers that bloom in late spring and early summer.

Zantedeschia rehmannii is 12 to 16 inches high and has narrow spotted leaves and 4- or 5-inch flowers in light rosy-pink (sometimes almost red). It blooms in mid-to-late spring. Variety *superba* is a more intense pink. Plant the rhizomes of these two callas about 3 inches deep.

Grow calla lilies in meandering groups or drifts in the background, in borders, at the base of a fence or wall, in tall, mixed flower plantings, or adjacent to shrub groupings.

10. CAMASS (*Camassia*): In spring, these hardy members of the lily family produce long and slender basal leaves and clusters of flowers on erect stalks. They are widely distributed in the east, west, and south.

Camassia cusickii is 3 to 3½ feet tall and has brilliant clusters of 1-inch long, light blue flowers.

Camassia esculenta grows 1½ to 2 feet high with light blue flowers, and is found in many parts of the east and south.

Camassia leichtlinii reaches 3 to 3½ feet high with normal culture and has large clusters of sparkling bluish-violet flowers. Occasionally they are creamy-white.

Camassia quamash grows 2 to 2½ feet high and displays rich tones of dark blue flowers.

Plant camassia bulbs 4 to 4½ inches deep in late fall. In very cold winter climates, they may be started indoors in early spring and brought outdoors when the weather warms. Use them in background units, special featured informal plots, in a shrub bay, or near a water feature. Any of these locations may be in full sun or partial shade. Give them considerable moisture throughout their growing and blooming season.

11. CANNA: These summer-blooming tuberous plants are vigorous and half-hardy. They have wide leaves and tall-growing, eccentric clusters of lily-like flowers. There are many excellent varieties ranging in height from 18 inches in dwarfs to 5 or 6 feet in the tall species. Canna are available in a broad range of colors—in vari-ous shades of orange, pink, red, white, apricot, coral, and peach. The foliage varies from light green, bluish-green, and light or medium bronze.

In cold winter climates, cannas must be considered as tender. At frost time, lift the clumps, dry, and winter-store in very dry material such as peat moss or sawdust. In spring, divide the rootstock and replant 5 or 6 inches deep.

Because of their relative bulkiness, the taller cannas are best located in distant background groupings adjacent to shrubs or against walls and fences. The lower-growing ones are used in borders, plots, and special features.

12. CRINUM LILY (*Crinum*): These tender bulb plants are late spring- and summer-blooming relatives of the amaryllis family. The leaves average 3 inches wide and 2½ feet long. Flower stalks 2 or 3 feet high bear clusters of large, fragrant, trumpet-shaped flowers in shades of pink, red, rose, or white; some are striped.

These plants usually bloom in late spring and summer. Use them in shaded parts of the garden, in large borders or as individual clumps near low shrub areas, mixed with meandering flower drifts in the background, or in special featured units. Plant them in fall or spring in mild climates. In cold winter areas, plant them in spring when the ground warms. Set the bulbs 5 or 6 inches deep in loose and fertile soil.

13. CROCUS: These are hardy little cormous plants that grow almost anywhere. They bloom in spring, summer, or fall according to specie and variety. They have basal leaves and 3- to 5-inch long, expanded tubular flowers that grow above the foliage on short stems. Some kinds of crocus bloom before the foliage appears. Their wide color range includes blue, lilac, orange, yellow, white, and combinations such as blue-violet, lilac-purple, and pinkish-lavender.

Plant crocus in fall about 3 inches deep almost anywhere in the garden where 5-inch flowers are appropriate.

14. CYCLAMEN: These low-growing, spring-, fall-, and winter-blooming relatives of the *Primula* family have ornamental, rounded, heart-shaped leaves in a basal clump with shooting-star-like flowers on upright, slender stems that arise through the foliage.

Florist's cyclamen (*Cyclamen persicum*) is half-hardy and can be grown outdoors in temperate climates and with partial shade and considerable moisture. Many 6- or 7-inch flower stems progressively arise, beginning in the fall and continuing until early spring. Plant them in partly shaded edgings along walks and here and there beside paths, in patio plantings, under the open-growing species of rhododendrons and camellias, or under open, spreading trees such as Japanese maple.

Hardy kinds of cyclamen are almost as attractive. Nurseries offer them in various heights, leaf markings, and colors. They enjoy rich, moist, woodsy soil in filtered sunlight. Try them on the shady side of the house, under an apple tree in a patio, as a special feature around a birdbath, near a natural pool, or meandering beside a winding path.

Plant cyclamen in late spring or summer in organic-filled soil, and cover the corm-like tubers with ¼ to ½ inch of soil. Keep them moist.

15. DAHLIAS: These are vigorous and well-foliaged plants that produce magnificent flowers in many forms, sizes, and colors. They are organized into distinct classifications for specialized use and effect in gardens of any size. The classifications include terms such as anemone, ball, cactus, bedding, formal and informal decorative, mignon, and pompon. The plants differ in height and bushiness. Some of the dwarf bedding varieties are 12 to 16 inches high, while the tall ones reach 6 or 7 feet. There is an impressive difference in the flowers of each classification, from little button miniatures to huge specimens 9 or 10 inches across.

Dahlias are easy to grow either from seed, cuttings, or tubers. (The colors may not come true from seed.) They may be purchased in flats, but the select varieties are grown from tubers to assure maximum quality in size and true color. Dahlias can be grown almost anywhere under certain conditions: plant after final frost in deep and fertile soil, provide ample moisture, good drainage, protection from garden pests and diseases (snails consider dahlias a delicacy), and in full sun unless summers are very hot.

Begin by purchasing tubers of exceptional flowering varieties, prepare the soil well, and give the plants continuous attention as they grow, develop, and flower. Remove all but three or four stalks from each plant and disbud to the extent of leaving a flower bud on the tip of each branch and a pair of buds below the tip. If you wish a larger number of flowers, tip the stalks when they have developed three or four sets of leaves. Multiple branching will result. If all except terminal buds are removed from these branches, sizable flowers will result. However, if you wish to grow exhibition-quality plants and flowers, join a dahlia society and become familiar with their methods.

Exercise great care when lifting, dividing, and storing tubers, because they are delicate and easily bruised or broken. In late fall when the foliage has yellowed, cut the stalks 8 or 10 inches above the ground. Dig a circle 12 or 14 inches deep around the tuber clump, staying outside a 10- or 12-inch radius from the stalk. Gently lift the tuber ball, and carefully remove all soil. Permit the tubers to dry for a day. Observe the clump closely. You will see a number of expanded tubers, each with a long neck. The necks are attached to a central stalk. Near the point of attachment of each neck, you will notice one or two tiny nodules —a little round raised point, which is a bud or eye. Using a sharp knife (not a hacking implement), remove each tuber neck from the central stalk with a small part of the stalk and at least one bud attached and intact. Be sure the neck is not *broken* or *bruised*. Place the tubers in dry sand or other dry material and winter-store in a cool, dry, and relatively dark place.

When spring weather warms, prepare loose, fertile planting holes, place each tuber horizontally in the bottom of a hole, drive a 6-foot stake near the tuber, and cover the tuber with 5 inches of soil.

Some professional growers prefer to winter-store the entire tuber clump and divide just before planting. Dahlias can also be propagated by cuttings taken from young spring shoots.

Use low-growing dahlias in borders or beds and for wide edgings. The tall-growing kinds are excellent in background locations, in front of walls and fences, near shrub groupings or in foundation plantings (probably near the outside corners of the house). They are also very effective used as a special garden feature. Dahlias bloom in summer and fall and are of particular value in keeping the garden alive and beautiful through the summer-fall transitional period.

16. DOG'S-TOOTH VIOLET (*Erythronium denscanis*): These plants are known in various parts of the country as adder's tongue, avalanche lilies, Easter bells, and glacier lilies. They are very hardy, spring-blooming, low-growing plants, comprised of usually mottled leaves and erect 10- to 15-inch stems that support airy little flowers with recurved petals in delicate colors ranging through variations of cream-white, lavender, pink, light rose, and yellow. Several varieties are bicolored, some are fragrant.

Use these plants in any location in your garden that will naturally accommodate small, woodland-like flowers, and always group several together for a more effective display. The corms may be planted in fall or early spring, but fall is preferable. Cover them 2 or 3 inches deep, and supply continuous moisture.

17. ELEPHANTS-EAR (*Colocasia*): These tender and ornamental tuberous plants are grown primarily for their large arrow-like leaves that are heart-shaped at the base and 2 or 3 feet long. They are supported by sizable leaf stalks 2 feet long. The plants may grow 4 or 5 feet high. The flowers are inconspicuous. Plant them near a pool that is located on the sandy side of tall shrubs or small trees, or in a special area that is shaded. They require considerable moisture. In cold winter climates, lift the tubers in fall, dry, and winter-store for spring planting.

18. FREESIA: These are tender, fragrant, spring-blooming plants, 10 to 15 inches high, with slender basal leaves and wiry-branched flower stems that grow up from ground level to support 2-inch long, funnel-like flowers in lavender, shades of orange, pink, rose, yellow, and white. Use them in edgings, along paths, in the forepart of flower borders, in massed plantings among trees, or in rock gardens. Plant the corms 2 to 2½ inches deep in friable and fertile soil. In cold winter climates, grow them in pots of several corms each, timed for after-frost blooming. When weather permits, carefully remove the entire root-soil unit and replant in the garden. After the plants have completely died down, lift the corms for winter storage. In temperate climates, the corms may remain in the garden soil.

19. FRITILLARY (*Fritillaria*): These are hardy, spring blooming bulb plants of interest in any garden.

Fritillaria imperialis (Crown imperial) is particularly good. It sends up strong flower stalks 3 or 3½ feet high; from the foliaged tips hang clusters of large, bell-shaped light orange, red, or yellow flowers that bloom in mid-spring.

Fritillaria meleagris (Checkered-lily or snakehead) develops rather slender, 12- to 15-inch flower stalks bearing 2- or 3-inch bell-shaped flowers with a checkered and veined pattern in maroon and purple.

Fritillaria recurva (Scarlet fritillaria) produces 2- or 3-foot flower stalks with bell-shaped flowers in scarlet and yellow. Most bloom in late spring.

In cool summer climates, grow *Fritillaria* in full sun. In hot summer areas, give them partial shade. Plant the bulbs 3½ to 4½ inches deep in loose and fertile humus-filled soil. Use them in borders, wide edgings, mixed plantings of similar height, and shrub coves.

20. GLADIOLUS: Gladiolus are hardy and easy to grow. A series of corm plantings at three-week intervals beginning in early spring will provide continuous bloom from spring into fall. Purchase large, well-developed corms with raised centers. There is a wide range of varieties that include tall, medium, and small plants. The flowers are in almost any color you wish, with intriguing combinations. They are excellent for cutting.

Plant gladiolus almost anywhere in your garden if fertile soil, ample moisture, and good drainage are available. In cold winter zones, the corms should be lifted in early fall. Cut off the dead stalks; clean, dry, and dust the corms with a combination fungicide-pesticide powder; and winter-store.

Protect gladiolus from inevitable thrips. Begin by soaking the corms in a preplanting dip, such as Phaltan (liquid), and when the plants are a few inches high, begin a series of sprayings with an appropriate insecticide, such as Malathion. (Others are available at your garden supply store). Before planting, prepare the soil well by incorporating generous amounts of humus. Set the corms 4½ inches deep, and maintain adequate moisture.

21. GLOXINIA (*Sinningia speciosa*): These are magnificent flowering plants that only a few homeowners grow. This is unfortunate, for gloxinias are as easy to grow as tuberous begonias and are excellent companion plants. They have big bell-shaped flowers in variations of blue, pink, purple, red, or white, often freckled with harmonizing colors.

Gloxinias like warm weather and are rarely planted in the open garden. They have specialized uses—as pot plants for light and airy rooms, at special locations for display in covered or well-shaped parts of a patio, in a lounging shelter, and in warm and protected spots in outdoor furniture areas.

Handle gloxinias much the same as African violets: give them just enough, but not too much water; feed every two or three weeks with a balanced liquid fertilizer (some growers use fish emulsion); give them as much indirect light as possible, but not direct sunlight; and keep faded leaves and flowers picked off. Propagate by seeds, leaf cuttings, or preferably by purchased tubers of the best quality and size.

In early spring, set the tubers 1 inch deep in pots filled with a humus-soil mixture. After flowering, gradually reduce the moisture, and, when the plants become dormant, lift, dry, and winter-store the tubers in a cool, dark dry place for spring planting.

22. GLORY-LILY (*Gloriosa*): These tender, tuberous-rooted, climbing plants grow 5 or 6 feet high when attached to supports. They have narrow leaves, each terminated by a tendril, and produce attractive, bright red, 4- or 5-inch lily-like flowers with open segments edged with yellow.

Grow them in warm and wind-protected parts of the garden. After frost, set the tubers 4 or 5 inches deep in humus filled soil. In cold winter climates, earlier bloom can be obtained by starting the tubers indoors in pots before the last frost and replanting in the garden when the soil

warms. In fall, lift and winter-store the tubers.

23. GLORY-OF-THE-SNOW (*Chionodoxa*): These hardy, spring-blooming bulb plants are at their best in cold winter climates. They seem to follow the snow. They have slender leaves and 5- or 6-inch stems that support clusters of small, bright blue flowers with white centers.

Use them under and around open-based shrubs and trees, in little meadow-like parts of the garden, beside paths, in edgings, and in spots of special interest. Plant the bulbs 3 or 4 inches deep in fall.

24. GLORY-OF-THE-SUN (*Leucocoryne ixioides odorata*): These are excellent, half-hardy little plants with slender leaves and wiry 10- to 15-inch high stems that support clusters of fragrant, light blue, 2-inch flowers with white centers in spring. They grow well in full sun and require little moisture after flowering. In cold winter climates, lift and winter-store the bulbs for replanting as soon as weather permits in spring. In temperate climates, plant the bulbs in fall 3½ inches deep in rich and humus-filled soil.

Use these plants on small banks and slopes, in rock gardens, in hillside gardens near steps or beside paths, at the base of large rocks, or in a window box. They are very good pot plants.

25. GRAPE HYACINTH (*Muscari*): These hardy bulb plants have low-growing grass-like leaves and erect 5- to 10-inch high stems that bear small flowers in miniature hyacinth-like fashion in spring. They are easy to grow and multiply rapidly.

There are several excellent species and varieties in variations of blue and in white. Some are fragrant. Plant the bulbs 2 inches deep in fall almost any place in your garden that will accommodate 5- or 10-inch flowers.

26. HYACINTH (*Hyacinthus*): The several widely grown species and varieties of hyacinths offer fabulous compositions of color, fragrance, and form. Fat, fluffy clusters of little bell-shaped flowers are fashioned around a central stem 8 to 15 inches high and appear to be protected by a few upward-growing, strap-like leaves. The colors are in tones of blue, pink, purple, red, yellow, and white.

The several classifications of hyacinths differ a little in size, conformation, and adaptability, thus providing appropriate plants for different temperatures and other climatic conditions.

Use these flowers in the special places in your garden: in important parts of the patio or terrace; to parallel the front walk or the driveway; near the pool; or in long, meandering drifts. Plant the bulbs 5 inches deep in fall before frost. Prepare the soil well; it should be deeply fertile and generously supplied with peat moss or comparable humus. If moles or gophers are a problem, remove the soil and line the planting areas with mesh wire, then refill and plant.

27. JACOBEAN LILY (*Sprekelia formosissima*): This half-hardy, summer-blooming bulb plant has strap-like leaves from near ground level and sends up strong, erect, 10- or 12-inch stems. At the tip of each stem is a single bright crimson flower. Its three upper parts are upwardly spreading and outwardly curved. The lower three parts roll together and then spread widely in a drooping fashion. These brilliant red segments, together with long, down-sweeping anthers, form a beautiful 4- or 5-inch flower with a lily-like outline.

Use these plants at close-in, very special locations in full sun. They are excellent pot plants. Plant the bulbs 3 or 4 inches deep in humus-filled soil. Provide ample moisture and feed them with a balanced fertilizer every three weeks through the growing season. In cold winter climates, plant the bulbs as soon as possible after frost. Lift them in fall and winter-store in a cool, dark, dry place.

28. LILY (*Lilium*): The range of height, form, and color of lilies is wide. Many of the older specie lilies are still excellent—madonnas, for example. However, there are improved hybrids of extraordinary beauty and wide climatic adaptability. If planted at the appropriate time and given reasonable attention, they all are easy to grow.

The quality and patterns of coloring in the hybrid classifications are fantastic, and their heights vary from a few inches to 5 or 6 feet. Most kinds prefer full sun but will tolerate a small amount of open shade. Deep, fertile, moist, well-drained soil is mandatory. A sizable percentage of the soil body must be humus. Most varieties are planted 4 or 5 inches deep. Madonnas, however, do best 1 inch below soil surface. Feeding is so important that a calendar should be set up and marked for each three weeks during the growing season. A balanced fertilizer is adequate.

After blooming, remove seed cases, but do not immediately cut the stalks; foliage is required for proper bulb development. Cut them after they turn yellow. If the bulbs are left in the ground in cold winter zones, apply a heavy protective mulch.

Plant tall-growing lilies in front of a wall or fence, in meandering drifts in the background, in one or two small groups in the foundation planting, or associated with shrub units. Or, arrange a number of varieties in a special garden feature. Madonna lilies and other low-growing ones are excellent as patio plantings and in borders and wide edgings, they are especially attractive

grouped in numbers around a birdbath, in a planting section at the end of the pool, or in panels in a formal garden.

29. LILY-OF-THE-NILE (*Agapanthus*): These are half-hardy, tuberous rootstock plants that develop a sizable mound of strap-like leaves and send up strong 3- or 4-foot high stalks that carry large and loose terminal clusters of 1½- or 2-inch long, trumpet-shaped, blue or white flowers in summer and early fall. Dwarf varieties are small versions of the tall ones and are 1 or 2 feet tall. These are excellent in borders, to maintain color in foundation plantings, in special units, or in rock gardens. Because of their overall size, the large kinds are best located in the background and in shrub bays.

In cold winter climates, *Agapanthus*, particularly the dwarf varieties, can be grown in pots or larger containers and transferred to the garden when weather permits. Protect them from snails. Divide every three or four years when the plants become heavily overgrown. In cold winter zones, lift the outdoor growing plants and winter store by replanting them in moveable containers for indoor protection.

30. LYCORIS: These hardy to tender bulb plants have an unusual order of development. Their strap-like leaves grow in early spring, and by midsummer have completely died down. Then, in late summer, strong, leafless stalks suddenly appear, rapidly grow 2 or 3 feet high, and develop loose, terminal clusters of 3- or 4-inch long amaryllis-like flowers.

Lycoris aurea is a tender and warm climate relative that has yellow flowers.

Lycoris radiata, sometimes called red spider-lily, is half-hardy, has red flowers, and blooms in mid-fall. Its variety *alba* has white flowers.

Lycoris sanguinea has brilliant red flowers.

Lycoris squamigera, known in parts of the country as magic-lily, is hardy and grows well into the northern cold zones. It has clusters of deep pink flowers in late summer.

Use Lycoris in borders and background drifts or behind a water feature. *Lycoris squamigera* is very effective associated with low-growing shrubs. The tall flower stalks grow up through the shrubs and brighten the whole area. Plant them on banks or slopes or above a wall. Plant Lycoris bulbs in fall or spring according to hardiness and their adaptability to climate.

31. MARIPOSA LILY (*Calochortus*): These typically western, spring-flowering plants grow well into the north and east if planted in protected locations and heavily mulched in winter. In severe cold zones, the corms should be lifted in

fall and winter-stored. The plants have thin leaves and slender 12- to 24-inch high stems with terminal and shallow cup-shaped flowers 1½- to 2½-inches wide in colors ranging through lavender-blue, rosy-purple, light and dark yellow, and white.

Calochortus venustus, commonly called mariposa tulip, has flowers either in light lilac or white with near maroon markings at the base of the petals.

These flowering plants are excellent in borders or edgings, in rock gardens, along informal woodsy paths or beside meandering paths in hillside gardens, and in small retirement or mobile home designs. However, they should be in locations that are fairly dry in summer. Set the corms about 3 inches deep in woodsy soil.

32. MONTBRETIA (*Tritonia*): These are half-hardy, summer-blooming cormous plants with loose mounds of slender leaves and erect, usually branched flower stalks.

Tritonia crocata has sparsely branched, 2-foot stalks and loose clusters of 2-inch freesia-like flowers in orange and red. There are varieties in light or dark pink and some in yellow.

Tritonia crocosmaeflora has branched stalks that are taller than *Tritonia crocata,* and it has clusters of flowers in bright orangy-crimson. The flowers of its variety *aurantiaca* are dark orange.

Tritonia rosea has red flowers with yellow spots toward the base.

Plant montbretias in full sun in borders or adjacent to shrub plantings, in the forepart of the background, or in front of walls. They are long-lasting cut flowers. Plant the corms in fall in temperate climates. In cold winter areas, lift in fall and winter-store for spring planting.

33. NARCISSUS: The genus *Narcissus* comprises several important species that are separated into related divisions according to their special characteristics. Most home gardeners, however, refer to the different kinds of narcissus simply as daffodils, jonquils, Chinese sacred lilies, or poet, paper white, and polyanthus narcissus. Members of the divisions are closely related and yet somewhat different in size, color, form, perianth (petals), and cup (central crown). Some are large-cupped and others are medium- or small-cupped. Some species have large trumpets—King Alfred daffodils, for example—and with some, such as *Poeticus actaea,* the perianth and cup form almost a round, flat plane. There are double daffodils and *triandus* hybrids with their clustered flowers and reflexed perianths; *tazetta* hybrids, the bunch-flowered narcissus that produce clusters of flowers on a single stem; miniatures, and

others. All this is mentioned to whet your curiosity and encourage you to select those best suited to your garden.

All narcissus have quality petal colors—cream, pink, golden-yellow, or white, with either the same colored cup or beautifully harmonized colorings. There are scores of species, varieties, and hybrids, among which are plants adaptable to almost every climate, severely cold to warm. Narcissus enjoy worldwide popularity and are probably the most stable of all bulb plants. Use them anywhere in your garden. Plant the bulbs in fall in most parts of the country. Cover the smaller growing kinds 4 inches deep, the medium-height types 5 inches deep, and the tall ones, such as daffodils, 5 to 6 inches deep.

34. NERINE: These are half-hardy and fall-blooming, bulbous relatives of amaryllis. They have basal, strap-like leaves and strong 12- to 20-inch high stalks that support loose terminal clusters of amaryllis-shaped flowers with widely separated segments that turn backward at the tips. The stamens are gracefully long and tendril-like.

Nerine bowdenii has shiny, strap-like leaves 7 to 10 inches long and erect, 18- to 20-inch high stalks terminating in loose clusters of pink, light crimson, or near red flowers.

Nerine curvifolia has 18- or 20-inch stalks with terminal clusters of large scarlet flowers, and its variety *fothergillii major* has scarlet flowers with a golden shimmer. The flower segments of *Nerine curvifolia* spread widely to display long, light yellow anthers. The leaves appear after flowering.

Nerine sarniens is commonly known as Guernsey lily and has 18- or 20-inch stalks with clusters of eight or ten deep pink, crimson, or white flowers, according to variety. The flowers precede the leaves.

In temperate climates, grow nerines in the open garden and leave the bulbs in the ground over winter. In cold winter zones, grow them in pots and display them throughout the season, or try plunging the pots into garden soil in shaded areas after the soil warms in spring. After flowering, lift and move the pots into a greenhouse or other protected location. Keep the plants watered during winter, and begin a feeding schedule in early spring.

Use nerines in special places for display—in protected parts of the patio or terrace, near outdoor furniture, or indoors in light-filled rooms.

35. RAIN-LILY (*Cooperia*): These half-hardy, summer-blooming bulb plants have thin, bluish-green leaves and 7- or 8-inch high stalks that terminate in 2- or 3-inch lily-like flowers with

spreading segments. They are light pink with dark pink markings or yellow with purplish markings, according to variety.

Use rain-lilies in full sun in borders, edgings, or rock gardens, beside paths, in places of special interest, against walls, or as pot plants. The bulbs should be covered 1½ to 2 inches with humus-filled loam. In mild climates, plant them in early fall. In cold winter zones, lift in fall, and winter store.

36. RANUNCULUS ASIATICUS: These half hardy tuberous plants are commonly known as Asiatic ranunculus and sometimes called Persian buttercups. They have fragile-appearing compound leaves and 15- or 20-inch high stems that support several, mostly double, flowers resembling small camellias. Many European, Australian, and American strains offer magnificent form and colors that include variations of orange, pink, red, rose, yellow, and white.

Ranunculus bloom in late spring and prefer temperate climates and garden locations with morning sun and partial shade in the afternoon. Set the claw-like tubers 2 inches deep in richly prepared soil. In cold winter sections of the country, special timing and care are required if they are to be grown in the open garden. Start them indoors in small destructible planters well before the last spring frost. When the soil warms, replant them in the garden without breaking the soil from the growing tubers.

Use ranunculus in borders, edgings, or mixed bulb plantings, and for special garden features.

37. SCILLA: This is a group of hardy and half-hardy, widely distributed and popular bulb plants with narrow basal leaves and slender, leafless stems that support terminal clusters of small bell-like flowers with wide-spreading segments. They bloom in spring, summer, or fall, according to variety.

Scilla amoena, commonly called star-hyacinth, is quite small (6- or 7-inch stems) with loose terminal clusters of blue or nearly white flowers.

Scilla autumnalis has 6- or 7-inch high stems bearing light rose flowers; it blooms in autumn.

Scilla bifolia is an early spring-flowering kind that is taller—8 or 10 inches high—with star-shaped flowers in light blue, shades of pink, or white.

Scilla hispanica, or Spanish blue-bell, is exceptionally fine with 14- to 18-inch stems and large hyacinth-like clusters of blue, pink, or white flowers that appear in late spring.

Scilla nonscripta, or English blue-bell, is also commonly called wood-hyacinth. These are very attractive when grown in large quantities in meadow-like areas or in meandering drifts under trees. They are very hardy, spring-blooming, and suggestive of small, fragrant, loosely clustered hyacinths on 10- or 12-inch stems. They are grown principally in blue varieties, but are available in pink or white.

Scilla sibirica, or Siberian squill, is a very hardy and vigorously growing early flowering plant that grows well in colder climates—into the north and upper eastern parts of the country. It has intense blue flowers on 5- or 6-inch stems, and when mass planted, the blue carpet is spectacular. There are also pink varieties.

Grow scillas in any part of your garden that will accommodate 6- to 18-inch flowers. They are also excellent pot plants. Cover the bulbs 2 or 3 inches deep in loose soil in full sun or partial shade.

38. SNOWDROP (*Galanthus*): Early blooming and very hardy, these bulb plants have basal leaves and hanging, white, bell-shaped flowers borne singly on a stem. The inner flower segments overlap, are smaller than the outer segments, and have green tips.

Galanthus byzantinus has relatively broad leaves with turned margins and ½- to ¾-inch long white flowers with pale green inner segments.

Galanthus elwesii, the giant snowdrop, is larger. Its flowers are 1 to 1½ inches long, with some green on the inner segments. The flower stems are 10 or 12 inches high, and the bluish-green basal leaves are 7 or 8 inches long.

Galanthus nivalis is the common snowdrop. It has bluish-green leaves and ¾- to 1-inch flowers with a little green on the inner segments. They hang on 7- to 10-inch high stems.

Use snowdrops in sunny or partly shaded locations in your garden—in borders, for edging, along walks or paths, as rock garden plants, or in front of low shrub plantings.

39. SNOWFLAKE (*Leuocojum*): This hardy little bulb plant is very similar to snowdrop. However, its green-tipped white flowers may be two or three to a stem, the perianth segments are spread apart, and the plant has more leaves than snowdrops. Its uses in the garden are the same as those of snowdrops.

40. SPIDER-LILY (*Hymenocallis calathina*): Sometimes called basket-flower, this half hardy relative of amaryllis has 15- to 20-inch long, strap-like, basal leaves and clusters of fragrant tubular flowers with long narrow perianth segments that curve outward and back. The stamens are united at the base into a unique cup with delicately fringed edges, and the slender filaments arise free-standing. These summer-blooming

flowers are white with pale green markings and grow on 18 to 24 inch stalks.

Spider-lilies are useful in borders, wide edgings, and special little areas beside paths. Or grow them in pots for special displays. Plant in spring right after frost in good soil and merely cover the bulbs. In fall, lift and winter-store.

41. SPRING STAR-FLOWER (*Brodiaea uniflora*): These are spring-flowering plants with flat blue-green leaves and loose clusters of white, blue-tinged flowers 1 to 1½ inches wide on the tips of 7- or 8-inch high stems.

There are several good varieties: *elegans*, often called harvest brodiaea, with purplish flowers on 15- to 18-inch stems; *hyacinthina*, with clusters of white flowers that bloom in late spring to early summer; *laxa*, sometimes called triplet-lily, which has large clusters of violet flowers on 12- to 14-inch stems in mid-spring; *pulchella*, with tightly formed clusters of small, dark blue flowers on 18- to 30-inch stems in early spring; and others.

Use these attractive plants on drier banks and slopes. There are many such locations in hillside gardens, distant parts of farm landscapes, and rock gardens. Plant the corms 3 inches deep in fall. In very cold winter areas, give them a protective mulch. They prefer that the soil become dry in summer.

42. STAR-OF-BETHLEHEM (*Ornithogalum umbellatum*): This spring-blooming, hardy, old-time favorite has narrow basal leaves 6 to 10 inches long and dense clusters of 1-inch wide, white, star-like flowers at the tips of 12- or 14-inch stems. Some species and varieties have flowers in yellow and shades of red. They are good for cutting.

Use these plants here and there in individual plantings or in a perennial border. Cover the bulbs 4 inches deep in fall in loose, rich soil that will drain well. Mulch them in cold winter zones.

43. SUMMER HYACINTH (*Galtonia candicans*): This is a half-hardy, summer-blooming bulb plant with strap-like basal leaves 24 to 30 inches long and a sparse cluster of hanging bell-shaped flowers on the upper part of a strong 2- or 3-foot stem. The flowers are white and fragrant.

Summer hyacinths are useful in borders and wide edgings, near shrub plantings, in appropriate places in hillside gardens, or against a low wall. They may also be grown in pots for summer display. Plant the bulbs in fall in temperate climates and in spring after frost in cold winter areas. Set them 5 or 6 inches deep.

44. TIGER-FLOWER (*Tigridia pavonia*): This is a strikingly attractive, rather tender, summer-blooming plant with 10- to 15-inch long, sword-shaped basal leaves. The 18- to 30-inch high stalks support 5- or 6-inch wide flowers. Wide-spreading and recurved flower segments of brilliant red form a cup-like shape that fades into orange and is dashed with yellow and purplish spots. There are some elegant *Tigridia pavonia* hybrids in pink, shades of red, yellow, and white with harmonized spots.

Use groupings of tiger flowers near a wall or fence, associated with shrub plantings, or in appropriate parts of the foundation planting. Or place three or four in the back strip of a perennial border or in mixed flower areas. Although considered tender, *Tigridia* corms may remain in the soil in mild winter climates. In cold winter zones, plant after frost 4 inches deep. Lift and winter-store the corms in late fall.

45. TUBEROSE (*Polianthes tuberosa*): These fragrant, tender, tuberous-rooted plants bloom in summer and into fall. They have slender basal leaves 12 to 14 inches long and terminal clusters of small, white, tubular flowers on 20- to 30-inch upright stalks.

Plant tuberoses in warm and partly shaded places in the garden in spring. Set the tubers 2 to 2½ inches deep. In medium cold and severe winter climates, start them indoors in flats or shallow boxes containing sphagnum moss, and replant outside when the soil warms.

46. TULIP (*Tulipa*): It is possible to spring color a small to medium-size garden exclusively with a succession of tulips. The early blooming types open the season with single and double flowers in elegant shades of pink, red, yellow, and white. Mendels and Triumphs follow immediately. Then the main show begins, featuring the stars of the tulip divisions—Breeders, the magnificent flared flowers of Cottages, tall proud Darwins and lily-flowered tulips, Rembrandts displaying colored patterns on their petals. Next come Parrots with their soft and feathery ruffled flowers. The show concludes with a glowing display of late-blooming double or Peony-flowered tulips and their varieties in variations of orange, red, rose, and white.

Each division comprises many fascinating varieties in tints, shades, and delicate variations of color. Any garden will accommodate tulips—retirement, mobile home, hillside. Plant them in full sun in borders, plots, meandering drifts, edgings, in front of your house, in the patio, near a water feature, along paths and walks, in a raised bed—in almost any sunny part of the garden.

Purchase the finest quality bulbs in October, put them in the 40 degree part of your refrigerator for three or four weeks, and plant them at a depth of about two or three times their diameter. If you give tulips rich, deep, friable, and well-drained, humus-filled loam; ample water; an occasional feeding (particularly at the beginning of their growth); and protection against pests, diseases, and underground rodents that will move them around, they will reward you extravagantly.

47. WAND-FLOWER (*Sparaxis tricolor*): These are half-hardy, late spring-blooming plants with slender basal leaves and spikes of small flowers with widely spread segments on 12- to 18-inch high stems. Their colors include blue, purple, red, and yellow.

Use these plants in borders, mixed flower plantings, wide edgings, or rock gardens, as a part of special garden features, at the base of large rocks, in front of a low wall, or in raised beds. In mild winter areas, plant the corms in fall. Cover them 2 to 2½ inches deep. In cold winter zones, plant them in pots in very early spring and, when flowering, display them in various parts of the garden. Or plant in open garden soil when the weather warms.

48. WINDFLOWER (*Anemone*): These fine tuberous and fibrous rooted plants have thin, airy, and mostly divided or dissected leaves. The major portion of the foliage is clustered around the base of the plant. Quantities of delicately composed flowers are supported singly on upright branched stems.

Japanese anemone (*Anemone japonica*) is a fibrous-rooted type that grows tall—to 3 feet— and is delicately handsome with pink, mauve, red, rose, or white saucer-shaped flowers that appear in fall. It performs well in temperate climates and in moist soil.

The spring-blooming, hardy, tuberous-rooted group includes *Anemone apennina*, with 1½ inch wide, light blue flowers borne on 8- or 10-inch stems; *Anemone blanda*, with 1½- to 2-inch wide, deep blue flowers on 5- or 6-inch stems; and *Anemone nemerosa*, which has smaller flowers on 6- or 8-inch stems in mid-spring. The several varieties of *nemerosa* have flowers in variations of lavender, reddish-purple, rose, and white. Plant these anemone tubers in fall, 1½ inches deep in humus-filled soil that is well drained.

High on the list of the less cold-hardy tuberous group are *Anemone coronaria*, or Poppy anemone, with light, airy, compound leaves and 2- to 3-inch wide, poppy-like flowers in shades of blue, red, yellow, and white borne on 10- to 20-inch stems; *Anemone fulgens*, or scarlet anemone, with semi-double flowers—near scarlet, with black stamens —2½ inches across on 8- to 12-inch stems in late spring; *Anemone hortensis*, or garden anemone, with purple, red, rose, or white flowers on 8- to 10-inch stems in spring. Plant tubers of this group 2 inches deep in late fall.

Select the kind of anemone that is most adaptable to your climate and garden situation. Use them in wide borders, in front of foundation shrub plantings, in clumps on either side of the front yard, in patio, pool, or lounging shelter units, or in rock gardens. In really cold or more difficult climates, grow them in containers and, when they begin to bloom, display them in protected places.

49. WINTER ACONITE (*Eranthis hyemalis*): These are hardy, tuberous-rooted plants with a basal pattern of sharply divided leaves and 1- to 2-inch wide, yellow to golden-yellow flowers resembling large buttercups on 4- to 8-inch high stems. They bloom in late spring about crocus time or in late winter in warm climates.

Use winter aconite in edgings, in rock gardens, or beside paths, preferably in partial shade. Plant the tubers in early fall, 4 inches deep in loose, humus-filled soil that readily drains.

50. ZEPHYR-LILY (*Zephyranthes*): This half-hardy, crocus-like little bulb plant has slender basal leaves and small amaryllis-like flowers in pink, rose, yellow, or white. The flowers appear singly on the tips of 8- to 10-inch erect stems. In some parts of the country, they are referred to as fairy lilies, and because they appear suddenly after a rain, they are sometimes called rain lilies. Zephyr-lilies bloom in spring, summer, and fall, according to variety.

In temperate climates, plant the bulbs in fall. In cold winter zones, plant them after spring frosts, setting the bulbs 2 inches deep in rich, woodsy soil that is well drained. When the foliage has died back, lift and winter-store the bulbs.

Use zephyr-lilies in borders and edgings, in rock gardens, near water features, beside paths, or in patio plantings.

Figure 10.1 TYPICAL LOCATIONS FOR HERBS (AND SOME VEGETABLES) WITHIN THE LANDSCAPED GARDEN

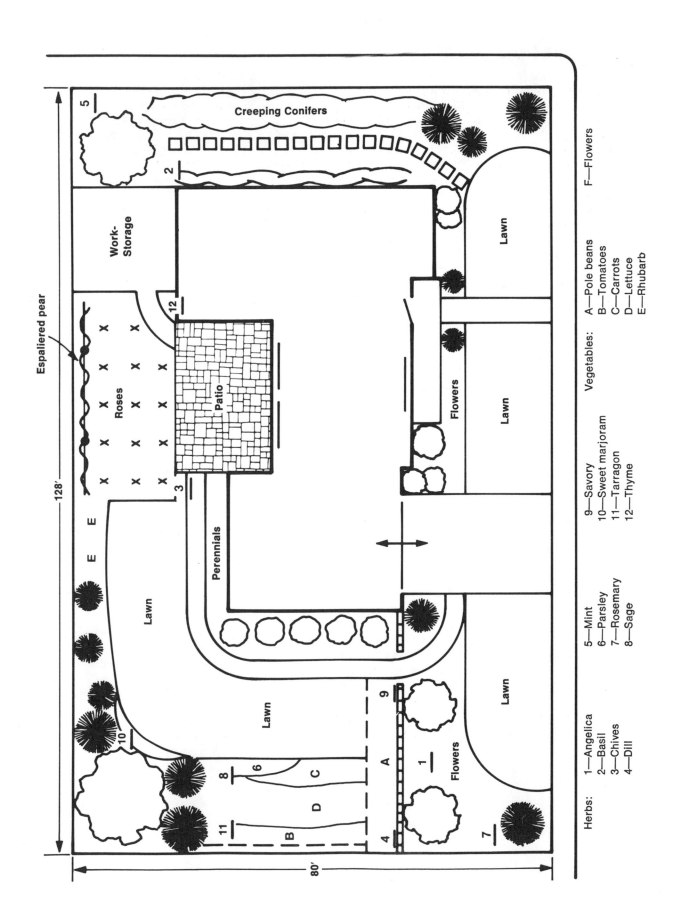

Herbs:
1—Angelica
2—Basil
3—Chives
4—Dill

5—Mint
6—Parsley
7—Rosemary
8—Sage

9—Savory
10—Sweet marjoram
11—Tarragon
12—Thyme

Vegetables:
A—Pole beans
B—Tomatoes
C—Carrots
D—Lettuce
E—Rhubarb

F—Flowers

Herbs and Vegetables

HERBS WITHIN THE LANDSCAPED GARDEN

Herbs are an increasingly popular and useful addition to today's gardens. Formerly they were assembled within intriclly formed designs of modified squares, wheels, or patchwork patterns—special areas more or less set aside in the manner of a vegetable unit. However, in modern land-scaping, where everything combines to promote both beauty and service, herbs have a natural place in the general organization of plants. Integrating the zestful foliage, color, and fragrance of herbs with conventional plants increases the interest and vitality of any garden. Planted along a path, they are exclamation points of interest; beside the pool, they freshen the atmosphere; and near the kitchen door, one can almost taste their savory flavor in hot soups and stews.

Like other plants, herbs range from creeping mats to small shrubs, and their species include annuals, biennials, and perennials. It's easy to find appropriate kinds to combine with regular annual, perennial, or mixed plantings throughout your garden. Figure 10.1 indicates little plots, strips, and bays suitable for herbs in a typical garden. Figure 10.2 includes a formal herb garden as part of the overall landscape design.

Nurseries offer packaged collections of tiny herbs growing in small paper pots with instructions for kitchen use. Their cultivation requirements are simple—ordinary fertile loam, moderate moisture, and protection from pests. In addition, many herbs can be successfully grown on a sunny window sill. Sketch 10.1 offers some suggestions.

Herbs for Your Garden

The following chart lists twelve common herbs for planting within your landscaped garden or in

HERB SELECTION CHART

Flavoring Herbs	Height	Annual	Biennial	Perennial	Sun	Part shade	Growable in pots indoors	Fragrant	Method of Propagation*
Angelica	3–5'		+			+			S—Sp,F
Basil	12–14"	+			+	+			S—Sp
Chives	10–12"			+	+	+	+		D—Sp,F
Dill	2–3'	+							S—Sp
Mint	8–10"			+	+	+	+	+	L—Sp
Parsley	8–15"		+			+	+		S—Sp
Rosemary	2–3'			+	+	+		+	S,C—Sp
Sage	10–15"			+	+		+		C—Sp
Savory	12–18"	+		+	+		+		S—Sp
Sweet marjoram	10–12"			+	+	+	+	+	S—Sp
Tarragon	16–18"			+	+				C,D—Sp
Thyme	7–10"			+	+	+	+		S,C—Sp

* Propagation of Herbs: S=seed in Sp=spring—F=fall
D=division in Sp=spring—F=fall C=cuttings in Sp=spring—F=fall
L=layering in Sp=spring—
F=fall (Preferable to buy plants from a nursery)

a specially designed herb garden. Detailed descriptions of these herbs follow the chart.

Here are details about the twelve herbs on the Selection Chart. All are of exceptional value to both garden and kitchen:

1. ANGELICA (*Angelica archangelica*): This 3- to 5-foot high biennial prefers a cool location and considerable moisture. Sow seed in spring or fall. Angelica is often used in salads.

2. BASIL (*Ocimum basilicum*): This annual grows to 12 or 14 inches high and prefers fertile, well-drained soil in a sunny location. Plant seed in spring. Try basil fresh or dry for seasoning cheese souffles, cream cheese, croutons, eggplant dishes, French omelets, hamburgers, and potato soup.

3. CHIVES (*Allium schoenoprasum*): This is a 10- or 12-inch high, onion-like perennial that may

Figure 10.2   **A FORMAL HERB GARDEN (WITH SOME VEGETABLES) WITHIN THE LANDSCAPED GARDEN**

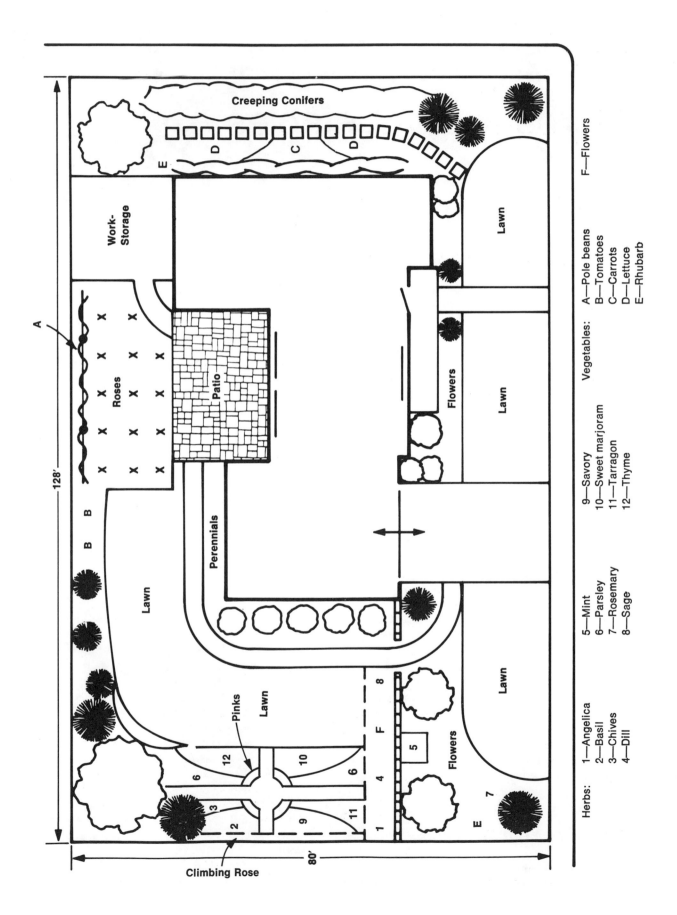

Herbs:
1—Angelica
2—Basil
3—Chives
4—Dill
5—Mint
6—Parsley
7—Rosemary
8—Sage
9—Savory
10—Sweet marjoram
11—Tarragon
12—Thyme

Vegetables:
A—Pole beans
B—Tomatoes
C—Carrots
D—Lettuce
E—Rhubarb
F—Flowers

Sketch 10.1 **HERBS FOR THE WINDOW SILL**

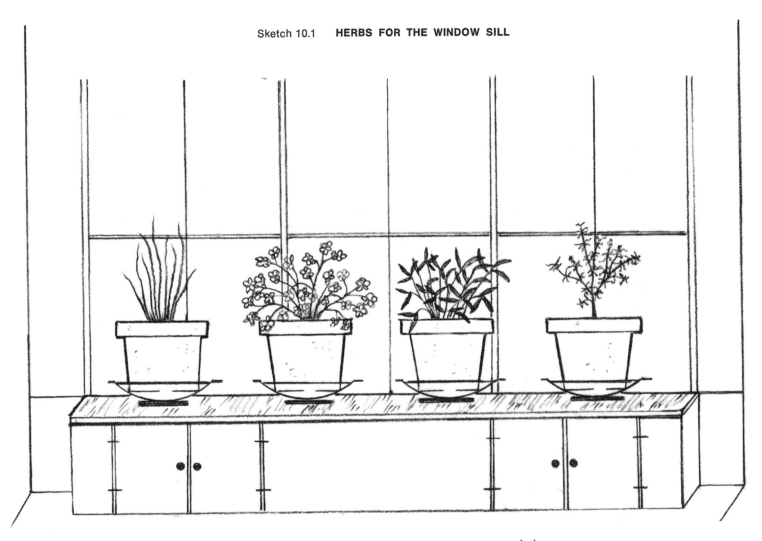

Typical herb plants that can be grown on a sunny window sill: from left to right—chives, parsley, basil, sage.
Use at least 5- or 6-inch pots with drain holes. Set the pots in saucers to catch excess water—large clear-glass ash trays are excellent.
For drying herb leaves, make a simple drying frame by removing the bottom from a bedding-plant flat and re-placing it with fine-mesh wire (such as window screen).

be grown here and there along the edge of a path or the patio. It requires good soil, sunshine, considerable moisture, and a feeding two or three times a year. Cut back to near the ground after flowering. New growth will soon appear. When it becomes too thick, lift and replant the bulbs. Chives can also be started from seed.

Cut the leaves into segments for flavoring salads, sauces, omelets, and sandwich fillings.

4. DILL (*Anethum graveolens*): This slender-growing annual, 2 or 3 feet high, develops loose and attractive flower heads that produce seeds used for seasoning. Plant a clump or two in the background for aesthetic effect. Use dill to flavor pickles, and try it in coleslaw, cottage cheese, and tomato juice cocktails.

5. MINT: There are several valuable varieties of mint; the two commonly grown in the landscape are Peppermint (*Mentha piperita*) and Spearmint (*Mentha spicata*). Plant them where their growth can be controlled as they spread rapidly by stolons. The aromatic leaves are ❧

valuable for flavoring cold drinks, jellies, and sauces, and for serving with meats.

6. PARSLEY (*Petroselinum hortense*): Although this plant is biennial, most gardeners grow it as an annual. It grows 8 or 10 inches high, has rather fragile, medium green foliage, and blends well into edgings, borders, or mixed plantings of any kind. Parsley is widely used for garnishing and flavoring, as in salads, cream cheese, chicken dumplings, meats, and stews. Pot it as an indoor plant for winter use.

7. ROSEMARY (*Rosmarinus officinalis*): This 2- to 4-foot high, spreading shrub has small aromatic leaves and blue flowers. It is an attractive garden shrub (or creeper) and may be located near the pool, in front of a shrub grouping, on a slope, or to help frame a doorway.

The leaves are used to flavor meats, stews, some Italian foods, and soups. Also try adding rosemary to meat loaf, cauliflower, and corn bread.

8. SAGE (*Salvia officinalis*): This is a 1- to 2-foot high, multi-branched perennial with grayish-green leaves that have a beaded texture. It prefers full sun and gives a change in foliage color in regular low plantings. The fresh or dried leaves are used in cooking poultry, pork, and other meats, and in poultry stuffing, cheese casseroles, and dressings.

9. SAVORY (*Satureja*): Two varieties are grown for food seasoning—summer savory (*Satureja hortensis*), which is a 1- to 1½-foot annual started from seed in early spring, and winter savory (*Satureja montana*), a small shrub-like perennial. Add two or three of these plants to any small shrub planting. Savory is often used to flavor consommé, hash, pork roast, and meat balls; some people like it in scrambled eggs.

10. SWEET MARJORAM (*Origanum vulgare*): This is a 10- or 12-inch high perennial, but grow it as an annual in cold winter zones. Start the plants from seed in early spring. The small aromatic foliage is delightful along a path or in the rock garden. The leaves are used for flavoring foods such as cheese casseroles, fish, fried chicken, hash, pork roast, poultry stuffing, and soufflés.

11. TARRAGON (*Artemisia dracunculus*): This multi-branched perennial is 16 or 18 inches high, with linear leaves that have a flavor similar to anise. They are often used to flavor fish, salads, salad dressing, and vinegar. Dried tarragon leaves lose their flavor.

12. THYME (*Thymus*): Two varieties are commonly grown—*Thymus serpyllum*, a low, creeping plant with purplish flowers, and *Thymus vulgaris*, a more erect plant (to 7 or 8 inches high) with lilac-purple flowers. Both are little perennials that look well in small coves beside a path or in the patio. Try thyme to flavor beef stew, cheese spread, eggplant dishes, fish chowder, fried chicken, pork chops, and poultry stuffing.

There are many other popular herbs. Look over the selections offered by your nursery dealer. You may wish to add two or three additional ones to your garden.

Herbs are occasionally attacked by garden pests, but do *not* apply poison sprays to the plants. Use other methods, such as forceful spraying with water, repeated until the plants are pest-free. When using sprays on regular garden plants, cover herbs with thin sheet plastic (available at paint stores for a few pennies per sheet).

VEGETABLES FOR THE LANDSCAPE

In every country and climate, homeowners with a piece of land experience the urge to grow at least a few vegetables. It isn't so much the economic value as the profound satisfaction of sitting at their own table and enjoying their own garden-grown produce. The real delight is the true flavor experience—rich, delectable, and zestful—the kind you can't buy.

What to Grow and How

If a plot of open land extends beyond or to one side of your landscaped garden, you are in luck. You can grow a variety of vegetables from late spring into fall, particularly if two or three successive plantings are made at three-week intervals.

If your property lacks such open spaces—as is the case for most of us—there is no reason why a limited number of vegetables cannot be distributed advantageously over the landscape. The same plant food and water that nourish the ornamentals benefit the adjacent vegetables. It is principally a matter of including them in your garden plan and becoming acquainted with the proper methods of cultivation.

Cool and Warm Season Vegetables

Some vegetables grow and develop more satisfactorily in cool weather, others during the warmer months. Beets, cabbage, cauliflower, chard, lettuce, onions, peas, potatoes, radishes, rhubarb, and turnips are among the cool weather vegetables. In cold winter climates, these should be started early in spring while the weather is still sharp. In mild climates, they often are started in fall and grown as winter crops.

Beans, cantaloupes, cucumbers, eggplant, peppers, squash, sweet potatoes, and tomatoes are warm weather vegetables. Their seeds require warm soil for germination, and the plants need warm weather and long days for vigorous development and a rich harvest. If you grow eggplant, peppers, and tomatoes from seed, give them a head-start indoors because they require a fairly long time to develop from seed to maturity. However, for the average homeowner, it is much easier to purchase young plants at planting time.

Soil Preparation

The quality of vegetables relies, at least in part, upon rapid growth, which, in turn, depends upon availability of water and nutrients. Therefore, proper soil preparation is extremely important. Work quantities of organic material, barnyard fertilizers, compost, and sand (if your soil is heavy) deeply into the soil in fall or at least a month in advance of planting time, and keep the ground moist. In cold winter zones, particularly, it is advantageous to spade the soil deeply before rains and frost begin and then to rework it in the spring.

If your soil is currently fertile and friable, a surface sprinkling of chemical fertilizer, such as a 10-10-5 formula, at the rate of about 2 pounds per 100 square feet, prior to the spring spading, is beneficial. Avoid using manures with a large quantity of straw. The straw may deplete the supply of nitrogen. Commercially prepared manures are easy to handle and weed free; odors are at a minimum; and the nutrient factors are more quickly available to the plants.

Pest Control

Be extremely careful with pesticides! Some of those used on ornamental plants might leave a poisonous residue on vegetables. This phase of vegetable gardening is so important that you are urged to call your county or state agricultural agent for information on the latest recommended sprays for your specific vegetable pest problem.

Constant research is in progress for safer and more efficient sprays. State and federal controls govern pesticides in many states.

Thinning and Weeding

Because they compete with each other for water and nutrients, overcrowded plants cannot grow rapidly or properly develop the luscious, tender vegetables you envision. Thin out excess plants when they are small. As a guide, thin large root vegetables, such as beets and turnips, to 4 inches apart, carrots to 3 inches, radishes to 2 inches, and head lettuce to 12 or 14 inches.

To conserve moisture and plant nutrients, remove weeds when quite small, before they become deeply rooted. Exercise considerable care in weeding. If done carelessly, the delicate root systems of the vegetable plants may be disturbed to the point of only partial recovery.

Where to Plant Vegetables

Many gardens are of sufficient size to accommodate separate vegetable areas within their boundaries. In such cases there is very little, if any, problem. However, in the great majority of home gardens, a complete vegetable unit either would not seem appropriate, or there is simply inadequate space. If this is your situation, do not abandon the idea of growing vegetables. Simply work them into your existing design.

The majority of vegetables require full sun, deep fertile soil, adequate moisture, and good drainage. Study your garden design and you will probably find several locations that meet these requirements: warm bays in front of a fence or wall, the outer edge of a low shrub grouping, and so on. Figure 10.3 suggests feasible locations for eight of the more attractive-appearing kinds of vegetables.

If you group vegetables in a plot that is in full view of the house, border them with flowers. Many home gardeners merely distribute little clumps or runs of beets, carrots, chard, eggplant, peppers, radishes, and turnips among low shrubs and perennials in an informal, scattered fashion. Usually they are unnoticed by guests. However, plant a few pepper plants at the turn of a path, and they become a conversation piece.

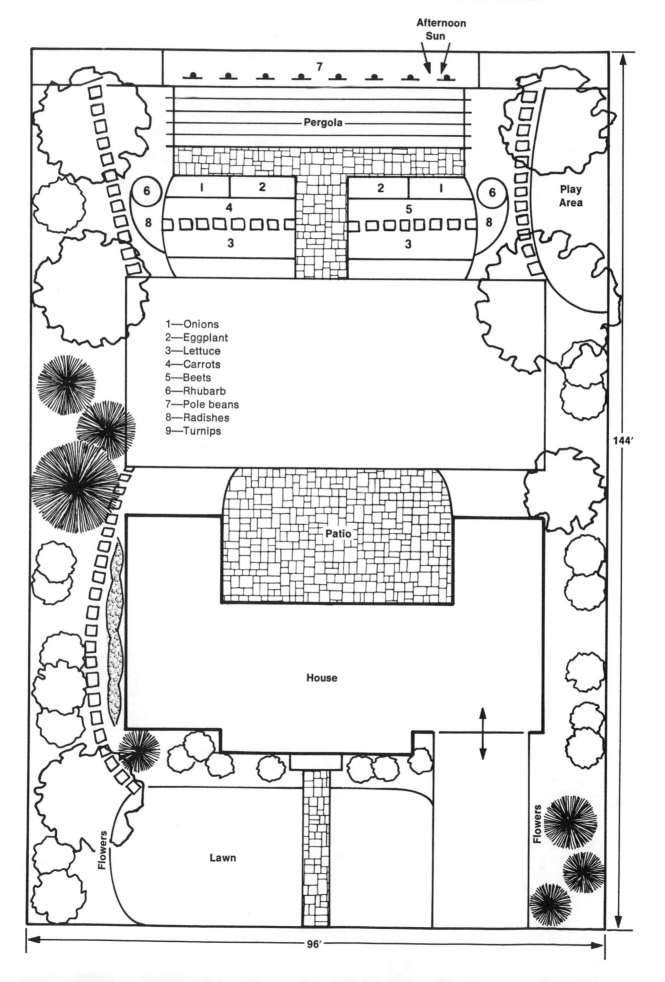

Figure 10.3 TYPICAL LOCATIONS FOR VEGETABLES WITHIN THE GARDEN

1—Onions
2—Eggplant
3—Lettuce
4—Carrots
5—Beets
6—Rhubarb
7—Pole beans
8—Radishes
9—Turnips

VEGETABLE PLANTING CHART
If you are planting *within* your landscaped garden, select and plant according to available space.

Name	Plant hardi-ness	Seed for 25' row	Seed plants roots in ground	Depth of seed—roots	Dis-tance between rows	Dis-tance apart of plants	Days to mature	Succes-sive plant-ings	Yield for family of 4
Beans, pole	Tender	¼ lb	May	1¼"	30"	2'	60–70	July	25' row
Beets	Tender	½ oz	April	1"	18"	4"	45–65	June	15' row
Cabbage	Hardy	¼ oz	March	¼"	30"	1'	130–150	—	15' row
Cantaloupe	Tender	¼ oz	May	¾"	5'	5'	100–120	—	6 hills
Carrots	Hardy	¼ oz	April	½"	2'	2"	80–90	June	25' row
Cauliflower	Tender		Plants/ in May		3'	2'	120–140	—	15 plants
Chard	Hardy	½ oz	April	¾"	2'	10"	110–120	July	10' row
Cucumber	Tender	¼ oz	June	¾"	4'	3'	70–90	July	6 plants
Eggplant	Tender		Plants/ in May		3'	2'	120–140	—	8 plants
Lettuce	Hardy	⅛ oz	April	½"	2'	10"	80–90	July	20' row
Onions	Hardy		Sets/ in April	2"	2'	3"	30–45	July	30' row
Peas	Hardy	½ lb	April	2"	3'	2'	35–45	June	50' row
Peppers	Tender		Plants/ in May		3'	2'	120–140	—	10 plants
Radishes	Hardy	¼ oz	April	½"	18"	2"	30–40	June	6' row
Rhubarb	Hardy		Roots/ in April	Top of root/2"	4'	3'	Second spring	—	4 plants
Squash (Sum)	Tender	¼ oz	June	½"	4'	3'	90–100	—	6 plants
Tomatoes	Tender		Plants/ in May		4'	4'	120–140	—	12 plants
Turnips	Tender	¼ oz	April	½"	2'	3"	60–80	July	15' row

Selecting Vegetables for Your Garden

Even if your growing space is unlimited, it is not advisable to include too many kinds of vegetables. Select around five or ten that you and your family really like. The Vegetable Planting Chart on this page will assist you.

Among the most popular and appropriate vegetables for small to medium gardens are beets, carrots, eggplant, lettuce, onions, peas, pole beans, radishes, rhubarb, squash, tomatoes, and turnips. It is not difficult to include a few of any of these in your garden. Most start readily from seed planted in the open ground after frost in spring. The exceptions are eggplant, onions, rhubarb, and tomatoes, which are handled a little differently.

Eggplant

Although eggplant is started from seed indoors in early March, young plants of the best variety for your area are available in nurseries at planting time. They are usually in individual paper pots that are easily cut away, permitting the plant to be transplanted without disturbing the roots. Plant them in a location that has sun at least two-thirds of the day.

Onions

Two types are of interest to the homeowner. Within the landscaped area where room is at a premium, the small bunching type for fresh eating are usually chosen. These are easily started from *sets*, which are small bulblets harvested by commercial growers for this purpose. Plant them 2 inches deep in fertile and friable loam.

The second type results in mature, fully developed onions, the kind used for slicing and cooking. These are also planted by means of *sets* and take 120 to 140 days to reach maturity.

Rhubarb

Rhubarb is usually propagated by division of fleshy roots taken from older plants. However, young plants may be purchased at garden supply stores in spring. Rhubarb is a perennial that lasts for years if its major root system is not periodically disturbed.

There are some important culture requirements. The soil must be deep and very fertile, and an abundance of moisture is mandatory. Shallow cultivation is beneficial. Feed the plants every three weeks during spring and early summer with a high nitrogen fertilizer to promote rapid stalk growth. It is not advisable to pull stalks the first season after planting. Be sure to cut away seed stems to prevent exhaustion of the plant. If the plant persists in growing seed stems, lift and replant in another location.

Tomatoes

There are varieties of tomatoes that will grow well in your garden. It is merely a matter of finding a few feet of space in *full sun*. Left to their own natural growth habit, tomato plants may spread out 3 or 4 feet in each direction. However, they can be trained up against a wall, trellis, or fence, or tied to stakes. Carefully attach the branches to their supports and prune lateral branches to keep the vines from becoming massively heavy. With this treatment, they will develop into 5- or 6-feet high, very productive plants. They must have warmth and protection from winds.

Prepare the soil well, working in a generous amount of organic fertilizer and humus to a depth of at least 2 feet. If you overfeed, lush growth with very little fruit will result. Perhaps one feeding of a low-nitrogen fertilizer will be adequate. Keep the soil deeply moist, and place a mulch over the root system.

Tomato vines are subject to certain pests and diseases. Your garden supply store has a highly effective spray or dust specifically formulated for the control of leafspot, mildew, and wilts on tomatoes. As a preventive measure, begin using it when the plants are quite small. Three-inch long, light green, fat, and incredibly voracious tomato worms may appear. Just pick them off by hand, and keep a watchful eye for more.

It is preferable to purchase tomato plants from your nursery dealer at planting time. He is aware of the varieties that grow and fruit well in your locality. However, tomato plants are not difficult to start from seed in an improvised little hotbed placed indoors in a light and warm place. Six inches of loose, humus-filled loam in a wooden box will do. Sow the seed sparingly and cover with ¼ inch of fine, sandy soil. Place a pane of glass over the box, keep the soil moist, and in a few days the young plants will appear. At this time, raise the glass during the day for circulation of air around the plants. When they reach 2 inches in height, replant them in flats or pots. Use light, sandy loam. When they are 5 or 6 inches in height and if there is no chance of frost, transplant them to their permanent outdoor location. Cutworms like newly transplanted tomato plants. To thwart their destructive intentions, wrap a paper collar around each stem and extend it ½ inch below the soil surface and ½ inch above.

Timing is important in planting tomato seed. Determine the approximate date of final frost and plant the seed indoors six or seven weeks before that date.

Some Suggested Varieties of Vegetables

Climate and other environmental factors may influence your variety selections. However, the following are good growers and universally used:

Beans—pole type—Blue Lake, Kentucky
      Wonder
Beets—Detroit Dark Red, Early Wonder
Cabbage
    Early: Early Jersey Wakefield, Golden Acre,
        Medium Round Dutch, Round Red
        Dutch
    Late: Danish Ballhead, Slow Bolting Flat
        Dutch
Cantaloupes—Casaba, Hales Best, Honey Dew,
      Persian
Carrots—Chantenay, Imperator, Nantes
Cauliflower
    Early: Snowball

Late: November-December
Chard—Fordhook Giant, Large Ribbed Dark
       Green
Cucumbers—Ashly, Lemon, Marketer
Eggplant—Black Beauty
Lettuce
    Head types: Bibb, Great Lakes, Matchless
    Loose heading and Leaf: Black seeded Simp-
      son, Cos (Romaine), Parris Island, Prizehead
Onions
    Early: California Early Red, Early Grano
    Late: Southport White Globe, Sweet Spanish
Peas
    Bush: Little Marvel, Progress
    Vine: Alderman, Melting Sugar
Peppers
    Bell type: Pimiento, Yolo Wonder
    Hot type: Hungarian Yellow Wax
Potatoes, Sweet

Moist type: Puerto Rico
Dry type: Yellow Jersey
Potatoes, White—Kennebec, Pontiac, Red La-
      Soda, White Rose
Radishes
    Red: Comet, Red Prince
    White: White Icicle
Rhubarb—Cherry, Strawberry
Squash
    Summer: Early Prolific Straight Neck, Early
      Bush, Scallop, Zucchini
    Winter: Butternut, Pink Banana, Table
      Queen
Tomatoes—Earlypak, Pearson Improved, Red
      Cherry
Turnips—Purple Top White Globe
Watermelons—Klondike, Solid Dark Green,
      Striped, Light and Dark-green
      Stripes

This book has hopefully made gardening easier and has helped you to create the environment that you most want around your own home. I've put my best skill and knowledge into this information but, just as with people, no two gardens or plots of ground are alike. And just as with people, gardens grow best when they receive love, food, and reassurance.

The nice thing about landscaping is that you can change your mind and replant or relocate plants and garden features as your interests change. The garden that is suitable for you now might be unusable or out of place in five years. So, landscaping can be a developing reflection of your own needs and interests.

Bibliographical Notes

The following publications have been consulted by the author for guidance in spelling, nomenclature, and appropriate plant selection. They are listed here by way of acknowledgment and to suggest to the reader helpful sources for reference and further reading.

For a concise dictionary of gardening and horticulture in general, see L. H. Bailey and Ethel Zoe Bailey, *Hortus, Second* (New York: The Macmillan Company, 1941). Expert advice is presented in simple terms in Norman Taylor, ed., *Taylor's Encyclopedia of Gardening* (Boston: The American Guild and Houghton-Mifflin Company, 1948). A complete, practical, and convenient guide to every detail of gardening can be found in E. L. D. Seymour, ed., *The Garden Encyclopedia* (New York: William H. Wise and Company, 1936), and Gretchen Fischer Harshbarger, *McCall's Garden Book* (New York: Simon and Schuster, 1967) is a uniquely specific, how-to-do-it garden book for everyone.

As for landscape design, Henry Vincent Hubbard and Theodora Kimball, *Landscape Design* (New York: The Macmillian Company, 1927) presents general instruction in landscape design and a skillful explanation of the principles of design. For reliable identification and information on trees and shrubs of North America, see Alfred Rehder, *Manual of Cultivated Trees and Shrubs*, Second Edition (New York: The Macmillan Company, 1956). Conifers used in England and in the United States are described in H. J. Welch, *Dwarf Conifers* (London: Faber & Faber, 1966). Further information on conifers can be found in Adrian Bloom, *Conifers for Your Garden* (New York: Charles Scribner's Sons, 1967). This book provides magnificent color photographs and suggests how conifers can be used effectively in gardens of any size.

A highly practical discussion of shrubs and vines used in the United States and Canada can be found in Donald Wyman, *Shrubs and Vines for American Gardens* (New York: The Macmillan Company, 1956), and suggestions for harmonious combinations of plant colors are provided in Harold D. Givens, *The Secrets of Artistic Gardens* (New York: Van Nostrand Reinhold Company, 1969).

The flowering plants of Hawaii are presented in color in Dorothy and Bob Hargreaves, *Hawaii Blossoms* (Portland, Oregon: Hargreaves Industries, 1958). For information on the installation, fertilizing, pest control, watering, mowing, weeding, renovation and general care of lawns, *Lawns and Groundcovers*, produced by the Sunset Editorial Staff (Menlo Park, California: Lane Book Company, 1964) is a useful text, and instruction on how bulbs can be used to achieve garden color the year round is given in *How to Grow Bulbs*, produced by the Sunset Editorial Staff (Menlo Park, California: Lane Book Company, 1962).

There are a number of United States Government Publications that will prove extremely helpful to gardeners. See, for example, the *Plant Hardiness Zone Map* (Miscellaneous Publication No. 814) for zoned lists of shrubs and trees. See also *Flowering Annuals* (Home and Garden Bulletin No. 91), *Spring Flowering Bulbs* (Home and Garden Bulletin No. 136), *Summer Flowering Bulbs* (Home and Garden Bulletin No. 151), *Flowering Perennials* (Home and Garden Bulletin No. 114), *Indoor Gardens* (Home and Garden Bulletin No. 133), and *Trees for Shade and Beauty* (Home and Garden Bulletin No. 117). These and many other concise and helpful publications can be obtained from: Superintendent of Documents, Agricultural Research Service, U.S. Department of Agriculture, Washington, D.C.

Index